Programming and Interfacing the 8086/8088 Microprocessor

A Product-Development Laboratory Process

PROGRAMMING AND INTERFACING THE 8086/8088 MICROPROCESSOR

A PRODUCT-DEVELOPMENT LABORATORY PROCESS

ROY GOODY
Mission College

Merrill, an imprint of
Macmillan Publishing Company
New York

Maxwell Macmillan Canada
Toronto

Maxwell Macmillan International
New York Oxford Singapore Sydney

Cover photo insert copyright: Allen-Bradley
Editor: Dave Garza
Production Editor: Rex Davidson
Art Coordinator: Vincent A. Smith
Cover Designer: Cathleen Norz
Production Buyer: Patricia A. Tonneman

This book was set in Times Roman by Bi-Comp, Inc. and was printed and bound by Semline, Inc., a Quebecor America Book Group Company. The cover was printed by Phoenix Color Corp.

Printed in the United States of America

Macmillan Publishing Company
866 Third Avenue
New York, NY 10022

Macmillan Publishing Company is part of the
Maxwell Communication Group of Companies.

Maxwell Macmillan Canada, Inc.
1200 Eglinton Avenue East, Suite 200
Don Mills, Ontario M3C 3N1

Library of Congress Cataloging-in-Publication Data
Goody, Roy W.
Programming and interfacing the 8086/8088 microprocessor / Roy Goody.
p. cm.
Includes index.
1. Intel 8086 (Microprocessor) 2. Intel 8088 (Microprocessor)
I. Title.
QA76.8.I292G66 1992
005.265—dc20 91-34776
CIP

Printing: 1 2 3 4 5 6 7 8 9 Year: 2 3 4 5

MERRILL'S INTERNATIONAL SERIES IN ENGINEERING TECHNOLOGY

ADAMSON
Applied Pascal for Technology, 0-675-20771-1
The Electronics Dictionary for Technicians, 0-02-300820-2
Microcomputer Repair, 0-02-300825-3
Structured BASIC Applied to Technology, 0-675-20772-X
Structured C for Technology, 0-675-20993-5
Structured C for Technology (w/disks), 0-675-21289-8

ANTONAKOS
The 68000 Microprocessor: Hardware and Software Principles and Applications, 0-675-21043-7

ASSER/STIGLIANO/BAHRENBURG
Microcomputer Servicing: Practical Systems and Troubleshooting, 0-675-20907-2
Microcomputer Theory and Servicing, 0-675-20659-6
Lab Manual to accompany Microcomputer Theory and Servicing, 0-675-21109-3

ASTON
Principles of Biomedical Instrumentation and Measurement, 0-675-20943-9

BATESON
Introduction to Control System Technology, Third Edition, 0-675-21010-0

BEACH/JUSTICE
DC/AC Circuit Essentials, 0-675-20193-4

BERLIN
Experiments in Electronic Devices to accompany Floyd's Electronic Devices and Electronic Devices: Electron Flow Version, Third Edition, 0-02-308422-7
The Illustrated Electronics Dictionary, 0-675-20451-8

BERLIN/GETZ
Experiments in Instrumentation and Measurement, 0-675-20450-X
Fundamentals of Operational Amplifiers and Linear Integrated Circuits, 0-675-21002-X
Principles of Electronic Instrumentation and Measurement, 0-675-20449-6

BERUBE
Electronic Devices and Circuits Using MICRO-CAP II, 0-02-309160-6

BOGART
Electronic Devices and Circuits, Second Edition, 0-675-21150-6

BOGART/BROWN
Experiments in Electronic Devices and Circuits, Second Edition, 0-675-21151-4

BOYLESTAD
DC/AC: The Basics, 0-675-20918-8
Introductory Circuit Analysis, Sixth Edition, 0-675-21181-6

BOYLESTAD/KOUSOUROU
Experiments in Circuit Analysis, Sixth Edition, 0-675-21182-4
Experiments in DC/AC Basics, 0-675-21131-X

BREY
Microprocessors and Peripherals: Hardware, Software, Interfacing, and Applications, Second Edition, 0-675-20884-X
The Intel Microprocessors-8086/8088, 80186, 80286, 80386, and 80486-Architecture, Programming, and Interfacing, Second Edition, 0-675-21309-6

BROBERG
Lab Manual to accompany Electronic Communication Techniques, Second Edition, 0-675-21257-X

BUCHLA
Digital Experiments: Emphasizing Systems and Design, Second Edition, 0-675-21180-8
Experiments in Electric Circuits Fundamentals, Second Edition, 0-675-21409-2
Experiments in Electronics Fundamentals: Circuits, Devices, and Applications, Second Edition, 0-675-21407-6

BUCHLA/McLACHLAN
Applied Electronic Instrumentation and Measurement, 0-675-21162-X

CICCARELLI
Circuit Modeling: Exercises and Software, Second Edition, 0-675-21152-2

COOPER
Introduction to VersaCAD, 0-675-21164-6

COX
Digital Experiments: Emphasizing Troubleshooting, Second Edition, 0-675-21196-4

CROFT
Getting a Job: Resume Writing, Job Application Letters, and Interview Strategies, 0-675-20917-X

DAVIS
Technical Mathematics, 0-675-20338-4
Technical Mathematics with Calculus, 0-675-20965-X
Study Guide to Accompany Technical Mathematics, 0-675-20966-8
Study Guide to Accompany Technical Mathematics with Calculus, 0-675-20964-1

DELKER
Experiments in 8085 Microprocessor Programming and Interfacing, 0-675-20663-4

FLOYD
Digital Fundamentals, Fourth Edition, 0-675-21217-0
Electric Circuits Fundamentals, Second Edition, 0-675-21408-4
Electronic Devices, Third Edition, 0-675-22170-6
Electronic Devices: Electron Flow Version, 0-02-338540-5
Electronics Fundamentals: Circuits, Devices, and Applications, Second Edition, 0-675-21310-X
Fundamentals of Linear Circuits, 0-02-338481-6
Principles of Electric Circuits, Electron Flow Version, Second Edition, 0-675-21292-8
Principles of Electric Circuits, Third Edition, 0-675-21062-3

FULLER *Robotics: Introduction, Programming, and Projects,* 0-675-21078-X
GAONKAR *Microprocessor Architecture, Programming, and Applications with the 8085/8080A, Second Edition,* 0-675-20675-8
The Z80 Microprocessor: Architecture, Interfacing, Programming, and Design, 0-675-20540-9
GILLIES *Instrumentation and Measurements for Electronic Technicians,* 0-675-20432-1
GOETSCH *Industrial Supervision: In the Age of High Technology,* 0-675-22137-4
GOETSCH/RICKMAN *Computer-Aided Drafting with AutoCAD,* 0-675-20915-3
GOODY *Programming and Interfacing the 8086/8088 Microprocessor,* 0-675-21312-6
HUBERT *Electric Machines: Theory, Operation, Applications, Adjustment, and Control,* 0-675-21136-0
HUMPHRIES *Motors and Controls,* 0-675-20235-3
HUTCHINS *Introduction to Quality: Management, Assurance and Control,* 0-675-20896-3
KEOWN *PSpice and Circuit Analysis,* 0-675-22135-8
KEYSER *Materials Science in Engineering, Fourth Edition,* 0-675-20401-1
KIRKPATRICK *The AutoCAD Book: Drawing, Modeling and Applications, Second Edition,* 0-675-22288-5
Industrial Blueprint Reading and Sketching, 0-675-20617-0
KRAUT *Fluid Mechanics for Technicians,* 0-675-21330-4
KULATHINAL *Transform Analysis and Electronic Networks with Applications,* 0-675-20765-7
LAMIT/LLOYD *Drafting for Electronics,* 0-675-20200-0
LAMIT/WAHLER/HIGGINS *Workbook in Drafting for Electronics,* 0-675-20417-8
LAMIT/PAIGE *Computer-Aided Design and Drafting,* 0-675-20475-5
LAVIANA *Basic Computer Numerical Control Programming, Second Edition,* 0-675-21298-7
MacKENZIE *The 8051 Microcontroller,* 0-02-373650-X
MARUGGI *Technical Graphics: Electronics Worktext, Second Edition,* 0-675-21378-9
The Technology of Drafting, 0-675-20762-2
Workbook for the Technology of Drafting, 0-675-21234-0
McCALLA *Digital Logic and Computer Design,* 0-675-21170-0
McINTYRE *Study Guide to accompany Electronic Devices, Third Edition* and *Electronic Devices, Electron Flow Version,* 0-02-379296-5
Study Guide to accompany Electronics Fundamentals, Second Edition, 0-675-21406-8
MILLER *The 68000 Microprocessor Family: Architecture, Programming, and Applications, Second Edition,* 0-02-381560-4
MONACO *Essential Mathematics for Electronics Technicians,* 0-675-21172-7
Introduction to Microwave Technology, 0-675-21030-5
Laboratory Activities in Microwave Technology, 0-675-21031-3
Preparing for the FCC General Radiotelephone Operator's License Examination, 0-675-21313-4
Student Resource Manual to accompany Essential Mathematics for Electronics Technicians, 0-675-21173-5
MONSSEN *PSpice with Circuit Analysis,* 0-675-21376-2
MOTT *Applied Fluid Mechanics, Third Edition,* 0-675-21026-7
Machine Elements in Mechanical Design, Second Edition, 0-675-22289-3
NASHELSKY/BOYLESTAD *BASIC Applied to Circuit Analysis,* 0-675-20161-6
PANARES *A Handbook of English for Technical Students,* 0-675-20650-2
PFEIFFER *Proposal Writing: The Art of Friendly Persuasion,* 0-675-20988-9
Technical Writing: A Practical Approach, 0-675-21221-9
POND *Introduction to Engineering Technology,* 0-675-21003-8
QUINN *The 6800 Microprocessor,* 0-675-20515-8
REIS *Digital Electronics Through Project Analysis,* 0-675-21141-7
Electronic Project Design and Fabrication, Second Edition, 0-02-399230-1
Laboratory Manual for Digital Electronics Through Project Analysis, 0-675-21254-5
ROLLE *Thermodynamics and Heat Power, Third Edition,* 0-675-21016-X
ROSENBLATT/FRIEDMAN *Direct and Alternating Current Machinery, Second Edition,* 0-675-20160-8
ROZE *Technical Communication: The Practical Craft,* 0-675-20641-3
SCHOENBECK *Electronic Communications: Modulation and Transmission, Second Edition,* 0-675-21311-8
SCHWARTZ *Survey of Electronics, Third Edition,* 0-675-20162-4
SELL *Basic Technical Drawing,* 0-675-21001-1

SMITH	*Statistical Process Control and Quality Improvement,* 0-675-21160-3
SORAK	*Linear Integrated Circuits: Laboratory Experiments,* 0-675-20661-8
SPIEGEL/LIMBRUNNER	*Applied Statics and Strength of Materials,* 0-675-21123-9
STANLEY, B.H.	*Experiments in Electric Circuits, Third Edition,* 0-675-21088-7
STANLEY, W.D.	*Operational Amplifiers with Linear Integrated Circuits, Second Edition,* 0-675-20660-X
SUBBARAO	*16/32-Bit Microprocessors: 68000/68010/68020 Software, Hardware, and Design Applications,* 0-675-21119-0
TOCCI	*Electronic Devices: Conventional Flow Version, Third Edition,* 0-675-20063-6
	Fundamentals of Pulse and Digital Circuits, Third Edition, 0-675-20033-4
	Introduction to Electric Circuit Analysis, Second Edition, 0-675-20002-4
TOCCI/OLIVER	*Fundamentals of Electronic Devices, Fourth Edition,* 0-675-21259-6
WEBB	*Programmable Logic Controllers: Principles and Applications, Second Edition,* 0-02-424970-X
WEBB/GRESHOCK	*Industrial Control Electronics,* 0-675-20897-1
WEISMAN	*Basic Technical Writing, Sixth Edition,* 0-675-21256-1
WOLANSKY/AKERS	*Modern Hydraulics: The Basics at Work,* 0-675-20987-0
WOLF	*Statics and Strength of Materials: A Parallel Approach,* 0-675-20622-7

PREFACE

INTRODUCTION

You have completed a basic 8-bit course in microcomputers and would like to continue your studies into the 16-bit world. Or, perhaps you wish to begin or continue your studies at the 16-bit level and would like a more practical, product-development-oriented approach. This text was written with you in mind.

PURPOSE AND APPROACH

Condensed into a single paragraph, here is a brief, ''snapshot'' look at the book's purpose and content: The text is introductory in nature; yet, due to its organization into layers of difficulty and its gradual step-by-step approach, the material is appropriate for 2-year or 4-year technician, technology, or engineering students. It covers hardware and interfacing, but with a strong emphasis on software development. The content is based on the Intel family of 16- and 32-bit microprocessors, the IBM PC development system, and programming in assembly-language and C. Depending on your background and on the objectives of your class, you can use this book as a laboratory supplement, or as a text, workbook, and laboratory manual all rolled into one.

Besides its overall content and purpose, as summarized above, a textbook also has a ''personality''—that which makes it different from other texts in the field. In this text we introduce the world of the 16-bit microprocessor in the only way that is practical: A hands-on, product-development, problem-solving (critical-thinking) approach that parallels the methods of industry. In other words, most of your time will be spent in front of a computer performing ''real-world'' tasks. For this reason, the majority of this text is organized around experimentally-based activities rather than theory-based chapters.

To better appreciate the text's approach—its personality—let us *dream* for just a moment. Would it not be grand if we could solve a variety of ''real-world'' problems in the laboratory? For example, a robotics project that requires us to interface a stepper motor to an external binary port, write basic movement routines in assembly-language and store them in a library, compose the main control program in C, command the motor's operation by way of the IBM PC keyboard and monitor, interrupt the motor's operation during an emergency, and have this robotic system "learn" the routine by storing in real time the sequence of commands in a file—all within the troubleshooting environment of a symbolic debugger. It is the intent of this text to turn such dreams into reality, and to do it in a way that everyone can follow.

The approach is one of "mix-and-match": The combining of *embedded* and *non-embedded* systems, methods of input and output, hardware and software, and assembly-language and C programming in any way we wish. Into this best-of-all-worlds brew, we throw in liberal amounts of *structured design,* including the use of *libraries* to modularize our programs and to make *mixed-language* programming (combining assembly and C) possible.

Now that we have an overview of what this text is about, let's sharpen our focus in several areas.

ORGANIZATION

The activities are divided into eight parts as follows: The first four parts cover *structured design* and are based on assembly-language and binary (embedded) ports. Part IV brings in *modularization, top-down design,* and the use of libraries, and Part V adds data I/O by way of the IBM PC keyboard and monitor. Part VI deals with more advanced mathematics, code conversion, and sign-number operations. Part VII introduces the C language and allows us to program in a mixed-language environment, and Part VIII gives us an opportunity to apply all that we have learned through a variety of projects. A quick glance at the Table of Contents will give you a more detailed overview of the material covered.

This text can be used by a variety of students, from technician and technology to engineering and science. First of all, to give all students a chance to "get up to speed," the earlier activities are straightforward and cover very basic material. As we progress through the activities, from the simpler to the more advanced, we find new material building on older material until we have all the tools and skills we need to perform more complex activities and projects. Second, all activities include many levels of difficulty from simple to complex, allowing all students to work at a level that provides both successful accomplishment and a challenging environment.

Also important is the laboratory equipment. To make sure we are in the "mainstream," we use the most popular, inexpensive, and readily-available development system tools. On the hardware side, we use the IBM PC and 8086 Intel microprocessor family. On the software side we use assembly-language and C, presently the most popular languages of the programming community. To streamline troubleshooting we use a powerful symbolic debugger.

COVERAGE

As stated earlier, this text is designed for both embedded and non-embedded systems. Let's make sure the distinction is clear. A non-embedded system is one in which the program is stored on disk, and input and output are in ASCII by way of keyboard and monitor. Most textbooks deal exclusively with non-embedded systems; engineers and technicians, however, usually work in an embedded environment, with program stored in an EPROM and input and output in binary by way of IC ports. As indicated, this lab/text manual includes both sides of this programming coin.

The reason that embedded system development is often neglected is that it includes a hardware component and requires a *development system.* A true embedded system is one dedicated to a specific application, built around a microcontroller chip (such as the 8051), with program stored in an EPROM, port access by way of ICs, and the entire development process under control of a full-fledged in-circuit-emulator (ICE).

Because such a system is impractical for a student laboratory, we greatly simplify the setup by using the technique of *emulation.* The only hardware absolutely required is an IBM PC or clone. For some of the activities, we suggest the use of a *bus-extender* to access external ports and to drive peripheral devices (such as a stepper motor), but in many cases even these can be bypassed using simulation techniques. Everything you need to know to perform both embedded and non-embedded product-development using emulation is presented within.

All the programs within this manual were written and tested using Microsoft software (MASM, QuickC, Codeview, and utilities). Although Microsoft software is recommended, and occasional reference is made to this specific product, the majority of activities in this manual are "software generic," and most any assembler, C compiler, and debugger can be used. For example, Turbo Assembler from Borland is 100% MASM-compatible. If you wish to perform mixed-language programming, introduced in Activity 26, make sure that your chosen software has the ability to combine (link) modules written in either assembly or C.

PREREQUISITES

Although this manual is introductory in nature, we assume some prerequisite knowledge. Recent completion of an introductory course in digital and 8-bit microprocessors (preferably the 8085) would be an ideal background. We also assume access to literature in such topics as a text editor, batch files, and simple DOS commands. Little or no previous knowledge of hardware interfacing, 8086 assembly-language programming, C programming, or a development system is necessary.

To keep report-writing to a minimum, there is sufficient space to enter all information and record all results. However, the "advanced activities" section of each activity and the applications projects of Part VIII do require a separate sheet to report results. The form of this report is to be specified by each instructor.

I would like to thank the following for reviewing the manuscript: Michael Batchelder, South Dakota School of Mines and Technology; David Delker, Kansas State University; Frank Gergelyi, Metropolitan Technical Institute; Charles Javens, Haywood Community College; Nazar Karzay, Indiana Vocational-Technical College; and Ron Moody, Pima Community College.

To the reader: Good luck and good success.

Roy W. Goody
Instructor
Mission College
Computer/Electronics Technology

CONTENTS

SECTION 1

SECTION 2

SECTION 1

Section 1 consists of two chapters based on the central theme of *product development*. The chapters are brief and limited in scope; their primary objective is to smooth our way into the experimental activities of Section 2.

Chapter 1 covers the early stages of product development, with a review of 8086/88 hardware design and an introduction to the format of assembly-language programs.

Chapter 2 covers the final stages of product development by using a *development system* for hardware/software integration, testing, and troubleshooting.

CHAPTER 1

HARDWARE/SOFTWARE DEVELOPMENT

This chapter begins the product development process. We assemble the hardware and examine the assembly-language format.

Product Development Overview

Product development begins with an idea. For non-embedded systems [Figure C1.1(a)], the process is all software development, with the end product a program on a floppy disk. The program is executed on the IBM PC, and all input and output is by way of keyboard and screen (or other standard I/O device such as a mouse).

For embedded systems [Figure C1.1(b)], the design effort is more complex because it is split into two components: hardware design and software design. During the integration phase, the hardware and software components are combined, the system is tested, and modifications are made. The final product is a dedicated system, with a customized program stored in an ''embedded'' EPROM (electrically programmable read-only memory), and input/output (I/O) by way of binary ports.

Following the embedded system approach, we review both hardware and software design in this chapter.

Hardware Design

As shown by Figure C1.2, all microcomputer systems, regardless of their complexity, consist of three core components: a central processing unit (CPU), ROM/RAM memory, and I/O ports. The address, data, and control buses connect these three types of components and are used by the CPU to access memory and I/O. In this section we begin with a discussion of the 8086/88 microprocessor, followed by a review of ROM, RAM, and I/O port interfacing. We conclude with a brief overview and comparison of the 8086, 80286, 80386, and 80486 microprocessors.

Maximum versus minimum modes

The 8086/88 offers two modes of operation controlled by the MN/$\overline{\text{MX}}$ pin: minimum and maximum. When MN/$\overline{\text{MX}}$ is high, we are in the minimum mode [Figure C1.2(a)] and only a single 8086/88 can interface the system bus. When MN/$\overline{\text{MX}}$ is low, we are in the maximum mode [Figure C1.2(b)] and several pins are redefined to support

FIGURE C1.1

The product development process. (a) Nonembedded systems. (b) Embedded systems.

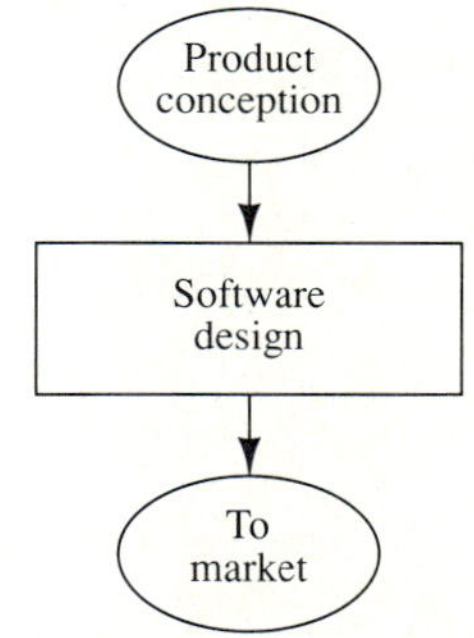

(a) Non-embedded systems

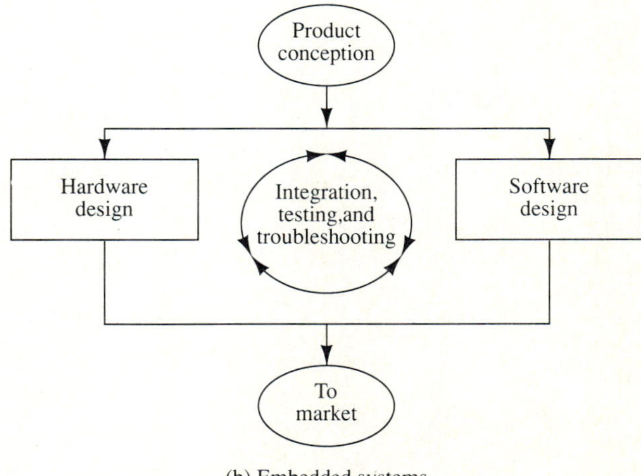

(b) Embedded systems

FIGURE C1.2

Microcomputer systems. (a) Single-processor (minimum) system. (b) Multiprocessor (maximum) system.

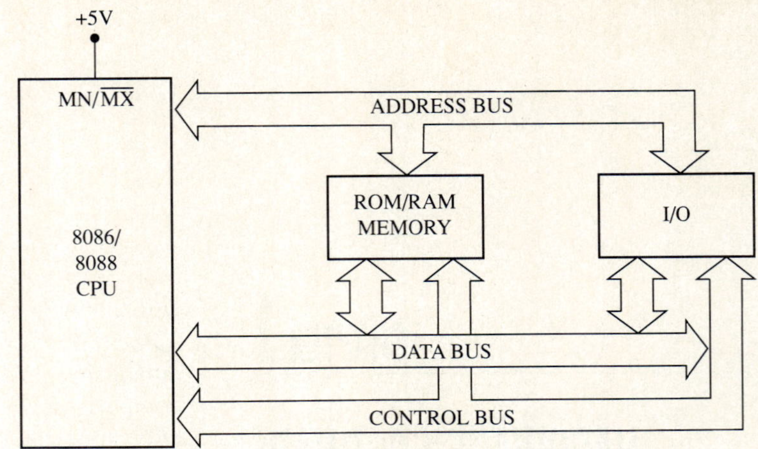

(a) Single-processor (minimum) system

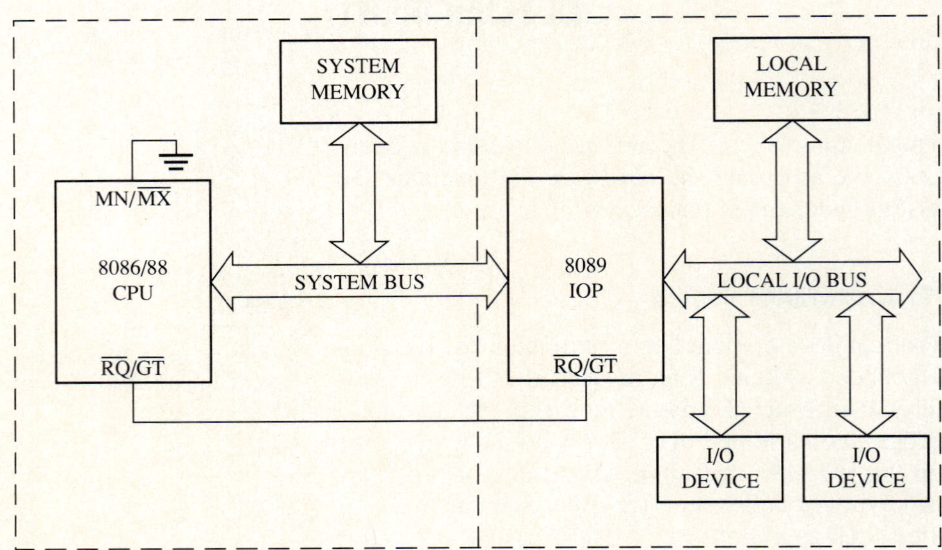

(b) Multi-processor (maximum) system

FIGURE C1.3

8086 addressing using high- and low-memory banks.

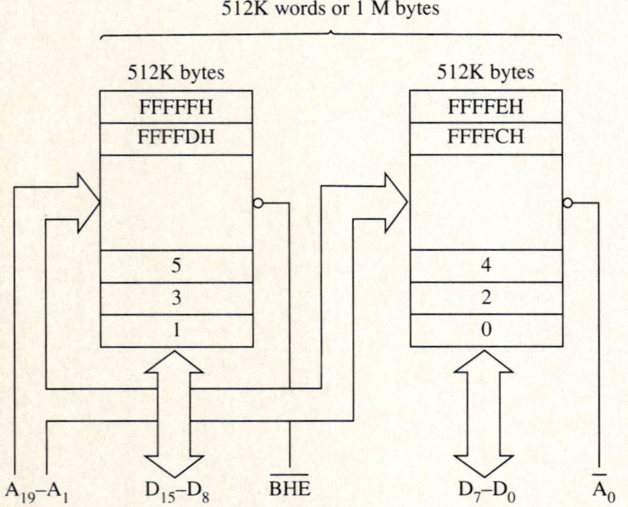

FIGURE C1.4

8086/8088 prefetching architecture.

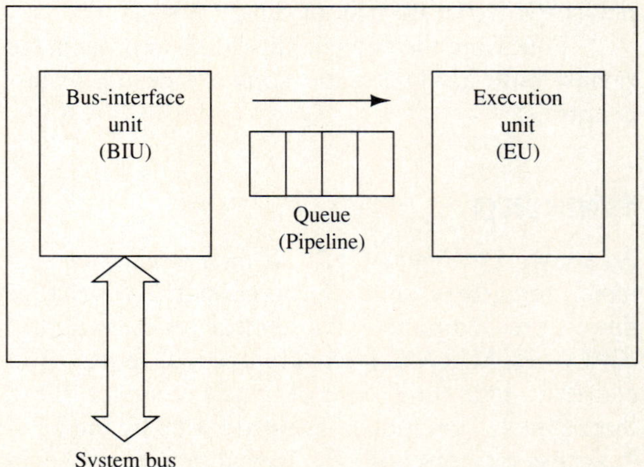

multiprocessing. In this mode, the 8089 input/output processor, the 8087 math *coprocessor*, or other 8086/88 slave processors can share the system bus with the 8086/88 master processor. *Request/grant* ($\overline{RQ}/\overline{GT}$) handshaking lines and the 8289 bus arbiter synchronize the use of the shared system bus.

The 8088 versus the 8086

The 8088 is 100% software compatible with the 8086. The only major difference is the size of the external data bus—8 bits for the 8088 and 16 bits for the 8086. To transfer a 16-bit word, the 8088 must perform two data transfer operations.

Because it is useful for the 8086 to access 8-bit bytes as well as 16-bit words, it uses the *bank-select* method to organize memory. Referring to Figure C1.3, address lines A1 through A19 select the desired word location and bank-select lines A0 and $\overline{BHE}$ *(bank high enable)* select either the low-order byte (A0 low), the high-order byte ($\overline{BHE}$ low), or the entire word (A0 and $\overline{BHE}$ low).

The internal architecture

Looking inside the 8086/88 (Figure C1.4), we see three major sections: a *bus interface unit* (BIU), an *execution unit* (EU), and an *instruction queue* (pipeline) linking the two. The reason for this novel structure is speed. The BIU *prefetches* instruction bytes whenever the EU is not using the bus and stores them in the queue. When the EU completes the execution of the present instruction, the next instruction's operation code and operand are usually waiting "in the wings" (the queue). Because future instructions are fetched while present instructions are executed, the instruction fetch times are normally "invisible."

The next level of detail (Figure C1.5) reveals the internal register set. The four-word (or eight-byte) registers (AX, BX, CX, and DX) are used for general-purpose data storage and to hold dedicated information required by certain instructions. The source index (SI) and destination index (DI) registers support indexed addressing and are used specifically by the string instructions. The stackpointer (SP) and base pointer (BP) are used for stack operations, and the flags are used primarily for conditional branching. The four *segment* registers (CS, DS, SS, and ES) along with the *instruction pointer* (IP) are used to locate instructions and data and are based on *segmented addressing*.

Segmented addressing

Referring to Figure C1.6, the 1 megabyte (Mbyte) of 8086/88 memory space contains up to four 64K *segments*. The bottom (lowest memory address) of each segment is known as its *segment base* and always begins at a memory address evenly divided by 16—which means that the 4 least significant bits are zero. Therefore, only the upper 16 bits are stored in the 16-bit segment registers. Once a segment is selected by specifying its segment base, we

FIGURE C1.5

8088 functional block diagram. (Courtesy Intel Corporation.)

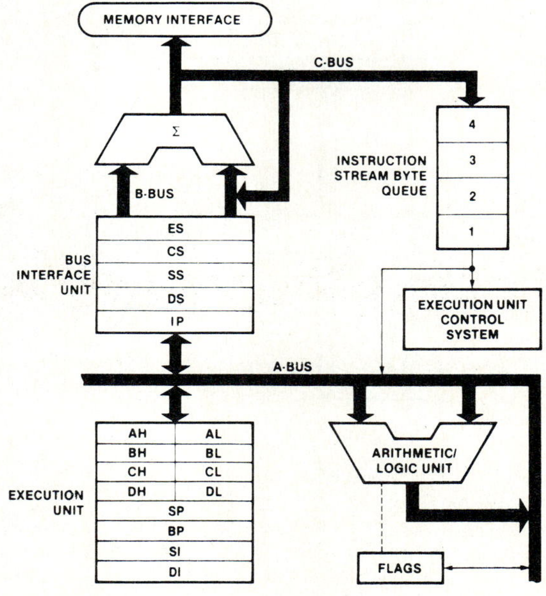

FIGURE C1.6

The 8086/8088 memory segmentation model. (Courtesy Intel Corporation.)

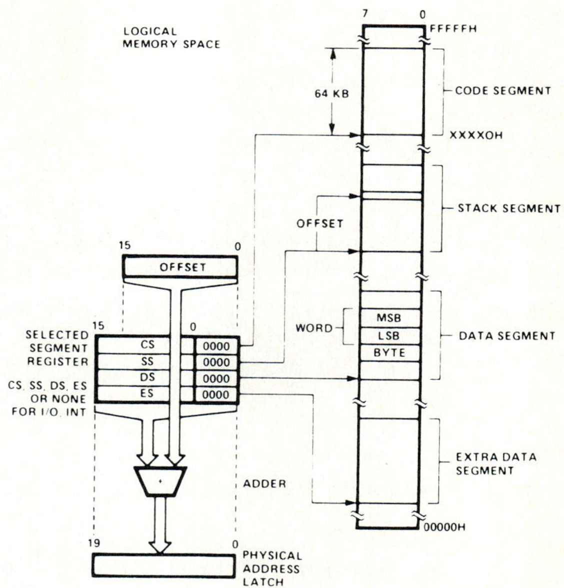

FIGURE C1.7

Generating the 20-bit physical address. (Courtesy Intel Corporation.)

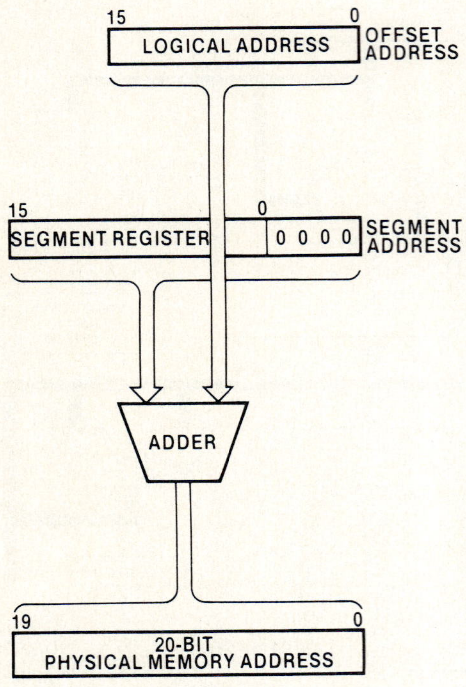

locate a byte or word within the segment by specifying its 16-bit *offset*.

The 20-bit *physical* address, to be released to the external address bus, is generated from the segment and offset addresses as shown in detail in Figure C1.7. Determination of which of the four segment registers is used is accomplished by default and follows the segment selection rules of Figure C1.8. A special *segment override prefix* added to an instruction will override the default condition for those operations that allow an alternate segment base. Also listed in Figure C1.8 are the sources of the offset address. (Be aware that the terms *offset, logical address,* and *effective address* all refer to the same item: the distance from the segment base given as a 16-bit address.)

Input/output ports are subject to segment addressing if they use *memory-mapped I/O,* in which ports are treated as individual memory locations. If using *isolated I/O,* in which the port address space is separate from the memory space, the addresses are not segmented but are a simple linear sequence of the 16-bit numbers from 0 to FFFFH. Isolated I/O is automatic when using the special IN/OUT instructions.

Timing and multiplexing

The *instruction cycle* is the time it takes to process one complete instruction. Because of prefetching, this is usually the time it takes to execute the instruction. Within the instruction cycle are one or more *machine cycles.* Each machine cycle carries out a single data transfer and performs other operations (such as arithmetic or logical) as needed. Within each machine cycle are three or more *states*; each state lasts for one clock cycle.

The timing/waveform diagram of the 8086/88 (Figure C1.9) is based on a single "generic" machine cycle and shows how address, data, and status information are *multiplexed.* Early in each memory or port-access machine cycle, low-level address and status information is output and latched into external circuitry by the ALE *(address latch enable)* signal. Later in the same machine cycle, data are transferred during the time the $\overline{RD}$ or $\overline{WR}$ control signal is active.

Pinout

We complete our discussion of the CPU by looking at the pins and signals of the 8088 (Figure C1.10), first in the minimum mode.

FIGURE C1.8

Segment selection rules. (Courtesy Intel Corporation.)

TYPE OF MEMORY REFERENCE	DEFAULT SEGMENT BASE	ALTERNATE SEGMENT BASE	LOGICAL ADDRESS
Instruction Fetch	CS	NONE	IP
Stack Operation	SS	NONE	SP
String Source	DS	CS,ES,SS	SI
String Destination	ES	NONE	DI
BP Used As Base Register	SS	CS,DS,ES	Effective Address
General Data Read/Write	DS	CS,ES,SS	Effective Address

FIGURE C1.9

The 8086/8088 machine cycle waveforms.

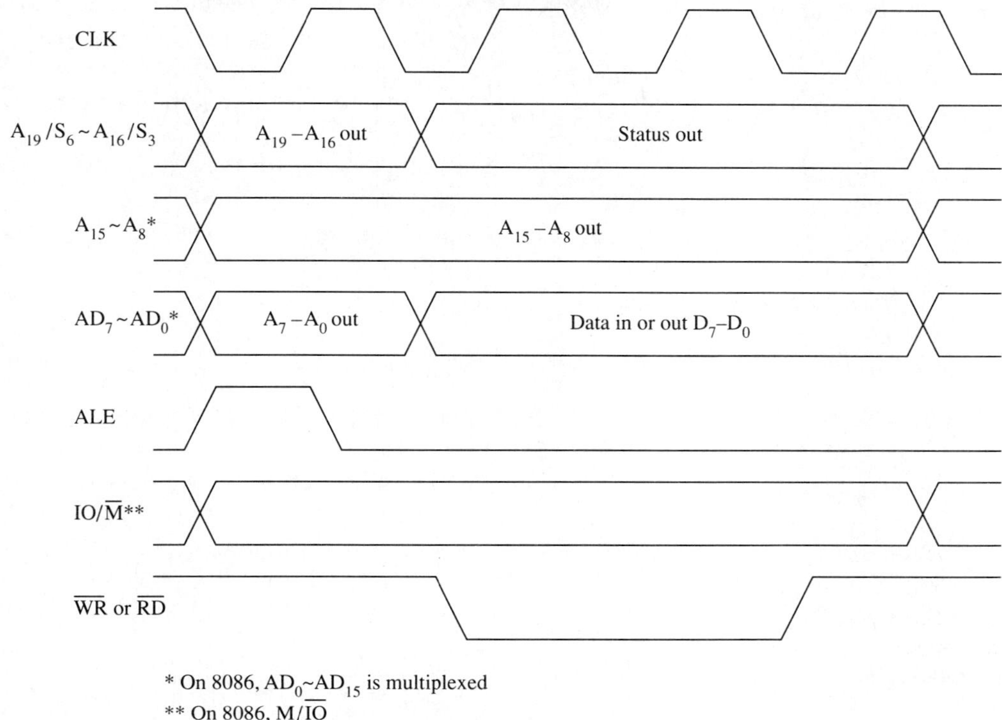

- The "AD" pins are multiplexed lines in which low-level address and data share the same pins.
- The "AS" pins are multiplexed lines in which high-level address and status share the same pins. Status information is used to identify the type of operation under way.
- The "A" lines are nonmultiplexed medium-level address lines and are combined with the demultiplexed "AD" and "AS" lines to form a 20-bit physical address.
- The IO/$\overline{M}$ line (M/$\overline{IO}$ for the 8086) determines if a given machine cycle is accessing a memory location or a port location. IO/$\overline{M}$ is active only during the execution of the IN or OUT instructions. (In a memory-mapped system, it is not used.)
- The $\overline{RD}$ and $\overline{WR}$ control lines time the flow of memory or port information to or from the 8086/88. They go active-low after the address has stabilized. The IBM PC decodes the IO/$\overline{M}$, $\overline{RD}$, and $\overline{WR}$ signals to generate the "8080-type" bus signals $\overline{MEM/R}$, $\overline{MEM/W}$, $\overline{IO/R}$, and $\overline{IO/W}$.
- HOLD tri-states (floats) the address, data, and control pins for DMA (direct memory access) operations. HLDA (hold-acknowledge) acknowledges the DMA state.
- READY is used to stretch the active part of a machine cycle (when $\overline{RD}$ or $\overline{WR}$ are low) by add-

FIGURE C1.10

The 8088 pinout. (Courtesy Intel Corporation.)

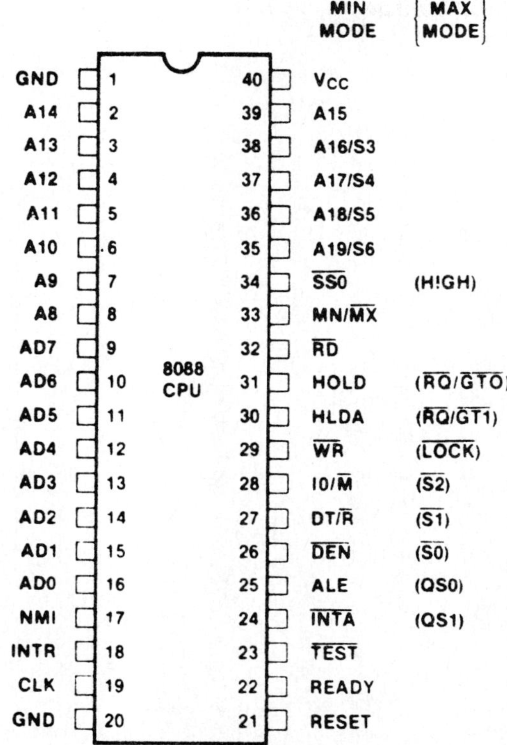

ing special wait states. It is often used in conjunction with slow memory.

- RESET sets CS to FFFFH and IP to 0000H and begins an instruction fetch machine cycle from that location.
- DEN and DT/$\overline{\text{R}}$ are used to control optional external address and data buffers.
- $\overline{\text{TEST}}$ is a 1-bit input port examined by the *wait* instruction. If $\overline{\text{TEST}}$ is high, the 8086/88 enters an ''idle'' state. $\overline{\text{TEST}}$ and *wait* are used by the 8087 math coprocessor to coordinate activities with the 8086/88.
- NMI (non-maskable-interrupt), INTR (interrupt-request), and $\overline{\text{INTA}}$ (interrupt-acknowledge) process external interrupts.

In the maximum mode, several of these pins take over handshaking duties in order to coordinate bus access between multiple processors.

- $\overline{\text{RQ0}}/\overline{\text{GT0}}$ and $\overline{\text{RQ1}}/\overline{\text{GT1}}$ are bidirectional handshaking lines that arbitrate the use of the system bus between the 8086/88 and coprocessor.
- $\overline{\text{LOCK}}$ is an instruction prefix that causes the

FIGURE C1.11

The major signals and buses of the 8088. (a) Minimum mode. (b) Maximum mode. (Courtesy Intel Corporation.)

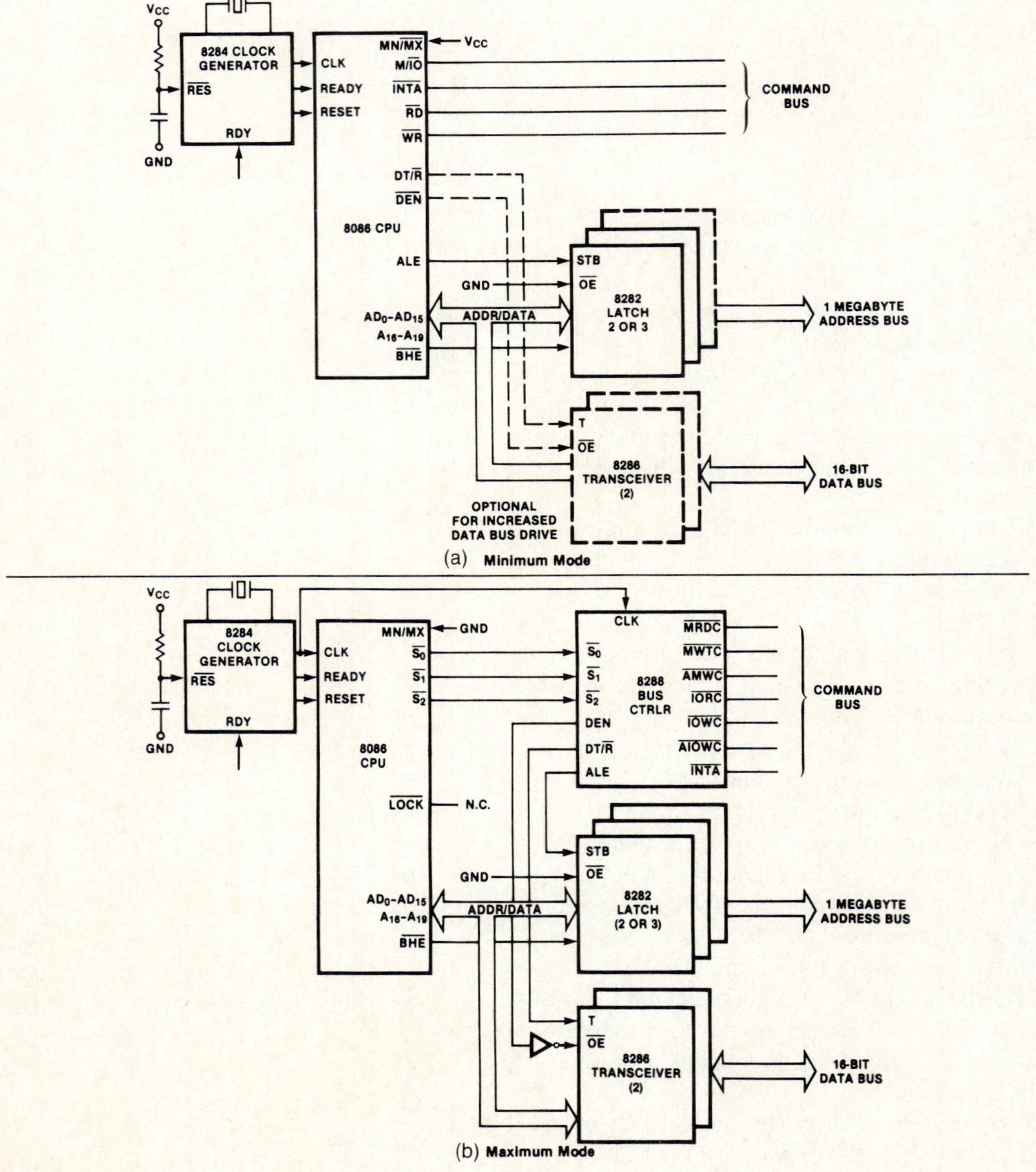

$\overline{\text{LOCK}}$ pin to go low, preventing another processor from using the system bus.

- QS0 and QS1 are *queue status* signals that track the progress of an instruction through the queue. They are used by coprocessors that receive their instructions by way of the ESC prefix (such as the 8087).
- $\overline{\text{S0}}$, $\overline{\text{S1}}$, and $\overline{\text{S2}}$ are *status* output signals to the 8288 *bus controller*. They are encoded signals that provide the information lost (such as the port and memory read/write control signals) when certain pins are redefined in the maximum mode.

These various pins and signals are summarized by the diagrams of Figure C1.11. The 8282 latch demultiplexes the data/address bus, the 8284 clock generator provides a crystal-controlled clock, the 8286 transceiver provides extra buffering, and the 8288 bus controller decodes the status output lines to provide maximum-mode control bus signals.

RAM, ROM, and I/O port interfacing

By interfacing ROM, RAM, and ports to the minimum-mode system of Figure C1.11(a), we design the 7-chip bare minimum "embedded" system of Figure C1.12. The 8155A provides 256 bytes of RAM and three programmable I/O ports, the 2732A gives 4K × 8 of ROM (EPROM), and the two 8205 decoders provide high-level addressing. The 8155A is a special chip that decodes the low-order address lines internally. Because A10 and A11 to the 2732A are tied high to reduce the number of address bus lines required, the chip is effectively a 1K × 8 ROM.

A major responsibility of the hardware designer is to place the RAM, ROM, and I/O ports at

FIGURE C1.12

8088-based minimum system.

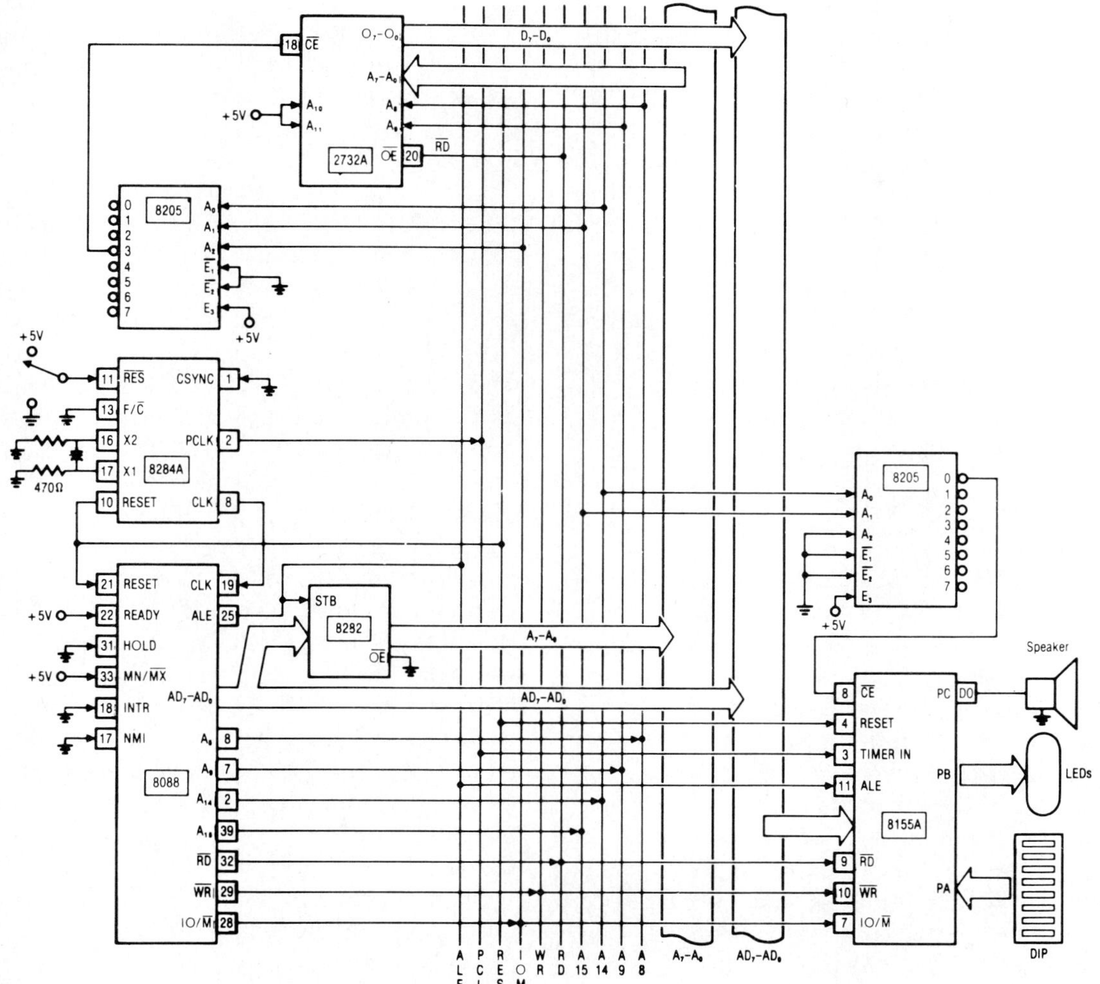

FIGURE C1.13

2732A addressing.

High-level

A_{19}	A_{18}	A_{17}	A_{16}	A_{15}	A_{14}	A_{13}	A_{12}	A_{11}	A_{10}
X	X	X	X	1	1	X	X	X	X

Don't care — Don't care

Low-level

A_9	A_8	A_7	A_6	A_5	A_4	A_3	A_2	A_1	A_0
0									0
				to					
1									1

the desired addresses. We begin with ROM.

Referring to Figure C1.13, we divide the 20-bit address into ten high-level address lines (to select the chip), and ten low-level address lines (to select the desired location within the chip). Since only high-level lines A14 and A15 are used, we have a partially decoded system that results in a great deal of "foldback" (multiple address blocks that point to the same physical memory).

Because ROM must be placed at the top of memory to hold the "bootstrap jump" (a jump from the FFFF0H reset location to the start of the program), the 2732A is selected when both A14 and A15 are high. Arbitrarily setting the remaining high-level lines to "1" places the ROM chip at FFC00H to FFFFFH.

Turning to the 8155A RAM I/O chip, the 256 bytes of RAM must be placed at the bottom of memory to hold the interrupt vectors. Therefore, the chip is selected when A14 and A15 are low, giving an address range of 00000H to 000FFH. Because a single chip select enables both RAM and I/O ports, the port addresses "tag along" at the bottom of the I/O space (0, 1, 2, and 3). Because the 8155A accepts the IO/$\overline{\text{M}}$ signal, the ports use isolated I/O and are accessed by the IN/OUT instructions.

By adding specialized ports and peripherals, the system is customized for dedicated operation.

The 80286, 80386, and 80486 microprocessors

Since the 8086/88 was introduced, microprocessor applications have increased from a single user performing a single task to a multiuser, multitasking environment requiring virtual-memory management, memory protection, and task switching. The 80286 was designed with these needs in mind.

The 80286 offers two modes of operation: *real* and *protected*. The real mode mimics the 8086 and is based on the same 1 Mbyte of memory space. In the protected mode, the real address space expands to 16 Mbyte, which in turn maps into a full gigabyte of virtual memory per task. (A virtual-memory system stores most instructions in secondary memory and brings blocks of them into main memory as needed.) All programs written for the 8086 will run in either mode without modification.

When we compare the conventional 8086 memory system with the protected memory mode of the 80286 (Figure C1.14), we see a significant change. Instead of segment registers, we have *segment selectors* that use 14 of their 16 bits to point to one of the 16K *segment descriptors* located in physical memory. Each segment descriptor represents one 64K segment of virtual memory. To map a 64K segment of virtual memory to the 16 Mbyte of physical memory, the segment descriptor sends a 24-bit segment base address to the CPU. The offset then locates a value within the selected segment.

The memory protection feature of the 80286 allows the programmer to specify each data or code segment at one of four levels of privilege. A program may access data at only the same or less privileged level.

To support multitasking, the 80286 can save the state of one task, load the state of another, and resume execution in less than 17 microseconds (μs). It can respond to an interrupt in less than 4 μs.

Although in widespread use because of the IBM AT class of computers, the 80286 is overshadowed by the more powerful 80386. The 80386 offers 32-bit architecture, runs at 20 MHz, executes 5 million instructions per second, and accesses 4 gigabytes (Gbyte) of physical memory. Its improved pipelined architecture and on-chip memory management unit (MMU) greatly enhance its throughput. Programmers will be glad to know that nearly all programs written for the 8086 and 80286 will also run on the 80386. In fact, 16-bit programs written to run under DOS can run concurrently with 32-bit programs written to run under UNIX.

The 80386 expands the number of memory models over the 80286. Its virtual-memory capacity is an astounding 64 terabytes. When using segmented addressing, each segment can be up to 4 Gbyte. It even offers straight linear addressing (no segments) of its 4 Gbytes of physical memory. A protection and privilege scheme similar to that of the 80286 provides a system of security for sensitive applications.

FIGURE C1.14

8086/88 versus 80286/88 address generation. (a) 8086/88. (b) 80286/88.

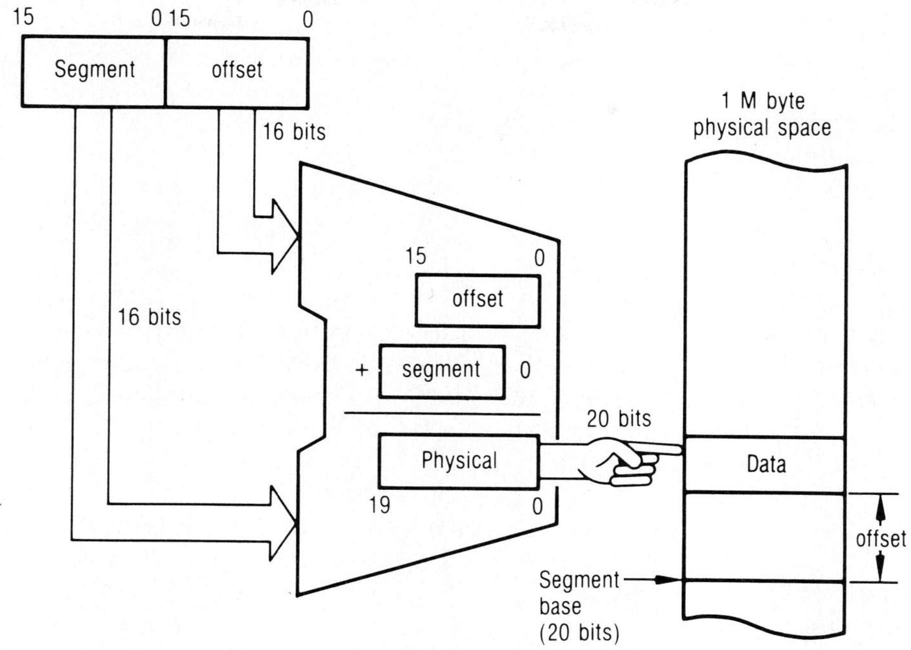

a. 8086/88.

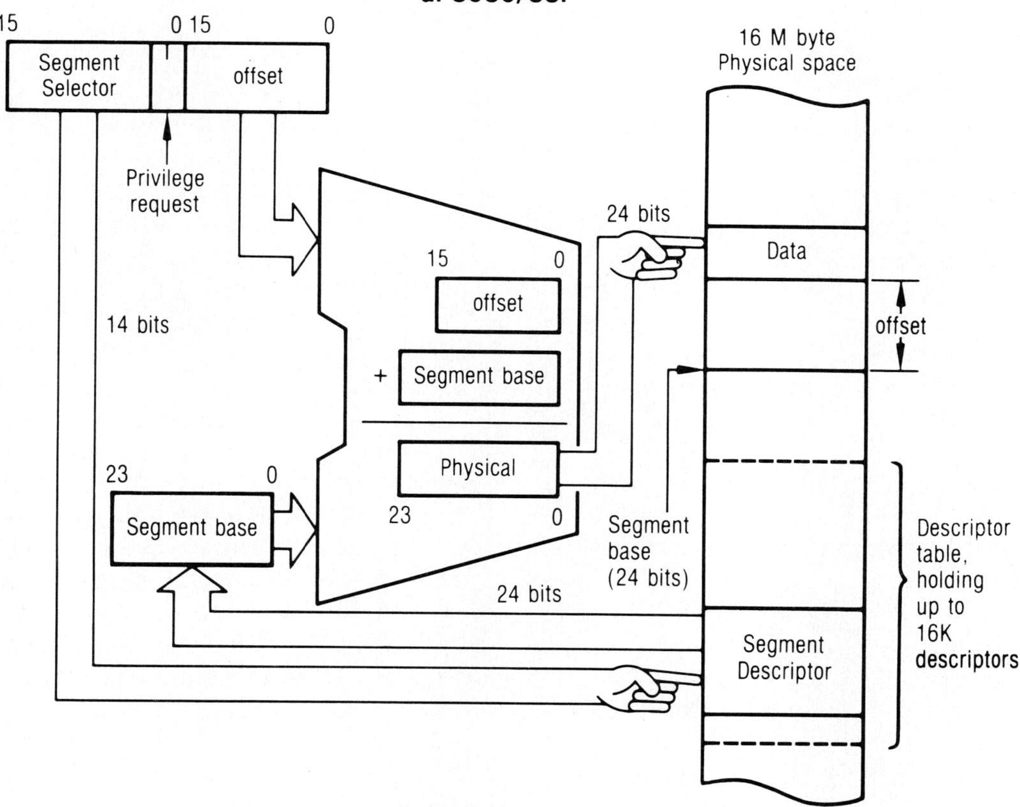

b. 80286/88.

The latest offering from Intel Corporation is the 80486 CPU, essentially a faster, more refined, more integrated 80386 microprocessor. Most impressive is the on-chip 387 math coprocessor, 8K on-chip cache (superfast memory that stores the group of instructions currently being executed), streamlined RISC (reduced instruction set computer) core, and the ability to run 80386 programs.

Software Design

In this section we cover the one area of software design not presented in detail within the activities: the assembly-language format. This will allow us to concentrate on the instruction set and programming techniques within the activities. The discussion is specific to Microsoft's assembly-language (MASM) and, therefore, may be slightly different from the format used by other assemblers.

To maintain compatibility with C, our assembly-language format must conform to a specific *segmentation model*. We can choose among TINY, SMALL, MEDIUM, COMPACT, LARGE, and HUGE. Because our programs are limited in size, we chose the default model SMALL. (The SMALL mode is also the most common model for embedded-systems applications.)

Program structure

The simple demonstration program of Figure C1.15 will allow us to refer to specific data and addresses

FIGURE C1.15

Assembly-language format and the relationship between logical segments and physical segments.

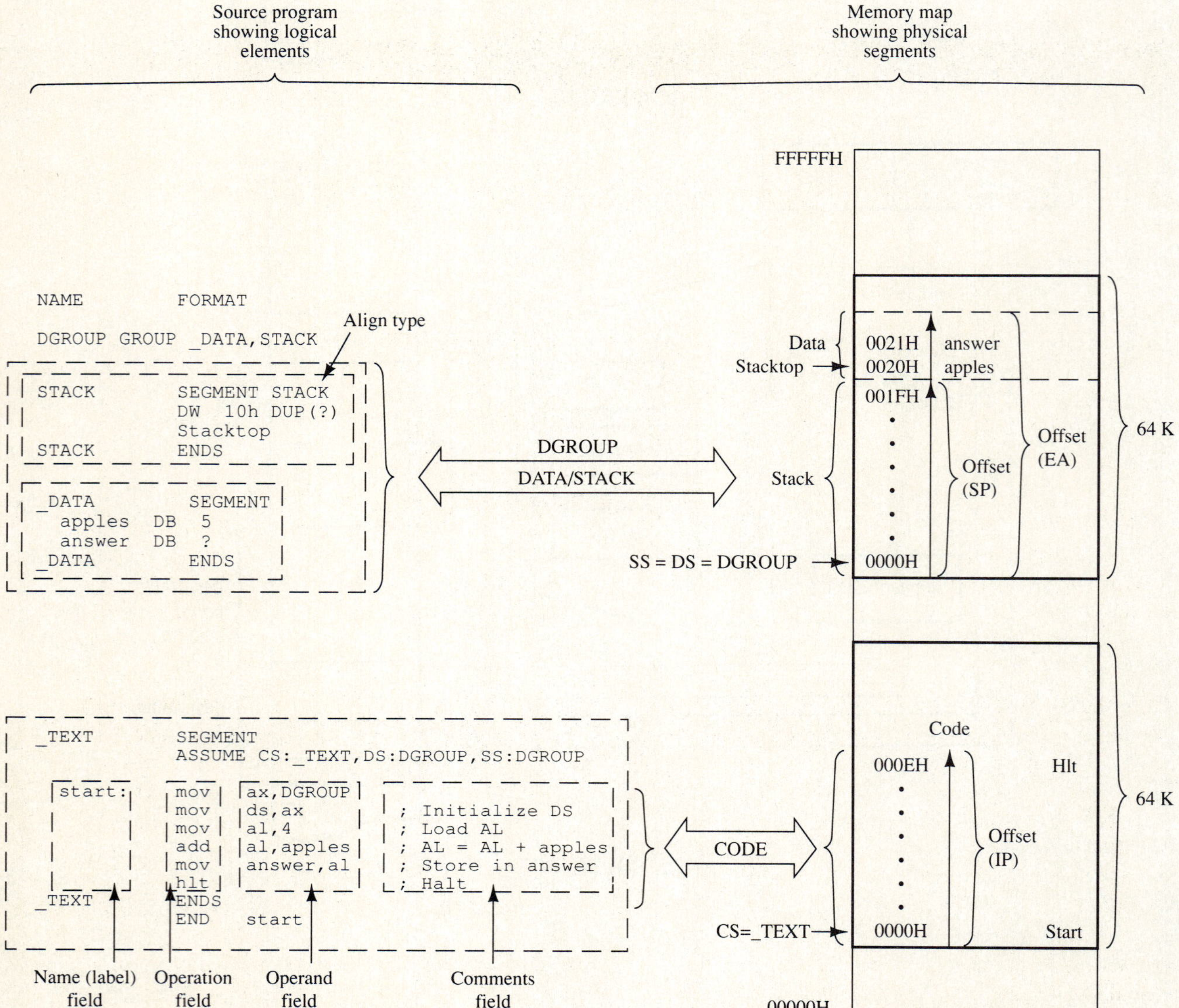

as we study the assembly-language format. The program initializes the DS register, loads 4 into register AL, adds byte variable *apples* to AL, and stores the result in byte variable *answer*. Although the stack is not used, we nevertheless set aside 32 bytes of stack space.

Overall, the most important feature of the program is *segmentation*. The source program consists of three *logical* segments. The _TEXT segment holds code, the _DATA segment holds variables, and the STACK segment holds stack data. Each logical segment of the source program corresponds to a *physical* segment of the memory map. We now focus on each section of the source programs in greater detail.

Referring to Figure C1.15, we first examine the top, where each program is named by entering a symbol (such as FORMAT) after the NAME directive.

The next line defines a GROUP. A GROUP is simply one or more segments combined so that they share a common base location and occupy no more than 64K. Because SMALL model programs are of limited size, this model combines segments _DATA and STACK into group DGROUP. When DGROUP is used within the program, it represents the common base address of this group, and offset values are automatically calculated relative to DGROUP. As shown, the first item listed in DGROUP is at offset zero.

The STACK segment, within group DGROUP, sets aside 20H (32) bytes of memory for stack operations. Locations 0 through 1FH hold stack data, and location 20H represents the top of the stack (STACKTOP). The stack pointer register (SP) is initialized to the value of STACKTOP and holds the offset address of the stack data. Note that by convention offset addresses go from top to bottom in the source program, but from bottom to top in the memory map. (When using MASM, the STACK *align type* causes initialization of the SP and SS registers.)

Moving to the _DATA segment, we find variables *apples* and *answer* defined and stored. Because segment _DATA belongs to the same group as segment STACK, these two byte variables are placed "on top of" the stack at locations 20H and 21H. (Variable *apples* can reside at location STACKTOP because only locations 0 through 1FH are actually used by the stack.) The offset addresses corresponding to variables *apples* and *answer* are calculated during assembly and are known as *effective addresses* (EAs). To locate the variables properly within group DGROUP, the assembler automatically adds 20H to their effective addresses.

The last segment (_TEXT) holds the executable code in source language format. Moving into the _TEXT segment, the ASSUME directive checks for errors during assembly. We tell the assembler what should be in the various segment registers at run time, and it checks to see if a piece of data or an instruction is accessible. For example, suppose we store a piece of data in segment DATA1, but we tell the assembler that register DS holds segment address DATA2 (ASSUME DS: DATA2). The assembler would catch the error and tell us that the data is not currently accessible. Because our SMALL model of segmentation allows only a single code, data, and stack segment, the role of the ASSUME statement is diminished.

Next comes the source code, arranged in four *fields*:

- The *name* field holds symbolic *labels* that "point to" instructions. Here, *start:* points to the first executable instruction. The same symbol after the END directive (marking the end of the program) causes the assembler to generate special code to initialize the CS and IP registers to point to *start:*.
- The *operation* field holds mnemonic op codes (such as *mov* and *add*).
- The *operand* field specifies the data to be operated on by the op code (such as *al,4* and *al,apples*).
- The *comments* field holds any statement desired by the programmer (such as *Load AL*). As shown, each comment must be preceded by a semicolon.

Address notations

In Figure C1.15, we refer to the offset, segment, and physical addresses in a number of ways. Listed below are several examples of address notations that are commonly used:

`0001H`	Numerical offset
`apples`	Symbolic offset
`0050H`	Numerical segment
`_TEXT`	Symbolic segment
`FF000H`	Numerical physical
`FF00:0000H`	Physical address split into numerical segment (FF00H) and numeric offset (0000)
`DGROUP:apples`	Physical address split into symbolic segment and symbolic offset
`DS:0001H`	Physical address split into "contents of DS" segment and numerical offset

Name: ______________________

Date: ______________________

Class: ______________________

QUESTIONS AND PROBLEMS

1. Does embedded-system product development usually include a hardware component?
2. For embedded-system product development, input/output (I/O) is usually accomplished by:
   a. IC ports using binary.
   b. keyboard and screen using ASCII.
3. To support multiprocessing, we must be in the:
   a. minimum mode.
   b. maximum mode.
4. If a program executes on an 8088 microprocessor, what changes have to be made to execute the program on an 8086?
5. On the 8086, what address line could logically be called *bank low enable*?
6. On the 8086/88, why are instruction fetch times normally "invisible"?
7. Which of the following registers would most likely be called the *accumulator*?
   a. SI
   b. CS
   c. AX
   d. DX
8. If the segment address is 1223H and the offset address is 3445H, what is the physical address?
9. What segment register is used by default during instruction-fetch operations?
10. I/O ports are treated as individual memory locations when using:
    a. isolated I/O.
    b. memory-mapped I/O.
11. What is always performed during a *machine cycle*?
12. Draw a waveform diagram for a typical input-port machine cycle. (Refer to Figure C1.9.)
13. What two pins on the 8086/88 are used for DMA operations?

14. When the 8086/88 is reset, the first op code is fetched from what *physical* address?

15. What is the purpose of *high-level* address lines?

16. What is *virtual memory*?

17. What normally is stored in the _TEXT segment?

18. What two reserved words bracket every segment?

19. Referring to the variable definitions below, at what *offset* addresses will the variables *apples* and *peaches* normally be placed?

```
_DATA   SEGMENT
   apples  DW ?
   peaches DB ?
_DATA ENDS
```

20. All segments belonging to the same GROUP have a common ____________ ____________ address.
21. When used in a program, what is the difference between ENDS and END?

22. Referring to Figure C1.15, what does label *start:* ‘‘point to’’?

Advanced Section

NOTE: For this and all future activities, research may be necessary to answer any of the questions and problems in the advanced section.

23. Why does the bus interface unit (BIU) operate independently from the execution unit (EU)?

24. When using the SMALL model of segmentation, what symbol defines the segment base address of the stack segment?

25. During which of the following could the $\overline{RD}$ control line be active low?
    a. Wait (Ready pulled low)
    b. Hold
26. What is the difference between the SMALL and LARGE models of segmentation?

CHAPTER 2

THE IBM PC DEVELOPMENT SYSTEM

This chapter completes the product development process started in Chapter 1. We move to the laboratory to write the program, integrate the hardware and software, and test the final product—all with the assistance of the IBM PC *development system.*

The Development System

A development system is a specialized computer that brings leverage to the process of product development. When the computer does what it does best (repetitive, menial tasks), we are free to spend more time in the world of inspiration, intuition, and creativity.

In this chapter we introduce the IBM PC development system, and we provide detailed information on the technique we call *emulation.*

For this discussion, we assume the following baseline system:

- IBM PC/XT/AT/386 or clone with 640K, black-and-white monitor, and single (or dual) 1.4M $3\frac{1}{2}$-in. floppy drive.
- PC-Write editor (ED) and the following software from Microsoft Corporation: MASM assembler, Codeview debugger, and all associated utilities (LINK, LIB, etc.).

At the end of this chapter, we make some suggestions concerning the use of alternative configurations.

Emulation

To *emulate* is to copy or imitate with the goal of equaling or surpassing the original. We emulate embedded system hardware by borrowing the resources of the IBM PC. Using emulation, we create executable (EXE) programs, and we test and troubleshoot those programs on the IBM PC using a symbolic debugger (such as Codeview). For I/O operations we use the keypad/monitor of the IBM PC or external binary ports.

Access to external binary I/O ports and other peripheral circuitry is through an optional bus-extender system. The bus-extender is optional because these external binary ports can be simulated and need not actually exist. However, if you are performing certain hardware activities—such as driving a stepper motor—true bus-extender ports must be present.

The Bus-Extender

A bus-extender is a buffered plug-in board that brings out the full IBM PC bus signals of Figure C2.1 to an external protoboard array. The hardware designer "looks at" these bus signals rather than the pins of the microprocessor. The important differences, when compared to the pins of the 8086, 80286, or 80386, are:

- All address lines are demultiplexed.
- The control lines $\overline{RD}$, $\overline{WR}$, and $IO/\overline{M}$ are decoded to $\overline{IOR}$, $\overline{IOW}$, $\overline{MEMR}$, and $\overline{MEMW}$.
- The interrupt inputs feed an 8259A interrupt controller.

FIGURE C2.1

The IBM PC/XT/AT bus.

$A_{19} \sim A_0$
$D_7 \sim D_0$
DRQ3 ~ DRQ1
IRQ7 ~ IRQ2
ALE
OSC
T/C
Clock
Reset
I/O ready
I/O check
DACK3 ~ DACKØ
$\overline{MEMW}$
$\overline{MEMR}$
$\overline{IOW}$
$\overline{IOR}$
AEN
+5V
GND

FIGURE C2.2

Suggested bus-extender ports.

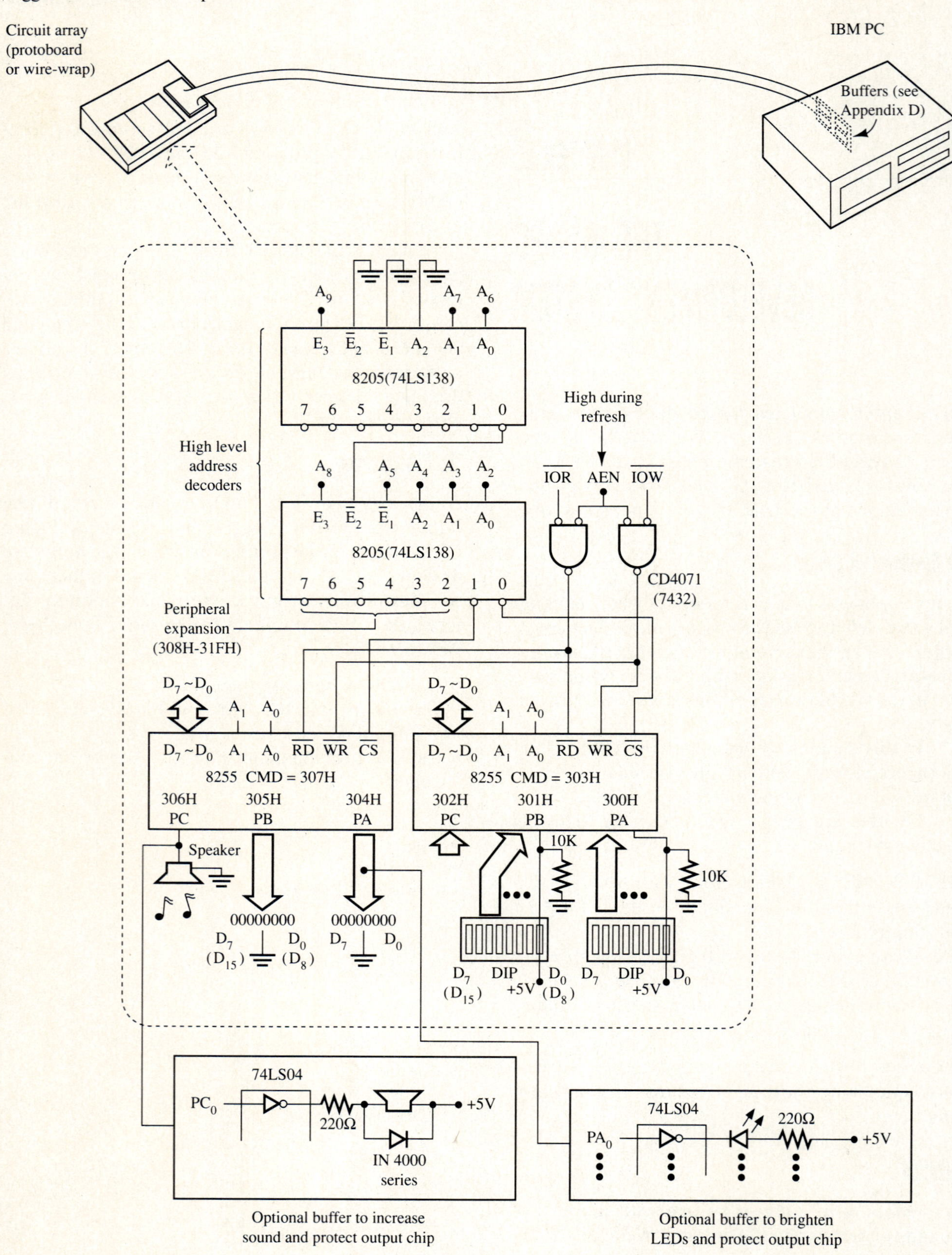

FIGURE C2.3

The 8255A programmable peripheral interface. (a) Pinout and block diagram. (b) Mode definition format. (Courtesy Intel Corporation.)

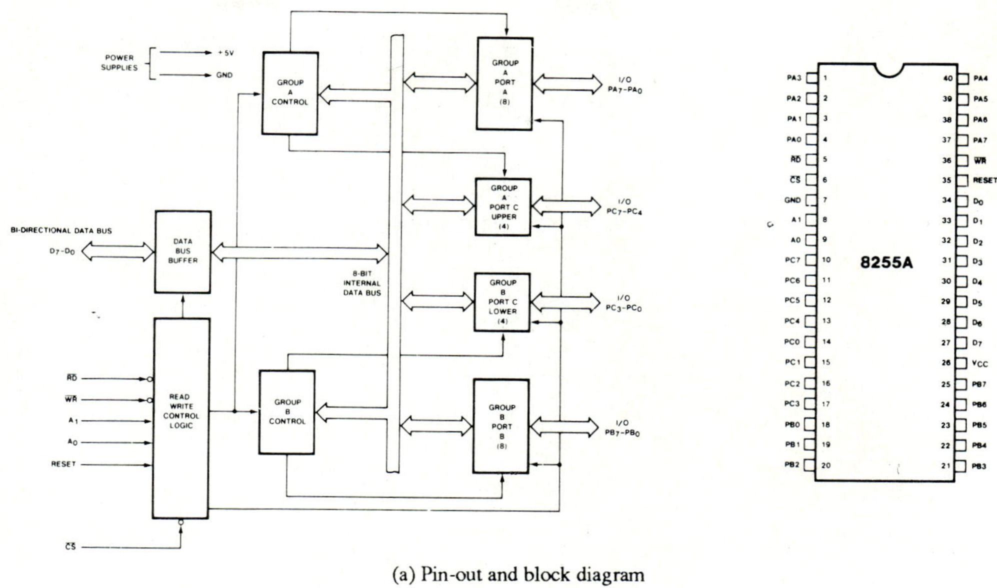

(a) Pin-out and block diagram

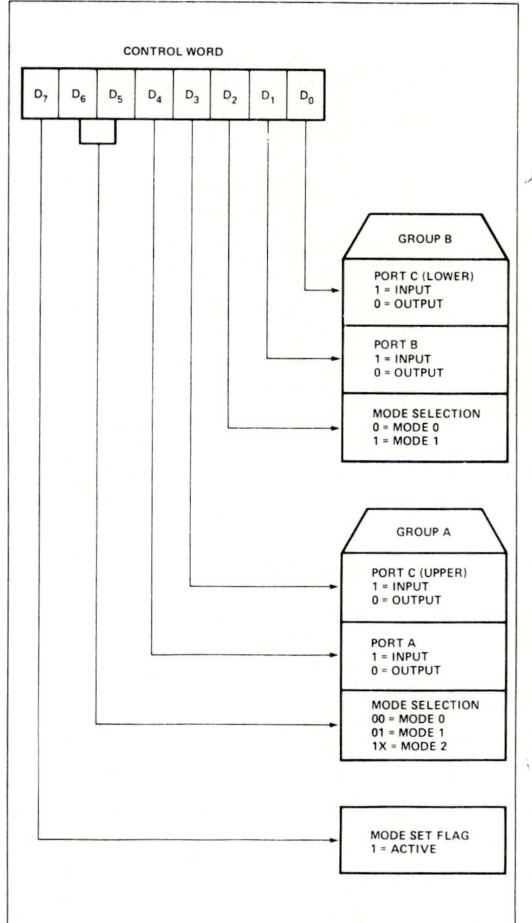

(b) Mode definition format

FIGURE C2.4

Demonstration program NEXT_WEEK showing I/O port alternatives. (a) Port simulation. (b) Bus-extender ports. (c) Variable substitution. (d) Screen simulation ports.

```
; output = input + seven_days (7)
; Port simulation under a symbolic
; debugger.  All port addresses are
; arbitrary.

NAME        NEXT_WEEK

DGROUP GROUP _DATA

_DATA       SEGMENT
  seven_days DB  7                 ; Define variable
_DATA       ENDS

_TEXT       SEGMENT
            ASSUME CS:_TEXT,DS:DGROUP
   start:   mov   ax,DGROUP
            mov   ds,ax            ; Initialize ds
   again:   in    al,0             ; Input from port 0000
            add   al,seven_days ; Add 7
            out   1,al             ; Output to port 0001
            jmp   again            ; Loop forever
_TEXT       ENDS
            END   start
```

(a) Port simulation

```
; output = input + seven_days (7)

NAME        NEXT_WEEK

DGROUP GROUP _DATA

_DATA       SEGMENT
  seven_days DB  7
_DATA       ENDS

_TEXT       SEGMENT
            ASSUME CS:_TEXT,DS:DGROUP
   start:   mov   ax,DGROUP
            mov   ds,ax            ; Initialize ds
            mov   dx,303h          ; Cmd port address (low)
            mov   al,9bh           ; Data for input 8255A
            out   dx,al            ; Initialize input 8255A
            mov   dx,307h          ; Cmd port address (high)
            mov   al,80h           ; Data for output 8255A
            out   dx,al            ; Initialize output 8255A
   again:   mov   dx,300h          ; Point to INLOW
            in    al,dx            ; Input
            add   al,seven_days ; Add 7
            mov   dx,304h          ; Point to OUTLOW
            out   dx,al            ; Output result
            jmp   again            ; Loop forever
_TEXT       ENDS
            END   start
```

(b) Bus-extender ports

Most 80286-based ATs and 80386-based clones offer several slots for PC/XT plug-in boards and are therefore fully compatible with bus-extender systems designed for the PC/XT. The IBM-built PS/2 system uses microchannel architecture and is not compatible with the PC/XT bus system.

An easy-to-build circuit based on the 8255A Programmable Peripheral Interface is diagrammed in Figure C2.2. As shown in Figure C2.3(a), each 8255A offers an 8-bit command register and three 8-bit I/O ports (A, B, and C). Ports A and B can be combined for 16-bit access, and port C can be programmed for handshaking applications. Port A addresses 300H and 304H access either the low-order byte ports (PA) or the combined word ports (PA and PB), depending on how the instruction is written.

FIGURE C2.4

(continued)

```
; outvariable = invariable + seven_days (7)
; Variables substituted for I/O ports.
; Access by way of symbolic debugger.

NAME         NEXT_WEEK

DGROUP GROUP _DATA

_DATA        SEGMENT
  invariable   DB  ?     ; Input variable
  outvariable  DB  ?     ; Output variable
  seven_days   DB  7
_DATA        ENDS

_TEXT        SEGMENT
             ASSUME CS:_TEXT,DS:DGROUP
   start:    mov    ax,DGROUP
             mov    ds,ax            ; Initialize ds
   again:    mov    al,invariable    ; Get "input"
             add    al,seven_days    ; Add 7
             mov    outvariable,al   ; Send to "output"
             jmp    again            ; Loop forever
_TEXT        ENDS
             END    start
```

(c) Variable substitution

```
; Output = input + seven_days (7)
; DIP/LED ports simulated using keyboard
; and screen of IBM PC.

NAME         NEXT_WEEK

DGROUP  GROUP   _DATA,STACK

STACK        SEGMENT STACK 'STACK'
             DW  100h  DUP(?)
STACK        ENDS

_DATA        SEGMENT PUBLIC 'DATA'
  seven_days  DB  7
_DATA        ENDS

_TEXT        SEGMENT PUBLIC 'CODE'
             ASSUME CS:_TEXT,DS:DGROUP,SS:DGROUP

    EXTRN _setupsim:NEAR,_dipblsim:NEAR,_ledblsim:NEAR

  start:     mov    ax,DGROUP
             mov    ds,ax
             call   _setupsim       ; Initialize screen
    again:   call   _dipblsim       ; Input from keyboard
             add    al,seven_days   ; Add 7
             push   ax              ; Send to LEDs
             call   _ledblsim       ; Show on screen
             add    sp,2            ; "Clean up" stack
             jmp    again           ; Loop forever
_TEXT        ENDS
             END    start
```

(d) Screen simulation ports

By writing the proper data to the command register according to the format of Figure C2.3(b), one 8255A is configured for input and the other for output.

If you choose other bus-extender circuitry, you will find that the only important differences are the port addresses and initialization data.

Demonstration Programs and I/O Alternatives

The earlier activities deal primarily with I/O from simple binary DIP/LED ports. Because true bus-extender ports may not always be available, the four versions of *source* program NEXT_WEEK of Figure C2.4 demonstrate four ways of accessing, simulating, or bypassing these ports. In all cases, today's date is input, added to variable *seven-days*, and next week's date is output. (Of course, the program does not give the correct result for the last week of each month—a deficiency we overcome in a future activity.)

The first version [Figure C2.4(a)] is designed for port simulation under a symbolic debugger and therefore uses arbitrary port addresses. The second version [Figure C2.4(b)] is designed to run on the bus-extender circuit of Figure C2.2 and uses specific initialization data and port addresses. The third version [Figure C2.4(c)] simply substitutes variables for I/O ports and relies on a symbolic debugger to enter values and obtain results. The fourth version [Figure C2.4(d)] is designed to simulate DIP and LED ports using the keyboard and screen of the IBM PC. (The home keys toggle the bits of the screen-simulated DIP.)

When performing the activities of this text, use whichever of these four methods is most appropriate. Although the fourth method (screen simulation) is not formally introduced until Activity 18, it can be used in the earlier activities if desired.

Following the example of Microsoft, and for maximum compatibility with the C language, all instructions, variables, and labels are written in lower case. All programs and development processes are based on the SMALL model of segmentation.

Development Sequence

Referring to Figure C2.5, the following is a brief description of the emulation development sequence based on the port simulation version of program NEXT_WEEK [Figure C2.4(a)] and using Microsoft software.

STEP 1: We enter the editor (such as PC-Write or WordStar), create the relocatable source program [Figure C2.4(a)], and store on disk using a file name of our choice (with ASM extension). For this exercise we choose DEMO.ASM. (A *relocatable* program can be run from a number of different memory locations.)

STEP 2: We evoke the assembler (MASM) and translate the relocatable source code to relocatable object (binary) code, generating files DEMO.OBJ [Figure C2.6(a)] and DEMO.LST [Figure C2.6(b)]. DEMO.LST shows the original source program, the translated code in hexadecimal format, a symbol table, and all syntax errors (none were found). The offset addresses of segments _TEXT and _DATA are temporarily set to 0 and the segment addresses are unspecified. (Because the program does not define a stack segment, variable *seven-days* is placed at location 0000H in DGROUP.)

If the object code had been an independently assembled procedure (subroutine), we would use the LIB (library) utility to store the module in a library. (The use of libraries is introduced in Activity 15.)

STEP 3: The LINK utility combines all required relocatable object modules into a single relocatable object module, generating files DEMO.EXE [Figure C2.6(c)] and DEMO.MAP [Figure C2.6(d)]. DEMO.EXE is in a special "executable" format that is ready to be loaded into the IBM PC.

FIGURE C2.5

The emulation development sequence.

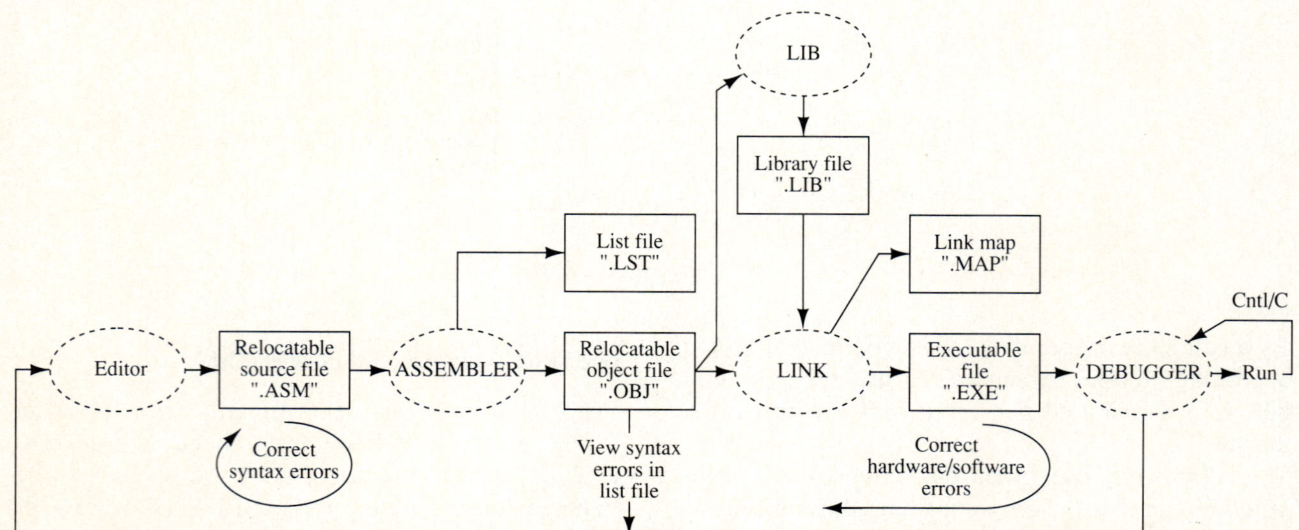

FIGURE C2.6

Emulation development sequence files. (a) DEMO.OBJ (relocatable object file). (b) DEMO.LST (list file). (c) DEMO.EXE (relocatable executable file). (d) DEMO.MAP.

```
demoa.ASMWCV75DEBSYMDEBTYPDGROUP$$TYPES
$$SYMBOLS_DATA_TEXTA'w h')O'1
```

(a) Demo.obj (object file)

```
 1                      ; output = input + seven_days (7)
 2                      ; Port simulation under Codeview.
 3                      ; All port addresses are arbitrary.
 4
 5                      NAME        NEXT_WEEK
 6
 7                      DGROUP GROUP _DATA
 8
 9 0000                 _DATA       SEGMENT
10 0000  07                seven_days DB  7            ; Define variable
11 0001                 _DATA       ENDS
12
13 0000                 _TEXT       SEGMENT
14                                  ASSUME CS:_TEXT,DS:DGROUP
15 0000  B8 ---- R         start:   mov   ax,DGROUP
16 0003  8E D8                      mov   ds,ax          ; Initialize ds
17 0005  E4 00             again:   in    al,0           ; Input from port 0000
18 0007  02 06 0000 R                add   al,seven_days ; Add 7
19 000B  E6 01                      out   1,al           ; Output to port 0001
20 000D  EB F6                      jmp   again          ; Loop forever
21 000F                 _TEXT       ENDS
22                                  END   start

Segments and Groups:

                N a m e                Length     Align    Combine Class

DGROUP . . . . . . . . . . . . .        GROUP
  _DATA . . . . . . . . . . . . .       0001     PARA      NONE
_TEXT  . . . . . . . . . . . . .        000F     PARA      NONE

Symbols:

                N a m e                Type       Value     Attr

AGAIN  . . . . . . . . . . . . .        L NEAR  0005       _TEXT

SEVEN_DAYS . . . . . . . . . . .        L BYTE  0000       _DATA
START  . . . . . . . . . . . . .        L NEAR  0000       _TEXT

@CPU . . . . . . . . . . . . . .        TEXT  0101h
@FILENAME  . . . . . . . . . . .        TEXT  demoa
@VERSION . . . . . . . . . . . .        TEXT  510


     22 Source  Lines
     22 Total   Lines
     15 Symbols

  47538 + 420985 Bytes symbol space free

      0 Warning Errors
      0 Severe  Errors
```

(b) Demo.1st (List file)

```
MZXdkvNBOOwDEMOA.OBJSEVEN_DAYS
AGAIN
START      demoa.ASMNBOO)
```

(c) Demo.exe (Relocatable executable file)

```
LINK : warning L4021: no stack segment

 Start  Stop   Length Name                         Class
 00000H 00000H 00001H _DATA
 00010H 0001EH 0000FH _TEXT

 Origin   Group
 0000:0   DGROUP

Program entry point at 0001:0000
```

(d) Demo.map

DEMO.MAP summarizes the link process, showing all segments and their sizes. For our single-module demonstration program, the LINK utility simply prepares the EXE file for loading.

STEP 4: We enter Codeview, load DEMO.EXE, and test and troubleshoot the program. If necessary, hardware/software integration also takes place during this step. *Locating* the program (converting all temporary and unspecified addresses into absolute and permanent addresses) is done automatically when the EXE program is loaded. (Normally, segment addresses are chosen by the

FIGURE C2.7

Emulation development package. (a) Disk storage. (b) Templates (.ASM). (c) Batch file (.BAT). (d) Config.sys.

```
Template    (.ASM)
Batch file  (.BAT)
CONFIG.SYS
ED.EXE
MASM.EXE
LINK.EXE
LIB.EXE
CV.EXE (Plus all related
        utilities.)
```

(a) Disk storage

```
NAME

DGROUP GROUP _DATA

_DATA         SEGMENT
_DATA         ENDS

_TEXT         SEGMENT
              ASSUME CS:_TEXT,DS:DGROUP
  start:      mov    ax,DGROUP
              mov    ds,ax
              nop

_TEXT         ENDS
              END    start
```

Standard

```
              TITLE
              DOSSEG
              .MODEL SMALL
              .DATA

              .CODE
  start:      mov    ax,@DATA
              mov    ds,ax
              nop

              END    start
```

optional for MASM 5.1 or later

(b) Template (.ASM)

```
:BEGIN
ED %1.ASM
MASM /MX /Zi %1.ASM,,,;
IF ERRORLEVEL 1 GOTO STOP
LINK /CO %1,,,;
CV /B /W %1
ERASE %1.OBJ
ERASE %1.LST
ERASE %1.EXE
ERASE %1.CRF
ERASE %1.MAP
GOTO END
:STOP
REM Assembler error detected; display list file and re-enter editor.
REM Ctrl-S will control scrolling of list file.
COPY %1.LST CON
GOTO BEGIN
:END
```

(c) Batch file (.BAT)

```
buffers = 10
files = 15
```

(d) Config.sys

IBM PC based on available memory, and the first item in each segment or group remains at offset 0000H.)

In this text we automate all four steps by using a *batch file*.

System Preparation

- If you intend to use external ports, interface a buffered bus-extender port system to the IBM PC. Use the suggested circuit of Figure C2.2 or one of your own choosing. (Appendix D lists a number of companies that market bus-extender hardware.)
- Using DOS, format a disk (FORMAT /S) and add the files shown in Figure C2.7(a). (Use the editor to create the template, batch, and config.sys files.) If using screen-simulation for port I/O, see Activities 15 and 18 for full details.

Alternative Configurations

If your development system configuration is different from the baseline configuration presented earlier, note the comments below:

- *Hardware:* If using dual 360K $5\frac{1}{4}$-in. floppy drives, split up the files on four separate disks and modify the batch file as shown in Figure C2.8. If using 720K $3\frac{1}{2}$-in. disks, your configuration will be somewhere between the baseline and 360K systems. If using a hard disk, place all files in a directory. Consider placing appropriate "environment variables" in AUTOEXEC.BAT.
- *Software:* In general, almost any 8086 assembler, C compiler, and debugger can be substituted for MASM, QuickC, and Codeview. For example, Turbo Assembler from Borland Corporation is 100% compatible with MASM. However, be aware that not all systems allow mixed-language programming (Activity 26).
- *Development process:* If necessary, modify the development package of Figure C2.7 to match your development system.

The Appendixes

The appendixes at the back of this text contain the following useful information:

Appendix A: Major DOS commands

FIGURE C2.8

Dual 360K system. (a) Disk storage. (b) Batch file.

```
Disk 1: USER
  Template     (.ASM)
  Batch file   (.BAT)
  CONFIG.SYS
  AUTOEXEC.BAT
Disk 2: EDITOR/ASSEMBLER
  MASM.EXE
  ED.EXE
Disk 3: UTILITIES
  LINK.EXE
  LIB.EXE
Disk 4: CODEVIEW
  CV.EXE (Plus all related
          utilities.)
```

(a) Disk storage

```
IF EXIST B:MASM.EXE GOTO CONTINUE
PAUSE Put EDITOR/MASM disk in drive B
:CONTINUEzx
B:MASM /MX /Zi %1.ASM,,,;
IF ERRORLEVEL 1 GOTO STOP
PAUSE Put UTILITIES disk in drive B
B:LINK /CO %1,,,;
PAUSE Put CODEVIEW disk in drive B
B:CV /B /W %1
GOTO END
:STOP
REM Assembler error detected; display list file and re-enter editor.
REM Ctrl-S will control scrolling of list file.
COPY %1.LST CON
B:ED %1.ASM
:END
```

(b) Batch file

Appendix B: Summary of the major PC-Write editor commands
Appendix C: Summary of the major Codeview commands
Appendix D: Bus-extender hardware
Appendix E: The instruction set
Appendix F: Data sheets
Appendix G: Codeview sample session
Appendix H: ASCII code table

PROCEDURE

In this section, we run through the development sequence of Figure C2.5 using the emulation development package of Figure C2.7 and the demonstration program NEXT_WEEK of Figure C2.4(a). To help when giving example commands, we use the generic file names EDITOR, BATCH, and DEMO for the editor, batch, and demonstration program file names, respectively.

1. Place your disk in drive A. Turn on the computer or reboot (Ctrl/Alt/Del) to execute CONFIG.SYS. This step need only be done once at the beginning of each laboratory session.
2. As a first step to writing a program, use the DOS copy command to make a copy of the template file (using another file name of your choice, but keeping the .ASM extension). This will protect the original template file so it can be used over and over.

   The NOP—no operation—instruction in the template is recommended if you are using the Codeview debugger because Codeview may skip the first instruction after *mov ds,ax* when single-stepping (executing one instruction at a time). By letting it skip NOP, we do not miss the first "real" instruction. For simplicity, the NOP instruction is not shown in the demonstration programs.
3. To carry out the development sequence, enter the name of the batch file followed by the program file name. (Do not use extensions.)

   Example: A>BATCH DEMO ⟨E⟩ (If necessary, be sure to substitute your chosen file names for the generic words BATCH and DEMO.)

   The batch file electronically sequences through the commands (like a player piano). To make the batch file work for any program, note that the file name after the batch command (currently DEMO) is automatically substituted for the %1 parameters. Press Ctrl/C to exit the batch process at any time and return to DOS.
4. The first step performed by the batch process is to enter the editor and bring up source file DEMO.ASM (presently holding the template). Using the facilities of the editor, enter the instructions and variables of demonstration program NEXT_WEEK of Figure C2.4(a), but deliberately include at least one syntax error (for example, spell "add" as "ad"). Exit the editor.
5. The batch process continues to the assembly step. Because at least one syntax error is found by the assembler, the IF batch file operator causes a branch to label :STOP. The system displays the list file and jumps to label :BEGIN to reenter the editor. (Use Ctrl/S to control the scrolling of the list file.) Use the clues presented by the list file to correct the errors. Exit the editor and reassemble the program.
6. When all syntax errors are eliminated, we exit the "syntax correction loop." Under batch file control, the software development process continues through the link step, generates DEMO.EXE, enters Codeview, and loads the program. (Ignore all warnings concerning the stack.)
7. Using the debugger commands, test the system. If *logic* errors are found or the program is to be modified, exit the debugger and reenter the batch process. To keep the disk "clean," note that all files but the source file are erased. (Appendix C contains a sample Codeview session based on demonstration program NEXT_WEEK. The Codeview user's manual provides more detailed information.)

Always remember, you are free to modify the batch file in any way you wish to more closely match the development process to your specific needs.

Name: ______________________

Date: ______________________

QUESTIONS AND PROBLEMS

Class: ______________________

1. What purpose do the buffers of Figure C2.2 serve?

2. Are the port addresses of Figure C2.2 folded back over other locations? Why or why not?

3. What do we mean when we say a program is *relocatable*?

4. Referring to the list file of program NEXT_WEEK [Figure C2.6(b)]:
   a. What OFFSET addresses were chosen by the assembler for the first item in the _TEXT and _DATA segments?

   b. Were SEGMENT addresses assigned by the assembler to the _TEXT and _DATA segments, or did they remain completely unspecified?

5. How does the 8088 access a word port?

6. With the help of Figure C2.5, explain the purpose and outcome of each line of the batch file of Figure C2.7(c).

7. How could the batch file of Figure C2.7(c) be modified to execute the program directly, rather than first entering Codeview?

8. For each of the files listed below, state what utility generated each, and explain briefly what each contains:
   a. DEMO.ASM
   b. DEMO.LST
   c. DEMO.OBJ
   d. DEMO.MAP
   e. DEMO.EXE
9. Referring to the standard template of Figure C2.7(b), explain the purpose or function of each line.

Advanced Section

10. When using Codeview, what is accomplished by F10?

11. Why do the object files of Figures C2.6(a) and (c) contain such unusual symbols? Are these files useful for documentation?

12. What is the difference between the SMALL, COMPACT, MEDIUM, and LARGE segmentation models?

13. Why does Microsoft place an underbar (_) before the segment names?

14. What is the purpose of running CONFIG.SYS?

15. What is the purpose of the AEN signal (as shown in Figure C2.2)?

16. How would the circuit of Figure C2.2 change if the PC used an 8086 rather than an 8088?

17. If we execute a program directly (rather than under Codeview), how do we return to DOS?

18. What is the purpose of each of the controls /MX, /Zi, and /CO in the batch file commands of Figure C2.7(c)?

19. During the development sequence, when does the *locate* process (establishing absolute addresses for all memory references) take place?

20. Under Codeview, what is the difference between a *watchpoint* and a *tracepoint*?

SECTION 2

Section 2 carries out the major objectives of the text, and consists of 42 experimental activities divided into eight parts. The central theme of Section 2 is *structured design*.

Structured design is comprised of the *structure theorem* (all programs can be fashioned from single-entry/single-exit nested combinations of *sequence, selection,* and *repetition*) and *top-down design* (programs are broken down into levels of modules from the general to the specific).

With structured design in mind, the eight parts are organized as follows: The first three parts cover the structure theorem and the basic instruction groups and are based on assembly-language and binary (embedded) ports. Part IV brings in top-down design, and Part V adds data I/O by way of the IBM PC keyboard and monitor. Part VI covers advanced mathematics, and Part VII introduces the C language and allows us to program in a mixed-language environment. Part VIII gives us an opportunity to apply all we have learned through a variety of projects.

PART I

THE STRUCTURE THEOREM / THE FOUR BASIC INSTRUCTION GROUPS / EMBEDDED PORTS

When we complete the six activities of Part I and gain access to the four basic instruction groups, we will have the ability to write structured programs using elementary mathematical, logical, and decision-making operations on data stored in a variety of locations.

Binary ports are used exclusively in the earlier activities because, from a programmer's viewpoint, they are by far the simplest to use. For Parts I through III, use the data I/O methods of your choice for each program that accesses binary ports (see Figure C2.4).

ACTIVITY 1

THE DATA TRANSFER GROUP / INSTRUCTION FORMATS / ADDRESSING MODES

OBJECTIVES

- To use the data transfer group of instructions.
- To hand assemble using the 8086/88 instruction set format.
- To operate on *variables* in the *data segment.*
- To compare the addressing modes of the 8086/88.
- To use the BYTE and WORD PTR directives.
- To use the segment override prefix.

PARTS AND EQUIPMENT

- None (This activity uses hand assembly exclusively.)

DISCUSSION

In this activity we use hand assembly techniques to study the 8086/88 instruction set format. If knowledge of instruction formats and hand assembly is not desired, complete the discussion, answer the appropriate questions and problems, and proceed to Activity 2.

The Data Transfer Instructions

Within a computer, data can reside in only three places: internal registers, memory locations, and ports. The 14 data transfer instructions of Figure 1.1 handle transfers of data between these three locations. In this activity we concentrate on the IN, OUT, and MOV instructions. The others will be introduced as needed.

The IN/OUT instructions are used to access binary ports in an embedded system. They use a 16-bit linear (nonsegmented) address from 0000 through FFFFH in the isolated I/O address space. During transfer of data, they drive the IO/$\overline{M}$ line active. There are two types of IN/OUT instructions: the *fixed port* type with a fixed address from 0 to 255, and the *variable port* type in which the 16-bit port address—held by the DX register—can be changed during execution. An example of each is given below:

fixed: in al,4 (Input a byte from the port whose address is 4 to AL.)
variable: out dx,ax (Output a word from AX to the port whose address is in DX.)

Note that only the accumulator is used to transfer port data (AL for bytes, AX for words). The powerful MOV instruction handles most transfers of data between registers and memory and will be the major subject of this activity.

The Data Segment

As we learned in the first two chapters, the 8086/88 uses *segmented* addressing for all memory references. *Variables* (data items that can change) are normally stored in RAM within the *data segment.* When a memory location is accessed using the MOV instruction, the data segment register is used by default to supply the segment base address.

Figure 1.2(a) reviews the segment selection rules. When an instruction byte (op code or operand) is fetched, the code segment is used by default; when a variable is accessed, the data segment is used by default. However, should the variable lie in the code segment, we can override the default condition with the *segment override prefix* of Figure 1.2(b). One use of the segment override prefix is to fetch constants permanently stored in ROM (in the code segment).

8086/88 Addressing Modes

To locate data within a register, port, or memory location, the instructions of the 8086/88 use the nine

FIGURE 1.1

The data transfer instructions. (Courtesy Intel Corporation.)

GENERAL PURPOSE	
MOV PUSH POP XCHG XLAT	Move byte or word Push word onto stack Pop word off stack Exchange byte or word Translate byte
INPUT/OUTPUT	
IN OUT	Input byte or word Output byte or word
ADDRESS OBJECT	
LEA LDS LES	Load effective address Load pointer using DS Load pointer using ES
FLAG TRANSFER	
LAHF SAHF PUSHF POPF	Load AH register from flags Store AH register in flags Push flags onto stack Pop flags off stack

FIGURE 1.4

An example of physical address calculation using base/displacement addressing. (a) Using the instruction format. (b) Using the memory map.

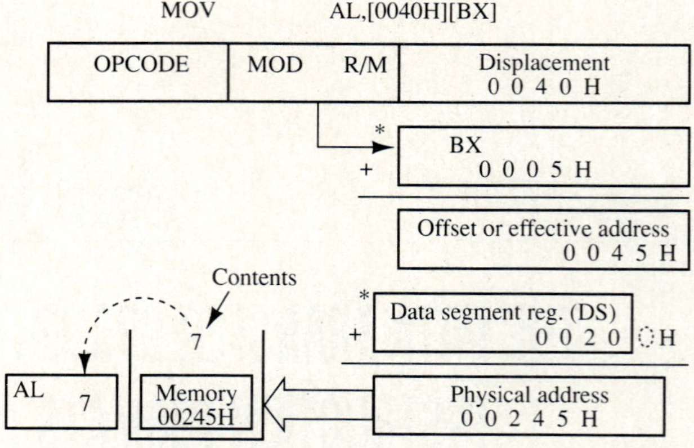

(a) Using the instruction format

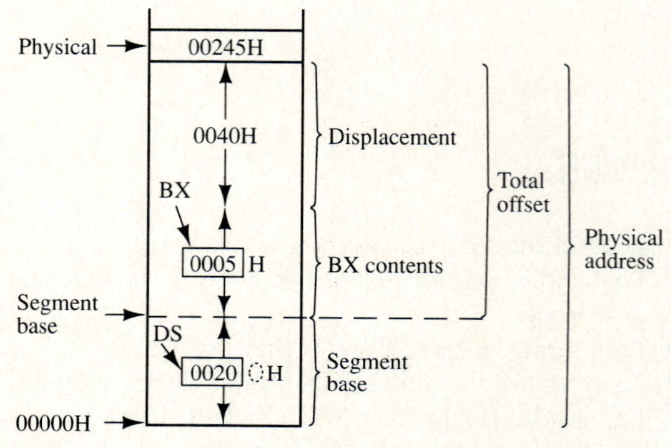

(b) Using the memory map

FIGURE 1.2

Segment and offset selection rules. (a) Sources of segment and offset addresses. (b) Segment override prefix.

Type of memory reference	Default segment base	Alternate segment base	Offset
Instruction fetch	CS	None	IP
Variable	DS	CS	Effective address

(a) Sources of segment and offset addresses

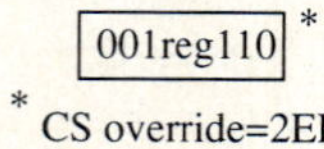

(b) Segment override prefix

FIGURE 1.3

The nine addressing modes.

```
Mode                            Example
IMMEDIATE                       *mov  al,07h
REGISTER                        *mov  ax,bx
DIRECT                          *mov  [0004h],cx
INDIRECT
  base                          *mov  cl,[bx]
  index                          mov  [si],dx
  base/index                     mov  [bx][di],al
  base/displacement             *mov  al,[0020h][bx]
  index/displacement             mov  [0005h][di],cl
  base/index/displacement        mov  al,[0008h][bx][di]
```

* Most commonly used

FIGURE 1.5

Tables for hand assembly. (Courtesy Intel Corporation.) (a) Addressing formats of the *mov* and *in/out* instructions. (b) Operand field table.

DATA TRANSFER

MOV = Move

Register/memory to/from register

1 0 0 0 1 0 d w	mod reg r/m

Timing (clocks): register to register 2; memory to register 8+EA; register to memory 9+EA

Immediate to register/memory

1 1 0 0 0 1 1 w	mod 0 0 0 r/m	data	data if w 1

Timing: 10+EA clocks

Immediate to register

1 0 1 1 w reg	data	data if w 1

Timing: 4 clocks

Memory to accumulator

1 0 1 0 0 0 0 w	addr-low	addr-high

Timing: 10 clocks

Accumulator to memory

1 0 1 0 0 0 1 w	addr-low	addr-high

Timing: 10 clocks

Register/memory to segment register

1 0 0 0 1 1 1 0	mod 0 reg r/m

Timing (clocks): register to register 2; memory to register 8+EA

Segment register to register/memory

1 0 0 0 1 1 0 0	mod 0 reg r/m

Timing (clocks): register to register 2; register to memory 9+EA

IN = Input to AL/AX from

Fixed port

1 1 1 0 0 1 0 w	port

Timing: 10 clocks

Variable port (DX)

1 1 1 0 1 1 0 w

Timing: 8 clocks

OUT = Output from AL/AX to

Fixed port

1 1 1 0 0 1 1 w	port

Timing: 10 clocks

Variable port (DX)

1 1 1 0 1 1 1 w

Timing: 8 clocks

(a) Addressing formats of the *mov* and *in/out* instructions

OPERAND SUMMARY

"reg" field Bit Assignments:

16-Bit (w = 1)	8-Bit (w = 0)	Segment
000 AX	000 AL	00 ES
001 CX	001 CL	01 CS
010 DX	010 DL	10 SS
011 BX	011 BL	11 DS
100 SP	100 AH	
101 BP	101 CH	
110 SI	110 DH	
111 DI	111 BH	

SECOND INSTRUCTION BYTE SUMMARY

mod	xxx	r/m

mod	Displacement
00	DISP = 0*, disp-low and disp-high are absent
01	DISP = disp-low sign-extended to 16-bits, disp-high is absent
10	DISP = disp-high: disp-low
11	r/m is treated as a "reg" field

r/m	Operand Address
000	(BX) + (SI) + DISP
001	(BX) + (DI) + DISP
010	(BP) + (SI) + DISP
011	(BP) + (DI) + DISP
100	(SI) + DISP
101	(DI) + DISP
110	(BP) + DISP*
111	(BX) + DISP

DISP follows 2nd byte of instruction (before data if required)

*except if mod = 00 and r/m = 110 then EA = disp-high: disp-low

OTHER BIT FIELDS:

D = 0: DESTINATION IS FIRST OPERAND 1: DESTINATION IS SECOND OPERAND	
S = 0: DATA = DATA HI, DATA LO 1: DATA = DATA-LO SIGN EXTENDED	APPLIES IF W = 1

(b) Operand field table

addressing modes of Figure 1.3. Referring to the MOV instruction examples, the source is on the right and the destination is on the left. Note the use of square brackets ([ ]) to indicate a *pointer* (a register or memory location that holds the offset address of the data, rather than the data itself). The five addressing modes marked by asterisks are the most commonly used by this text.

Always remember that when an operand references memory it gives only the *offset* portion of the physical address. The *segment* portion is obtained from a segment register (DS in this case).

Using arbitrary addresses, Figure 1.4(a) gives an example of how the physical address is calculated when using *base/displacement* addressing. As shown by Figure 1.4(b), three items must be added to give the final physical address: the *displacement,* register BX, and segment register DS.

Instruction Symmetry

Mastering the 8086/88 instruction set is made easier because the instruction operands are symmetric. That is, in all cases except *immediate,* the source and destination can be reversed by writing the operands in opposite order. For example:

```
mov   al,[bx]   ; Move from
                  memory to al
mov   [bx],al   ; Move from
                  AL to memory
```

Instruction Formats

Figure 1.5(a) lists the instruction formats for the MOV and IN/OUT instructions, and Figure 1.5(b) shows the operand coding scheme. An example of hand assembly, using the instruction of Figure 1.4, is diagrammed in Figure 1.6. After assembling the instructions of this experiment by hand, the reader will greatly appreciate a machine assembler.

The BYTE and WORD PTR Directives

The BYTE PTR and WORD PTR directives are used whenever it is unclear whether the instruction is to operate on a byte or word in memory. This knowledge is necessary to set the "w" field in the instruction format properly ("1" for a word operation and "0" for a byte operation). Consider the instruction mnemonic below:

```
mov   [bx],7
```

FIGURE 1.6

Example of hand assembly.

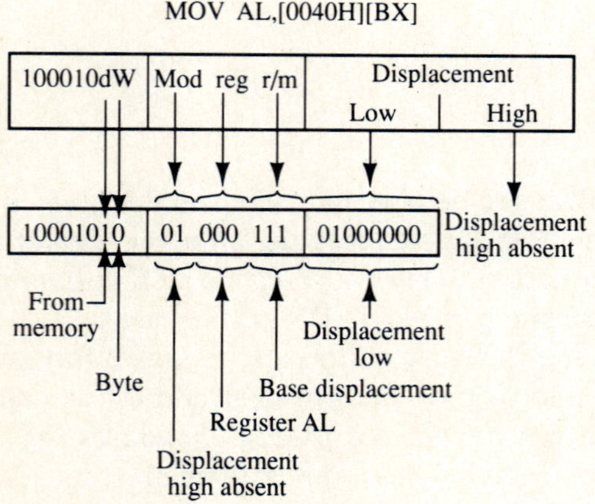

FIGURE 1.7

Loading registers immediately.

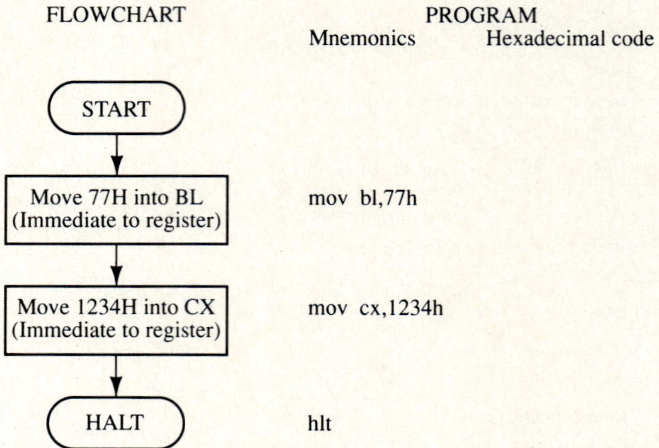

Is 7 to be moved to a byte memory location (to hold 07H) or a word memory location (to hold 0007H)? Neither a human nor a machine has any way of knowing. By using either the BYTE PTR or WORD PTR directive, the uncertainty is removed:

```
mov   BYTE PTR[bx],7   (move 07H)
mov   WORD PTR[bx],7   (move 0007H)
```

PROCEDURE

NOTE: With the help of Figure 1.5, hand assemble all instructions and place the machine code in the "Hexadecimal code" column of the appropriate figure (Figures 1.7 through 1.10). Check your answers

FIGURE 1.8

Loading memory immediately.

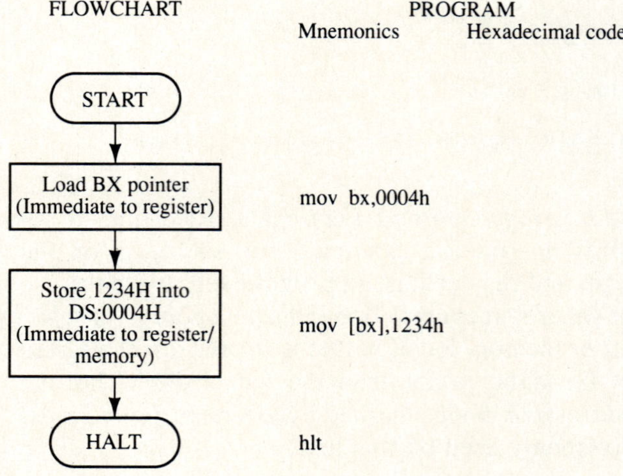

FIGURE 1.9

Memory-to-memory transfer using direct addressing.

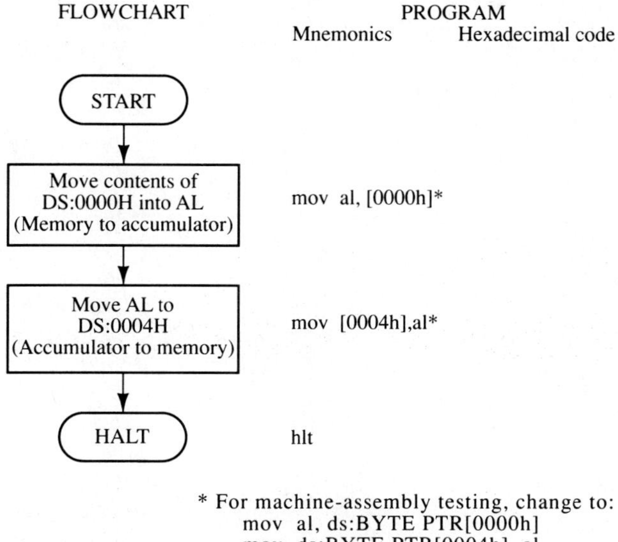

FIGURE 1.10

Memory-to-memory transfer using base/displacement addressing.

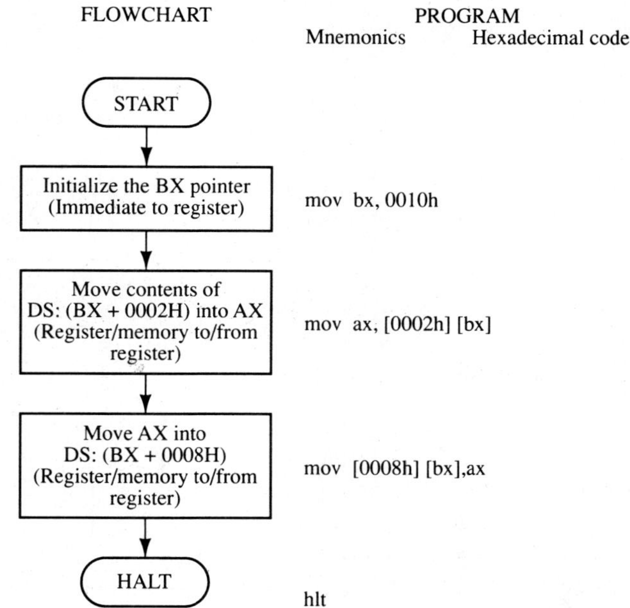

with your instructor, or machine assemble your code and examine the list file.

1. Referring to Figure 1.7, use immediate addressing to place data byte 77H into register BL, and data word 1234H into register CX.
2. Referring to Figure 1.8, use based addressing to place word 1234H into offset location 0004H in the data segment.
3. Referring to Figure 1.9, use direct addressing to move the contents of offset location 0000H to offset location 0004H (both in the data segment).
4. Referring to Figure 1.10, use base/displacement addressing to move the contents of offset location 0012H to offset location 0018H (both are word locations in the data segment).

Advanced Activities

5. Write and hand assemble a program that outputs the contents of the byte variable in the data segment whose 16-bit *offset address* is input. (For testing purposes, preload several memory locations beginning at DS:0 with data of your choice.)
6. Building on the program of step 5, write and hand assemble a centigrade-to-Fahrenheit conversion program that inputs the centigrade temperatures from 0 to 9 and outputs the corresponding Fahrenheit equivalents in hexadecimal. (*Hint:* Load the Fahrenheit temperatures corresponding to centigrade temperatures 0 to 9 into DS:0 to DS:9.)

Name: ______________________

Date: ______________________

Class: ______________________

QUESTIONS AND PROBLEMS

1. What is the difference between the following two instructions?

```
mov   ax,bx
mov   ax,[bx]
```

2. Why would the verb *copy* be a more accurate way of describing the action of the MOV instruction?

3. How are the source and destination of a data transfer indicated by position in the assembly-language mnemonic?

4. Which of the following instructions are illegal? Why?

```
a. mov cx,[bx]
b. mov [bx],cl
c. mov dh,[bl]
d. mov dl,ax
e. mov bl,BYTE PTR[0003h]
f. mov [bx + 0003h],al
g. mov [bx],[bx + 0004h]
```

5. State in your own words what is accomplished by the following instruction sequence:

```
mov   al,9bh
mov   dx,303h
out   dx,al
```

6. For each of the following instructions, indicate the format category [from Figure 1.5(a)] and the addressing mode (from Figure 1.3).

	FORMAT CATEGORY	ADDRESSING MODE
a. `mov cx,1234h`		
b. `mov [bx],1234h`		
c. `mov [0004h],al`		
d. `mov ax,[bx][0002h]`		

7. What instruction format field determines if an instruction operates on a byte or a word?
8. When using base/displacement addressing (see Figure 1.4), is it correct to say that the displacement is part of the offset?
9. Variable *apples* can be defined in either the _TEXT or _DATA segment. Which one requires the use of a segment override prefix?

Advanced Section

Remember that research may be necessary to answer any of the questions and problems of the advanced sections.

10. What is the difference (if any) between each of the following?

    a. `mov ax,[bx][0010h]`
    b. `mov ax,[bx + 0010h]`

11. Referring to Figure 1.5(b), what addressing mode is generated when mod = 00 and r/m = 110? Give an example of a data transfer (mov) instruction that uses this special addressing mode.

ACTIVITY 2

RELOCATABLE PROGRAMS AND SYMBOLIC VARIABLES

OBJECTIVES

- To write relocatable data transfer programs using symbolic variables.
- To use the OFFSET operator.

PARTS AND EQUIPMENT

- IBM PC (bus-extender optional).
- Assembler, debugger, and utilities.

DISCUSSION

In this and all activities to follow, we assume machine assembly or compilation for all programs.

Relocatable Programs

A program is *relocatable* if it can be stored and executed at many different memory locations. The use of segmented addressing makes relocation automatic. To relocate a program, we simply change the segment addresses in the segment registers. All offsets, of course, remain unchanged.

Because all offset addresses remain unchanged during relocation, they can be written as numbers (as we did in Activity 1). However, the use of numerical addresses makes it difficult to read, write, and modify a program. (All addresses must be calculated by hand.) Furthermore, many of the modularization activities of Part IV could not be performed at all. The solution is to use symbols—not numbers—for all memory references, and to let the development system perform all address calculations.

Based on symbolic variable *apples,* Figure 2.1 uses a variety of MOV instructions to summarize the nine addressing modes. In all cases, the symbol *apples* represents the *displacement* portion of the offset address of the variable (see Figure 1.4).

FIGURE 2.1

The nine addressing modes, using symbolic variable *apples* to specify the displacement.

```
Mode                         Example
IMMEDIATE                    mov   al,07h
REGISTER                     mov   ax,bx
DIRECT                       mov   apples,cx
INDIRECT
  base                       mov   cl,[bx]
  index                      mov   [si],dx
  base/index                 mov   [bx][di],al
  base/displacement          mov   al,apples[bx]
  index/displacement         mov   apples[di],cl
  base/index/displacement    mov   al,apples[bx][di]
```

Defining and Initializing Variables

All symbolic variables must be *defined* (or *declared*). As shown in Figure 2.2, all variables are normally defined (stored) in the data segment. The DB (define byte), DW (defined word), and DD (define double word) directives allocate space in memory and specify the type of information each variable can contain. Initialization data follows the directives; the "?" indicates no initial value. As part of its error-checking capability, the assembler makes sure that the variables are *used* in the same manner in which they are *defined.* [Data types DQ (8 bytes) and DT (10 bytes) are used in Activity 22, where the 8087 math coprocessor is used to perform calculations on numbers that range from very small to very large.]

The last definition shows how a sequence of variables (an *array*) is defined. As shown, *variable4* has three array elements (numbered 0, 1, and 2). Elements 0 and 2 are uninitialized, and element 1 is initialized with 77H. The elements of an array are conveniently accessed using base/displacement addressing. (Arrays are covered in detail in Activity 10.)

The OFFSET Operator and LEA Instruction

The OFFSET operator is an assembler directive that returns the offset address of a variable rather than its contents. Comparing the two instructions below, the first places the *contents* of word variable *apples* into AX, and the second places the *offset address* of *apples* into AX.

```
mov   ax,apples
mov   ax,OFFSET DGROUP:apples
```

Note that the group name is used in the second case. This is required to return the proper offset address (the distance between segment base address DGROUP and the variable).

If a variable uses based or indexed addressing, then we cannot determine its offset address at assembly time (the value of BX, SI, or DI is not known at assembly time). In this case, as shown by the example below, we use the LEA (*load effective address*) instruction to load the offset address into AX at run time:

```
lea   ax,apples[bx]
```

Intel Corporation suggests that the LEA instruction be used only when run-time calculation is required.

Instruction Symmetry

The 8086/88 instruction set is symmetric and therefore simple to use. For example, a single mnemonic (MOV) performs most data transfer operations, and in most cases the direction of movement is reversed by switching the source and destination. To demonstrate this flexibility, all of the following are legal operations that move (copy) the right-hand source operand to the left-hand destination operand:

```
mov   al,bl              ; Copy byte BL to byte AL
mov   apples,bl          ; Copy byte BL to byte variable apples
mov   [bx],cx            ; Copy word CX to word pointed to by BX
mov   BYTE PTR[bx],7     ; Place 7 into byte pointed to by BX
mov   peaches[bx],2222h  ; Place data word 2222H into word
                           variable peaches[bx]
mov   dh,pears           ; Copy byte variable pears to byte DH
mov   bx,grapes[bx]      ; Copy word variable grapes[bx] to
                           word BX
mov   grapes[bx],bx      ; Copy word BX to word variable
                           grapes[bx]
```

FIGURE 2.2

Symbolic variable definitions.

```
_DATA        SEGMENT
    variable1  DB  ?
    variable2  DW  1234h
    variable3  DD  12345678h
    variable4  DB  ?, 77h, ?
_DATA        ENDS
```

Remember that memory-to-memory operations, such as those listed below, are not allowed:

```
mov   peaches,apples   ; Not allowed
mov   apples,[bx]      ; Not allowed
```

Instead, we must use two instructions and a "middle-man" register, such as that shown below for the first example:

```
mov   al,apples
mov   peaches,al
```

Number Systems

The machine assembler has the ability to recognize numbers entered in a variety of formats and to convert them into "machine language" (binary). The list at the top of page 43 includes the major allowed number formats. In the comments field, we specify the contents of AL in hexadecimal after the instruction is executed.

Segment Override Prefix

When writing programs for machine assembly, we use the DS or CS prefix to specify a segment override. One use of the segment override prefix is to access instruction bytes in the code segment as if

```
mov   al,20          ; AL = 14H
mov   al,0ah         ; AL = AH  (A ''0'' must precede all
                       hexadecimal numbers that begin with a
                       letter so the assembler will know they are
                       not symbols.)
mov   al,01110001B ; AL = 71H
mov   al,-10         ; AL = F6H (Assembler took 2's complement of
                       +10).
mov   al,'A'         ; AL = 41H (ASCII for the letter ''A.'')
```

they were data. (In an embedded system, one way to permanently store data in ROM is to define the data in the _TEXT segment.) The following instruction uses the segment override prefix to retrieve data from byte variable *peaches* (defined in the _TEXT segment):

```
mov   al,CS:peaches
```

In most cases, the machine assembler knows where the variable is defined and generates the segment override prefix automatically.

Demonstration Program

Demonstration program HOPSCOTCH of Figure 2.3 reviews the major topics introduced in this ac-

FIGURE 2.3

Demonstration program HOPSCOTCH. (a) Diagram. (b) Program.

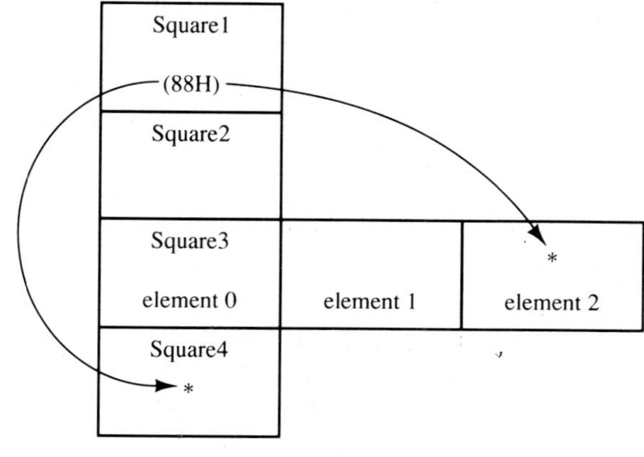

(a) Diagram

```
NAME          HOPSCOTCH

DGROUP GROUP _DATA

_DATA         SEGMENT
  square1  DB   88h
  square2  DB    ?
  square3  DB  ?,?,?
  square4  DB    ?
_DATA         ENDS

_TEXT         SEGMENT
              ASSUME CS:_TEXT,DS:DGROUP
   start:     mov   ax,DGROUP
              mov   ds,ax
              mov   al,square1          ; Using direct addressing
              mov   bx,OFFSET DGROUP:square4
              mov   [bx],al             ; Using based addressing
              mov   bx,2
              mov   square3[bx],al      ; Using base/displacement addressing
              hlt
_TEXT         ENDS
              END   start
```

(b) Program

tivity. Using a variety of addressing modes, the contents of variable *square1* (88h) is moved to variable *square4* and to element 2 of array *square3*.

Reporting Programs

For simplicity (in this and all future activities) when you are asked to enter an assembly-language program in a procedure step, you may wish to enter only the instructions and variable definitions, leaving out all template information. However, when testing your programs on the development system, all template information must be included (as shown in demonstration program HOPSCOTCH of Figure 2.3b).

PROCEDURE

NOTE: Test all programs using machine assembly.

1. Using *immediate* addressing, write the single instruction required to place 77H into byte variable *eagle*. (Remember to define variable *eagle*.)

   ASSEMBLY-LANGUAGE INSTRUCTION

2. Using *direct* addressing for both variables, write the two-instruction sequence that moves the data in word variable *coffee* to word variable *cup*. (Remember, memory-to-memory operations are not allowed.)

   ASSEMBLY-LANGUAGE INSTRUCTIONS

3. Using the OFFSET operator to generate pointers and *based* addressing for all movements to or from memory, show the four-instruction sequence that moves the data in word variable *ball* to word variable *basket*. (*Hint:* The sequence is *point, move, point, move*.)

   ASSEMBLY-LANGUAGE INSTRUCTIONS

4. Using *base/displacement* addressing for memory access, write the two-instruction sequence that places the contents of AL into the fourth element of array *eagle*. (The fourth element is element number 3.)

   ASSEMBLY-LANGUAGE PROGRAM

5. Operation "Tour de Computer" of Figure 2.4(a) takes data byte 77H on a journey through a variety of registers, memory locations, and ports of the 8086/88. Using the addressing modes designated, write the routine beside the flowchart of Figure 2.4(b).
6. Single-step the program "Tour de Computer" and examine the appropriate registers and memory locations at each step. Test successful? ____________

Advanced Activity

7. Write an "examine memory" monitor routine that inputs an offset address and displays the corresponding instruction byte (in the _TEXT segment).

FIGURE 2.4

Operation "Tour de Computer." (a) Diagram. (b) Program.

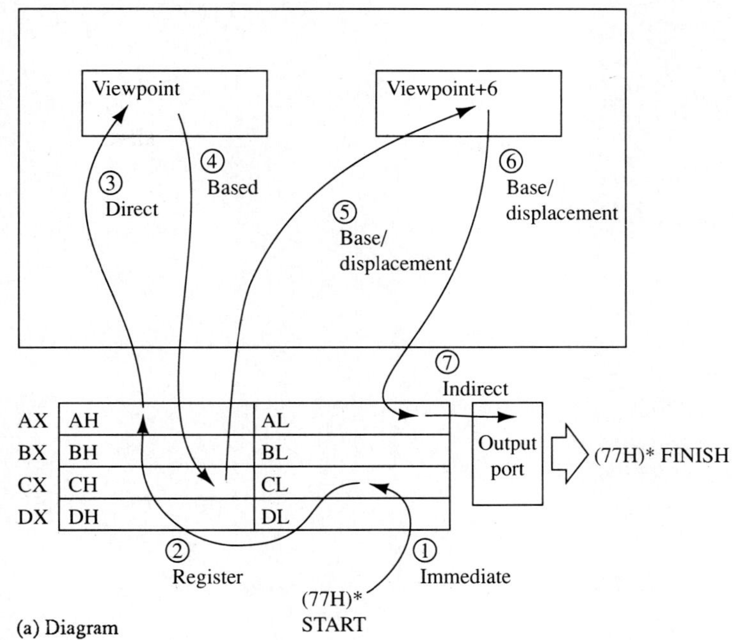

(a) Diagram

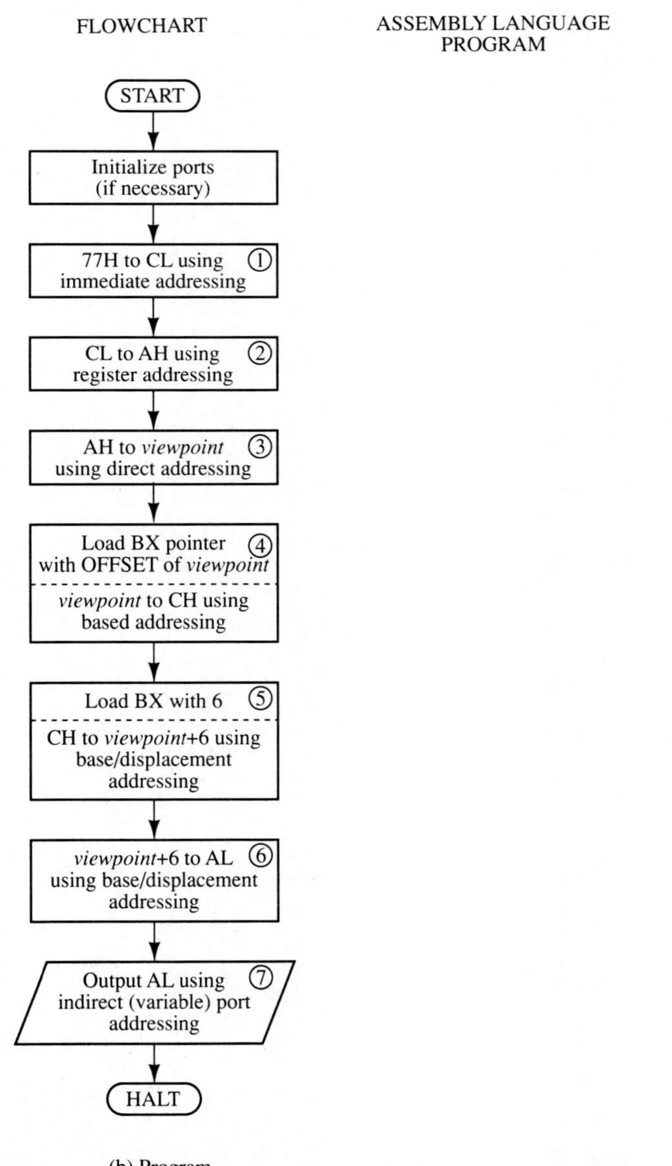

(b) Program

Name: ______________________

Date: ______________________

QUESTIONS AND PROBLEMS

Class: ______________________

1. Fill in the following with *segment* or *offset*.

   To relocate a program, change the ____________ address.
2. Can a variable be stored in the _TEXT segment? If so, how does the computer find the variable?

3. If the data segment is located at 00A00H (00A0:0000H), what numerical *offset, segment,* and *physical* addresses correspond to each of the following two byte variables?

```
_DATA     SEGMENT
  apples   DB  ?
  peaches DB  ?
_DATA     ENDS
```

4. Repeat question 3 assuming variables *apples* and *peaches* are defined as words.

5. If DS = 447BH, BX = 9, and byte variable *peaches* represents a displacement of 0007H, what physical address is accessed by the instruction below?

```
mov  al,peaches[bx]
```

6. What is accomplished by the following instruction?

```
mov  [bx],bx
```

7. What addressing mode is generated by the *mov bx,OFFSET DGROUP:peaches* instruction? (*Hint: OFFSET DGROUP:peaches* reduces to a numerical offset address when assembled.)

8. Array *apples* contains the four elements shown below:

```
apples DB  1,2,3,4
```

   Using the instruction *apples[bx],* what is placed into BX in order to access the "1"? the "3"?

9. Why must all hexadecimal numbers that begin with a letter (A through F) be preceded by a 0?

10. The two instructions listed below both place the offset address of variable *apples* into BX. What is the difference between them?

```
mov   bx,OFFSET DGROUP:apples
lea   bx,apples
```

Advanced Section

11. In the instruction below, variable *apples* is defined in the _TEXT segment. Why is the use of the CS override prefix optional?

```
mov   bl,cs:apples
```

12. Variables can be stored in internal registers or in memory (usually as symbolic variables). What are the advantages of storing variables in memory? in internal registers?

13. If *apples* is a word variable, what is accomplished by the following?

```
mov   BYTE PTR apples,al
```

14. The SMALL model of segmentation also provides for segments CONST and MEMORY. What is the purpose of each?

15. Are the programs of this experiment *dynamically relocatable*? (That is, will they run from any memory location without modification?) Explain your answer.

16. Is a program relocatable (or dynamically relocatable) if the code occupies more than one segment, such as when using the LARGE model of segmentation?

17. How would the answers to question 8 change if *apples* were a word array?

ACTIVITY 3

LABELS AND THE UNCONDITIONAL JUMP

OBJECTIVES

- To contrast *labels* and *variables*.
- To introduce unconditional *branches* and *loops*.
- To compare the five types of unconditional jump instructions.

PARTS AND EQUIPMENT

- IBM PC (bus-extender optional).
- Assembler, debugger, and utilities.

DISCUSSION

Labels

A *label* is similar to a *variable*. Consider the following statement, containing label *here* and variable *apples*:

```
here:   mov   al,apples
```

They are similar because both represent symbolic offset addresses. However, they differ in their definition and use:

- Variable *apples* is usually defined in the _DATA segment with the DB directive. When variable *apples* appears within an instruction, it "points to" a memory location in the data segment whose *contents* are used in the operation.
- Label *here* usually is defined in the _TEXT segment by writing the symbol in the label field (to the left of an instruction). In our example, label *here* "points to" the MOV op code in the code field. A label usually appears as the operand of a jump instruction to give the target address of the jump.

In future activities, we will further refine our understanding of variables and labels.

The Unconditional Jump

A program *branch* is a break in the normal sequential flow and is caused by a *jump* instruction. If the branch always occurs, it is known as an *unconditional jump,* which is the subject of this activity. If the branch *may* occur, it is known as a *conditional jump* and is the subject of a future activity.

Figure 3.1 shows examples of the five kinds of unconditional jumps. A brief description of each is given below:

a. An *intra*segment (NEAR) jump causes a branch *within* the current segment (from −32K to +32K) and changes only the instruction pointer (IP). The label *alabel* is a label that represents a 16-bit *relative* offset address in two's-complement notation. If the target is within −128/+127 the assembler may generate a special 2-byte SHORT jump, using an 8-bit relative offset address.
b. An *intra*segment (NEAR) indirect (register) jump uses the BX register to hold the *absolute* (as opposed to relative) 16-bit target offset address. Note the use of the OFFSET operator and the label (*alabel*) as one way of initializing the BX register.
c. An *intra*segment (NEAR) indirect (variable) jump is similar to routine b, but holds the absolute 16-bit target offset address in data segment variable *avariable*. Besides direct addressing of the variable (as shown), any addressing mode can be used. Note the use of *alabel* as one way of initializing *avariable* with the correct target address.
d. An *inter*segment (FAR) direct jump can branch anywhere (to the same segment or another segment) and, therefore, may change both the CS and IP registers. The label *alabel* represents the 32-bit (offset:segment) *absolute* target address.
e. An *inter*segment (FAR) indirect jump holds the 32-bit *absolute* target address in the double-word

FIGURE 3.1

Unconditional jump demonstration routines. (a) Intrasegment (NEAR) direct. (b) Intrasegment (NEAR) indirect (register). (c) Intrasegment (NEAR) indirect (variable). (d) Intersegment (FAR) direct. (e) Intersegment (FAR) indirect (variable).

```
NAME        NEAR_DIRECT

DGROUP GROUP _DATA

_DATA       SEGMENT
_DATA       ENDS

_TEXT       SEGMENT
            ASSUME CS:_TEXT,DS:DGROUP
  start:    nop
  alabel:   nop
            nop
            jmp   alabel
_TEXT       ENDS
            END   start
```

(a) Intra-segment (NEAR) direct

```
NAME        NEAR_INDIRECT_REGISTER

DGROUP GROUP _DATA

_DATA       SEGMENT
_DATA       ENDS

_TEXT       SEGMENT
            ASSUME CS:_TEXT,DS:DGROUP
  start:    mov   bx,OFFSET alabel
  alabel:   nop
            nop
            jmp   bx
_TEXT       ENDS
            END   start
```

(b) Intra-segment (NEAR) indirect (register)

```
NAME        NEAR_INDIRECT_VARIABLE

DGROUP GROUP _DATA

_DATA       SEGMENT
  avariable  DW  alabel
_DATA       ENDS

_TEXT       SEGMENT
            ASSUME CS:_TEXT,DS:DGROUP
  start:    mov   ax,DGROUP
            mov   ds,ax
  alabel:   nop
            nop
            jmp   avariable
_TEXT       ENDS
            END   start
```

(c) Intra-segment (NEAR) indirect (variable)

```
NAME        FAR_DIRECT

DGROUP GROUP _DATA

_DATA       SEGMENT
_DATA       ENDS

_TEXT       SEGMENT
            ASSUME  CS:_TEXT,DS:DGROUP
  start:    nop
  alabel LABEL FAR
            nop
            nop
            jmp   alabel
_TEXT       ENDS
            END   start
```

(d) Inter-segment (FAR) direct

```
NAME        FAR_INDIRECT

DGROUP GROUP _DATA

_DATA       SEGMENT
  avariable  DD  alabel
_DATA       ENDS

_TEXT       SEGMENT
            ASSUME  CS:_TEXT,DS:DGROUP
  start:    mov   ax,DGROUP
            mov   ds,ax
  alabel LABEL FAR
            nop
            nop
            jmp   avariable
_TEXT       ENDS
            END   start
```

(e) Inter-segment (FAR) indirect (variable)

FIGURE 3.2

Contrasting the direct and indirect jumps. (a) The NEAR direct jump. (b) The NEAR indirect (register) jump.

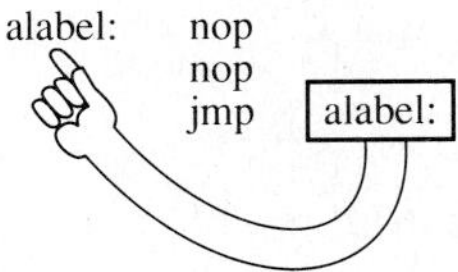

(a) The NEAR direct jump

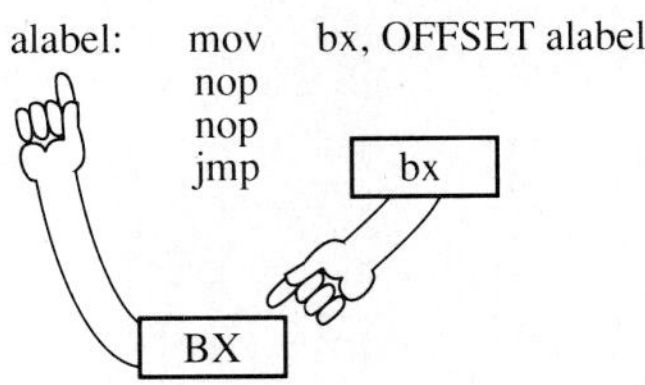

(b) The NEAR indirect (register) jump

data segment variable *avariable*. Besides addressing the variable in the direct mode (as shown), any addressing mode can be used. (Unlike routine b, a 16-bit internal register pair cannot be used to hold the 32-bit target address.)

Note that the target labels for both FAR jumps (routines d and e) must use the long form (*alabel* LABEL FAR). For NEAR jumps we can use either the long form (*alabel* LABEL NEAR) or the short form (*alabel:*).

The diagrams of Figure 3.2 contrast the direct and indirect jump processes.

Relative Addressing

The NEAR/SHORT direct jump of routine a is by far the most commonly used in this text. It is the only one that uses *relative* addressing. Because a relative address gives the distance *between* source and target, these instructions are automatically *dynamically relocatable* (can be stored and executed at any memory location without modification).

Forward-Referenced Jumps

All the demonstration programs of Figure 3.1 are loops; therefore, all jumps are *backward referenced*. However, if a *direct* jump is *forward referenced* (to a larger memory address), the assembler has no way of determining on its own the correct number of memory locations to set aside (the SHORT, NEAR, and FAR direct jumps require 2, 3, and 5 bytes, respectively).

If no additional information is given, the assembler assumes the jump is NEAR. Therefore, if a forward-referenced *direct* jump is to be SHORT or FAR, we must notify the assembler as follows:

```
JMP  SHORT alabel
JMP  FAR PTR alabel
```

If no information is given, the assembler defaults to NEAR and sets aside a word address. If it later finds that a SHORT jump will do, it places a NOP instruction in place of the high-order address.

PROCEDURE

1. Program "Loop 1" of Figure 3.3(a) uses the NEAR/SHORT DIRECT jump to perform a loop about the NOP instruction (NOP is not executed). Write your assembly-language program

FIGURE 3.3

Jump instruction problems. (a) Using direct jumps. (b) Using indirect jumps.

FLOWCHART

ASSEMBLY LANGUAGE PROGRAM

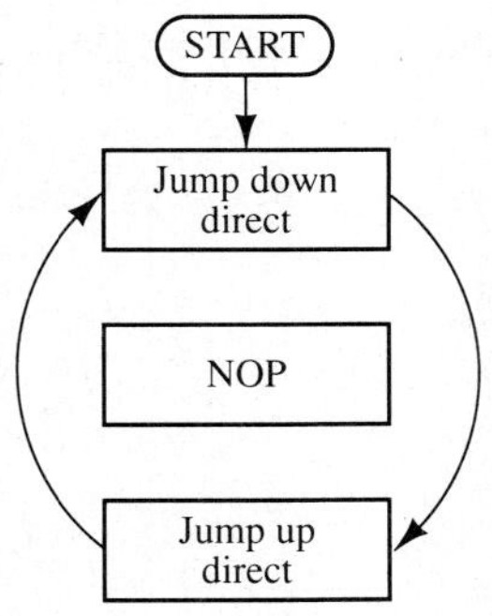

(a) Using direct jumps

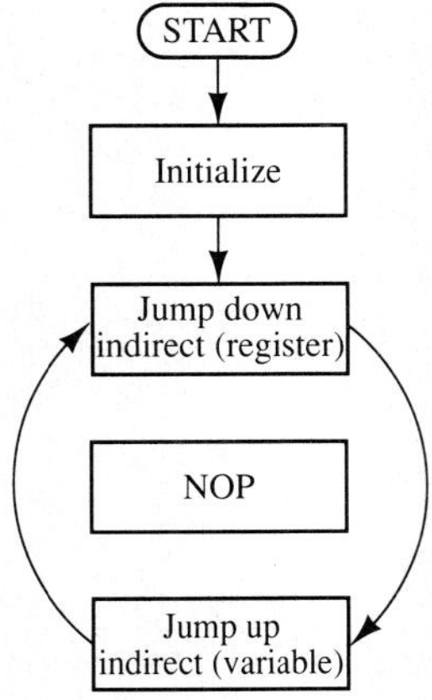

(b) Using indirect jumps

FIGURE 3.4

Program JITTERBUG.

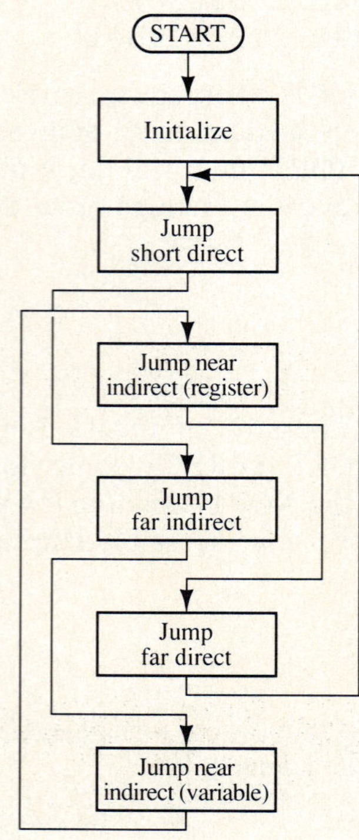

beside the flowchart and test by single-stepping.

Is the loop properly performed? ___________

2. Program "Loop 2" of Figure 3.3(b) uses the NEAR INDIRECT (register) instruction for the forward jump, and the NEAR INDIRECT (variable) instruction for the backward jump. Write your assembly-language program beside the flowchart and test by single-stepping. Is the loop properly performed? ___________

Advanced Activities

3. Examine the list file for program "Loop 1." How many memory locations were required (including any added NOP instructions) for each of the following?

   * The forward jump: ___________

   * The backward jump: ___________

4. Repeat program "Loop 2" of step 2, but using *base/displacement* addressing for the backward jump.

5. Write program JITTERBUG of Figure 3.4.

Name: ______________________

Date: ______________________

QUESTIONS AND PROBLEMS

Class: ______________________

1. Explain how the target address is determined for each type of jump listed below:
   a. NEAR direct:
   b. NEAR indirect (register):
   c. NEAR indirect (variable):
2. Write *direct* or *indirect* for each of the following:
   a. A label follows the jump mnemonic: ____________
   b. A variable or register follows the jump mnemonic: ____________
3. What is a *relative* address?
4. What is the advantage of the SHORT jump over the NEAR jump?
5. Name one advantage of an indirect jump over a direct jump.
6. Why does a FAR indirect jump require a double-word variable?
7. What changes would you make to the following forward-referenced instruction to generate a SHORT jump? a FAR jump?

   ```
   jmp mylabel
   ```

8. For backward-referenced jumps, why aren't the SHORT and FAR PTR directives required to distinguish among SHORT, NEAR, or FAR jumps?

Advanced Section

9. What will be in registers AX, BX, and CX after the following program is run? (Assume that *apples* and *start* are both at offset 0000 within the _DATA and _TEXT segments.)

```
NAME        VARIABLES_VS_LABELS

DGROUP GROUP _DATA

_DATA       SEGMENT
  apples DW 3333h
_DATA       ENDS

_TEXT       SEGMENT
            ASSUME CS:_TEXT,DS:DGROUP
 start:     mov  ax,DGROUP      ; 3-byte instruction
            mov  ds,ax          ; 2-byte instruction
```

```
peaches: mov   ax,apples
         mov   bx,OFFSET DGROUP:apples
         mov   cx,OFFSET peaches
         hlt
_TEXT    ENDS
         END    start
```

10. Which of the five jump options of Figure 3.1 results in a loop that is *dynamically relocatable*? Under what conditions are the others dynamically relocatable?

11. What happens to the instruction queue within the 8086/88 when a jump instruction is processed? Why?

12. When a relative address is calculated, the IP is incremented to point to the next instruction op code before the relative address is added. Based on this, what is the relative jumping range for both the direct NEAR and SHORT jumps *with respect to the jump op code*?

13. Examine the list file of program "Loop 1" of Figure 3.3(a) and explain how the assembler computed the address of the backward jump. (*Hint:* See question 12.)

14. What is the difference between an EXE file and a COM file and how does this relate to dynamic relocation?

ACTIVITY 4

THE ARITHMETIC GROUP

OBJECTIVES

- To write and execute a variety of programs using instructions from the arithmetic group.
- To introduce the EQU directive.

PARTS AND EQUIPMENT

- IBM PC (bus-extender optional).
- Assembler, debugger, and utilities.

DISCUSSION

The Arithmetic Group

The instructions of the arithmetic group are listed in Figure 4.1 and include the ability to perform a number of arithmetic processes on a variety of data types. In this experiment, we confine ourselves to signed and unsigned operations on bytes and words using the asterisked instructions. Future activities will extend arithmetic processing into BCD and ASCII numbers, multiple precision, data structures, advanced signed number operations, and the 8087 math coprocessor.

When using the instructions of the arithmetic group, keep in mind the following restrictions:

- The increment, decrement, add, and subtract instructions operate on both signed and unsigned numbers.
- The multiply and divide operations require separate instructions for signed and unsigned numbers.
- When multiplying bytes, the multiplier must be in the AL register. The multiplicand can be in any register or memory location, and the word product goes to AX. (With word multiplication, the answer goes to AX/DX.) The examples below show how multiplication is performed:

```
mul  bl       ; AX = AL * BL,
                where all values
                are unsigned
imul apples   ; AX = AL * apples,
                where all values
                are signed and
                apples is a byte.
```

- When dividing bytes, the dividend (number to be divided) must be a word in AX. If the dividend

FIGURE 4.1

The arithmetic instructions. (Courtesy Intel Corporation.)

ADDITION	
∗ADD	Add byte or word
ADC	Add byte or word with carry
∗INC	Increment byte or word by 1
AAA	ASCII adjust for addition
DAA	Decimal adjust for addition
SUBTRACTION	
∗SUB	Subtract byte or word
SBB	Subtract byte or word with borrow
∗DEC	Decrement byte or word by 1
∗NEG	Negate byte or word
CMP	Compare byte or word
AAS	ASCII adjust for subtraction
DAS	Decimal adjust for subtraction
MULTIPLICATION	
∗MUL	Multiply byte or word unsigned
∗IMUL	Integer multiply byte or word
AAM	ASCII adjust for multiply
DIVISION	
∗DIV	Divide byte or word unsigned
∗IDIV	Integer divide byte or word
AAD	ASCII adjust for division
∗CBW	Convert byte to word
CWD	Convert word to doubleword

* Instructions covered in this activity

begins as a byte in AL, it must be extended throughout AX by clearing AH for unsigned operations or using the CBW (*convert byte to word*) instruction for signed operations. After division, the quotient will be in AL and the remainder in AH. (Word division follows a similar process using register pair AX/DX.) The examples below show how division is performed:

```
div  bl        ; AL = AX/BL
                 (remainder in
                 AH), where all
                 values are
                 unsigned.
idiv apples    ; AL = AX/apples
                 (remainder in
                 AH), where all
                 values are
                 signed and
                 apples is a
                 byte.
```

Instruction Symmetry

As a further review of the symmetry and flexibility of 8086/88 assembly-language programming, the list below provides a sampling of legal operations. Where two operands are involved, the answer is found in the left-hand destination operand.

```
add  apples,55h       ; apples = apples + 55H
inc  BYTE PTR[bx]     ; Increment byte pointed to by BX
sub  apples[bx],cl    ; apples[bx] = apples[bx] - CL
sub  cl,apples[bx]    ; CL = CL - apples[bx]
dec  apples           ; Decrement apples
mul  peaches[bx]      ; AX = AL * peaches[bx]
div  cl               ; AL = AX/CL (remainder in AH)
add  dh,bl            ; DH = DH + BL
```

The EQU Directive

The *equate* (EQU) directive is used to substitute a descriptive English expression for any part of an instruction. It is especially useful when an item that appears many times in the program might be modified at a later time. Simply modify the single equate value, and all changes will be made during reassembly. In the example below, the assembler substitutes 365 wherever the symbol YEAR appears in the program. (How difficult would it be to make the program valid during leap years?)

```
YEAR EQU 365
```

FIGURE 4.2

Demonstration program ALGEBRA (using simulated binary ports).

```
; This version of program ALGEBRA uses
; simulated binary ports for input and
; output.

NAME          ALGEBRA

DGROUP GROUP _DATA

_DATA         SEGMENT
_DATA         ENDS

_TEXT         SEGMENT
              ASSUME CS:_TEXT,DS:DGROUP
              ADDCONST  EQU  5
     start:   mov    ax,DGROUP
              mov    ds,ax           ; Initialize ds
     again:   in     al,0            ; Input byte
              mul    al              ; Square
              add    ax,ADDCONST     ; Add 5
              out    1,ax            ; Output word
              jmp    again           ; Loop forever
_TEXT         ENDS
              END    start
```

The Arithmetic Operators

The arithmetic *instructions* (Figure 4.1) perform arithmetic operations *during execution*. The arithmetic *operators* (+, −, *, /, MOD) perform arithmetic operations *during assembly*. Some examples of arithmetic operators are given at the top of page 57.

```
mov  cx,3 * (16 / 7 + 3) ; Place 15 (FH) into CX.
mov  cx,apples + 4       ; Move into CX the contents of the
                           memory location whose offset address is
                           four greater than the offset address of
                           apples.
```

When using operators, be aware that the multiplication, division, and modulo operators can only be used with numerical (or equated) values.

Operators are used for two major reasons: to avoid hand calculation and for program documentation.

Demonstration Program ALGEBRA

Demonstration program ALGEBRA of Figure 4.2 uses arithmetic instructions and simulated binary ports to solve the following equation for input unsigned bytes:

$$\text{outputword} = (\text{inputbyte})^2 + 5$$

PROCEDURE

NOTE: Where appropriate, initialize variables and test your program on both signed and unsigned numbers.

FIGURE 4.3

Program ADD_SEVEN.

FLOWCHART ASSEMBLY LANGUAGE PROGRAM

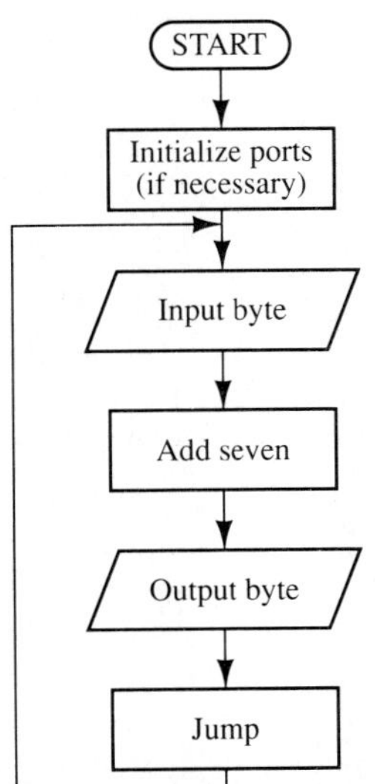

1. Making use of the ADD IMMEDIATE and IN/OUT instructions, write a loop program beside the flowchart of Figure 4.3 that adds +7 to each input byte prior to outputting. (Use ADDCONST EQU 7 in your program.)
2. Using the MUL, SUB, INC, and IN/OUT instructions, write a loop program that processes the equation below for input signed bytes. (*Hint:* Refer to Figure 4.2.)

$$\text{outputword} = (\text{inputbyte} - 3)^2 + 1$$

FLOWCHART ASSEMBLY-LANGUAGE PROGRAM

3. Using the DIV instruction, write a loop program in which unsigned word variable *miles* and unsigned byte variable *gallons* are divided and the resulting *miles-per-gallon* value (quotient and remainder) is stored in word variable *answer*. (Caution: Do not divide by zero.)

FLOWCHART ASSEMBLY-LANGUAGE PROGRAM

Advanced Activities

4. Using the DIV instruction, write a program that performs the R = A MOD B operation on unsigned bytes. (Divides byte variable A by byte variable B and reports the remainder in byte variable R.)

5. Making use of the IDIV and CBW instructions, write a program that displays (outputs) the average value of two input *signed* bytes (remainder also reported).

6. Write a program that processes the equation below to output the corresponding Fahrenheit temperature for all input centigrade temperatures between 0 and 25.

$$F = (9 \times C)/5 + 32$$

7. Using a single MOV instruction and the arithmetic *operators* (rather than the arithmetic *instructions*), have the assembler calculate the Fahrenheit equivalent of 3 degrees (deg) centigrade during assembly and place the result in variable location F + 4 during execution.

Name: ______________________

Date: ______________________

Class: ______________________

QUESTIONS AND PROBLEMS

1. Fill in the following: Adding -5 is the same as subtracting __________.
2. The hexadecimal number 81H could be interpreted as what two decimal numbers (depending on whether the number is signed or unsigned)?

3. Using signed number (two's-complement) notation, convert each of the following decimal numbers to hexadecimal:

   a. 0   c. +127
   b. −1   d. −128
4. What is accomplished by each of the following instructions:
   a. *add al.al*
   b. *neg apples*
5. What change must be made in the demonstration program ALGEBRA of Figure 4.2 if we wish to enter −3 as well as +3?

6. If the AL register is currently holding 81H, what would the AX register hold after the CBW instruction?

7. Using the OFFSET DGROUP and WORD PTR directives, show how to use based addressing to increment word variable *apples*.

Advanced Section

8. Why was the 8086 designed to issue an automatic interrupt when dividing by zero?

9. Over what range of numbers does an unsigned double word (DD) extend? a signed double word?

10. Why would it be improper to perform the temperature calculation of step 6 in the following manner:

$$F = ((9 / 5) \times C) + 32$$

11. Although not included in the 8086 instruction set, theoretically, can the MUL and DIV instructions use *immediate* addressing?

12. Contrast the reasons for performing mathematical operations during execution (*instructions*) versus during assembly (*operators*).

13. If BX holds 4, are the following instructions equivalent? ____________

    a. `MOV AX,APPLES + 4`
    b. `MOV AX,APPLES[BX]`

14. What is performed by the HIGH and LOW operators?

15. How are *words* divided?

ACTIVITY 5

THE LOGICAL GROUP

OBJECTIVE

- To write and execute a variety of programs involving instructions from the logical group.

PARTS AND EQUIPMENT

- IBM PC (bus-extender optional).
- Assembler, debugger, and utilities.

DISCUSSION

The 13 logical instructions of Figure 5.1 are used for three major purposes: mathematical processing, Boolean operations, and bit manipulation. (The TEST instruction is involved with decision-making and will be discussed in Activity 6.)

- For mathematical processing, the shift instructions multiply or divide by multiples of two. The logical shift instructions (SHL and SHR) process unsigned data, and the arithmetic shift instructions (SAL and SAR) process signed data. The NOT instruction performs the one's-complement process.
- For Boolean operations, the logical group includes the OR, XOR (exclusive or), and NOT instructions. To combine two Boolean variables logically, we use the shift instructions to place them into the same bit position, but in separate registers or memory locations.
- For bit manipulation operations, we take advantage of the following Boolean axioms:

```
A + 1 = 1    A * 1 = A
A + 0 = A    A * 0 = 0
```

An AND/OR sequence will set individual bits high, low, or unchanged in any combination we wish.

The Shift and Rotate Instructions

The diagrams of Figure 5.2(a) compare the arithmetic shift, logical shift, and rotate instructions. As shown by the examples of Figure 5.2(b), we can use any of the nine addressing modes to shift or rotate bytes or words once or by the number of times specified by register CL (the *count* register). The *carry flag* (CF) is a one-bit flip-flop used in decision-making and will be covered in the next activity.

The Logical and Shift Operators

Analogous to the arithmetic case, the logical and shift *instructions* perform operations *during execution*; the logical and shift *operators* (OR, XOR, AND, NOT, SHR, SHL) perform operations *during assembly*. The following examples at the top of page 62 show how the operators are used:

FIGURE 5.1

The logical group. (Courtesy Intel Corporation.)

LOGICALS	
NOT	"Not" byte or word
AND	"And" byte or word
OR	"Inclusive or" byte or word
XOR	"Exclusive or" byte or word
TEST	"Test" byte or word
SHIFTS	
SHL/SAL	Shift logical/arithmetic left byte or word
SHR	Shift logical right byte or word
SAR	Shift arithmetic right byte or word
ROTATES	
ROL	Rotate left byte or word
ROR	Rotate right byte or word
RCL	Rotate through carry left byte or word
RCR	Rotate through carry right byte or word

```
mov  cx,1234H SHR 8       ; cx = 0012H after execution
mov  cx,2233H and 00FFH   ; cx = 0033H after execution
```

Demonstration Program NAND_GATE

Demonstration program NAND_GATE of Figure 5.3 shows how logic and bit manipulation operations are used to simulate a two-input NAND gate. Note the following important points:

- All single-bit Boolean variables are lined up in the same bit position (D0 in our case) and in separate register or variable locations before Boolean operations are performed.
- The Boolean instructions operate on full bytes or words (performing 8 or 16 operations simultaneously), even though in our case only a single bit position is involved.
- The instruction *and al,00000001B* performs a special form of bit manipulation known as *masking*.

  Bits 1 through 7 are set to zero (masked out); bit 0 remains unchanged.

Storing and Processing Variables: Registers Versus Memory

Referring to Figure 5.3(d), we used both a register (AL) and a symbolic memory location (*temp*) to store our variables during processing. The question is: Is it best to store and process variables in registers or as symbolic variables in memory?

Registers have the advantage of speed—often the major reason for using assembly-language. However, registers are available in limited supply and are dedicated to other purposes and often not available (such as DX for port addressing, CL for shift/rotate counts, and BX for based addressing). At the expense of processing speed, symbolic variables overcome these problems, and they have the added advantage of making programs more readable.

Therefore, in the programs that follow we recommend a mixture of symbolic variable and register storage. (When we introduce library routines in Activity 15, this recommendation will be modified.)

FIGURE 5.2

The shift and rotate instructions. (a) Diagrams. (b) Examples.

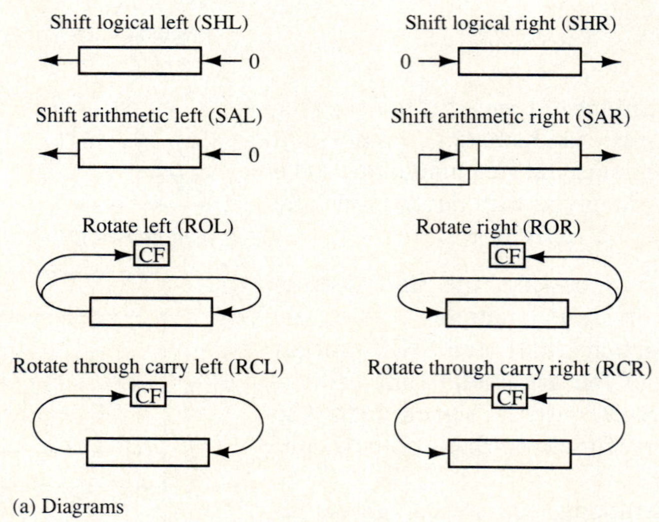

(a) Diagrams

```
rcl  bx,1              ;Rotate BX left through carry once         } Once only
sal  apples,1          ;Shift APPLES left arithmetically once
ror  apples[bx],cl     ;Rotate APPLES[BX] right CL times          } 0–255
rol  ax,cl             ;Rotate AX left CL times                     times
shl  BYTE PTR[bx],cl;Shift [bx] left logically CL times
```

(b) Examples

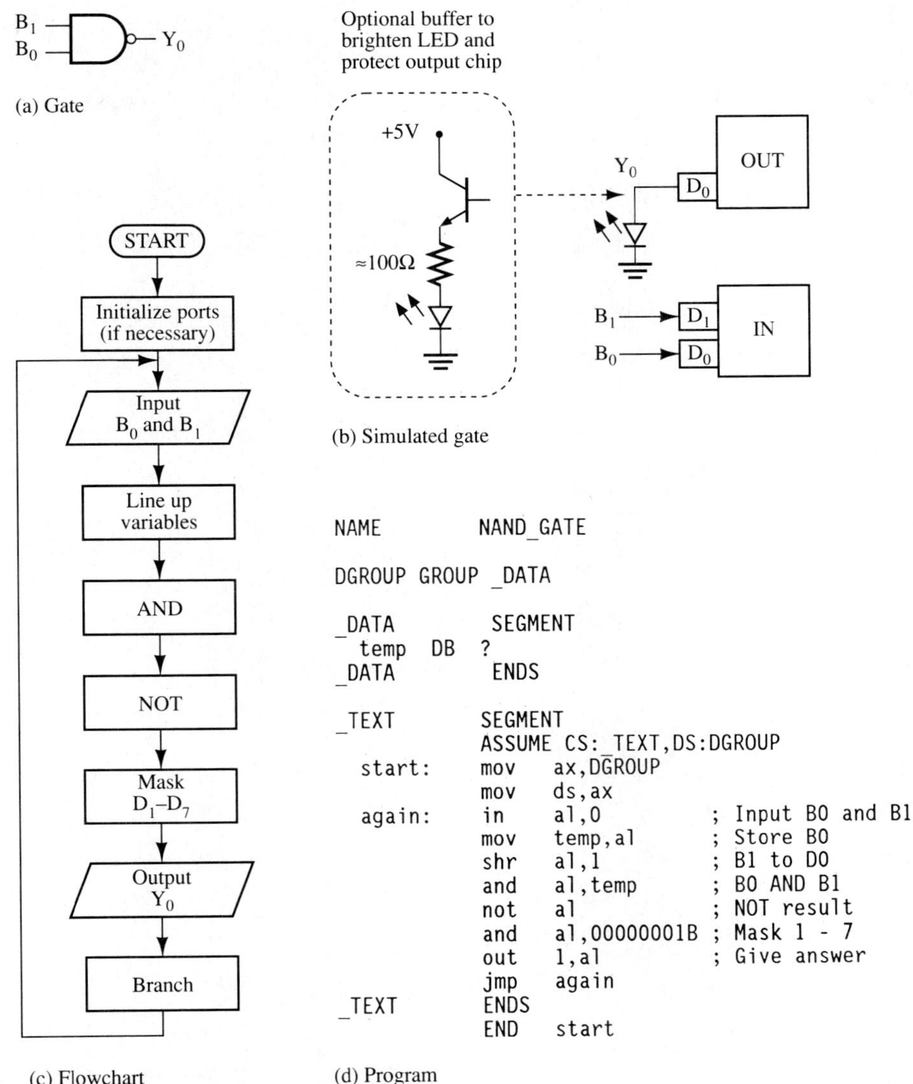

FIGURE 5.3

Demonstration program NAND_GATE. (a) Gate. (b) Simulated gate. (c) Flowchart. (d) Program.

Instruction Symmetry

As a final reminder of the symmetry and flexibility of the 8086/88 instruction set, all the operations listed below are legal. For the two-operand Boolean instructions, the result goes to the left-hand ("destination") operand.

```
not   apples             ; One's complement of apples
and   [bx],cl            ; [bx] = [bx] AND CL
or    apples[bx],44h     ; apples[bx] = apples[bx] OR 44H
shr   ax,cl              ; Shift AX logically right CL times
rcr   BYTE PTR[bx],1     ; Rotate through carry byte [bx] once
xor   bl,apples          ; BL = BL XOR apples
```

PROCEDURE

Mathematical Processing

1. Using the SAL instruction to multiply, solve the algebraic equation shown below. Test your program on both positive and negative bytes. (Whenever the output overflows, the answer is no longer valid.)

$$\text{outputbyte} = (8 \times \text{inputbyte}) + 2$$

FLOWCHART ASSEMBLY-LANGUAGE PROGRAM

Logic Gate Simulation

2. Using the space reserved in Figure 5.4(b), write the flowchart for a loop program that simulates the logic circuit of Figure 5.4(a). Write the program beside the flowchart. Test your program and verify proper operation by filling in the following truth table.

B2	B1	B0	Y0
0	0	0	
0	0	1	
0	1	0	
0	1	1	
1	0	0	
1	0	1	
1	1	0	
1	1	1	

FIGURE 5.4

Gate simulation program. (a) Logic circuit. (b) Flowchart and program.

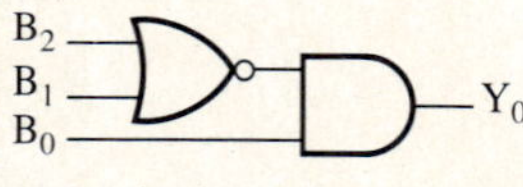

(a) Logic circuit

FLOWCHART ASSEMBLY LANGUAGE PROGRAM

(b) Program

Bit Manipulation

3. Each of the 8 bits (0 to 7) of an input port individually controls eight spotlights on the stage of a theater. Write a loop program that makes sure lights 0 and 1 are *always* on, lights 6 and 7 are *always* off, and the remaining four lights are controlled by input values.

FLOWCHART ASSEMBLY-LANGUAGE PROGRAM

4. The upper 4 bits of byte variable *uppermap* hold half the data required to locate buried treasure. The lower 4 bits of byte variable *lowermap* hold the other half. The remaining 4 bits of both variables hold useless data. Using a combination of AND and OR operations, write a program that properly combines the two halves and places the result in byte variable *treasuremap*.

FLOWCHART ASSEMBLY-LANGUAGE PROGRAM

Advanced Activities

5. Given Boolean variables *karen, sue,* and *homework,* use I/O ports to simulate the following logical situation:

    If Karen *or* Sue arrives (but *not both*), *and* I do *not* have homework, I will go to the movies.

6. Byte variable *security* holds 0FH (00001111B), the expected arrangement of normally on (1) and normally off (0) burglar alarm switches. Write a loop program that inputs data from the eight switches and outputs a 1 at whatever bit positions do not match the expected condition. (*Hint:* Use the XOR instruction.)
7. Using feedback from output port back to input port, simulate the RS latch shown in Figure 5.5(a) with the port configuration of Figure 5.5(b).
8. Using a single MOV instruction and both the logical and shift *operators* (rather than the logical and shift instructions), have the assembler process word 1234H and move 0340H into AX during execution.

FIGURE 5.5

RS latch hardware. (a) Circuit. (b) Simulated circuit.

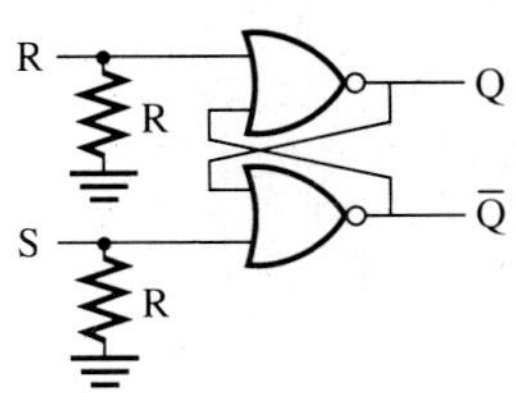

(a) Circuit

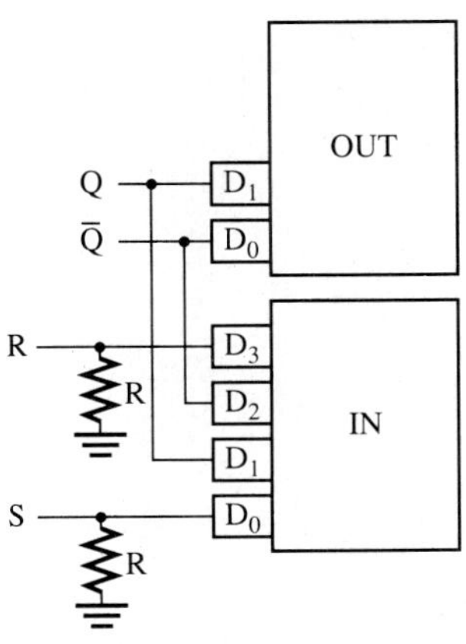

(b) Simulated circuit

Name: ____________________

Date: ____________________

QUESTIONS AND PROBLEMS

Class: ____________________

1. What is the *one's-complement*? What instruction performs the one's-complement process?

2. One way to clear the accumulator (set all positions to zero) using an instruction from the logical group is to AND immediate all zeros. Can you think of another *logical* instruction that will accomplish the same result?

3. What logical instruction will set all accumulator bit positions to 1?

4. If AL holds 10001110B and CL = 2, what will be in AL after each of the following?

   a. `shr al,cl`
   b. `sar al,cl`
   c. `ror al,cl`

5. When implementing a four-input AND gate, why does diagram (b) of Figure 5.6 correspond more closely to the software-oriented method used by a computer?

6. What is the result when we shift −20 once using the SHR instruction? using the SAR instruction? Which one properly divides by two?

7. What are several of the advantages of storing variables in memory as symbols? of storing variables in registers?

FIGURE 5.6

Four-input AND gate configurations.

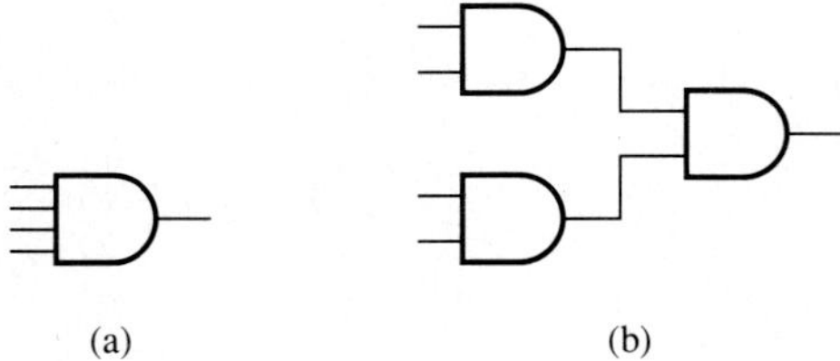

Advanced Section

8. Referring to the equation of procedure step 1, what are the largest unsigned and signed input bytes that will not cause loss of data (overflow)?

9. Are the following two statements equivalent? Prove your answer using DeMorgan's theorem.
   a. If it is NOT raining AND it is NOT snowing, I will go to the beach.
   b. If it is raining OR snowing, I will NOT go to the beach.

ACTIVITY 6

DECISION-MAKING
The Conditional Jump Instruction and Flags

OBJECTIVE

- To write and execute programs involving decision-making.

PARTS AND EQUIPMENT

- IBM PC (bus-extender optional).
- Assembler, debugger, and utilities.

DISCUSSION

The *structure theorem* tells us that all programs, no matter how complex, are fashioned from single-entry/single-exit nested combinations of *sequence, selection,* and *repetition.* As shown by Figure 6.1, decision-making—the subject of this activity—is central to both selection and repetition.

As diagrammed by Figure 6.2, decision-making is a two-step process:

- The first step (set flags) is accomplished with an instruction from the arithmetic or logical groups. When the instruction is processed, selected flags (Figure 6.3) are set or reset according to the result of the operation.
- The second step (branch) is accomplished when a conditional transfer (jump) instruction from the list of Figure 6.4(a) examines the flags and jumps if the condition is true. All conditional jumps are SHORT direct jumps that use relative addressing.

Choosing the Right Set Flags/Branch Combination

The programmer selects the correct set flags/branch combination to carry out each decision. The following tips should help you make the right choice:

- An especially useful flag-setting instruction is COMPARE. Compare performs an "invisible subtraction" (the flags are set, but the destination operand is not changed and is used for less-than/greater-than/equal-to decision-making. Those conditional jumps using the words *above, below, equal, greater,* or *less* are "high level" (English-related) and are specifically intended to follow the *compare* flag-setting instruction. For example, the following combination says "jump to *there* if register AL is not below variable *apples*":

```
cmp  al,apples
jnb  there
```

  (Those conditional jumps that contain *above* or *below* refer to the comparison of unsigned values; those containing *greater* or *less* refer to the comparison of signed values.)
- The TEST instruction performs an "invisible" AND operation and is used to determine the state of individual bits. The conditional jumps JZ or JNZ most often follow TEST. For example, the following combination says "jump to *there* if bit D2 of variable *peaches* is high":

```
test  peaches,00000100B
jnz   there
```

- Many instructions have more than one form. For example, *jump if above* (JA) is logically equivalent to *jump if not below or equal* (JNBE). Also, *jump equal* (JE) is equivalent to *jump zero* (JZ). We use the high-level JE when COMPARE is the flag-setting instruction and the low-level JZ otherwise.

The Relational Operators

Similar to the arithmetic and logical groups, the relational *instructions* of Figure 6.4(a) perform true/false operations *during execution,* and the relational *operators* of Figure 6.4(b) perform true/false operations *during assembly*. The examples on page 70 show how the operators are used:

FIGURE 6.1

The three basic patterns of structured programming.

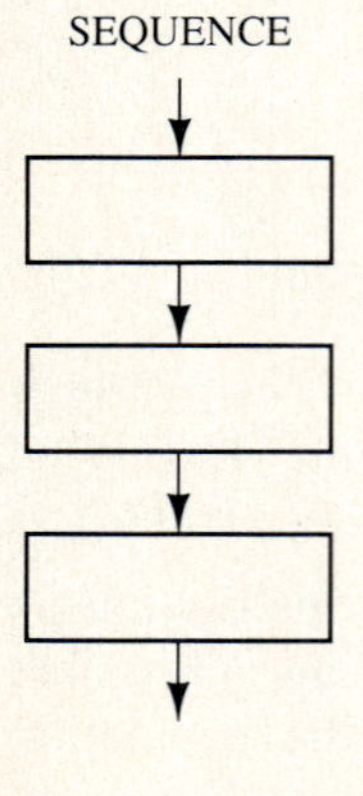

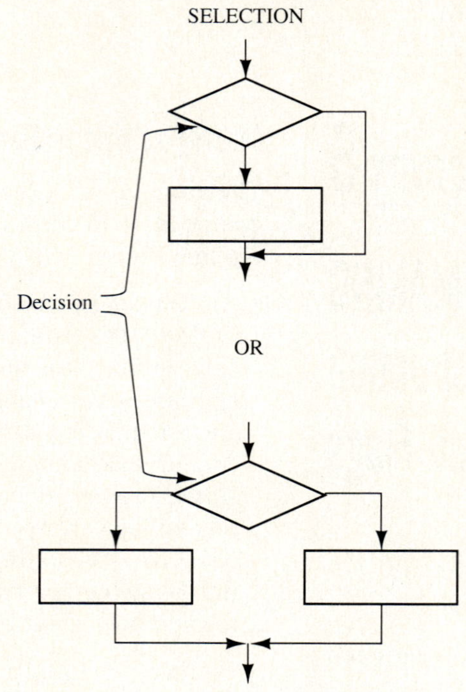

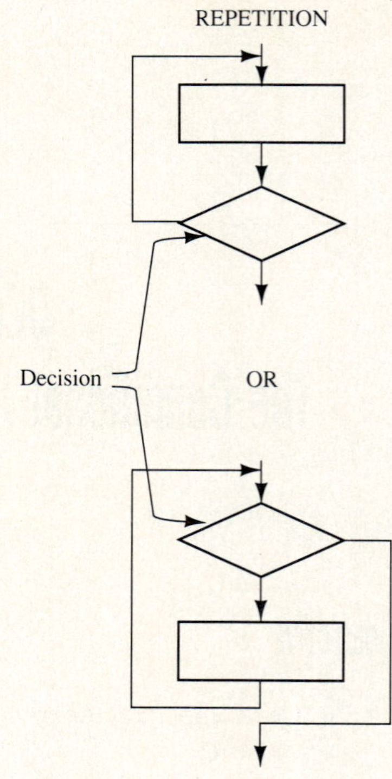


```
mov  al,18 GT 9 * 2        ; After execution, AL contains 00H
                             (false) because 18 is not greater
                             than 9 * 2.
mov  al,128 EQ (1 SHL 7) ; After execution, AL contains FFH
                             (true) because 128 = (1 SHL 7).
```

As before, operators are used for documentation and to avoid error-prone hand calculations.

Demonstration Programs

Program TOP_SCORE of Figure 6.5 demonstrates the two-step decision-making process by placing the largest of the two variables *first* and *second* into variable *biggest*. The CMP/JA decision-making pair is equivalent to the statement "Jump to *over* if *first* (in AL) is above *second*." (What happens when *first* and *second* are equal?)

FIGURE 6.2

The two-step decision-making process.

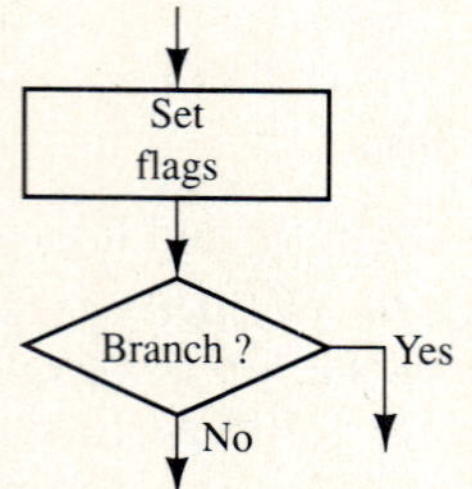

FIGURE 6.3

The 8086 flag register. (Courtesy Intel Corporation.)

15								7							0
X	X	X	X	OF	DF	IF	TF	SF	ZF	X	AF	X	PF	X	CF

X = Don't Care

AF: AUXILIARY CARRY — BCD
CF: CARRY FLAG
PF: PARITY FLAG
SF: SIGN FLAG
ZF: ZERO FLAG
} 8080 FLAGS

DF: DIRECTION FLAG STRINGS
IF: INTERRUPT ENABLE FLAG
OF: OVERFLOW FLAG CF ⊕ SF
TF: TRAP — SINGLE STEP FLAG
} 8086 FLAGS

FIGURE 6.4

The decision-making process. (a) The conditional jump instructions (Courtesy Intel Corporation). (b) The relational operators.

CONDITIONAL TRANSFERS	
JA/JNBE	Jump if above/not below nor equal
JAE/JNB	Jump if above or equal/not below
JB/JNAE	Jump if below/ not above nor equal
JBE/JNA	Jump if below or equal/ not above
JC	Jump if carry
JE/JZ	Jump if equal/zero
JG/JNLE	Jump if greater/not less nor equal
JGE/JNL	Jump if greater or equal/not less
JL/JNGE	Jump if less/not greater nor equal
JLE/JNG	Jump if less or equal/not greater
JNC	Jump if not carry
JNE/JNZ	Jump if not equal/ not zero
JNO	Jump if not overflow
JNP/JPO	Jump if not parity/ parity odd
JNS	Jump if not sign
JO	Jump if overflow
JP/JPE	Jump if parity/parity even
JS	Jump if sign

(a) The conditional jump instructions

Description	Format
Equal:	Operand EQ operand
Not equal:	Operand NE operand
Less than:	Operand LT operand
Less than or equal:	Operand LE operand
Greater than:	Operand GT operand
Greater than or equal:	Operand GE operand

(b) The relational operators

FIGURE 6.5

Demonstration program TOP_SCORE. (a) Flowchart. (b) Program.

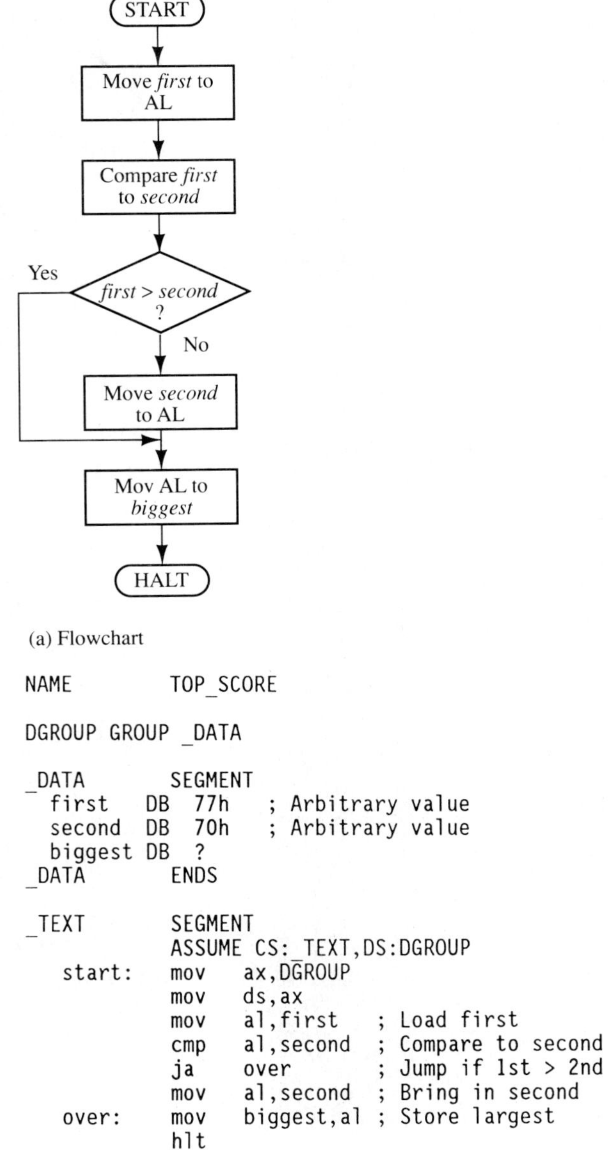

(a) Flowchart

```
NAME          TOP_SCORE

DGROUP GROUP _DATA

_DATA         SEGMENT
  first   DB  77h     ; Arbitrary value
  second  DB  70h     ; Arbitrary value
  biggest DB  ?
_DATA         ENDS

_TEXT         SEGMENT
              ASSUME CS:_TEXT,DS:DGROUP
   start:     mov    ax,DGROUP
              mov    ds,ax
              mov    al,first    ; Load first
              cmp    al,second   ; Compare to second
              ja     over        ; Jump if 1st > 2nd
              mov    al,second   ; Bring in second
   over:      mov    biggest,al  ; Store largest
              hlt
_TEXT         ENDS
              END    start
```

(b) Program

Demonstration program ROBOT_HAND of Figure 6.6 shows how the TEST instruction determines the state of individual bits. Bits D0 through D4 represent the five fingers on a robot hand—each fitted with a pressure sensor. Our task is to issue a "pickup" command when an object is sensed. Our algorithm is: An object is sensed whenever the thumb (bit D0) and one or more of the four fingers (bits D1 through D4) senses pressure.

We input the sensor values and first test for thumb pressure. If no pressure is sensed (logic 0), we jump back and try again. When the thumb senses pressure, we then test for pressure on any combination of fingers. If no pressure, we jump back and try again; if pressure, we issue a "pickup" command (FFH) and exit the routine.

FIGURE 6.6

Demonstration program ROBOT_HAND. (a) Flowchart. (b) Program.

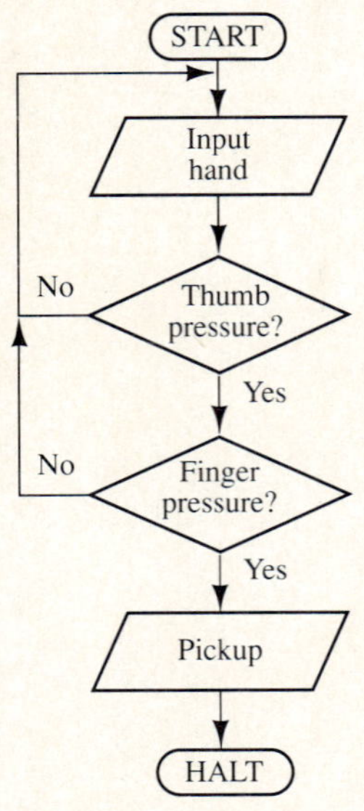

(a) Flowchart

```
; Issue "pickup" if thumb and any combination
; of fingers senses an object.  (Thumb is bit
; 0 and fingers are bits 1 - 4.)

NAME        ROBOT_HAND

DGROUP GROUP _DATA

_DATA       SEGMENT
_DATA       ENDS

_TEXT       SEGMENT
            ASSUME CS:_TEXT,DS:DGROUP
   start:   mov    ax,DGROUP
            mov    ds,ax
   back:    in     al,0
            Test   al,00000001B ; Thumb pressure?
            jz     back         ; Jump back if no
            test   al,00011110B ; Finger pressure?
            jz     back         ; Jump back if no
            mov    al,0ffh
            out    1,al         ; Issue "pickup"
            hlt
_TEXT       ENDS
            END    start
```

(b) Program

PROCEDURE

NOTE: Be sure to initialize all variables where appropriate.

1. Guided by the flowchart of Figure 6.7, write program COMBINATION LOCK, which waits in a loop until a number equal to byte variable *combination* is input. The correct input causes OPEN (FFFFH) to be output. (Initialize variable *combination* with a byte value of your choice.)
2. Write a loop program that simulates a three-input NOR gate using only conditional jump strategy. You may use Boolean operations only for masking. (*Hint:* Use the TEST instruction to determine the one unique input state.)

   FLOWCHART ASSEMBLY-LANGUAGE PROGRAM

3. For additional practice in writing decision-making programs, choose one or more of the following problems. If required, report the flowchart and assembly-language program on a separate sheet of paper.

FIGURE 6.7

COMBINATION LOCK flowchart and program.

FLOWCHART ASSEMBLY LANGUAGE PROGRAM

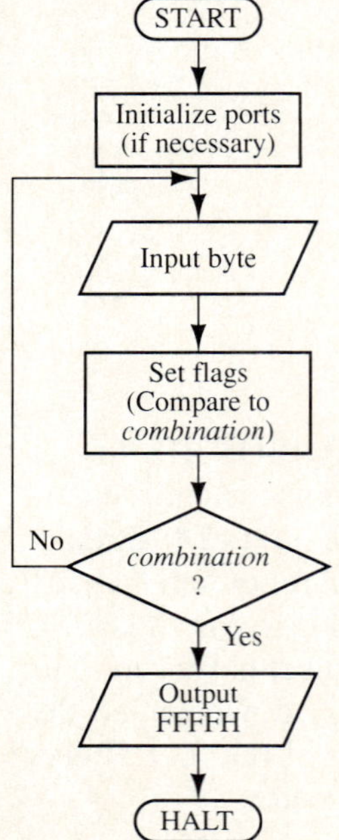

a. Write a loop program that inputs bytes and passes on to the output only the two "lucky" numbers, 7 or 11. All other input values cause zero to be output.
b. Modify original demonstration program NEXT_WEEK to report the correct date when seven days are added to any day of the present month. For example, if seven is added to April 27, the computer should show four (for May 4) rather than 34, an illegal date.
c. Write a loop program that inputs bytes and passes on to the output only those that are positive and of even parity. All other input values cause zero to be output. (*Hint:* Use the sign and parity flags.)
d. Write a loop program that inputs bytes and outputs the number of bit positions that contain a 1. (For example, if the input number is 11011100, a 5 would be output).
e. Write a loop program that inputs bytes and passes on to the output only those in which the upper 4 bits are greater than the lower 4 bits. All other input values cause a zero to be output.
f. Write a "bandpass" program that inputs bytes and passes on to the output only those that are below byte variable *upperrange* and above byte variable *lowerrange*. (Select arbitrary values for *upperrange* and *lowerrange*.)
g. Based on the configuration of Figure 6.8, simulate a level-active D latch.
h. Write a program to simulate a Schmitt trigger: The input byte must go above 64 (40H) to turn on (output 1), but must go below 16 (10H) to turn off (output 0).

Advanced Activities

i. Write a loop program that outputs FOUND (FFFFH) for all input words with exactly five ones in a row anywhere (and zeros elsewhere).
j. Write program GUESS in which the "quizmaster" preloads a number between 0 and 255 into byte variable *unknown*. Your task, as "contestant," is to enter numbers and determine the unknown value as quickly as possible. To help the contestant, if the entered number is below the unknown number, 0FH is output; if above, F0H is output; and if equal, FFH is output and the program halts.
k. Using based addressing, write a loop program that scans *itself*, reporting the number of instruction bytes equal to various input values of your choice.
l. Write a decision-making program of your own choosing.

FIGURE 6.8

D latch simulation.

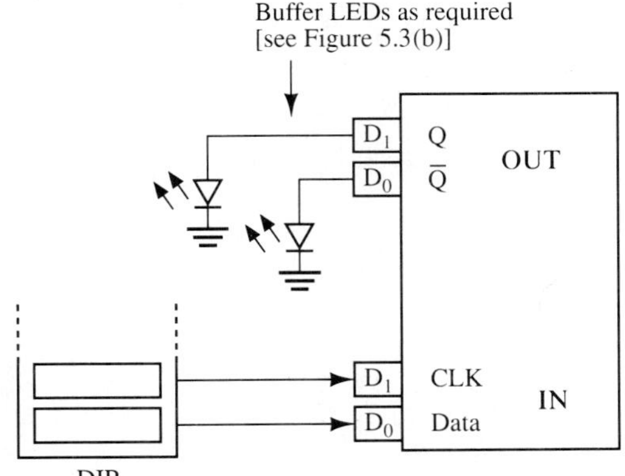

4. Using a single MOV instruction and the relational *operators* (rather than the relational *instructions*), have the assembler place 0FFH (true) in AL during execution if the average value of 4, 15, 3, 7, and 8 is greater than or equal to 6. Otherwise, zero is placed in AL.

Name: ______________________

Date: ______________________

Class: ______________________

QUESTIONS AND PROBLEMS

1. How does the MOV instruction affect the flags?

2. What are the two steps involved in every decision-making process?

3. Is it necessary for the Jcondition addr instruction to *immediately* follow the set flag instruction? Explain.

4. Regarding the CARRY flag, what is the net result of a ROR instruction followed by a ROL instruction? of ROL followed by ROR?

5. Why is the COMPARE instruction called an "invisible subtraction" and the TEST instruction called an "invisible AND"? (Why is the TEST instruction said to perform nondestructive bit testing?)

6. How does the Jcondition addr instruction itself affect the flags?

7. Referring to Appendix E, what do the CLC, STC, and CMC instructions accomplish?

8. The accumulator is holding A2H. What are the states of the ZF and CF flags after running the following instruction?

```
cmp  al,0a7h
```

9. When the ZF flag goes to one as the result of an arithmetic or logical operation, what do we know about the *result* of the operation?

10. Using a flowchart diagram, show how a computer uses decision-making to choose the right path among three possible choices.

11. What set flags/Jcondition combination will determine if a number in AL is even or odd?

12. Referring to Figure 6.4(a), why is there more than one mnemonic form for many of the instructions (such as JE/JZ and JAE/JNB)?

13. Referring to Figure 6.1, summarize the differences between the two types of selection and the two types of repetition.

Advanced Section

14. With respect to the location of the SHORT jump op code, why is the target range from −126 through +129?

15. If the target of a conditional branch lies beyond the short/relative −126/+129 range, how is the branch made?

16. Is the conditional jump process dynamically relocatable? Explain your answer.

PART II

WAVEFORMS AND TIMING

Like the precise biological clocks that control the rhythms of the animal kingdom, a crystal-controlled computer is also governed by exact and regular cycles and pulses. In the three activities of Part II we will view the computer's waveforms and calculate its timing cycles, and we will see how the steady beat of processing leads to the generation of a musical note. In keeping with our "mix-and-match" theme, we may use the internal speaker of the IBM PC for sound generation.

ACTIVITY 7

WAVEFORMS

OBJECTIVE

- To view 8086/88 waveforms on the oscilloscope.

PARTS AND EQUIPMENT

- IBM PC with bus-extender.
- Assembler, debugger, and utilities.
- Dual-trace oscilloscope with delay (or logic analyzer).

DISCUSSION

The flashes of a strobe light can "freeze" the action of a hummingbird's wings, allowing it to be studied under normal dynamic conditions in real time. The waveforms of a computer also can be frozen on an oscilloscope screen by placing the program into a loop and strobing the trigger input with a signal that occurs once each program cycle. The I/O loop program of Figure 7.1(a) (designed to access the bus-extender ports of Figure C2.2) satisfies these requirements.

Waveforms are composed of program cycles, instruction cycles, and machine cycles. As shown by Figure 7.1(b), prefetching makes it difficult to interpret instruction cycle waveforms. Therefore, we will limit our waveform studies to the program and machine cycles. The waveforms are further complicated by the periodic *refreshing* signals of the IBM PC.

The Microprocessor Versus the IBM PC Bus

As shown by the "generic" waveform sets for 8088-type systems (Figure 7.2), several changes take place in going from the pins of the microprocessor (Figure 7.2(a)) to the IBM PC bus (Figure 7.2(b)):

- The multiplexed address/data lines of the microprocessor are demultiplexed by ALE (address latch enable) before they appear on the IBM PC bus.
- The $\overline{RD}$, $\overline{WR}$, and IO/$\overline{M}$ pins of the microprocessor are decoded to $\overline{IOR}$, $\overline{IOW}$, $\overline{MEMR}$, and $\overline{MEMW}$ on the IBM PC bus.

In this activity, we use the signals of the IBM PC bus for all waveform analysis.

Memory Refresh

Approximately every 15 μs, the IBM PC performs a dynamic memory refresh operation using DMA (direct memory access). To prevent other devices (such as external ports) from responding to the DMA signals, AEN (address enable) is driven high during all DMA transfers.

Clock Rates

For waveform analysis we assume the standard 4.77-MHz clock rate, giving a 0.21-μs clock cycle time. For faster clock signals, adjust the sweep rate of the oscilloscope accordingly.

PROCEDURE

NOTE: If using a logic analyzer, follow the instructions of the user's guide.

1. Load and execute the loop program of Figure 7.1(a).

The Program Cycle

2. Assign $\overline{IOW}$ to channel A and ALE to channel B. Trigger internally off $\overline{IOW}$. Set both channels to 5 V/div and the main time base to 2 μs. ($\overline{IOW}$ must be qualified with AEN as shown in Figure C2.2.)

   Approximately how many program cycles are displayed on the oscilloscope? (Hint: $\overline{IOW}$ goes low once each program cycle.)

   ____

FIGURE 7.1

Waveform analysis sample program. (a) The loop mimic program. (b) Machine-cycle diagram of loop portion of mimic program showing prefetching.

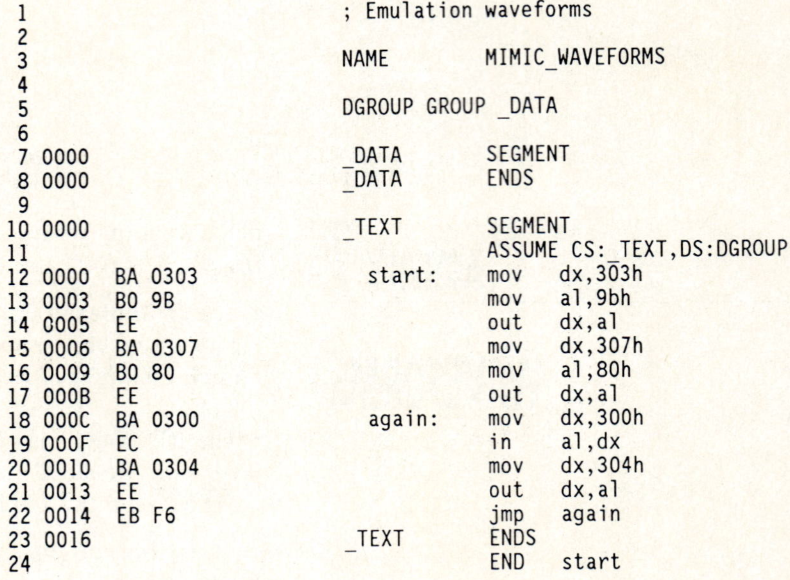

```
                           ; Emulation waveforms

                           NAME       MIMIC_WAVEFORMS

                           DGROUP GROUP _DATA

0000                       _DATA      SEGMENT
0000                       _DATA      ENDS

0000                       _TEXT      SEGMENT
                                      ASSUME CS:_TEXT,DS:DGROUP
0000  BA 0303                start:   mov   dx,303h
0003  B0 9B                           mov   al,9bh
0005  EE                              out   dx,al
0006  BA 0307                         mov   dx,307h
0009  B0 80                           mov   al,80h
000B  EE                              out   dx,al
000C  BA 0300                again:   mov   dx,300h
000F  EC                              in    al,dx
0010  BA 0304                         mov   dx,304h
0013  EE                              out   dx,al
0014  EB F6                           jmp   again
0016                       _TEXT      ENDS
                                      END   start
```

(a) The loop-mimic program

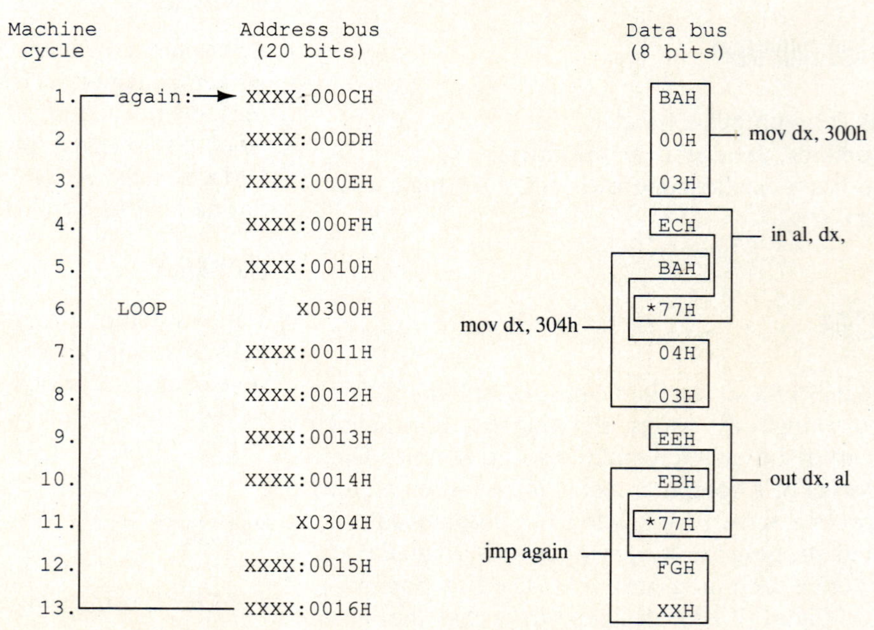

(b) Machine-cycle diagram of loop portion of mimic program showing pre-fetching

3. Can you count the 13 ALE pulses that correspond to the 13 machine cycles belonging to one program cycle? (This may prove difficult due to the effects of refreshing.) ____________

The Machine Cycle

4. To zoom in on the output machine cycle, set the delay time base to .2 μs (main time base remains at 2 μs).
5. Enter the delay mode and adjust the delay control until the ALE and $\overline{IOW}$ traces match those of Figure 7.3. The beginning of the output machine cycle is now at the far left of the screen.
6. Move the B probe to the lines shown and complete the graph. Show the waveform for the D0 bus line when the corresponding DIP input is toggled high and low (dotted line for high, solid line for low). Answer the following questions:

FIGURE 7.2

Typical machine-cycle waveform sets for 8088-type systems. (a) The microprocessor. (b) The IBM PC bus.

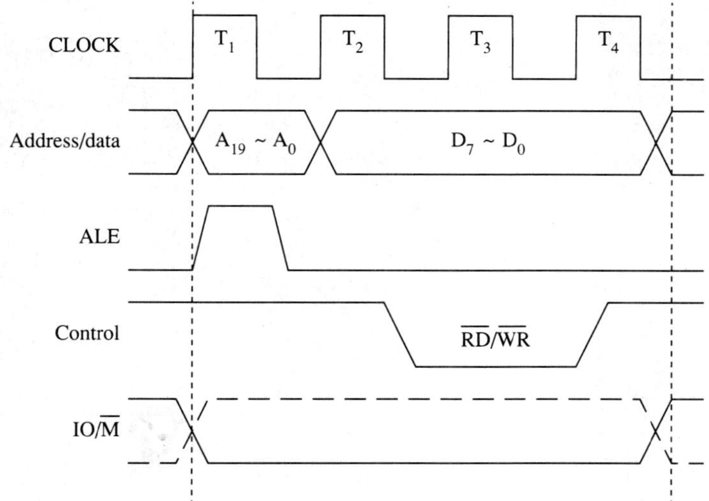

(a) The microprocessor

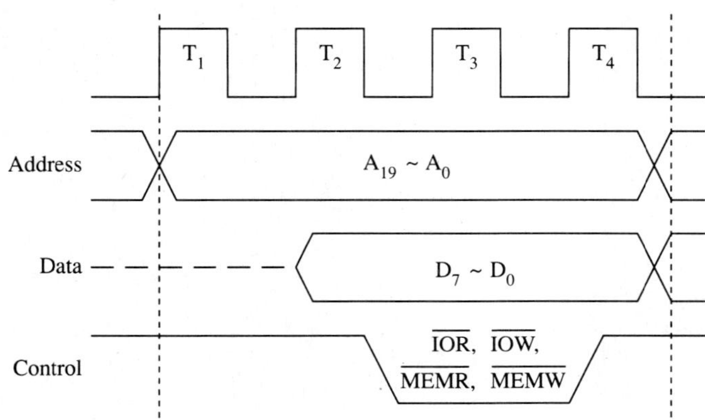

(b) The IBM PC bus

FIGURE 7.3

Output machine-cycle waveforms.

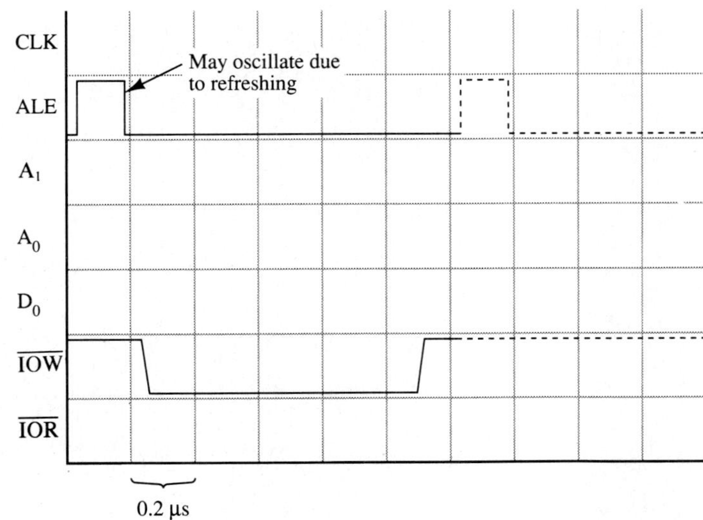

a. How many clock cycles make up the output port machine cycle? ____________
b. Are A0 and A1 correct for the port address used? ____________
c. Is $\overline{IOR}$ high during the output port machine cycle?

Refreshing

7. Exit the delay mode. Using channel A, trigger off AEN (main time base remains at 2 μs). How often does refreshing occur? ____________

8. Expand the main time base to .2 μs. After viewing any of the following bus signals from channel B, summarize what happens during a refresh operation. (For this step, the control signals are not qualified with AEN.)
   - A0–A15
   - $\overline{IOR}$, $\overline{IOW}$
   - $\overline{MEMR}$, $\overline{MEMW}$
   - DACK0 (DMA channel 0 acknowledge)

Name: ______________________

Date: ______________________

Class: ______________________

QUESTIONS AND PROBLEMS

1. Why did we use the $\overline{\text{IOW}}$ signal as a trigger?

2. Why does prefetching increase throughput?

3. What is the major advantage of a multiplexed bus?

4. What is accomplished by the negative-going edge of ALE?

5. What takes place during every *machine cycle*?

Advanced Section

6. Why doesn't the IBM PC use static RAM in order to eliminate the need for refreshing?

ACTIVITY 8

LOOPS, TIMING, AND DEBOUNCING
A Musical Tone

OBJECTIVES

- To use a delay loop to generate a musical tone.
- To determine program timing.
- To debounce a mechanical switch.

PARTS AND EQUIPMENT

- IBM PC (bus-extender optional).
- Assembler, debugger, and utilities.

DISCUSSION

Conditional Loops

Using the decision-making techniques of Activity 6, we can form a *conditional loop* (a loop that can be exited). The simplest task performed by a conditional loop is to generate a delay, as shown by the flowchart of Figure 8.1.

A Musical Tone

As diagrammed in Figure 8.2, a steady musical tone is generated by a repeating output/toggle/delay sequence. The delay portion of the sequence uses the delay loop of Figure 8.1 to set the frequency of the note.

Timing

Program timing is determined by counting total clock cycles and multiplying by the clock period. Referring to Appendix E, the number of clocks required to execute each instruction is included in the assembly-language reference card. Because nearly all instructions are prefetched, the clock cycles listed are for execution only. To determine the EA (effective address) portion of the clock equation, we turn to the *Effective Address Calculation Time* table (also in Appendix E).

For example, let's determine the number of clock cycles required to carry out the following instruction:

```
mov   bl,apples
```

Turning to the MOV instruction in Appendix E, we see that this *memory-to-register* operation requires 8+EA clocks. From the *Operand Address Timing* table we find that *direct* (*immediate offset* or *displacement only*) addressing requires six clock cycles. Therefore, the total clocks required are $8 + 6 = 14$.

Debouncing

When a mechanical switch is closed or opened, the contacts bounce for a short period of time. If an event must occur once and only once for each switch cycle, the switch must be debounced. The simplest way to debounce a switch is the software-only method: Place a short delay after the first closing and the first reopening are detected. For greater reliability, we can choose the hardware/software method. By adding either of the hardware circuits of Figure 8.3, we eliminate the delay loop from our debounce routines.

The Internal Speaker of the IBM PC

As an alternative to an external speaker interfaced to a bus-extender port, we can access the IBM PC's internal speaker by writing a high or low to bit D1 of port 61h, with bit D0 = 0 (making sure we do not disturb bits D2 through D7).

The routine below performs a toggle/output of the internal speaker each time it is run:

FIGURE 8.1

The simple delay loop.

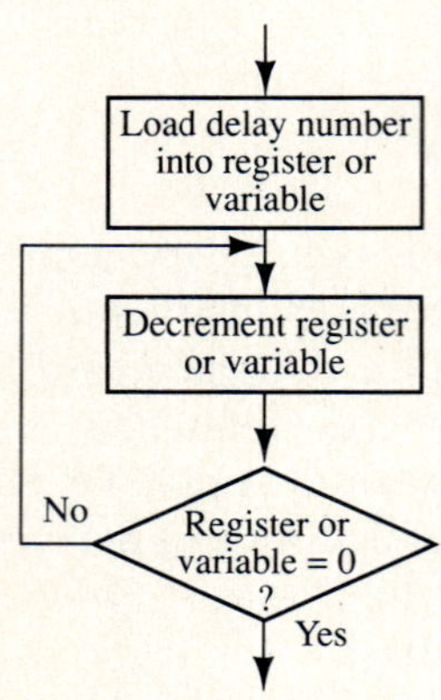

FIGURE 8.2

A musical tone is generated by a toggle/output/delay sequence.

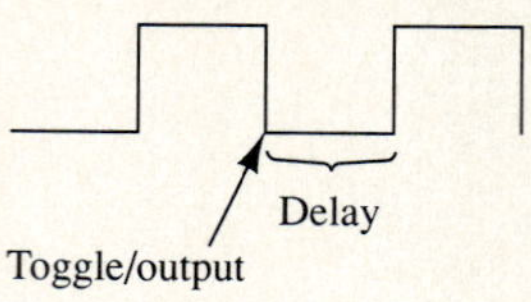


```
in    al,61h   ; Fetch present
                 value of D1
xor   al,2     ; Toggle D1
and   al,0feh  ; D0 = 0
out   61h,al   ; D1 to speaker
```

If you wish to eliminate the slight warble caused by the clock-tick interrupts, disable the external interrupts using CLI, but realize that this disrupts the computer's sense of time.

PROCEDURE

NOTE: Use either the external or internal speaker.

A Musical Tone

1. Based on the flowchart of Figure 8.4, write program STEADY_TONE, in which a continuous musical tone is sent to the speaker. Temporarily place an arbitrary value in byte variable *delay*.

Timing

2. In the CLOCKS column of Figure 8.4, write the number of clock cycles required to execute each instruction. (*Caution:* If using Appendix E, the timing for all conditional jumps should read *Jump is taken 16,* rather than 8.)
3. Using the equation of Figure 8.5, calculate the delay number (N) required to produce the tone-of-A (440 Hz). (If N is greater than approximately 150, choose 880 Hz or 1760 Hz for the tone-of-A.)

   Delay number for tone-of-A: ____________
4. Execute the program and note the tone. If a pitch pipe, tuning fork, oscilloscope, or other means is available, how close is the tone to true A? ____________.

FIGURE 8.3

Hardware debouncing using positive feedback. (a) Using inverters. (b) Using NAND gates.

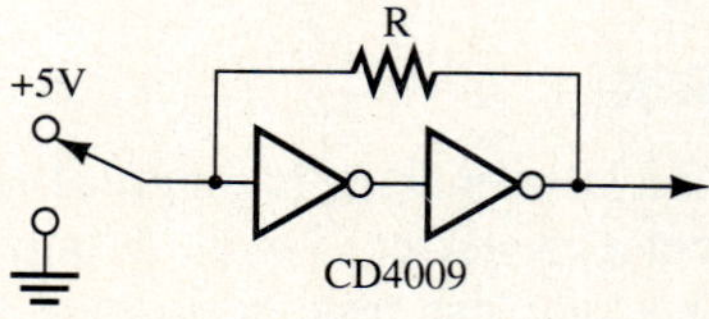

(a) Using inverters

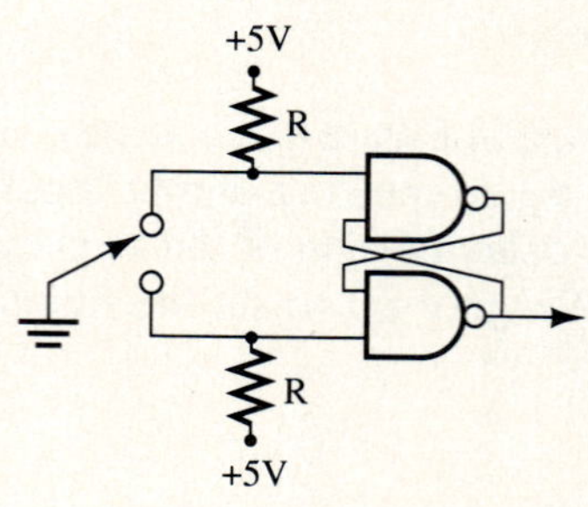

(b) Using NAND gates

FIGURE 8.4

Program STEADY_TONE.

FLOWCHART | ASSEMBLY LANGUAGE PROGRAM | Clocks

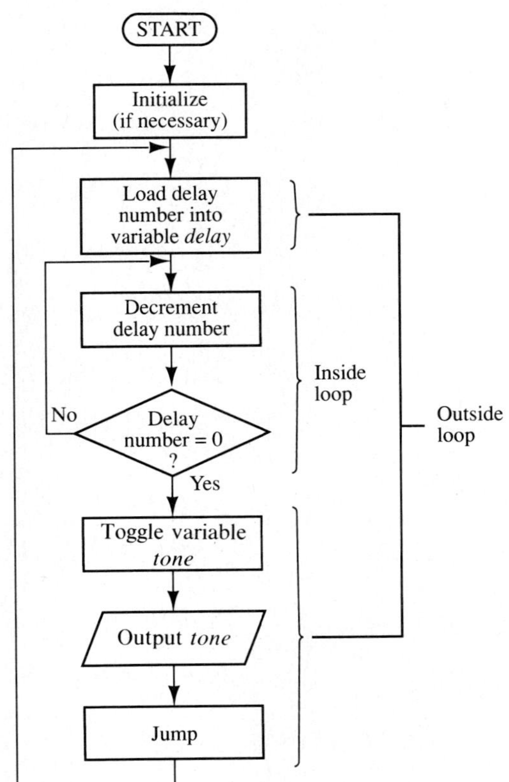

5. Modify program STEADY_TONE of Figure 8.4 so the frequency of the tone depends on the value stored in a variable or register. A change in the value changes the tone. (If using a bus-extender port, the tone is varied in real time by changing the input value.) Does the input value for the tone-of-A closely match that of the calculated value of step 3?

Debouncing (Requires bus-extender.)

6. Based on the strategy of Figure 8.6, write program COUNT_UP. The program uses software-only debouncing to count up by one for each cycling of the D0 bit of a byte port. (*Hint:* Use the TEST instruction to determine switch closing and opening.)

FIGURE 8.5

Frequency-of-tone equation.

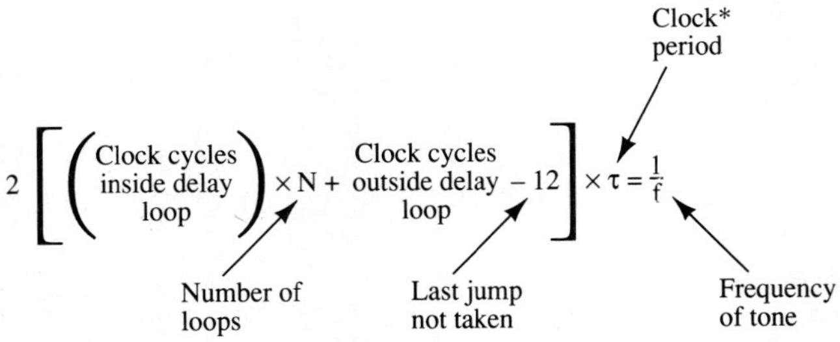

$$2\left[\left(\begin{array}{c}\text{Clock cycles}\\ \text{inside delay}\\ \text{loop}\end{array}\right)\times N + \begin{array}{c}\text{Clock cycles}\\ \text{outside delay}\\ \text{loop}\end{array} - 12\right]\times \tau = \frac{1}{f}$$

Number of loops (N); Last jump not taken (− 12); Clock* period (τ); Frequency of tone (f)

*The baseline clock rate for the IBM PC is 4.77 MHz, giving a 0.21 μs clock cycle time. Adjust as required for your system.

FIGURE 8.6

Program COUNT_UP using software-only debouncing.

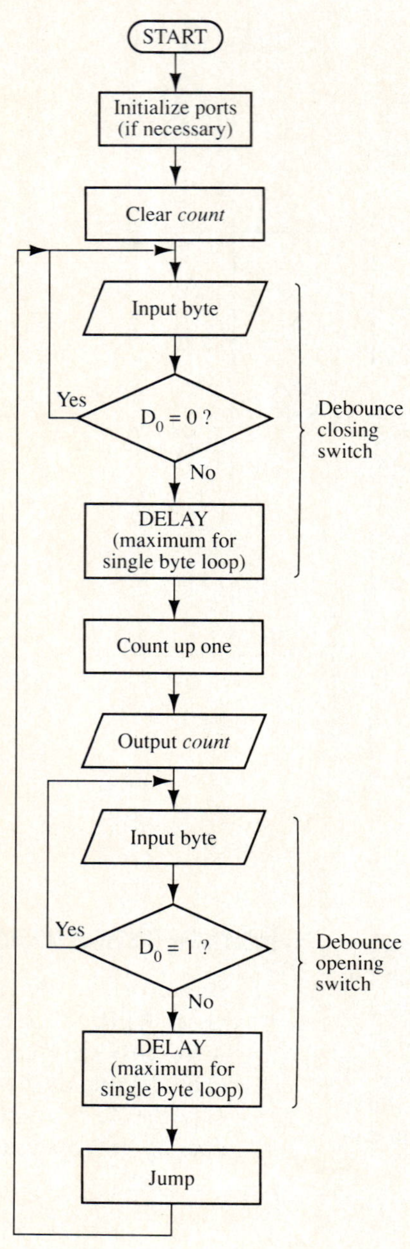

Advanced Activities (Some steps require bus-extender ports.)

7. Develop program SIREN in which a tone rapidly increases in frequency, instantly drops back to a lower frequency, and repeats the cycle.
8. Experimentally determine the approximate smallest delay number (N) that reliably debounces the switch of step 6. From this, calculate the time required for the switch to settle down (stop bouncing).

FIGURE 8.7

Generating tone combinations.

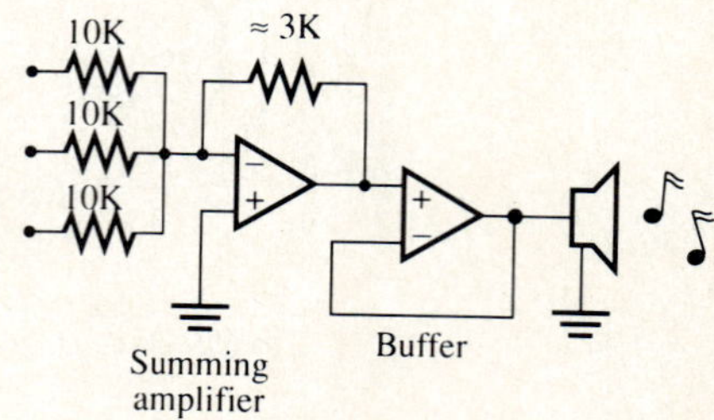

9. Repeat program COUNT_UP of step 6 using the hardware/software debouncing technique. (Add one of the circuits of Figure 8.3.)
10. Write program INCREASE_TONE, in which each open/close cycle of an input port switch causes the frequency to approximately double (increase one octave). When the frequency reaches the maximum, it decreases to the minimum value and the process repeats. Use the debouncing technique of your choice.
11. Making sure the program of step 5 uses the increment instruction for the toggle step, install the summing amplifier circuit of Figure 8.7, and experiment with the note combinations (chords) that can be produced by summing together various bit positions of the output port.

Name: ____________________

Date: ____________________

Class: ____________________

QUESTIONS AND PROBLEMS

1. Based on the program of Figure 8.4, what is the musical relationship between the various bit positions (D0 to D7) of the output port? (The program uses the external speaker and the increment instruction to toggle the note.)

2. What is the purpose of the 2 on the left-hand side of the delay number equation of Figure 8.5?

3. Approximately how many three-clock NOP (*no operation*) instructions would have to be substituted for the delay loop of Figure 8.4 in order to produce the tone-of-A (440 Hz)?

4. Calculate the maximum delay possible for the simple delay loop of Figure 8.1 for each of the following cases:

   a. The delay number is held in a 16-bit register: __________
   b. The delay number is held in a 16-bit memory location (symbolic variable): __________

Advanced Section

5. Based on the hardware of procedure step 11, can we generate a major chord? (As with any of the advanced questions and problems, research may be required.)

6. When using a symbolic word variable to hold the delay number (Figure 8.1), what delay number value (N) will generate a delay as close as possible to 1 ms?

7. In our timing calculations, why can we ignore the time it takes to fetch instructions?

ACTIVITY 9

NESTING
A Musical Note

OBJECTIVES

- To nest delay loops.
- To write a program that generates a musical note.

PARTS AND EQUIPMENT

- IBM PC (bus-extender optional).
- Assembler, debugger, and utilities.

DISCUSSION

Nesting and Musical Notes

In computer programming, *nesting* refers to one program branch, subroutine, or loop inside another. When loops are nested, the basic delay times of the previous experiment can be greatly expanded.

A note is a tone of specified duration and is generated by the use of the following delay loops:

- a single-nested byte loop for producing the frequency and
- a double-nested word loop for generating the duration.

The delay number for frequency will be loaded into byte variable *period*, and the delay numbers for duration will be loaded into word variables *dur1* and *dur2*. The following mathematical relationships determine the frequency and duration:

- Frequency is proportional to 1/*period*.
- Duration is proportional to *dur1* × *dur2*.

The *structured* flowchart of Figure 9.1 shows how the note is generated. Careful examination of the program strategy will reveal that the frequency and duration are independent (the frequency number does not affect duration). Figure 9.2 shows the same program using a conventional flowchart.

In the applications activities of Part VIII, we will see how the 8253 programmable timer chip provides a hardware alternative to the purely software techniques of this activity. We will also apply the lessons learned in this and future activities to the generation of computer music.

PROCEDURE

1. Beside the conventional flowchart of Figure 9.2, write program SINGLE_NOTE. (Variables *period, dur1,* and *dur2* are temporarily set to 100, 1000, and 1000.)
2. Run program SINGLE_NOTE and indicate the approximate frequency and duration of the note.

   Note frequency: ______________

   Note duration: ______________
3. Using simple ratios, determine the values of *period, dur1,* and *dur2* required to generate the note-of-A (440 Hz) for one *whole note* time span (approximately 2 s). (Assume that *dur1* = *dur2*.)

   Value of *period* for note-of-A: ______________

   Value of *dur1* and *dur2* for whole note: ______________
4. Load the values for *period, dur1,* and *dur2* obtained from step 3 and experimentally verify the results. Make any necessary corrections to your values.
5. Using different values for *period* and *dur1*/*dur2* answer the following question: Is the frequency independent of the duration? (Can *period* be changed without affecting the duration?): ______________

Advanced Activities

6. By modifying the program of Figure 9.2, generate a continuous note/rest sequence. Control the

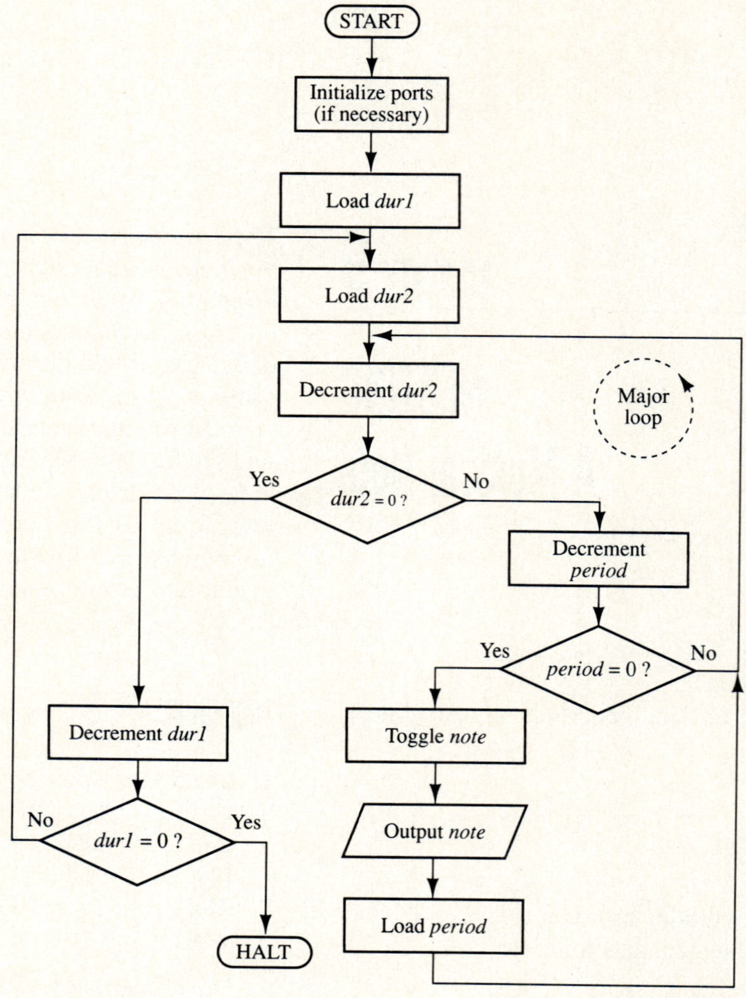

FIGURE 9.1

Program NOTE_OF_A structured flowchart.

tempo (durations of notes and rests) by inputting values (or changing memory values).

7. By sampling a square-wave input, write a program that acts as a frequency counter for frequencies between 1 and 255 Hz. (*Hint:* So your program works for signals of any duty cycle, count the number of signal transitions in 0.5 s).
8. Write program ROULETTE in which $25 is displayed in the low-order LED port, and a single light of the high-order LED port rotates very rapidly (too rapidly to track with the eye).

When the player places a bet by setting one bit of the low-order DIP port high, the rotating light gradually slows down to stop at one bit position. If the light lands at the same position as the player bet, 6 is added to the total score and displayed; otherwise, 1 is subtracted and the result displayed. When the player clears the low-order port, the "wheel" spins again and the cycle is repeated. The game is over when you either lose or double your money.

FIGURE 9.2

Program NOTE_OF_A standard flowchart.

FLOWCHART

ASSEMBLY LANGUAGE PROGRAM

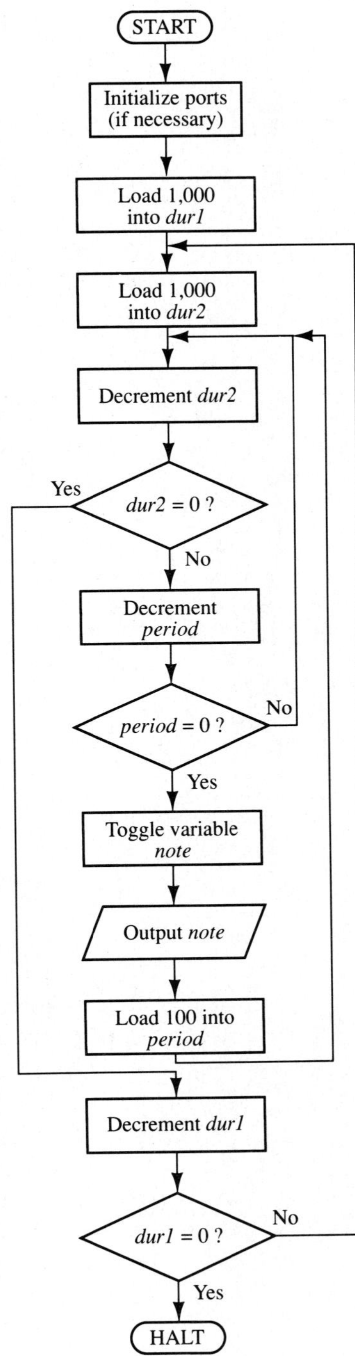

Name: ____________________

Date: ____________________

Class: ____________________

QUESTIONS AND PROBLEMS

1. What is the difference between the terms *branch, loop,* and *nest*?

2. If a single-byte-wide delay loop generates a 1-ms delay, approximately how large a delay can be produced by a byte-wide delay loop nested 10 deep? (Why should you not attempt to verify your answer in the laboratory?)

3. If *period, dur1,* and *dur2* of Figure 9.2 are all cut in half, what happens to the duration and the frequency?

4. Why does setting *dur1* and *dur2* to zero result in a slightly larger duration than setting each to FFFFH?

5. Why is it not necessary to initialize *period* at the beginning of the program of Figure 9.2?

Advanced Section

6. By counting the number of clock cycles within the ''major loop'' of Figure 9.1 (where the processor spends most of its time), calculate the value of *period* required to generate the note-of-A. Compare this value to the values of procedure steps 3 and 4.

7. Based on the description of procedure step 8, what advantage in odds does the ''house'' enjoy?

PART III

DATA STRUCTURES

In the English language, simple objects—such as a *table* or a *chair*—are referred to as nouns. We also have ways of referring to more complex objects: the *array* of six planes that makes up the Blue Angels, and the *string* of sled dogs that pulls as one. In programming, as in English, there are also more complex data types than the simple byte and word. In the three activities of Part III, we will process such complex data types as *arrays, structures, tables, strings,* and *records*.

ACTIVITY 10

ARRAYS AND TABLES

OBJECTIVES

- To write assembly-language programs that process arrays and look-up tables.
- To introduce the American Standard Code for Information Interchange (ASCII).
- To use the iteration control instructions.

PARTS AND EQUIPMENT

- IBM PC (bus-extender optional).
- Assembler, debugger, and utilities.

DISCUSSION

Arrays

An *array* is a group of related variables stored in sequential memory locations. As shown by the examples of Figure 10.1, arrays are defined by listing initialization information after the type directive. The *elements* of an array are numbered starting from zero. For example, array *apples* contains four elements numbered from zero to three. The name of the array points to the zeroth element of the array, and the question marks indicate no initial value. As demonstrated by the next array (*peaches*), question marks and initial values can be mixed-and-matched in any order. Moving to array *pears,* writing 100 DUP(?) is a shorthand method of listing 100 question marks in a row. Array *grapes* demonstrates that the DUP directive can be mixed with individual initial values. The single quotes in the final example (*names*) command the assembler to convert the character string to ASCII (see Appendix H).

In a typical application, the elements of the array are accessed using base/displacement addressing and scanned by incrementing BX, SI, or DI within a loop. As an advanced activity, we use based/indexed/displacement addressing to access a two-dimensional array.

The Iteration Control Instructions

The processing of arrays can be streamlined by using the *iteration control* instructions of Figure 10.2. The simple LOOP instruction is especially useful when the number of loops is a set value. First, we initialize CX with the number of iterations in the loop. Each time a LOOP instruction is processed, CX is automatically decremented by 1. When CX reaches 0, we exit the loop.

By means of this technique, demonstration program POKER_HAND of Figure 10.3 counts the number of nines in array *hand* and returns the answer to the AL register. To produce a more "generic" program, assembler directive TYPE returns a 1 for byte arrays and a 2 for word arrays. As shown by programs (a) and (b), we have the option of accessing an array using either *base/displacement* or *based* addressing. Of course, either of the index registers (SI or DI) could have been used instead of BX.

The LOOPE/LOOPZ and LOOPNE/LOOPNZ instructions test both the CX register and ZF flag and therefore provide two exit conditions: Either the CX register is counted down to zero or a condition turns false. Demonstration program RADAR of Figure 10.4 uses the LOOPNE instruction to search array *return* for the "signature" 7777H. As soon as the signature is found, we exit the loop and report its offset location. The JNE instruction is used to test the exit condition. If the signature was found (ZF = 1), we report its location in register AX; otherwise (ZF = 0), we jump to *notfound* and report FFFFH in AX.

Look-up Tables

A *look-up table* is a special kind of *byte* array in which the position (address) of each array element is related to its contents. Demonstration program NUMBER_SQUARED of Figure 10.5 shows us the details. The contents of each element of array *squares* holds the square of its array position. To look up the square of the numbers from 0 to 9, we

FIGURE 10.1

Examples of array definitions.

```
_DATA       SEGMENT
   apples  DB  ?,?,?,?
   peaches DW  2222h, ?, 10000
   pears   DW  100 DUP(?)
   grapes  DB  10 DUP(?), 6, 15, 12 DUP(23)
   names   DB  'BILL, JANE, TAI'
_DATA       ENDS
```

first initialize register BX to point to the beginning of the table. The XLAT (*translate*) instruction replaces the element number in AL with the contents of the corresponding array element. Note the use of the multiply operator (*) to command the assembler (rather than the programmer) to generate the square of each element position. Also demonstrated is the technique for listing the elements of a single array on multiple lines.

PROCEDURE

Arrays

NOTE: Where appropriate, initialize arrays with bytes or words of your choice. (Using Codeview, FIO steps through a LOOP, and *DB* or *DW variable_name* displays an array.)

1. Write program ADD_SMALL, which scans the ten-element byte array *list* and places into the AL register the sum of all the elements that are equal to or below 25.

   ASSEMBLY-LANGUAGE PROGRAM

2. Write program TOP_GUN, which scans the eight-element word array *scores* and returns the largest score found to the AX register.

   ASSEMBLY-LANGUAGE PROGRAM

3. Using the proper iteration control instructions, write program MEMORY_CHECK, which scans the ten elements of byte array *eprom* looking for a memory cell that is not erased (not = FFH). If none is found, it returns FFFFH (chip good) to the AX register; otherwise, it returns the location (0 to 9) of the first bad memory cell to AX.

   ASSEMBLY-LANGUAGE PROGRAM

FIGURE 10.2

The iteration control instructions.

Iteration Controls	
LOOP	Loop
LOOPE/LOOPZ	Loop if equal/zero
LOOPNE/LOOPNZ	Loop if not equal/ not zero
JCXZ	Jump if register CX = 0

FIGURE 10.3

Counting the number of nines in array *hand*. (a) Using base/displacement addressing. (b) Using based addressing.

```
; Using base-displacement addressing, this program
; places the number of nines found in array hand
; in the AL register.

NAME          POKER_HAND

DGROUP GROUP _DATA

_DATA         SEGMENT
  hand    DB  4,9,7,9,9,2,9
  count   DB  0
_DATA         ENDS

_TEXT         SEGMENT
              ASSUME CS:_TEXT,DS:DGROUP
  start:      mov   ax,DGROUP
              mov   ds,ax
              mov   bx,0           ; Point to 1st card
              mov   cx,7           ; Load number of cards
  again:      cmp   hand[bx],9     ; 9?
              jne   over           ; Jump if not.
              inc   count          ; 9 found
  over:       add   bx,TYPE hand   ; Next
              loop  again          ; Done?
              mov   al,count
              hlt
_TEXT         ENDS
              END   start
```

(a) Using base/displacement addressing

```
; Using based addressing, this program places
; the number of nines found in array hand into
; the AL register.

NAME          POKER_HAND

DGROUP GROUP _DATA

_DATA         SEGMENT
  hand    DB  4,9,7,9,9,2,9
  count   DB  0
_DATA         ENDS

_TEXT         SEGMENT
              ASSUME CS:_TEXT,DS:DGROUP
  start:      mov   ax,DGROUP
              mov   ds,ax
              mov   bx,OFFSET DGROUP:hand ; Point to 1st card
              mov   cx,7                  ; Load number of cards
  again:      cmp   BYTE PTR[bx],9        ; 9?
              jne   over                  ; Jump if not.
              inc   count                 ; 9 found
  over:       add   bx,TYPE hand          ; Next
              loop  again                 ; Done?
              mov   al,count
              hlt
_TEXT         ENDS
              END   start
```

(b) Using based addressing

FIGURE 10.4

Searching for "signature" 7777H in array *return*.

```
; This program searches for 7777H in word array return.
; When found, it places its element number (0 to 4)  in AX.
; If not found, it places FFFFH in AX.

NAME        RADAR

DGROUP GROUP _DATA

_DATA       SEGMENT
  return  DW  4234H,9930H,1118H,7777H,6629H
_DATA       ENDS

_TEXT       SEGMENT
            ASSUME CS:_TEXT,DS:DGROUP
  start:    mov   ax,DGROUP
            mov   ds,ax
            mov   bx,0FFFEH          ; Point to 1st element
            mov   cx,5               ; Number of elements
  again:    add   bx,TYPE return     ; Next word
            cmp   return[bx],7777H   ; Loop for signature
            loopne again             ; Found or done?
            jne   notfound           ; Which?
            mov   ax,bx
            sar   ax,1               ; Divide by 2
            hlt
  notfound: mov   ax,0FFFFH          ; Not found
            hlt
_TEXT       ENDS
            END   start
```

FIGURE 10.5

Using a look-up table to generate squares.

```
; This program uses table look-up to input
; a number and output its square.

NAME        NUMBER_SQUARED

DGROUP GROUP _DATA

_DATA       SEGMENT
  squares  DB  0*0,1*1,2*2,3*3,4*4
           DB  5*5,6*6,7*7,8*8,9*9
_DATA       ENDS

_TEXT       SEGMENT
            ASSUME CS:_TEXT,DS:DGROUP
  start:    mov   ax,DGROUP
            mov   ds,ax
            mov   bx,OFFSET DGROUP:squares ; Point to squares
  again:    in    al,0
            xlat  squares                  ; Get number squared
            out   1,al                     ; Output answer
            jmp   again
_TEXT       ENDS
            END   start
```

4. The scores achieved in two rounds of nine-hole golf are listed in byte arrays *round1* and *round2*. Write a program that writes to byte array *best* the best (lowest) score obtained *at each hole*.

ASSEMBLY-LANGUAGE PROGRAM

Look-up Tables

5. Using look-up table techniques, write a program that inputs a centigrade (C) temperature from 0 to 9 and outputs its corresponding Fahrenheit (F) temperature. (Using the equation $F = 9 * C / 5 + 32$, have the assembler initialize each of the ten elements of array *Fahrenheit*.)

ASSEMBLY-LANGUAGE PROGRAM

Advanced Activities

6. Write a program that counts the number of names in the list defined below and returns the answer to AL. (*Hint:* The ',' directive will command the assembler to generate the ASCII character for a comma.)

```
census DB 'Jack, Mary, Tai,'
       DB 'George, Ed, Karen,'
       DB 'Jose'
```

7. Use the *bubble sort* technique and the XCHG instruction to arrange the ten elements of byte array *rank* from lowest to highest. (The bubble sort technique involves comparing adjacent elements of the array: If the lower element is larger than the higher element, they are exchanged. After nine passes through the array, the smaller numbers have "bubbled up" to the lower locations.)
8. Array *suspectprint* holds the 5 bytes of data describing a fingerprint found at the scene of a crime. Array *fileprint* holds the 5-byte fingerprint data of an individual in the police files. Write a program that returns the number of corresponding elements that match to the AL register.
9. A four-by-four matrix of digits is defined below as a two-dimensional array. Using based/indexed/displacement addressing, write a program that places into AL the sum of the diagonal elements (upper left to lower right).

```
matrix DB 6,1,9,3
       DB 9,4,9,9
       DB 4,7,2,3
       DB 6,0,1,7
```

Name: ______________________

Date: ______________________

QUESTIONS AND PROBLEMS

Class: ______________________

1. Which two of the following array variables are illegal and why?
   - apples[si]
   - apples[bl]
   - apples[ds]

2. Using assembly-language instructions, show how to move element number 3 (the fourth element) of array *apples* to element number 6 (the seventh element) of array *peaches*.

3. What common address mode is represented by both of the following instructions?

```
mov bx,OFFSET DGROUP:apples
add bx,TYPE apples
```

4. When using the XLAT instruction, what is in the AL register before and after the instruction is executed?

5. Referring to Figure 10.4, what value does "TYPE return" generate? What value would be returned if array *return* were a double-word array?

6. What is in BX when we exit the following routine?

```
apples DW  6, 3, 17, 9, 8, 10, 8, 2
       mov   cx,8
       mov   bx,0
       sub   bx,2
back:  add   bx,TYPE apples
       cmp   bx,apples[bx]
       loopne back
       hlt
```

7. How did the "bubble-sort" technique get its name?

8. Why is the JCXZ (jump if CX zero) instruction often placed at the beginning of a loop? (*Hint:* If CX is zero when we enter a loop, do we wish to process the loop at all?)

9. The LOOPE instruction combines what two instructions?

10. What advantages do the directives OFFSET and TYPE offer?

Advanced Section

11. Which of the programs of Figure 10.3 is more readable and refers to the elements of the array in a more logical manner? Which executes the program faster?

12. Why can't we use the JCXZ instruction *after* the LOOPE/LOOPNE instruction to test the exit condition? (*Hint:* What happens when the element we are searching for is the last element?)

13. We wish to search array *stocks* and exit when we find the first element *under* 100. Why can't we make use of the LOOPE/LOOPNE instructions?

ACTIVITY 11

STRUCTURES AND RECORDS

OBJECTIVE

- To write assembly-language programs that process structures and records.

PARTS AND EQUIPMENT

- IBM PC (bus-extender optional).
- Assembler, debugger, and utilities.

DISCUSSION

Structures

A *structure* is a collection of variables that are logically related. These variables are accessed symbolically as a single "data object." Using structures, complex data objects are handled in a more readable and logical manner.

Demonstration Program

Program AVERAGE_GRADE of Figure 11.1 is a case in point. First we define structure *student grades* of *fields quiz* and *lab*. We then define variables (arrays) *john* and *mary*, with each variable initialized with quiz and lab grades following the structure format.

Within the program, we use *structure variables* such as *john.lab* to refer to the data. Variable *john* (to the left of the period) locates a structure of data, and field name *lab* (to the right of the period) gives the "distance" into the structure. The purpose of the program is to report in AL the average lab grade of students John and Mary (67).

As an option, we have the ability to define and initialize the arrays using the special format shown below:

```
john student_grades <85,55>
mary student_grades <60,80>
```

Figure 11.1(b) shows why a structure is known as a *template*. Note that field names *quiz* and *lab* are permanently etched on the template. When we place template *student grades* over any appropriate structure variable—such as *john* or *mary*—the data "show through."

Mixing Data Types

Especially useful is the ability of data elements within a structure to be of different types. Program TOTAL_SCORE of Figure 11.2 demonstrates this important feature.

This time structure *student grades* consists of a 3-element byte array (*quiz*) and a word variable (*final*). If we initialize a variable (such as array *mary*) with quiz and final scores according to the structure format, then we can use structure variables (such as *mary.quiz*[*bx*]) to conveniently access the data. The program adds the three quiz grades and the final grade and places the total (461) in AX.

As before, the assembler has no trouble computing the offset address of any member of the structure varible. For example, the offset address of any quiz value is the sum of the offset of variable *mary*, the offset from the beginning of the structure to field *quiz*, and the contents of the BX register. The structure template of Figure 11.2(b) shows clearly how the initialized data and structure format are related.

Records

Suppose a doctor wishes to store the following information about each patient:

Gender (male or female)	1 bit
Weight (0 to 255 lbs)	8 bits
Height (0 to 127 inches)	7 bits

Using conventional byte/word storage, three bytes are required to hold the 16 bits of information.

FIGURE 11.1

Structure demonstration program. (a) Program. (b) Templates.

```
; This program places the average lab
; grade of students john and mary in AL.

NAME          AVERAGE_GRADE

DGROUP GROUP _DATA

_DATA         SEGMENT
  student_grades STRUC
     quiz  DB  ?
     lab   DB  ?
  student_grades ENDS
  john  DB  85, 55
  mary  DB  60, 80
_DATA         ENDS

_TEXT         SEGMENT
              ASSUME CS:_TEXT,DS:DGROUP
  start:      mov    ax,DGROUP
              mov    ds,ax
              mov    al,john.lab
              add    al,mary.lab
              shr    al,1          ; Divide by 2
              hlt
_TEXT         ENDS
              END    start
```

(a) Program

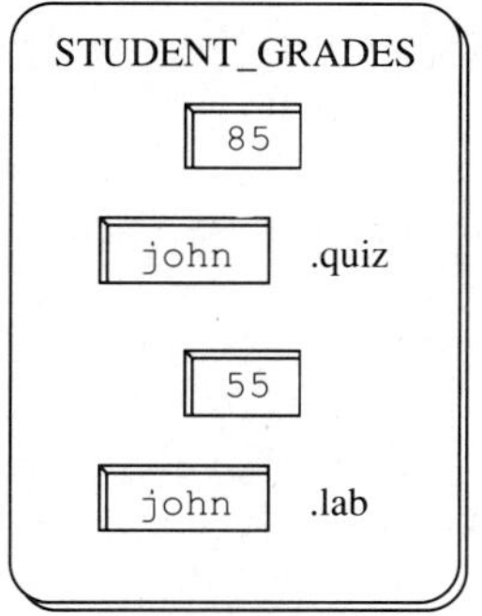

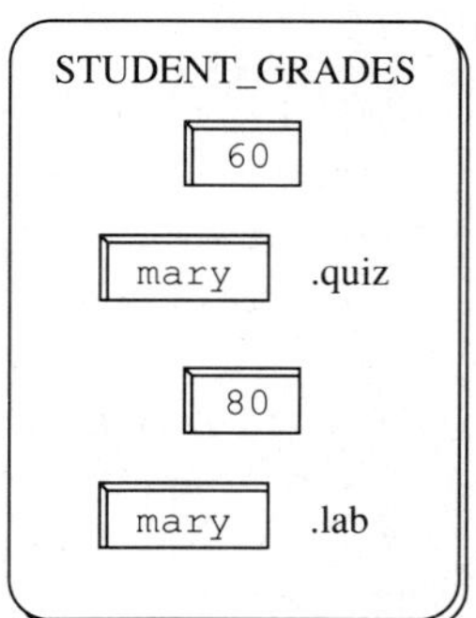

(b) Templates

Clearly, we are wasting 33% of the memory space. The solution is to store the information as a *record* and compact the three "fields" into a single word. As expected, we refer to the fields of the record using symbols.

Following this example, demonstration program FIND_WEIGHT of Figure 11.3(a) uses the RECORD directive to define a 16-bit record called *physical* of fields GENDER, WEIGHT, and HEIGHT. As specified by the record template, the fields are organized as shown in Figure 11.3(b).

Array *persons* is assigned the records of four people. Our task is to locate the only woman in the array and report her weight in register AX. To help us process the records, special MASK and shift-count operators use the record template to operate on the data. As shown, operation MASK GENDER generates the mask 1000000000000000B in order to isolate and test bit position D15, and MASK WEIGHT is used to isolate bits D7 through D14. Operation *mov cl,WEIGHT* places in CL the number of bit positions required to shift the WEIGHT field to the far right of AX for convenient display of results. (Which array element represents the woman, and what is her weight?)

PROCEDURE

Structures

1. Define structure *temperature* with byte fields *hight* and *lowt*. Using the technique of Figure 11.1, initialize arrays *today* and *tomorrow* with high and low temperatures of 88/54 and 75/37. Using structure variables (such as *today.lowt*), return to AL the average value of the low temperatures of today and tomorrow.

   ASSEMBLY-LANGUAGE PROGRAM

Records

2. The British secret service keeps records on its five top agents according to the format of Figure 11.4. Using record *secret_service,* with fields NUMBER, RUSSIAN, and MARKSMANSHIP, write a program that processes the data listed below and returns to AX the number of the agent who speaks Russian and also has a marksmanship score of greater than 500. (If no agent is found with these qualifications, FFFFH is returned.)

```
agents DW 6498H, 0BAECH, 1C51H
       DW 3ED9H, 41FDH
```

FIGURE 11.2

Mixing data types example. (a) Program. (b) Template (showing structure variable *mary*).

```
; This program adds the final exam grade
; and three quiz grades of student mary
; and places the total in AX.

NAME          TOTAL_SCORE

DGROUP GROUP _DATA

_DATA         SEGMENT
  student_grades STRUC
     quiz  DB  3 DUP(?)
     final DW  ?
  student_grades ENDS
  mary  DB  61,76,54
        DW  270
_DATA         ENDS

_TEXT         SEGMENT
              ASSUME CS:_TEXT,DS:DGROUP
  start:      mov    ax,DGROUP
              mov    ds,ax
              mov    al,0      ; Clear answer register
              mov    bx,0      ; Point to 1st element
              mov    cx,3      ; Three quizzes
   back:      add    al,mary.quiz[bx]
              inc    bx
              loop   back
              mov    ah,0
              add    ax,mary.final
              hlt
_TEXT         ENDS
              END    start
```

(a) Program

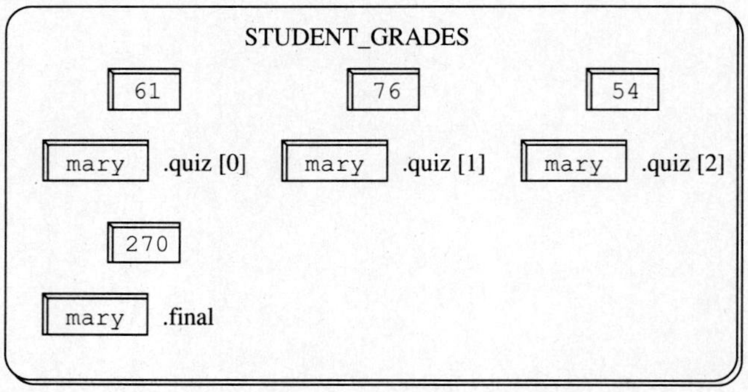

STUDENT_GRADES		
61	76	54
mary .quiz [0]	mary .quiz [1]	mary .quiz [2]
270		
mary .final		

(b) Template (showing structure variable *mary*)

ASSEMBLY-LANGUAGE PROGRAM

Advanced Activities

3. Using structure *weeks-pay,* with fields *hours-per-day* (5-element byte array), *payrate* (byte variable), and *weekly-bonus* (work variable), write a program that places in AX the average weekly pay of two employees. (Define and initialize the data with names and values of your own choice.)

FIGURE 11.3

Record example. (a) Program. (b) Template (showing *persons[0]*).

```
; Program FIND_WEIGHT searches for the first woman
; in the record, and places her weight in AX.

NAME        FIND_WEIGHT

DGROUP GROUP _DATA

_DATA       SEGMENT
  physical  RECORD  GENDER:1, WEIGHT:8, HEIGHT:7
  persons   DW  4649H, 0C0C0H, 632EH, 2D10H
_DATA       ENDS

_TEXT       SEGMENT
            ASSUME CS:_TEXT,DS:DGROUP
  start:    mov    ax,DGROUP
            mov    ds,ax
            mov    cx,4
            mov    bx,0FFFEH
  next:     add    bx,TYPE persons           ; Next
            test   persons[bx],MASK GENDER   ; Woman?
            loopz  next                      ; If not, try again
            jz     nowoman                   ; Jump if no woman
            mov    ax,persons[bx]            ; Woman found
            and    ax,MASK WEIGHT            ; Isolate weight
            mov    cl,WEIGHT                 ; CL = 7
            shr    ax,cl                     ; Weight to D0-D6
            hlt                              ; Weight in ax
  nowoman:  mov    ax,0FFFFH                 ; No woman code
            hlt
_TEXT       ENDS
            END    start
```

(a) Program

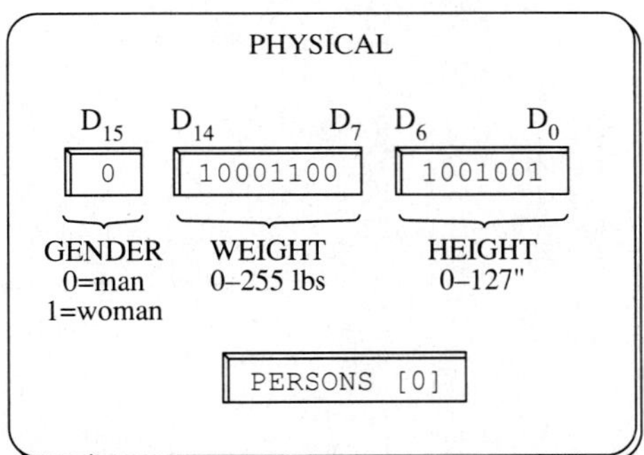

(b) Template (showing PERSONS[0])

FIGURE 11.4

Record *secret_service* format.

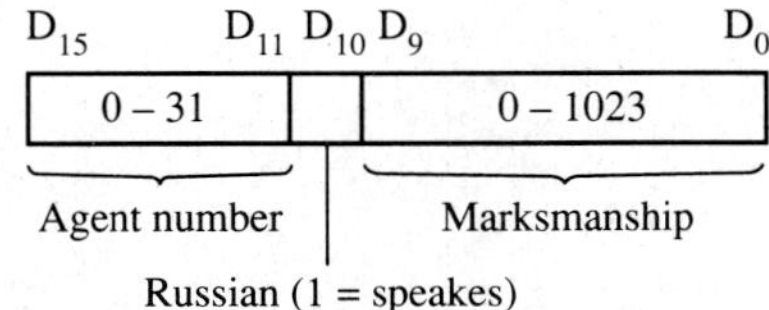

4. Record *salary* contains right-most bit field *number* (employee number, 6 bits), middle bit field *years* (years of service, 5 bits), and left-most bit field *payrate* (pay per hour, 5 bits). Write a program that scans the records of five employees (shown below) and doubles the pay rate of all with ten or more years of service.

```
employees DW 5811H, 70F0H
          DW 5C53H, 7BA7H
```

Name: ______________________

Date: ______________________

QUESTIONS AND PROBLEMS

Class: ______________________

1. Referring to the program of Figure 11.1, what is the *physical* address of variable *john.lab*? (Assume the data segment is located at 00A00H.)

2. When storing a number of items, each requiring a very few bits to specify, why is a record more efficient than a structure?

Advanced Section

3. What is a "partial" record?

4. What is accomplished by the WIDTH operator?

5. During which of the following processes are we allocating memory?
   a. When using the STRUC directive to define the fields.
   b. When using DB or the special <> operator to define the variable name.

6. Referring to Figures 11.1, why did we perform division using the logical shift (*shr*) rather than the arithmetic shift (*sar*)?

7. Referring to Figure 11.2, explain how the computer locates Mary's quiz score of 54.

ACTIVITY 12

THE STRING INSTRUCTIONS

OBJECTIVE

- To use the string instructions for efficient processing of arrays.

PARTS AND EQUIPMENT

- IBM PC (bus-extender optional).
- Assembler, debugger, and utilities.

DISCUSSION

The Five Primitive String Operations

When an array (a linear sequence of bytes or words) is treated as a single object, it is known as a *string*. The 8086/88 instruction set includes the five *primitive* string operations listed below:

MOVS—move string
CMPS—compare string
SCAS—scan string
LODS—load string
STOS—store string

All strings are located using the following default conditions:

- Address of source string = DS:SI
- Address of destination string = ES:DI

(We can override the source segment, but not the destination segment.)

Each time a string instruction is run, both SI and DI are automatically incremented or decremented, depending on the state of the DF (direction flag). We use the CLD (clear direction) and STD (set direction) instructions to initialize the direction flag. For word operations, SI and DI are automatically incremented or decremented by two.

The Repeat Prefixes

The three prefixes that are normally used with a string instruction are:

- REP (repeat)
- REPE/REPZ (repeat while equal/repeat while zero)
- REPNE/REPNZ (repeat while not equal/repeat while not zero)

Each of these prefixes causes the string instruction to be repeated the number of times specified by the CX register. The last two are used with the SCAS and CMPS string instructions and provide a means of prematurely exiting the repeat loop when the zero flag (ZF) turns false.

Demonstration Programs

Demonstration program DIRECTORY of Figure 12.1 uses the REP MOVS instruction to transfer string 'William' from position *here* in the data segment to position *there* in the extra segment. Note the initialization of the ES register. (The operands *here* and *there* are used only to determine the data type and can be omitted if we use the optional mnemonics MOVSB or MOVSW.)

Demonstration program SEARCH of Figure 12.2 uses the REPNE SCAS string instruction to search array *numbers* for the word 7777H. Each string element is compared with the contents of the AX register (7777H), and the process repeats as long as they are not equal. When the loop is exited, the JNE instruction is used to determine the exit condition. If 7777H is found, its offset address is returned to AX; otherwise, FFFFH is returned.

PROCEDURE

1. Strings 'Mary' and 'William' are listed in order in the data segment. Write a program that moves

FIGURE 12.1

Using the MOVS instruction to relocate a string.

```
; This program moves string 'William' from
; here to there.

NAME        DIRECTORY

DGROUP GROUP _DATA

_DATA       SEGMENT
  here  DB  'William'
_DATA       ENDS

EXTRA       SEGMENT
  there  DB  7 DUP(?)
EXTRA       ENDS

_TEXT       SEGMENT
            ASSUME CS:_TEXT,DS:DGROUP,ES:EXTRA
  start:    mov   ax,DGROUP
            mov   ds,ax
            mov   ax,EXTRA
            mov   es,ax
            cld                     ; Increment si/di
            mov   si,OFFSET DGROUP:here  ; Point to here
            mov   di,OFFSET there ; Point to there
            mov   cx,7            ; Number of iterations
            rep movs there,here   ; Move 'William'
            hlt
_TEXT       ENDS
            END   start
```

FIGURE 12.2

Using the SCAS instruction to search for a word in an array.

```
; This program seraches for 7777h, and places
; its address (0, 2, 4, or 6) into AX.  If not
; found, FFFFH is placed into AX.

NAME        SEARCH

DGROUP GROUP _DATA

_DATA       SEGMENT
_DATA       ENDS

EXTRA       SEGMENT
  numbers  DW  1372H, 22ACH, 7777H, 0F029H
EXTRA       ENDS

_TEXT       SEGMENT
            ASSUME CS:_TEXT,DS:DGROUP,ES:EXTRA
  start:    mov   ax,DGROUP
            mov   ds,ax
            mov   ax,EXTRA
            mov   es,ax
            cld                     ; si/di incremented
            mov   di,OFFSET numbers ; Point to numbers
            mov   cx,4              ; Set array length
            mov   ax,7777H          ; Set target
            repne scas numbers      ; Search for 7777h
            jne   pass              ; Jump is not found
            dec   di
            dec   di                ; Back one
            mov   ax,di             ; Answer in ax
            hlt
  pass:     mov   ax,0FFFFH         ; Not found code
            hlt
_TEXT       ENDS
            END   start
```

both strings to the EXTRA segment, but in reverse order ('William' before 'Mary').

ASSEMBLY-LANGUAGE PROGRAM

2. Using the string instruction SCAS (with proper prefix), write program MEMORY_CHECK that searches the five-element word array *eprom* for any change from the normal erased condition (FFFFH). The offset address of the first bad memory cell found is returned to AX; if all memory cells are properly erased, FFFFH is returned to AX.

ASSEMBLY-LANGUAGE PROGRAM

Advanced Activities

3. The data segment holds the 5-byte string *suspectprint,* which specifies the fingerprint pattern found at the scene of a crime. The EXTRA segment holds the 5-byte string *fileprint,* which holds a fingerprint pattern from the police files. Write a program that returns 8001H to AX if they don't match and FFFFH if they do.
4. The string 'Violets are Blue' is stored in the DATA segment. Write a program that repeats the string ten times in a row in the EXTRA segment. (*Hint:* The DUP directive can be nested.)
5. Using the STOS (store string) instruction, write a program that fills the first page (256 locations) of the EXTRA segment with 44h.
6. Making use of the LODS, STOS, and XLAT instructions, write a program that converts a string of centigrade temperatures in array *ctemp* (_DATA segment) to Fahrenheit and stores them in array *ftemp* (EXTRA segment).

Name: ______________________

Date: ______________________

QUESTIONS AND PROBLEMS

Class: ______________________

1. The MOVS instruction alone (with no prefix) transfers how many bytes or words of information each time it is executed?

2. What two conditions will cause us to exit the following loop?

```
repne cmps apples,peaches
```

3. Referring to Appendix E, how much time is required to execute the REP STOS instruction? (Assume CX = 10.)

4. When using the MOVS string instruction, in what segment will the destination string be found?

Advanced Section

5. When using the MOVS instruction, can the source or the destination be in the _TEXT segment?

6. Why is the LODS string instruction not normally assigned a repeat prefix?

PART IV

TOP-DOWN DESIGN

When we carry out any complex task, such as building a skyscraper or traveling to the moon, it is vital that we separate the details from the overall concepts. Such a design method, in which we proceed from a general description through successively more detailed levels, is known as *top-down design*.

To achieve top-down design in programming, we subdivide the overall project into smaller, more manageable units known as *modules*. The high-level, more conceptual modules (at the "top") are broken down into successively smaller and smaller, more detailed modules (at the "bottom"). Each module performs a specific task and each is a self-contained "package," with well-defined inputs and outputs. By focusing on individual modules, rather than the entire task, program design is greatly enhanced.

In the four activities of Part IV, we see how the modularization techniques of *subroutines, parameters, libraries, macros,* and *include files* lead to *top-down programming* and greatly improved software design efficiency. From a "mix-and-match" standpoint, modularization is vital because it leads to the power and versatility of *mixed-language programming*.

ACTIVITY 13

SUBROUTINES

OBJECTIVES

- To write programs involving subroutines and nested subroutines.
- To use the PUSH and POP instructions to protect internal registers.

PARTS AND EQUIPMENT

- IBM PC (bus-extender optional).
- Assembler, debugger, and utilities.

DISCUSSION

A *subroutine* is a block of program code that is stored once but can be used many times in a program (like the chorus in a musical score). Subroutines save memory space and allow the program to be *modularized*—broken up into smaller pieces—to support top-down design and improve program documentation. When subroutines are nested (one subroutine calling another), the advantages are amplified.

To execute a subroutine, we *call* the subroutine from the main program and *return* to the main program using the CALL/RETURN instructions of Figure 13.1(a). All addressing modes found in the JMP instruction (except SHORT) are also available with a CALL.

To return to the proper location, the call process *pushes* the return address onto a special location in memory called the *stack*. During the return process, it is *popped* off the stack. A stack location is determined by the *stack segment* (SS) and *stack pointer* (SP) registers. To process subroutines, we must create a stack segment, set aside sufficient stack space, and initialize the SS and SP registers.

Demonstration program TONE of Figure 13.2 uses the toggle/output/delay sequence to emit a steady tone from the internal speaker. The delay operation is performed by subroutine DELAY—an ideal candidate for a subroutine because it represents a logical processing unit and can be used many times in the same program.

From program TONE, we note the following:

- For future compatibility with C (such as QuickC), the main program is labeled *main,* and underbars precede all subroutine labels.
- We set aside 256 words of stack space (more than sufficient to prevent stack overflow for this and all future programs).
- Because subroutine DELAY is in the same segment as the main program (the _TEXT segment), it is tagged NEAR—so MASM will generate a NEAR call and a NEAR return.
- When using QuickC, the STACK *align type* (after STACK SEGMENT) causes the system to initialize the SS and SP registers automatically.

The PUSH and POP Instructions

Suppose a main program holds crucial information in a register or flag when a call is made to a subroutine. If the subroutine also uses this same register or flag, the crucial main-program information may be destroyed. The solution is to protect all such registers and flags with PUSH/POP pairs.

Program COUNT_UP_SLOWLY of Figure 13.3 is a case in point. The main program uses AX to hold the count value, and the subroutine also uses AX to generate the delay. To protect AX, we use the PUSH/POP instruction pair of Figure 13.1(b). To save memory space should the subroutine be called many times in the same program, we place the PUSH/POP pair in the subroutine. Since information is PUSHed on the stack on a first-in/last-out basis, it is POPped off the stack in reverse order. (Note from this example that the subroutine can be placed either before or after the main program.)

FIGURE 13.1

The subroutine processing instructions. (Courtesy Intel Corporation.) (a) The CALL/RETURN pair. (b) The PUSH/POP instructions.

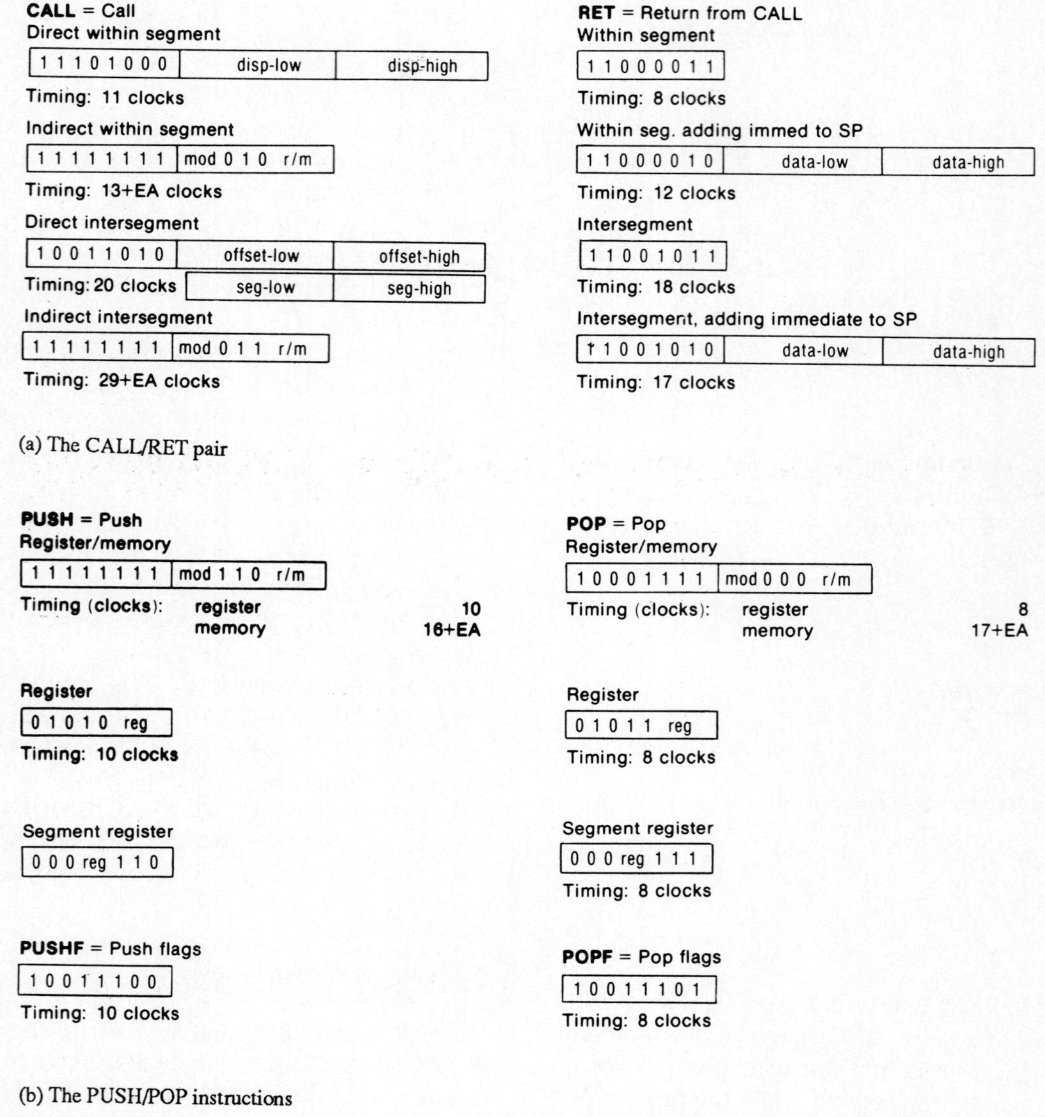

Real-Time Subroutine Processing

As an advanced topic, program ATM (automatic teller machine) of Figure 13.4 shows how indirect addressing of an *array of pointers* is used to carry out real-time subroutine selection. Recall from Activity 3 that when a variable is used as the CALL (or JMP) operand, the target address is given by the *contents* of the variable.

What is new here is the use of an array, rather than a simple variable. We store the target addresses of our two subroutines (DEPOSIT and WITHDRAW) in the two elements of array *table* and access them using base/displacement addressing. When we input a 0, we call subroutine DEPOSIT and deposit $10 to variable *savings*; when we input a 1, we call subroutine WITHDRAW and withdraw $10. Note the shorthand method of labeling a NEAR subroutine (e.g., _deposit:). (As shown, all "input" and "output" values may be stored in memory.)

PROCEDURE

NOTE: Key F10 under Codeview will single-step through subroutines.

1. Update your templates as shown in Figure 13.5. (The batch file requires no changes.)

FIGURE 13.2

Subroutine demonstration program TONE.
(a) Flowchart. (b) Program.

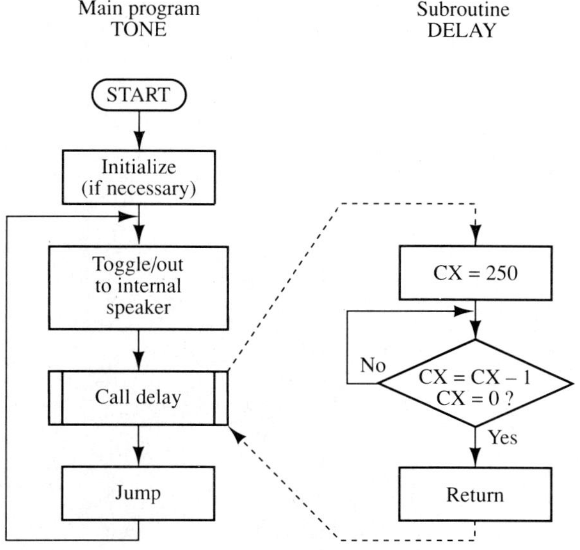

(a) Flowcharts

```
; Program TONE calls subroutine DELAY
; to generate a steady tone from the
; internal speaker.

NAME        TONE

DGROUP GROUP _DATA,STACK

STACK       SEGMENT STACK
            DW  100h DUP(?)
STACK       ENDS

_DATA        SEGMENT
_DATA        ENDS

_TEXT       SEGMENT
            ASSUME CS:_TEXT,DS:DGROUP,SS:DGROUP

  _delay PROC NEAR
            mov    cx,250      ; Load delay value
       self: loop   self       ; Delay
            ret                ; Return to main
  _delay ENDP

   main:   mov    ax,DGROUP
           mov    ds,ax
   again:  in     al,61h
           xor    al,2         ; Toggle
           and    al,0feh
           out    61h,al       ; Output
           call   _delay       ; Call delay
           jmp    again
_TEXT      ENDS
           END    main
```

(b) Program

2. Modify program TONE of Figure 13.2 so both the toggle/output sequence and the delay are called as subroutines. (The toggle/output routine to the internal speaker will be called SPEAKINT.)

ASSEMBLY-LANGUAGE PROGRAM

Subroutine Nesting

3. Figure 13.6 shows how program TONE is further modularized by nesting. Main-program TONE calls subroutine CYCLE, which in turn calls sub-subroutines SPEAKINT and DELAY. Write your program in the space provided. (Routines CYCLE, SPEAKINT, and DELAY can be listed in any order, either before or after MAIN.)

Advanced Activities

4. Single-step or breakpoint to a location in the main program of Figure 13.6 just before the CALL CYCLE instruction. Examine the SS:SP registers and write the value of *stacktop* in Figure 13.7 (using SS:SP notation). Predict the contents of the stack and the position of the stack pointer within sub-subroutine SPEAKINT (just before the RET instruction). Write these values in the Predictions column of Figure 13.7. Single-step or breakpoint to this location and write the actual values in the Measurements column. Explain and correct any differences.
5. Subroutines SUM, DIFFERENCE, MULTIPLY, and DIVIDE perform the indicated operations on bytes—generating a word result. Using the real-time subroutine selection process of Figure 13.4 as a guide, write a loop program that performs the indicated operations on two input bytes when 0, 1, 2, or 3 is input. The result is displayed. (Memory may be substituted for I/O ports.)

FIGURE 13.3

Protecting a register with a PUSH/POP pair.

```
; Since both modules use the AX register,
; it is protected with a PUSH/POP pair.

NAME        COUNT_UP_SLOWLY

DGROUP GROUP _DATA,STACK

STACK       SEGMENT STACK
            DW  100h DUP(?)
STACK       ENDS

_DATA        SEGMENT
_DATA        ENDS

_TEXT       SEGMENT
            ASSUME CS:_TEXT,DS:DGROUP,SS:DGROUP
    main:   mov   ax,DGROUP
            mov   ds,ax
            mov   ax,0
   again:   inc   ax
            call  _delay      ; Delay, but don't destroy AX
            out   1,ax        ; Display
            jmp   again

  _delay PROC NEAR
              push  ax        ; Protect AX
              mov   ax,0ffffh
        back: dec   ax
              jnz   back
              pop   ax        ; Restore AX
              ret
  _delay ENDP

_TEXT       ENDS
            END   main
```

FIGURE 13.4

Using a table of pointers (addresses) and an indirect call for real-time subroutine selection.

```
; An inported 0 will deposit $10 to variable
; savings.  An inported 1 will withdraw $10.
;
; All "input" and "output" values are stored in
; memory.

NAME        ATM

DGROUP GROUP _DATA,STACK

STACK       SEGMENT STACK
            DW  100h DUP(?)
STACK       ENDS

_DATA        SEGMENT
  savings  DW  100
  input_value  DW  ?
_DATA        ENDS

_TEXT       SEGMENT
            ASSUME CS:_TEXT,DS:DGROUP,SS:DGROUP

  _deposit:  add  savings,10
             ret

  _withdraw: sub  savings,10
             ret

  table   DW  _deposit
          DW  _withdraw

  main:       mov   ax,DGROUP
              mov   ds,ax
              mov   bx,input_value  ; "Input" selection parameter
              shl   bx,1       ; Multiply by 2 for word operation
              call  table[bx]  ; Call DEPOSIT or WITHDRAW
              hlt
_TEXT         ENDS
              END   main
```

FIGURE 13.5

Template update. (Place procedures in _TEXT segment either before or after main program.)

```
NAME

DGROUP GROUP _DATA,STACK

STACK         SEGMENT STACK*
              DW  100h DUP(?)
STACK         ENDS

_DATA          SEGMENT
_DATA          ENDS

_TEXT         SEGMENT                                **
              ASSUME CS:_TEXT,DS:DGROUP,SS:DGROUP

          PROC
          ENDP

  main:       mov    ax,DGROUP
              mov    ds,ax
              nop

_TEXT         ENDS
              END    main
```

STANDARD

* STACK align type causes SS : SP to be initialized.
**ASSUME of SS : DGROUP optional.

```
          TITLE
          DOSSEG
          .MODEL SMALL
          .STACK 100h
          .DATA

          .CODE

         PROC
         ENDP

main:     mov    ax,@DATA
          mov    ds,ax
          nop

          END    main
```

OPTIONAL (MASM 5.1 or later)

FIGURE 13.6

Program TONE, using nested subroutines. (a) Flowchart. (b) Program.

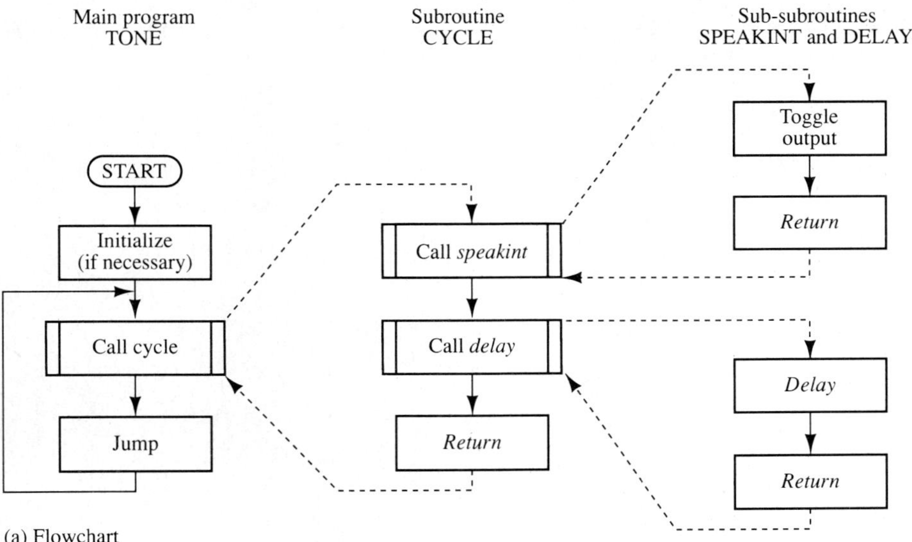

(a) Flowchart

(b) Program

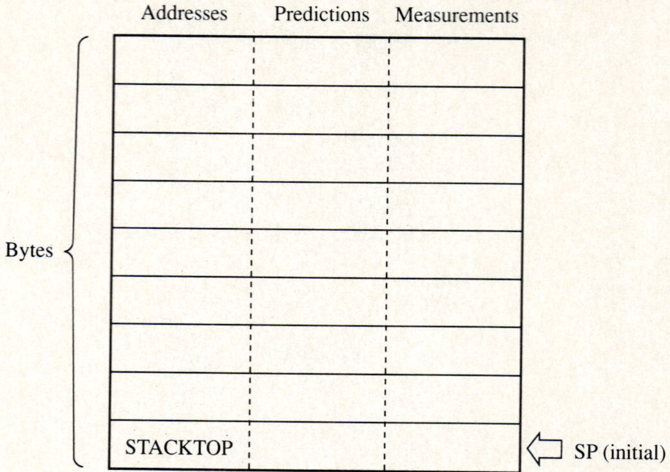

FIGURE 13.7

Program TONE stack contents.

6. Byte array *score* holds the eight scores (each between 0 and 10) given at an Olympic event. Using subroutines SMALLEST (deletes the smallest score), LARGEST (deletes the largest score), and AVERAGE (gives the average of the remaining six), write a program that deletes the lowest and highest scores and returns the average of the remaining scores to word variable *answer* (quotient in low order; remainder in high order). Subroutine AVERAGE will in turn call sub-subroutines SUM and DIVIDE.

Name: ______________________

Date: ______________________

QUESTIONS AND PROBLEMS

Class: ______________________

1. What is the difference between a NEAR call and a FAR call?

2. To implement a fourfold nested subroutine program using NEAR calls (main program and three nested subroutines), what is the minimum amount of memory space that must be reserved for the stack?

3. If we push AX, BX, and CX onto the stack in that order, in what order must they be popped off the stack?

4. Why can the stack pointer be initialized to a memory location that is reserved for other information?

5. What is the minimum amount of stack space required when processing a FAR call?

6. In a practical (real-world) situation, are we likely to create a subroutine if it is called only once? (Explain your answer.)

7. When writing complex programs with many nested subroutines, why is it good practice to set aside (define) more stack locations than you intend to use?

Advanced Section

8. After the program of Figure 13.4 passes through the assembler and locater, symbol *table[bx]* will be converted to a number. What will that number represent?

9. Why are PUSH/POP pairs normally placed in the called routine rather than in the calling routine?

10. What is ''bottom-up'' programming, and why is it often called ''tool building''? Given a large project, is it reasonable that ''top-down'' and ''bottom-up'' programming will take place simultaneously?

ACTIVITY 14

PARAMETER PASSING

OBJECTIVES

- To pass information between the main program and subroutine modules using parameters.
- To pass multiple parameters.

PARTS AND EQUIPMENT

- IBM PC (bus-extender optional).
- Assembler, debugger, and utilities.

DISCUSSION

Parameter Passing

Subroutine DELAY of Activity 13 can produce only a single delay value during execution and, therefore, is of limited use. For example, using subroutine DELAY, program TONE of Figure 13.2 generated only a single steady tone. To generate a more complex sound efficiently, such as a warble, we must pass a delay value from the main program to a subroutine. This type of data is known as a *parameter*.

The simplest way of passing a parameter is to use the *mailbox* technique: Place the information in a common register or memory location accessible to both modules. This straightforward technique is demonstrated by program WARBLE of Figure 14.1. To generate repeating cycles of increasing frequency, the main program decrements a variable and continuously passes it to procedure DELAY by way of mailbox variable *delay_value*. (The cycle re-

FIGURE 14.1

Passing a parameter by way of a mailbox variable.

```
; This version of program WARBLE uses a
; variable mailbox to pass a varying delay
; value from MAIN to DELAY, and thereby
; generate a warble.

NAME        WARBLE

DGROUP GROUP _DATA,STACK

STACK       SEGMENT STACK
            DW  100h DUP(?)
STACK       ENDS

_DATA         SEGMENT
  delay_value DB  ?
_DATA         ENDS

_TEXT       SEGMENT
            ASSUME CS:_TEXT,DS:DGROUP,SS:DGROUP

  _delay PROC NEAR
              mov   al,delay_value   ; Get parameter
       back:  dec   al
              jnz   back
              ret
  _delay ENDP

  _speakint PROC NEAR
              in    al,61h
              xor   al,2
              and   al,0feh
              out   61h,al
              ret
  _speakint ENDP

    main:   mov   ax,DGROUP
            mov   ds,ax
    again:  dec   delay_value   ; Decrease delay_value
            call  _delay        ; Call delay and pass parameter
            call  _speakint
            jmp   again
_TEXT       ENDS
            END   main
```

FIGURE 14.2

Passing a parameter by way of the stack. (a) Using the Pascal convention. (b) Using the C convention. (c) Stack contents within subroutine DELAY.

```
; This version of program WARBLE uses the
; Pascal convention to pass a parameter
; to DELAY by way of the stack.

NAME         WARBLE_PASCAL

DGROUP GROUP _DATA,STACK

STACK        SEGMENT STACK
             DW  100h DUP(?)
STACK        ENDS

_DATA         SEGMENT
  delay_value DW  ?
_DATA         ENDS

_TEXT        SEGMENT
             ASSUME CS:_TEXT,DS:DGROUP,SS:DGROUP

  _delay PROC NEAR
               push  bp
               mov   bp,sp
               mov   al,[bp + 4]   ; Get parameter
        back:  dec   al
               jnz   back
               pop   bp
               ret   2h            ; Clean up stack
  _delay ENDP

  _speakint PROC NEAR
               in    al,61h
               xor   al,2
               and   al,0feh
               out   61h,al
               ret
  _speakint ENDP

    main:    mov   ax,DGROUP
             mov   ds,ax
    again:   dec   delay_value      ; Decrease delay_value
             push  delay_value      ; Pass parameter
             call  _delay           ; Call delay
             call  _speakint
             jmp   again
_TEXT        ENDS
             END   main
```

(a) Using the Pascal convention

peats each time variable *delay_value* underflows from 0 and goes to FFH.)

Despite its simplicity, the mailbox method has several disadvantages. One is security: Because all modules have access to the mailbox, parameters can be inadvertently destroyed. Other disadvantages will become apparent in future activities.

To avoid the problems inherent in the use of mailbox (*global*) variables to pass information between modules, a parameter-passing technique that uses the stack has been developed and standardized.

Parameter Passing Using the Stack

As demonstrated by the two versions of program WARBLE of Figure 14.2, there are two methods for passing parameters on the stack. Method 1 of Figure 14.2(a) uses the older Pascal convention, and method 2 of Figure 14.2(b) uses the newer C convention.

The two methods are similar in many ways. In both cases, the main program passes the delay parameter by pushing it onto the stack. Subroutine DELAY retrieves the parameter using base/displacement addressing ([bp + 4]). Saving the base pointer (BP) with a PUSH/POP pair is necessary when parameters are passed between nested subroutines. As we go into and out of each nesting level, the top of each parameter set is saved and restored. (Because the location of the parameters is standardized, this method is used even when subroutines are not nested.) Figure 14.2(c) shows how

FIGURE 14.2

(continued)

```
; This version of program WARBLE uses the
; C convention to pass a parameter
; to DELAY by way of the stack.

NAME        WARBLE_C

DGROUP GROUP _DATA,STACK

STACK       SEGMENT STACK
            DW  100h DUP(?)
STACK       ENDS

_DATA        SEGMENT
  delay_value DW  ?
_DATA        ENDS

_TEXT       SEGMENT
            ASSUME CS:_TEXT,DS:DGROUP,SS:DGROUP

  _delay PROC NEAR
              push  bp
              mov   bp,sp
              mov   al,[bp + 4]   ; Get parameter
       back:  dec   al
              jnz   back
              pop   bp
              ret
  _delay ENDP

  _speakint PROC NEAR
              in    al,61h
              xor   al,2
              and   al,0feh
              out   61h,al
              ret
  _speakint ENDP

    main:   mov   ax,DGROUP
            mov   ds,ax
    again:  dec   delay_value       ; Decrease delay_value
            push  delay_value       ; Pass parameter
            call  _delay            ; Call delay
            add   sp,2              ; Clean up stack
            call  _speakint
            jmp   again
_TEXT       ENDS
            END   main
```

(b) Using the C convention

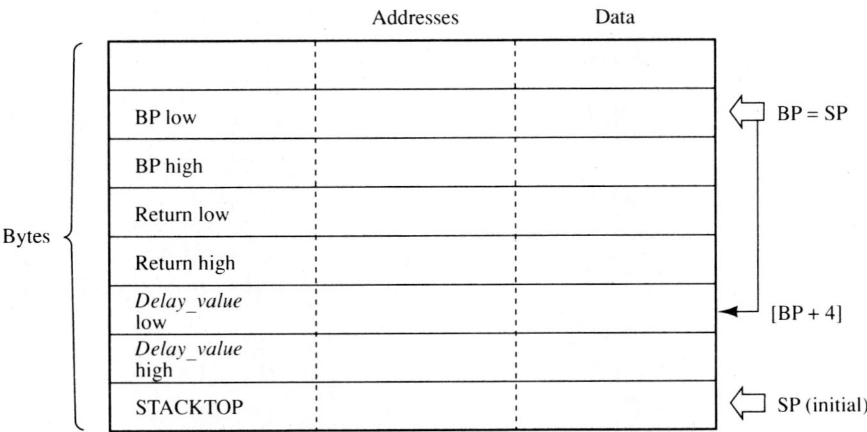

(c) Stack contents within subroutine delay

FIGURE 14.3

Implementing a function. (a) Demonstration program MATH_FUNCTION. (b) Stack contents within function PRODUCT.

```
; Math function product uses the C method of
; passing parameters to accept two byte
; parameters and return the word product in ax
; for main-program storage in variable answer.

NAME        MATH_FUNCTION

DGROUP GROUP _DATA,STACK

STACK       SEGMENT STACK
            DW  100h DUP(?)
STACK       ENDS

_DATA       SEGMENT
  first   DW  4
  second  DW  5
  answer  DW  ?
_DATA       ENDS

_TEXT       SEGMENT
            ASSUME CS:_TEXT,DS:DGROUP,SS:DGROUP

    _product PROC NEAR
              push  bp
              mov   bp,sp
              mov   al,[bp + 4]           ; Get second
              mul   byte ptr[bp + 6]      ; Times first
              pop   bp
              ret                         ; Return product in ax
    _product ENDP

  main:     mov   ax,DGROUP
            mov   ds,ax
            push  first                   ; Pass first
            push  second                  ; Pass second
            call  _product                ; Call subroutine
            add   sp,4                    ; Clean up stack
            mov   answer,ax               ; Store result
            hlt
_TEXT       ENDS
            END   main
```

(a) Demonstration program MATH_FUNCTION

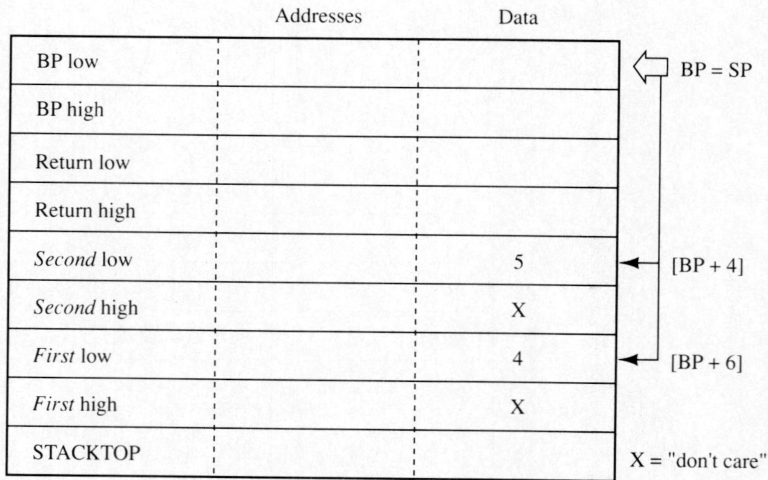

(b) Stack contents within function *product*.

subroutine DELAY locates the parameter on the stack.

The difference between the two methods relates to how each "cleans up" the stack. This cleanup is necessary because there is a PUSH (i.e., *push delay_value*) without a corresponding POP. To ensure that the original stack conditions are restored upon return to the main program, we increment the stack pointer (SP) two additional times (for each parameter pushed). To accomplish this, the Pascal convention uses the special *ret 2h* instruction at the end of the subroutine, and the C convention uses the special *add sp,2* instruction after the call in the main program.

Pascal or C?

Which convention shall we use, Pascal or C? The C convention has one advantage: Subroutines can be written to accept a variable number of parameters during execution. This is possible because the main program—not the subroutine—cleans up the stack. (We have an opportunity to write such a program as an advanced activity.) Because of this advantage, and because we wish to maintain compatibility with C (our chosen high-level language), we adopt the C convention for all future programs.

Passing Bytes as Parameters

The PUSH instruction can transfer only a *word* variable or register. If we wish to pass only a byte as a parameter (as with the routines of Figure 14.2), it must be sent as part of a word. The following examples show how the receiving routine picks up only what it wants, ignoring unwanted data:

```
mov  al,[bp + 4]  ; receive
                    low-order
                    byte
mov  al,[bp + 5]  ; receive
                    high-order
                    byte
mov  ax,[bp + 4]  ; receive
                    word
```

Procedures, Functions, and Multiple Parameters

Subroutine DELAY, which accepts parameters but does not return a value, is often called a *procedure*. When a subroutine does return a result, it is often called a *function*. Because the distinction is often blurred, in this text we use the terms "subroutine," "procedure," and "function" interchangeably when referring to assembly-language programming. In addition, we use the term "parameter" in a general way to refer to any value passed between modules as well as the variables that hold these passed values. Also common is the use of the term "formal parameter" to refer to the variable receiving a parameter, and the term "actual parameter" (or "argument") to refer to an actual value passed between modules.

By convention, the value returned from a function is always sent back to the calling program by way of the AL or AX register (AL for bytes; AX for words). For example, function PRODUCT of Figure 14.3(a) uses the C convention of passing parameters to accept word variables *first* and *second* (holding byte-size values), multiply their low-order bytes, and return the word result in the AX register for storage in variable *answer*. Figure 14.3(b) shows how these multiple parameters are stored and retrieved.

Passing Arrays as Parameters

When a data value is sent to a function as an argument (such as the delay value of program WARBLE), the process is known as *call by value*; when an address is passed as an argument, it is known as *call by reference*. One use of call by reference is to pass an array as a parameter. Rather than pass all the elements of the array, we pass only the array's address. As a case in point, program CALL_BY_REFERENCE of Figure 14.4 passes the address of ten-byte array *numbers* to function ADD_ARRAY, which returns the sum for storage in variable *answer*.

PROCEDURE

NOTE: Except for the first procedure step, all parameters are passed on the stack using the C convention. (Under Codeview, DW SP will display the stack contents.)

1. Write program MILES_PER_GALLON, which uses the mailbox technique to pass variables *miles* (word) and *gallons* (byte) to function MPG (miles per gallon). Function MPG divides the values and returns the quotient and remainder for storage in word variable *mileage*. (*Caution:* do not divide by zero.)

FIGURE 14.4

CALL_BY_REFERENCE demonstration program.

```
; Subroutine ADD_ARRAY receives the address
; of ten-byte array numbers and returns
; the sum for storage in variable answer.

NAME        CALL_BY_REFERENCE

DGROUP GROUP _DATA,STACK

STACK       SEGMENT STACK
            DW  100h DUP(?)
STACK       ENDS

_DATA       SEGMENT
  numbers DB  3, 8, 1, 3, 7, 7, 3, 5, 1, 2
  answer  DB  ?
_DATA       ENDS

_TEXT       SEGMENT
            ASSUME CS:_TEXT,DS:DGROUP,SS:DGROUP

    _add_array PROC NEAR
              push  bp
              mov   bp,sp
              mov   cx,10             ; Ten times
              mov   al,0              ; Clear answer register
              mov   bx,[bp + 4]       ; Get pointer
       again: add   al,[bx]           ; Add element
              add   bx,TYPE numbers   ; Look at next element
              loop  again             ; Do ten times
              pop   bp
              ret                     ; Return sum in al
    _add_array ENDP

  main:     mov   ax,DGROUP
            mov   ds,ax
            mov   ax,offset DGROUP:numbers
            push  ax                  ; Pass address
            call  _add_array          ; Call subroutine
            add   sp,2                ; Clean up stack
            mov   answer,al           ; Store result
            hlt
_TEXT       ENDS
            END   main
```

ASSEMBLY-LANGUAGE PROGRAM

2. Rewrite program MILES_PER_GALLON of procedure step 1, but use the stack method [Figure 14.2(b)] to pass all parameters. (Remember, although variable *gallons* holds byte values, it must nevertheless be defined as a word in order to be pushed.)

ASSEMBLY-LANGUAGE PROGRAM

3. Write a program that sends variable *number* (holding byte values) to function COUNT_

ONES, which returns the number of ones for storage in byte variable *answer*. (For example, parameter 10110011B would return 5.)

ASSEMBLY-LANGUAGE PROGRAM

Advanced Activities

4. By setting a breakpoint within function DELAY of main program WARBLE [Figure 14.2(b)], fill in the chart of Figure 14.2(c).
5. Byte array *names* holds a list of names (an ASCII string) separated by commas. By passing the address of array *names* to function COUNT_NAMES via the stack, write a call-by-reference program that returns the number of names (in AL) for main-program storage in byte variable *answer*. [*Hint:* Place a '$' (or other character) at the end of the string to determine EOS (end-of-string).]
6. Write a program that passes byte variables *hours, pay_rate*, and *bonus* (all holding byte values) to function WAGES, which returns the total pay in AX for main-program storage in word variable *answer*. Initialize the variables with values of your choice.
7. Taking advantage of the C convention of passing parameters, write the special function SUM, which accepts an arbitrary number of pushed arguments (as initialized variables) and returns the sum in AL for storage in main-program variable *answer*. (*Hint:* The last argument sent gives the total number of arguments to be added and is always located at BP + 4.)
8. Modify program CALL_BY_REFERENCE of Figure 14.4 so the number of elements of array *numbers* can be any value from 0 to 255.

Name: ______________________

Date: ______________________

Class: ______________________

QUESTIONS AND PROBLEMS

1. What is a *mailbox*?

2. When using base-pointer addressing (such as [bp + 4]), what segment register is used by default to determine the physical address?

3. Can we push variables as well as registers?

4. Why do we PUSH/POP register BP?

5. What instruction within a function retrieves the high-order byte of a single passed word parameter?

6. When using the stack method, does the receiving function have to know which register or memory location passed the parameter? What is the advantage of this?

7. When passing parameters on the stack, what is the advantage of the newer C convention over the older Pascal convention?

8. When information is sent to a function using the stack method of passing parameters, how is information usually returned to the main program?

9. When using a FAR call, why is the top argument (the last one pushed) located at [bp + 6]? What would be the location of the next argument?

10. Based on program MILES_PER_GALLON of procedure step 2, how are multiple parameters passed?

Advanced Section

11. If we PUSH parameters onto the stack, why don't we POP them off (rather than using an instruction such as *add sp,2*)?

12. When using the mailbox technique, what is the advantage of using symbolic variables rather than registers to pass parameters? Are there any advantages to using registers?

13. What is the difference between "call by value" and "call by reference"?

14. How can we convert routine DELAY of Figure 14.2(b) from a function that does not return a value to a function that does return a value? (Returning the value of the passed parameter is good practice because it may be needed for further processing. If not, it is simply ignored.)

15. How do functions return double-word (32-bit) values?

ACTIVITY 15

INDEPENDENTLY ASSEMBLED MODULES
The LINK and LIBRARY Utilities

OBJECTIVES

- To write programs involving independently assembled main modules and function modules.
- To use the LIBRARY utility to place independently assembled functions into a library.
- To use the LINK utility to combine main modules and library modules.
- To contrast *global* and *local* variables.

PARTS AND EQUIPMENT

- IBM PC (bus-extender optional).
- Assembler, debugger, and utilities.

DISCUSSION

Software productivity can be increased in two major ways:

- By using *parallel programming* techniques, in which several programmers work on separate portions of a program simultaneously.
- By including previously written modules into our present program (to avoid "reinventing the wheel").

To incorporate both of these techniques into our product development sequence, we write and assemble main-program and function modules as separate files, store the object modules in a *library,* and combine them using the *link* utility. As an added bonus, the use of library routines will greatly encourage top-down programming.

The Library Utility

After a function is independently assembled, the relocatable object module is placed into a library file. Based on Microsoft's LIB utility, listed at the bottom of the page are sample library commands for adding, deleting, and listing the modules of library MYLIB.LIB. (Any reference to file MYLIB automatically assumes an extension of .LIB.)

Consult the appropriate literature for complete information on the library utility you are using.

The LINK Utility (LINK.EXE)

After all independently assembled relocatable object modules have been stored in a library, they are combined with the main-program object module using the LINK utility. (The LINK utility searches for and links only the modules that are needed by the main program.) A single relocatable object module is generated (and converted to an EXE file for IBM PC execution).

Demonstration Program WARBLE

To demonstrate the process of independent assembly and linkage, we begin with the familiar WAR-

```
A>B:LIB
 Library name: mylib               (If new, LIB will create)
 Operations: +delay-msec-+beep     (Add  delay.obj,  delete msec.obj,
                                   and update beep.obj)
 List file: mylib.lst              (Display mylib.lst after returning
                                   to DOS)
 Output library:                   (Ignore-used only for changing
                                   the library name)
```

BLE program from Activity 14 (reproduced in Figure 15.1). Program WARBLE consists of three modules: the main module and functions DELAY and SPEAKINT. Figure 15.2 shows these same three modules split apart for independent assembly. We obeyed the following general rules:

- All shared (global) symbols (labels and variables) are declared PUBLIC in the module in which they are *defined,* and EXTRN (*external*) in the modules in which they are *used.*
- All external declarations must be typed NEAR or FAR, so the assembler will know what kind of CALL instruction to generate (e.g., _delay:NEAR).
- Modules DELAY and SPEAKINT lack a STACK segment because sufficient stack space (100H) is set aside by the main program. (The larger segmentation models may require that each module be responsible for setting aside additional stack space.)
- In the general case, all modules have a _DATA segment. Modules DELAY and SPEAKINT lack a _DATA segment because they do not use variables. ("Empty" stack and data segments can remain in each module if desired.)
- *Combine types* PUBLIC and STACK (written after the SEGMENT directives) ensure that all segments of the same name will be combined into sequential memory locations. Combine type STACK further ensures that the top of the stack will be 1 byte greater than the *combined* stack size.
- *Class* names 'STACK', 'DATA', and 'CODE' ensure that all segments of the same class will be placed together in memory. (Class is an important feature of the larger segmentation models, with their multiple segments of different names.)

FIGURE 15.1

Program WARBLE comprised of main module and subroutines DELAY and SPEAKINT.

```
; This version of program WARBLE uses the
; C convention to pass a parameter
; to DELAY by way of the stack.

NAME        WARBLE_C

DGROUP GROUP _DATA,STACK

STACK       SEGMENT STACK                                   MAIN module
            DW  100h DUP(?)
STACK       ENDS

_DATA        SEGMENT
  delay_value DW  ?
_DATA        ENDS

_TEXT       SEGMENT
            ASSUME CS:_TEXT,DS:DGROUP,SS:DGROUP

  _delay PROC NEAR
              push  bp
              mov   bp,sp
              mov   al,[bp + 4]   ; Get parameter DELAY module
       back:  dec   al
              jnz   back
              pop   bp
              ret
  _delay ENDP

  _speakint PROC NEAR
              in   al,61h
              xor  al,2                                SPEAKINT module
              and  al,0feh
              out  61h,al
              ret
  _speakint ENDP

    main:   mov   ax,DGROUP
            mov   ds,ax
    again:  dec   delay_value       ; Decrease delay_value
            push  delay_value       ; Pass parameter
            call  _delay            ; Call delay
            add   sp,2              ; Clean up stack
            call  _speakint
            jmp   again
 _TEXT      ENDS
            END   main
```

FIGURE 15.2

Program WARBLE using independently assembled modules. (a) Main. (b) Function DELAY. (c) Procedure SPEAKINT.

```
NAME        WARBLE_C

DGROUP GROUP _DATA,STACK

STACK       SEGMENT STACK 'STACK'
            DW  100h DUP(?)
STACK       ENDS

_DATA        SEGMENT PUBLIC 'DATA'
  delay_value DW  ?
_DATA       ENDS

_TEXT       SEGMENT PUBLIC 'CODE'
            ASSUME CS:_TEXT,DS:DGROUP,SS:DGROUP

  EXTRN _delay:NEAR,_speakint:NEAR

    main:   mov    ax,DGROUP
            mov    ds,ax
   again:   dec    delay_value
            push   delay_value
            call   _delay
            add    sp,2
            call   _speakint
            jmp    again
_TEXT       ENDS
            END    main
```

(a) Main module

```
; Function DELAY accepts a byte parameter,
; delays a period proportional to the
; parameter, and returns its value.

NAME        DELAY

_TEXT       SEGMENT PUBLIC 'CODE'
            ASSUME CS:_TEXT

  PUBLIC _delay

  _delay PROC NEAR
            push  bp
            mov   bp,sp
            push  bx         ; Protect BX
            pushf            ; Protect flags
            mov   al,[bp + 4]
            mov   bl,al      ; Don't change AL
     back:  dec   bl
            jnz   back
            popf
            pop   bx
            pop   bp
            ret              ; Return value in AL
  _delay ENDP

_TEXT       ENDS
            END
```

(b) Function DELAY

```
; Procedure SPEAKINT performs a
; single toggle/output operation
; on the internal speaker.

NAME        SPEAKINT

_TEXT       SEGMENT PUBLIC 'CODE'
            ASSUME CS:_TEXT

  PUBLIC _speakint

  _speakint PROC NEAR
              push ax    ; Protect AX
              pushf      ; Protect flags
              in   al,61h
              xor  al,2
              and  al,0feh
              out  61h,al
              popf
              pop  ax
              ret
  _speakint ENDP

_TEXT       ENDS
            END
```

(c) Procedure SPEAKINT

- Note that module DELAY returns the passed delay value (in AL) *in case it is needed by the main program for further processing*. Although the return value is not needed in our specific case, we must assume the most general case. After all, module DELAY is now PUBLIC and can be used by any main program—written now or in the future. If the return value is not needed by the main program, it is simply ignored.
- Within routines DELAY and SPEAKINT, all registers and flags used by each are protected by PUSH/POP pairs. Again, this is because we must

assume the most general ("worst") case in which these same registers and flags are holding vital main-program data at the time each function is called. (Of course, the accumulator and flags are not protected if they return values.)

- Segment register and stack initializations take place only in the main module.
- The starting location label (*main*) appears after END only in the main module.
- Because library routines are often of limited scope, we are encouraged to use "register variables" (to store and process variables in registers rather than in memory). This greatly speeds up library-routine execution times.

The Bus-Extender Port I/O Library Routines

Our first use of library routines is to access the bus-extender I/O ports. As always, a bus-extender is not absolutely required when using these routines because I/O operations can be simulated when running under a symbolic debugger.

Referring to Figure 15.3, the bus-extender I/O library routines are listed below. All port addresses and initialization data are based on the suggested bus-extender circuit of Figure C2.2.

PORTSET — A procedure that initializes ports, if necessary.

DIPBL — A function that returns a byte from the low-order DIP.

LEDBL — A function that accepts a byte argument, outputs it to the low-order LEDs, and returns the output value (in case it is needed for further processing by the main program).

SPEAKEXT — A function that performs the toggle/output sequence on the external speaker each time it is called. Note that this function has retained the data segment in order to hold variable *toggle*.

The demonstration program of Figure 15.4 uses several of these I/O library routines to carry out the familiar NEXT_WEEK process. Note that all external functions are declared EXTRN.

Global Versus Local Variables

A *global* variable is one shared between two or more modules; a *local* variable is one used only within a single module. To complicate matters, there are two kinds of local variables: *static* and *automatic* (*auto*).

To demonstrate global and local variables, the main program and function of Figure 15.5 include every possible variety. For each variable, the question is: *where* is it valid (its *visibility*) and *when* is it valid (its *lifetime*)?

* *first* — a global variable defined in the main module and used in function GLOLOC. Because it is declared PUBLIC, it is valid everywhere. Because it is defined in the data segment, it is permanent (has a "global lifetime"). Because it is declared EXTRN within function GLOLOC, it is "visible" (accessible) from function GLOLOC. It is initialized with "1".

* *second* — a local (static) variable defined in the main module. Because it is not declared PUBLIC, it is visible only to the main module. Because it is defined in the data segment, it has a global lifetime. It is initialized with "2".

* *third* — a local (auto) variable defined in function GLOLOC. Because it cannot be defined external, it is visible only to module GLOLOC. Because it is not defined in the data segment, it is temporary (has a "local lifetime"). The variable is created on the stack when we enter the module, and destroyed when we leave the module. It cannot be referenced by a symbol (*third* is used for identification only). It is initialized with "3".

Let's review these concepts by following through the programs of Figure 15.5. In this example, all three variable types are added to an input value, and the result is output.

Starting at the top of the main program, we input a byte from port 0 to register AL. We add the contents of global variable *first*, followed by the contents of local (static) variable *second*. We pass the sum (input + 1 + 2) to function GLOLOC. Within function GLOLOC, we create space on the stack for the automatic variable by subtracting 2 from SP, and we initialize this new variable with 3. We bring in the argument and place in AL. We again add the contents of global variable *first* (to show it is visible to function GLOLOC). We then add the contents of the local (auto) variable (called *third*). We destroy the automatic variable and re-

FIGURE 15.3

Bus-extender I/O library routines. (a) Procedure PORTSET. (b) Function DIPBL. (c) Function LEDBL. (d) Procedure SPEAKEXT.

```
; Procedure _portset initializes the
; two 8255s according to the standard
; configuration of Chapter 1.

NAME          PORTSET

_TEXT         SEGMENT PUBLIC 'CODE'
              ASSUME CS:_TEXT

     PUBLIC _portset

  _portset PROC NEAR
              push  ax
              push  dx
              mov   dx,303h
              mov   al,9bh
              out   dx,al
              mov   dx,307h
              mov   al,80h
              out   dx,al
              pop   dx
              pop   ax
              ret
  _Portset ENDP

_TEXT         ENDS
              END
```

(a) Portset

```
; Function _dipbl inputs a byte
; from the low-order DIP switch
; and returns the value in AL.

NAME          DIPBL

_TEXT         SEGMENT PUBLIC 'CODE'
              ASSUME CS:_TEXT

  PUBLIC  _dipbl

  _dipbl PROC NEAR
              push  dx
              mov   dx,300h
              in    al,dx
              pop   dx
              ret
  _dipbl ENDP

_TEXT         ENDS
              END
```

```
; Function _ledbl accepts a byte
; parameter and outputs it to the
; low-order LEDs.  The output value
; is returned (in AL) in case it is
; needed.

NAME          LEDBL

_TEXT         SEGMENT PUBLIC 'CODE'
              ASSUME CS:_TEXT

  PUBLIC  _ledbl

  _ledbl PROC NEAR
              push  bp
              mov   bp,sp
              push  dx
              mov   dx,304h
              mov   al,[bp + 4]
              out   dx,al
              pop   dx
              pop   bp
              ret
  _ledbl ENDP

_TEXT         ENDS
              END
```

(c) Ledbl

```
NAME        SPEAKEXT

DGROUP GROUP _DATA

_DATA         SEGMENT PUBLIC 'DATA'
  toggle DB   ?
_DATA         ENDS

_TEXT         SEGMENT PUBLIC 'CODE'
              ASSUME CS:_TEXT,DS:DGROUP

     PUBLIC _speakext

  _speakext PROC NEAR
              push  ax
              push  dx
              pushf
              inc   toggle
              mov   dx,306h
              mov   al,toggle
              out   dx,al
              popf
              pop   dx
              pop   ax
              ret
  _speakext ENDP

_TEXT         ENDS
              END
```

(d) Speakext

FIGURE 15.4

Bus-extender I/O library demonstration program.

```
NAME          NEXT_WEEK

DGROUP GROUP _DATA,STACK

STACK         SEGMENT STACK 'STACK'
              DW  100h DUP(?)
STACK         ENDS

_DATA         SEGMENT PUBLIC 'DATA'
  seven_days   DB  7
_DATA         ENDS

_TEXT         SEGMENT PUBLIC 'CODE'
              ASSUME CS:_TEXT,DS:DGROUP,SS:DGROUP

  EXTRN _portset:NEAR,_dipbl:NEAR,_ledbl:NEAR

  main:       mov    ax,DGROUP
              mov    ds,ax
              `all   _portset
  again:        ll   _dipbl
                     al,seven_days
              ush    ax
              call   _ledbl
              add    sp,2
              jmp    again
_TEXT         ENDS
              END    main
```

turn to the main program with the result (input + 1 + 2 + 1 + 3) in AL. The result is output to port 1, and we loop back.

In assembly-language, it is common for most local variables to be static; in a high-level language (such as C), it is common for most local variables to be automatic.

Nesting Library Routines

Can library routines call other library routines? The answer is yes—and this ability gives us the most powerful tool yet for modular design. For a demonstration of this important idea, let's return to program WARBLE. Referring to Figure 15.6, main program WARBLE_NESTED calls high-level library routine CYCLE, which in turn calls nested low-level library routines DELAY and SPEAKINT. Note that the delay argument and its returned value are relayed back and forth through module CYCLE. All modules are placed in MYLIB, and all are combined—regardless of nesting level—at link time.

Nesting means we never again have to "reinvent the wheel." Once a library routine is written and tested, we can use it again and again wherever needed—in the main program *or in another library routine*. Equally important is the idea that main programs themselves might be turned into library functions and used as building blocks for still more complex programs.

Because most of the programs in this manual are small, your opportunities to use nesting will be limited. However, nesting should be used wherever possible in the more complex advanced activities and in the projects of Activity 43.

Structure Charts

When using nested modules, the first design step is often a *structure chart,* as shown in Figure 15.6(d) for program WARBLE_NESTED. All modules are arranged in a top-down hierarchy, and all parameters are displayed.

After writing a structure chart, the designer may wish to write flowcharts for any of the modules whose complexity justifies their use.

Aided by the structure and flowcharts, the actual coding can begin. The general rule that applies here is *solve the problem before writing the program.*

Parameters—Another Look

Can you now see the real advantage of using the stack to pass parameters? It is this: Functions need not know what register or memory location passed the parameter. When using the mailbox, on the other hand, both the calling and called routines must have this information—not always readily available in a library environment. Add to this, of course, the ever-present security problem with global ("cookie jar") variables.

However, to be fair, there are times when global variables make sense. For example, if a large number of modules must share the same information, then global variables may be the preferred method of intermodular communication.

The Cross-Reference Listing

When a program includes a great number of variables and labels, a *cross-reference listing* can help locate symbols and resolve external references during debugging.

To create a cross-reference listing with Microsoft software we use the CREF.EXE utility. For example, if the demonstration program of Figure 15.2 is stored under file name WARBLE.ASM, the following command will convert the unreadable *cross-reference file* (.CRF) generated by MASM to a readable *cross-reference listing* (.REF):

```
CREF WARBLE;
```

FIGURE 15.5

Global versus local variables. (a) Main program. (b) Function GLOLOC.

```
; This main program defines (creates) global
; variable first and static-local variable
; second.  Variables first and second
; are added to an input value and function GLOLOC
; is called.  The returned value is output.

NAME        GLOLOC_DEMO

DGROUP GROUP _DATA,STACK

STACK       SEGMENT STACK 'STACK'
            DW  100h DUP(?)
STACK       ENDS

_DATA        SEGMENT PUBLIC 'DATA'
   first  DB  1   ; Define global variable
     PUBLIC first  ; Declare public
   second  DB  2   ; Define local variable
_DATA        ENDS

_TEXT       SEGMENT PUBLIC 'CODE'
            ASSUME CS:_TEXT,DS:DGROUP,SS:DGROUP

    EXTRN _gloloc:NEAR

  main:     mov   ax,DGROUP
            mov   ds,ax
  again:    in    al,0        ; Input value
            add   al,first    ; Add global variable
            add   al,second   ; Add local variable
            push  ax          ; Send partial result
            call  _gloloc     ; Call routine
            add   sp,2        ; Restore SP
            out   1,al        ; Output result
            jmp   again       ; Put into loop
_TEXT       ENDS
            END   main
```

(a) Main program

```
; In library routine GLOLOC, variables first
; (global), third (local-auto) are added and
; the result returned in AL.  The auto variable
; does not have a symbolic name.

NAME        GLOLOC

DGROUP GROUP _DATA

_DATA       SEGMENT PUBLIC 'DATA'
   EXTRN first:BYTE  ; Declare first global
_DATA       ENDS

_TEXT       SEGMENT PUBLIC 'CODE'
            ASSUME CS:_TEXT,DS:DGROUP

     PUBLIC _gloloc

  _gloloc  PROC NEAR
           push  bp
           mov   bp,sp
           sub   sp,2                 ; Create local (auto) variable
           mov   BYTE PTR[bp - 2],3 ; Initialize local (auto) variable
           mov   al,[bp + 4]          ; Bring in parameter (argument)
           add   al,first             ; Add global variable
           add   al,[bp - 2]          ; Add local (auto) variable
           mov   sp,bp                ; Destroy local (auto) variable
           pop   bp
           ret                        ; Return result in AL
  _gloloc  ENDP

_TEXT       ENDS
            END
```

(b) Function GLOLOC

FIGURE 15.6

Library routine nesting demonstration program. (a) Main program. (b) Midlevel routine CYCLE. (c) Low-level routines DELAY and SPEAKINT. (d) Structure chart.

```
NAME        WARBLE_NESTED

DGROUP GROUP _DATA,STACK

STACK       SEGMENT STACK 'STACK'
            DW  100h DUP(?)
STACK       ENDS

_DATA        SEGMENT PUBLIC 'CODE'
  delay_value DW  ?
_DATA        ENDS

_TEXT       SEGMENT PUBLIC 'CODE'
            ASSUME CS:_TEXT,DS:DGROUP,SS:DGROUP

   EXTRN _cycle:NEAR

     main:  mov    ax,DGROUP
            mov    ds,ax
    again:  dec    delay_value
            push   delay_value
            call   _cycle
            add    sp,2
            jmp    again
_TEXT       ENDS
            END    main
```

(a) Main program

```
; Mid-level function CYCLE calls nested
; functions DELAY and SPEAKINT. Function
; CYCLE accepts a parameter and passes it
; on to function DELAY.  Delay returns the
; delay_value back to CYCLE, which returns
; it back to MAIN.

NAME        CYCLE

_TEXT       SEGMENT PUBLIC 'CODE'
            ASSUME CS:_TEXT

  PUBLIC _cycle
  EXTRN _delay:NEAR,_speakint:NEAR

  _cycle PROC NEAR
            push   bp
            mov    bp,sp
            pushf                ; Protect flags
            mov    al,[bp + 4]   ; Get parameter
            push   ax            ; Send it on
            call   _delay
            add    sp,2
            call   _speakint
            popf
            pop    bp
            ret                  ; Delay-value in AL
  _cycle ENDP

_TEXT       ENDS
            END
```

(b) High-level library routine cycle

```
; Function DELAY accepts a byte parameter,
; delays a period proportional to the
; parameter, and returns its value.

NAME        DELAY

_TEXT       SEGMENT PUBLIC 'CODE'
            ASSUME CS:_TEXT

  PUBLIC _delay

  _delay PROC NEAR
            push   bp
            mov    bp,sp
            push   bx            ; Protect BX
            pushf                ; Protect flags
            mov    al,[bp + 4]
            mov    bl,al         ; Don't change AL
     back:  dec    bl
            jnz    back
            popf
            pop    bx
            pop    bp
            ret                  ; Return value in AL
  _delay ENDP

_TEXT       ENDS
            END
```

```
; Procedure SPEAKINT performs a
; single toggle/output operation
; on the internal speaker.

NAME        SPEAKINT

_TEXT       SEGMENT PUBLIC 'CODE'
            ASSUME CS:_TEXT

  PUBLIC _speakint

  _speakint PROC NEAR
            push ax      ; Protect AX
            pushf        ; Protect flags
            in   al,61h
            xor  al,2
            and  al,0feh
            out  61h,al
            popf
            pop  ax
            ret
  _speakint ENDP

_TEXT       ENDS
            END
```

(c) Low-level routines

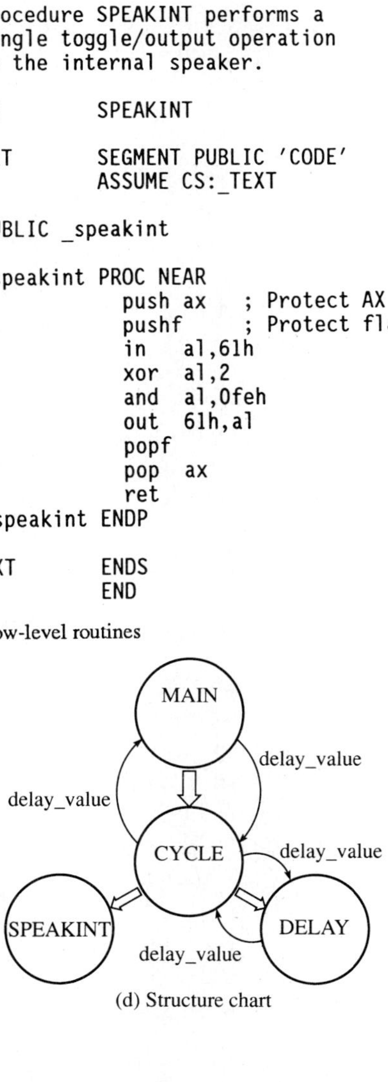

(d) Structure chart

FIGURE 15.7

Using the cross-reference listing to locate symbols in the list file. (a) Cross-reference listing (WARBLE.REF). (b) List file (WARBLE.LST).

```
 Symbol Cross-Reference          (# definition, + modification)

@CPU . . . . . . . . . . . . . .    1#
@VERSION . . . . . . . . . . . .    1#

AGAIN. . . . . . . . . . . . . .   23#     28

CODE . . . . . . . . . . . . . .   12      16

DELAY_VALUE. . . . . . . . . . .   13#     23+     24
DGROUP . . . . . . . . . . . . .    3      17      17      21

MAIN . . . . . . . . . . . . . .   21#     30

STACK. . . . . . . . . . . . . .    3       5#      5      10

_DATA. . . . . . . . . . . . . .    3      12#     14
_DELAY . . . . . . . . . . . . .   19#     25
_SPEAKINT. . . . . . . . . . . .   19#     27
_TEXT. . . . . . . . . . . . . .   16#     17      29


 12 Symbols
```

(a) Cross-reference listing

```
1                           NAME        WARBLE_C
2
3                           DGROUP GROUP _DATA,STACK
4
5 0000                      STACK       SEGMENT STACK 'STACK'
6 0000   0100[                          DW  100h DUP(?)
7            ????
8                                   ]
9
10 0200                     STACK       ENDS
11
12 0000                     _DATA        SEGMENT PUBLIC 'CODE'
13 0000  0000                   delay_value DW  ?
14 0002                     _DATA        ENDS
15
16 0000                     _TEXT       SEGMENT PUBLIC 'CODE'
17                                      ASSUME CS:_TEXT,DS:DGROUP,SS:DGROUP
18
19                                EXTRN _delay:NEAR,_speakint:NEAR
20
21 0000  B8 ---- R              main:   mov   ax,DGROUP
22 0003  8E D8                          mov   ds,ax
23 0005  FF 0E 0000 R           again:  dec   delay_value
24 0009  FF 36 0000 R                   push  delay_value
25 000D  E8 0000 E                      call  _delay
26 0010  83 C4 02                       add   sp,2
27 0013  E8 0000 E                      call  _speakint
28 0016  EB ED                          jmp   again
29 0018                     _TEXT       ENDS
30                                      END   main
```

(b) List file

Referring to ASCII file WARBLE.REF of Figure 15.7(a), we see a cross-reference listing of all the symbols defined in the program. Each symbol name is followed by a list of numbers representing the lines in the listing file of Figure 15.7(b) in which the symbol appears. The "#" indicates where a symbol is defined, and the "+" indicates where the symbol is modified. For example, local variable *delay_value* is defined in line 13, and modified (has its value changed) in line 23.

As with nested library routines, cross-reference listings are most useful when developing programs that are larger and more complex than most of those found within this manual.

FIGURE 15.8

Demonstration program POKER_HAND _MILESTONE.

```
; Milestone demonstration program POKER_HAND
; inputs a byte from 1 to 10 and outputs
; the number of cards in array hand
; equal to this value.

NAME        POKER_HAND_MILESTONE

DGROUP GROUP _DATA,STACK

STACK       SEGMENT STACK 'STACK'
            DW  100h DUP(?)
STACK       ENDS

_DATA        SEGMENT PUBLIC 'DATA'
  hand DB  9,1,4,4,7,4,9
  count DW ?
_DATA        ENDS

_TEXT       SEGMENT PUBLIC 'CODE'
            ASSUME CS:_TEXT,DS:DGROUP,SS:DGROUP

    EXTRN _portset:NEAR,_dipbl:NEAR,_ledbl:NEAR

    main:   mov   ax,DGROUP
            mov   ds,ax
            call  _portset
    again:  call  _dipbl        ; Input number
            mov   cx,7          ; 7 cards
            mov   bx,0          ; Start with first card
            mov   count,0       ; Initialize count
    next:   cmp   hand[bx],al   ; Check for match
            jne   over          ; Skip if no match
            inc   count         ; Found, so count
    over:   add   bx,TYPE DGROUP:hand  ; Next card
            loop  next          ; Next iteration
            push  count         ; Send answer as parameter
            call  _ledbl        ; Display answer
            add   sp,2          ; Clean up stack
            jmp   again         ; Keep it going
_TEXT       ENDS
            END   main
```

A Milestone Demonstration Program

Demonstration program POKER_HAND_MILESTONE of Figure 15.8 marks a milestone in our progress to date. It combines control flow, the array data type, and libraries—all important parts of *structured design*. You will write similar programs in the procedure steps that follow.

PROCEDURE

NOTE: To simulate the DIPBL and LEDBL ports under Codeview, use key F10 to execute through the subroutines, and load or view AL as appropriate.

1. Update your templates and batch files as suggested in Figure 15.9.
2. Assemble the bus-extender routines of Figure 15.3, as well as routine SPEAKINT, and generate object code for each. For example, if using MASM, the command line shown below assembles source file PORTSET.ASM:

   ```
   MASM /MX /Zi PORTSET,,,;
   ```

   (Modify port initialization data and I/O addresses if necessary.)
3. Create library MYLIB and add the object files generated in procedure step 2.
4. Using bus-extender library routines PORTSET, DIPBL, and LEDBL, write and test a loop program that inputs a byte and outputs the same byte inverted. (Use the NOT instruction.)

   MAIN-PROGRAM INVERT

FIGURE 15.9

Development package update. (a) Templates (.ASM). (b) Batch file (.BAT).

```
NAME

DGROUP GROUP _DATA,STACK

STACK       SEGMENT STACK 'STACK'
            DW  100h DUP(?)
STACK       ENDS

_DATA        SEGMENT PUBLIC 'DATA'
_DATA        ENDS

_TEXT       SEGMENT PUBLIC 'CODE'
            ASSUME CS:_TEXT,DS:DGROUP,SS:DGROUP

    EXTRN

  main:     mov   ax,DGROUP
            mov   ds,ax
            nop

_TEXT       ENDS
            END   main
```

Main program

```
        TITLE
        DOSSEG
        .MODEL SMALL
        .STACK 100h
        .DATA

        .CODE

EXTRN

main:   mov    ax,@DATA
        mov    ds,ax
        nop

        END   main
```

Main program

```
NAME

DGROUP GROUP _DATA

_DATA       SEGMENT PUBLIC 'DATA'
_DATA       ENDS

_TEXT       SEGMENT PUBLIC 'CODE'
            ASSUME CS:_TEXT,DS:DGROUP

      PUBLIC

          PROC
          ENDP

_TEXT       ENDS
            END
```

Library routine
STANDARD

```
    TITLE
    DOSSEG
    .MODEL SMALL
    .DATA

    .CODE

PUBLIC

       PROC
       ENDP

       END
```

Libary routine
OPTIONAL (MASM 5.1 or later)

(a) Template (.ASM)

```
:BEGIN
ED %1.ASM
MASM /MX /Zi %1.ASM,,,;
IF ERRORLEVEL 1 GOTO STOP
LINK /CO %1,,,MYLIB;
CV /B /W %1
ERASE %1.OBJ
ERASE %1.LST
ERASE %1.EXE
ERASE %1.CRF
ERASE %1.MAP
GOTO END
:STOP
REM Assembler error detected; display list file and re-enter editor.
REM Ctrl-S will control scrolling of list file.
COPY %1.LST CON
GOTO BEGIN
:END
```

(b) Batch file (.BAT)

5. Write library function SQUARE, which accepts an unsigned byte argument and returns its square (an unsigned word) in AX. Add to library MYLIB.

LIBRARY FUNCTION SQUARE

6. Using library routine SQUARE, write a program that solves the following equation, where x and y are unsigned byte variables and z is an unsigned word variable. (*Note:* To push bytes x and y as parameters, we can either redefine them as word variables or move the values to AL and push AX.)

$$z = (x^2 + y^2)$$

MAIN PROGRAM SUM_OF_SQUARES

7. Write library function ODDEVEN, which accepts a byte parameter and returns a 0 if even and a 1 if odd. Add to MYLIB.

LIBRARY FUNCTION ODDEVEN

8. Using function ODDEVEN, write a program that reports (outputs or places in a variable) the number of elements of 10-byte array *numbers* that are odd.

MAIN-PROGRAM ADD_ODD

9. By modifying function DELAY of Figure 15.2, write function MSEC, which accepts a single word argument and generates a delay in milliseconds equal to the argument value—which is returned in case it is needed. Add to library MYLIB. (*Hint:* Write a 1-ms byte loop and nest this within a loop controlled by the argument. Be sure to allow for a zero value argument.)

LIBRARY FUNCTION MSEC

10. Using library routines PORTSET, LEDBL, SQUARE, and MSEC, write a test program that counts up by squares (1, 4, 9, 16, . . . , 225) at the rate of once every 4 s. (*Note:* Although routine SQUARE returns a word, we display only the low-order byte with LEDBL.)

MAIN-PROGRAM MSEC_TEST

11. Write library routine BEEP, which emits a tone of short duration from the internal speaker. Add to library MYLIB. (You may wish to nest SPEAKINT within BEEP.)

LIBRARY ROUTINE BEEP

12. Using library routines BEEP and MSEC, write a program that "beeps" ten times, at time intervals specified by the 10-element word array *time*. (Initialize array *time* with values of your choice.)

MAIN-PROGRAM BEEP_INTERVAL

13. Write library routine AVERAGE and add to MYLIB. AVERAGE accepts two unsigned byte parameters and returns their unsigned byte average.

LIBRARY ROUTINE AVERAGE

14. Using library routines AVERAGE, MSEC, and BEEP, write a program that scans 10-byte arrays *score1* and *score2* at the rate of one element every 5 s. Whenever the average value of like elements is greater than 20, a beep is heard.

MAIN-PROGRAM AVERAGE_BEEP

15. Using library routines BEEP and MSEC, write program POKER_HAND_BEEP, in which the seven "cards" of array *hand* are scanned at the rate of one every 2 s. As each card is checked, a beep is heard; if the card is a 9, two beeps (closely spaced) are heard.

MAIN-PROGRAM POKER_HAND_BEEP

Advanced Activities

16. If using a bus-extender, create the following additional routines and add to MYLIB:

DIPBH	inputs a byte from the high-order DIP
DIPW	inputs a word from both DIPs
LEDBH	outputs a byte parameter to the high-order LEDs
LEDW	outputs a word parameter to the LEDs

17. Generate a cross-reference file for any of the programs developed so far and note the information contained.
18. The equation below gives the distance traveled versus time elapsed of an object dropped in Earth's gravity:

    $D = 16 \times T^2$
    (distance in feet, time in seconds)

    Making maximum use of library routines, write program FREE_FALL, which displays the distance as words in real time at 1-s intervals. Each second, when a new number is displayed, a beep is heard. (Use bus-extender ports, if available.)
19. Making use of library routines, write program REACTION_TIME, which displays a "trigger" (LEDBL), measures the time required to react and throw a switch (MSEC and DIPBL), and reports the reaction time in milliseconds (LEDBH). The process is repeated when the reaction switch is returned to low.
20. Write high-level library routine BEEPSQU, which accepts a byte parameter and generates a number of beep/rest cycles equal to the square of the parameter. Routine BEEPSQU nests low-level routines SQUARE and BEEP.

    Using routine BEEPSQU, write a main program that inputs (or reads from memory) a byte value and generates a series of beeps equal to the square of the value.

Name: ______________________

Date: ______________________

Class: ______________________

QUESTIONS AND PROBLEMS

1. Why must externally specified library routines be typed NEAR or FAR?

2. The STACK combine type guarantees that label *stacktop* will refer to what memory location after modules have been combined?

3. Why should all registers and flags be protected with PUSH/POP pairs when a subroutine module is independently assembled? When should the accumulator and flags not be protected?

4. Define the following:
   a. class

   b. combine type

5. How do we know from the file name that a certain file is a library file?

6. If a procedure is used here, but defined elsewhere, it is tagged ______________. If the procedure is defined here, but used elsewhere, it is tagged ______________.

7. How does the library process help programmers to avoid "reinventing the wheel"?

8. Referring to Figure 15.10, there are four categories of routines. Place each of the library routines used in this activity under the correct diagram.

9. Function LEDBL accepts a byte parameter, yet we must push a word. What happens to the high-order byte of the argument?

10. Referring to demonstration program NEXT_WEEK of Figure 15.4, what happened to the output value returned from function LEDBL? (*Hint:* Was it simply ignored?)

FIGURE 15.10

The four categories of procedures and functions.

Procedures

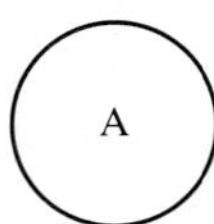

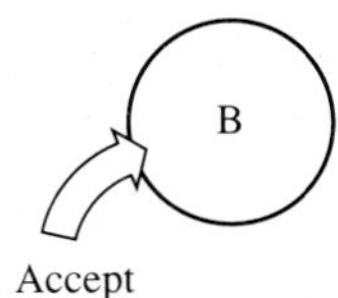

Functions

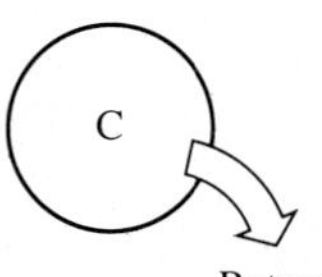

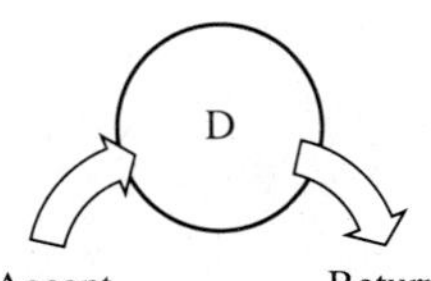

11. When high accuracy is desired, why might it be necessary to adjust the time delay of function MSEC depending on the main program that calls it?

12. Why do none of the library functions used in this and future experiments contain a stack segment?

13. Referring to routine AVERAGE of procedure step 13, does it matter in which order the two arguments are pushed? Will this be true for functions in general?

14. How do we use the PUBLIC/EXTRN directives to handle global variables?

15. If procedure MSEC is valid for one computer, is it valid for all computers? Explain your answer.

16. What is the difference between a *static* local variable and an *auto* local variable? What advantage do automatic variables have over static variables?

17. In a "real-world" situation (as opposed to simple "learning value"), why might the use of function SQUARE be considered "function overkill"?

Advanced Section

18. Can two independently assembled modules use the same name for a local variable? When combined (linked), does each symbol represent a distinct and separate memory location?

19. For a given symbol (label or variable), circle the statement that is true.
    a. It can appear only twice, once tagged PUBLIC and once tagged EXTRN.
    b. It can appear any number of times with the EXTRN tag, but only once with the PUBLIC tag.
    c. It can appear any number of times with the PUBLIC tag, but only once with the EXTRN tag.
    d. It can appear any number of times with either the PUBLIC or EXTRN tag.

20. When using independent assembly, why is parameter passing via the stack superior to parameter passing via a mailbox?

21. What is an *align type* and where is it placed in a program?

22. When writing routine SQUARE of procedure step 5, under what conditions would you *not* use a PUSH/POP pair to protect the flags?

23. What changes to routine AVERAGE of procedure step 13 would allow the routine to accept signed bytes and return a signed byte average in the range of −128 to +127?

ACTIVITY 16

MACROS AND INCLUDE FILES

OBJECTIVES

- To use macros and include files to modularize programs.
- To introduce *conditional assembly*.

PARTS AND EQUIPMENT

- IBM PC (bus-extender optional).
- Assembler, debugger, and utilities.

DISCUSSION

Macros

A function and a macro are similar. When using either, for example, a single symbol stands for a sequence of characters. The difference is that the sequence of characters represented by a function must be a set of instructions and is substituted during *execution*; the sequence of characters represented by a macro can be anything and is substituted during *assembly*.

Demonstration program MIMIC_DELAY of Figure 16.1(a), which places a simple delay between input and output, shows two of the primary uses of macros: to modularize header information and instruction sequences. Note how actual parameters (arguments) 100H and 0FFFFH are sent to formal parameters SIZE and NUMBER. The list file of Figure 16.1(b) shows the macros substituted in the program. (The 1s are nesting-level indicators.)

Include Files

The problem with macros, as used in Figure 16.1(a), is that they "clutter up" the source program. The solution lies in *include files*. Any section of a program can be placed in a separate file and "included" in the main program at assembly time. The demonstration program of Figure 16.2(a) is a case in point. Since the header information of Figure 16.2(b) will be found in all future programs, it is stored in a separate file and included in the main program at assembly time. The list file of Figure 16.2(c) shows the information included in the main program.

Functions, Macros, or Include Files?

Activities 15 and 16 introduced three major methods of modularizing a program: functions, macros, and include files. Which is best? The answer, of course, depends on the application at hand.

Macros and include files have several advantages. They can modularize any part of a program, whereas a function can modularize only instructions. A macro or an include file results in no loss of execution speed, whereas a function must pass through the call/return process. (To reduce main-program clutter, a library of macros can be placed in an include file.)

However, regardless of these advantages, a function (stored in a library) must be considered the most powerful of the three. The major reason was mentioned earlier: Functions are called during execution rather than during assembly, which means that only functions can accept real-time parameters from registers and symbolic variables. Another advantage is that no matter how many times a function is called, it uses up only one block of memory. This is not true of a macro or an include file.

In summary, if a program module is to be used only once or twice, execution speed is critical, and all parameters are constants, use a macro or an include file. Otherwise, use a function.

Conditional Assembly

As an advanced topic, special alternation and loop directives provide *conditional assembly*. Demonstration program MIMIC_DELAY of Figure 16.3 is such a program. If a "1" (true) follows the IF statement, a loop delay is generated. If a "0" (false) follows the IF statement, the REPT directive produces four NOP instructions in sequence.

Conditional assembly allows a single source program to represent any number of unique executable programs. For example, suppose a single source program is to run on either an 8088 machine or an 80386 machine. To take advantage of special 386 instructions (such as immediate multiply), these can be selected by conditional assembly.

The macro and include facilities are considerably more complex and powerful than represented by this single activity. For example, mathematical and logical operators can be used within macros, a number of built-in functions are available that return values, macro parameters can be other macros, and macros can be nested. Refer to the appropriate manuals for more detailed information.

In the procedure steps to follow, our goal is to write a single program that uses all three major modularization techniques: functions, macros, and include files.

PROCEDURE

1. A useful instruction-sequence macro is one that adds the elements of an array. By filling in the macro definition shown below with the appropriate instructions, write macro ADDARRAY, which accepts actual parameters ARRAYNAME and ELEMENTCOUNT and places the sum of the array elements in AL.

```
ADDARRAY MACRO   ARRAYNAME,ELEMENTCOUNT





         ENDM
```

2. Using macro ADDARRAY, include file HEADER, and function BEEP, write a main program that beeps if the sum of the elements of 8-byte array NUMBERS is above 10.

MAIN PROGRAM

Advanced Activity

3. Using conditional assembly techniques, write program WARBLE that selects either internal or external speaker operation.

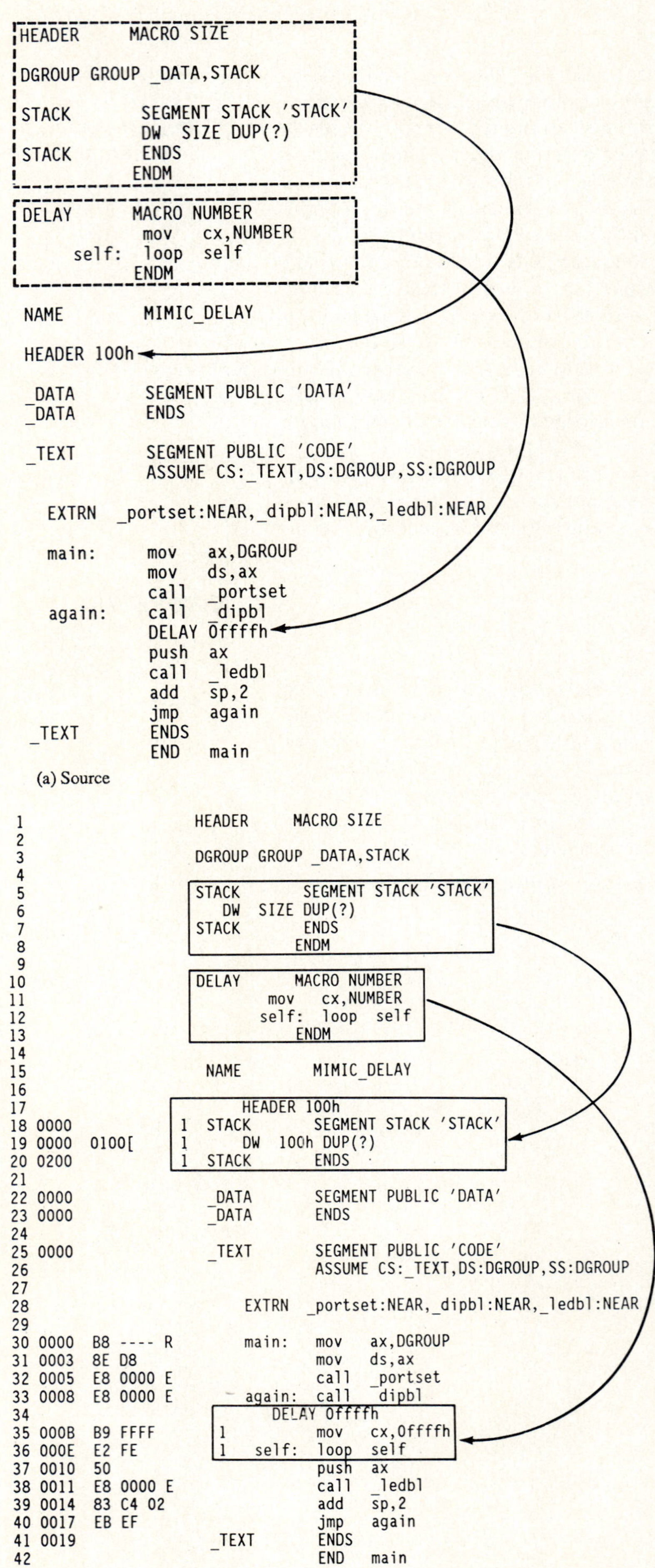

```
HEADER      MACRO SIZE

DGROUP  GROUP  _DATA,STACK

STACK        SEGMENT STACK 'STACK'
             DW   SIZE DUP(?)
STACK        ENDS
             ENDM

DELAY        MACRO NUMBER
             mov   cx,NUMBER
     self:   loop  self
             ENDM

NAME         MIMIC_DELAY

HEADER 100h

_DATA        SEGMENT PUBLIC 'DATA'
_DATA        ENDS

_TEXT        SEGMENT PUBLIC 'CODE'
             ASSUME CS:_TEXT,DS:DGROUP,SS:DGROUP

  EXTRN   _portset:NEAR,_dipbl:NEAR,_ledbl:NEAR

  main:      mov    ax,DGROUP
             mov    ds,ax
             call   _portset
  again:     call   _dipbl
             DELAY 0ffffh
             push   ax
             call   _ledbl
             add    sp,2
             jmp    again
_TEXT        ENDS
             END    main
```

(a) Source

```
                         HEADER      MACRO SIZE

                         DGROUP GROUP _DATA,STACK

                         STACK        SEGMENT STACK 'STACK'
                            DW  SIZE DUP(?)
                         STACK        ENDS
                                     ENDM

                         DELAY       MACRO NUMBER
                                 mov    cx,NUMBER
                                self:  loop  self
                                     ENDM

                           NAME        MIMIC_DELAY

                               HEADER 100h
0000                   1  STACK        SEGMENT STACK 'STACK'
0000   0100[           1      DW  100h DUP(?)
0200                   1  STACK        ENDS

0000                       _DATA       SEGMENT PUBLIC 'DATA'
0000                       _DATA       ENDS

0000                       _TEXT       SEGMENT PUBLIC 'CODE'
                                       ASSUME CS:_TEXT,DS:DGROUP,SS:DGROUP

                               EXTRN   _portset:NEAR,_dipbl:NEAR,_ledbl:NEAR

0000   B8 ---- R               main:   mov    ax,DGROUP
0003   8E D8                           mov    ds,ax
0005   E8 0000 E                       call   _portset
0008   E8 0000 E              again:   call   _dipbl
                                 DELAY 0ffffh
000B   B9 FFFF           1             mov    cx,0ffffh
000E   E2 FE             1    self:    loop   self
0010   50                              push   ax
0011   E8 0000 E                       call   _ledbl
0014   83 C4 02                        add    sp,2
0017   EB EF                           jmp    again
0019                       _TEXT       ENDS
                                       END    main
```

(b) List

FIGURE 16.1

Macro demonstration program. (a) Source file. (b) List file.

FIGURE 16.2

Include file demonstration program. (a) Main program. (b) Include file. (c) List file.

```
NAME        MIMIC_DELAY
INCLUDE HEADER

_DATA       SEGMENT PUBLIC 'DATA'
_DATA       ENDS

_TEXT       SEGMENT PUBLIC 'CODE'
            ASSUME CS:_TEXT,DS:DGROUP,SS:DGROUP

  EXTRN  _portset:NEAR,_dipbl:NEAR,_ledbl:NEAR

  main:     mov   ax,DGROUP
            mov   ds,ax
            call  _portset
  again:    call  _dipbl
            mov   cx, Offffh
   self:    loop  self
            push  ax
            call  _ledbl
            add   sp,2
            jmp   again
_TEXT       ENDS
            END   main
```

(a) Main program

```
DGROUP GROUP _DATA,STACK

STACK        SEGMENT STACK 'STACK'
             DW  100h DUP(?)
STACK        ENDS
```

(b) Include file

```
                           NAME        MIMIC_DELAY

                           INCLUDE HEADER
                        C  DGROUP GROUP _DATA,STACK
                        C
0000                    C  STACK      SEGMENT STACK 'STACK'     <- Included
0000  0100[             C     DW  100h DUP(?)
         ????           C
             ]          C
                        C
0200                    C  STACK          ENDS

0000                       _DATA       SEGMENT PUBLIC 'DATA'
0000                       _DATA       ENDS

0000                       _TEXT       SEGMENT PUBLIC 'CODE'
                                       ASSUME CS:_TEXT,DS:DGROUP,SS:DGROUP

                             EXTRN  _portset:NEAR,_dipbl:NEAR,_ledbl:NEAR

0000  B8 ---- R              main:     mov   ax,DGROUP
0003  8E D8                            mov   ds,ax
0005  E8 0000 E                        call  _portset
0008  E8 0000 E              again:    call  _dipbl
000B  B9 FFFF                          mov   cx, Offffh
000E  E2 FE                   self:    loop  self
0010  50                               push  ax
0011  E8 0000 E                        call  _ledbl
0014  83 C4 02                         add   sp,2
0017  EB EF                            jmp   again
0019                       _TEXT       ENDS
                                       END   main
```

(c) List file

FIGURE 16.3

Conditional assembly demonstration programs.

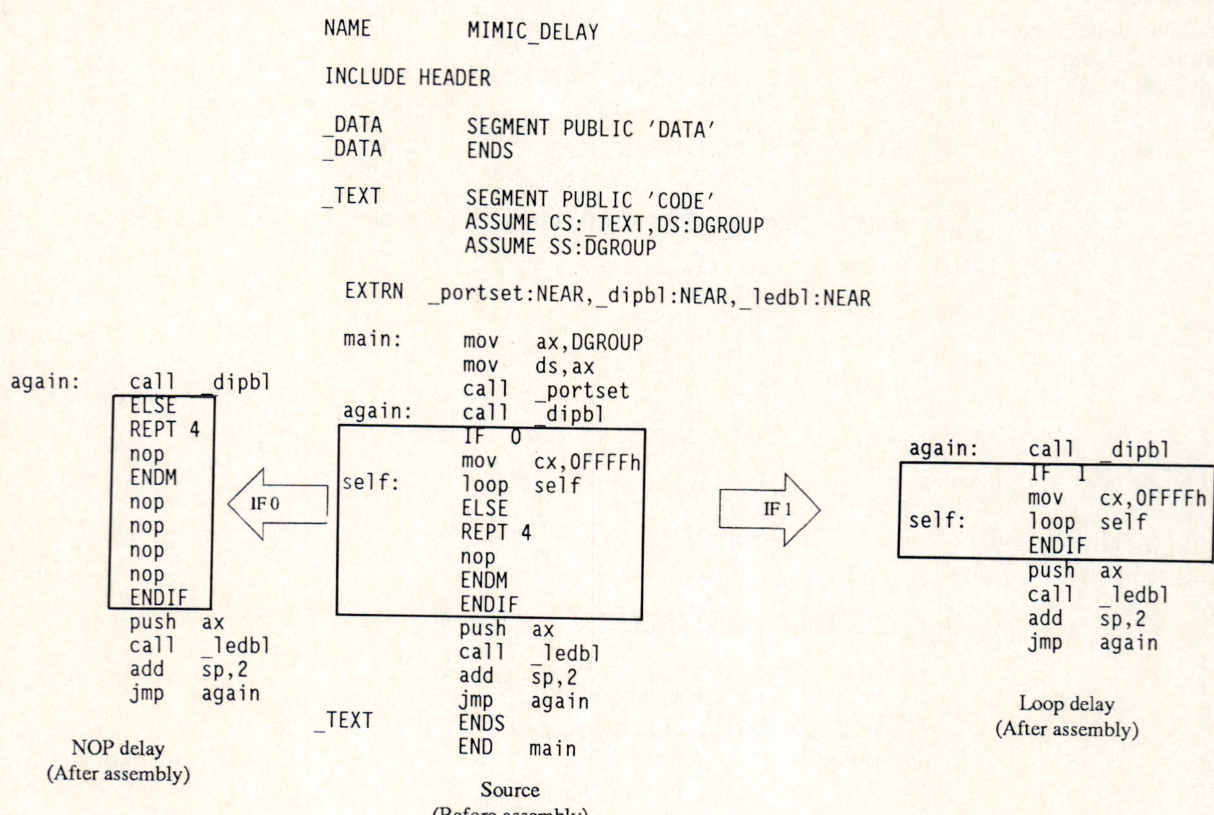

Name: ______________________

Date: ______________________

Class: ______________________

QUESTIONS AND PROBLEMS

1. Under what conditions would you use a function rather than a macro?

2. Does the use of macros result in any loss of execution speed? Is this true for functions?

3. Macro APPLES and function PEACHES each represent 100 bytes of code. If both APPLES and PEACHES are each used 20 times in a program, *approximately* how much memory is required to store the code represented by each?

4. Is there any part of a program that cannot be placed in an include file?

5. Can macros be placed in a library? in an include file?

Advanced Section

6. Can parameters be passed to an include file?

7. Can macros be nested?

PART V

INTERRUPTS, BIOS/DOS CALLS, KEYBOARD-MONITOR I/O, GRAPHICS

To thrive in a real-world environment, we must react to the unexpected and the unforeseen. The same holds true for a computer. In Part V we program our computer to accept *interrupts* and, therefore, to react to events that are unpredictable and irregular. To help us process interrupts, we make use of ROM-BIOS and DOS calls.

In Part V, our mix-and-match theme gets a big boost. Also using ROM-BIOS and DOS calls, we write numerous library routines that turn the IBM PC keyboard and monitor into I/O ports. As an added bonus, these same library routines turn the monitor into a *graphics* medium for the display of images.

To further enhance our mix-and-match theme, Figure 1 offers a suggested hardware/software design for an external seven-segment display that provides all 128 character combinations. Library routine *out7b* is a *device driver* for the hexadecimal character set. Because the system does not use multiplexing, the displays need not be continuously "refreshed."

FIGURE 1

Interfacing a hexadecimal 7-segment byte port. (a) Hardware. (b) Library routine OUT7B.

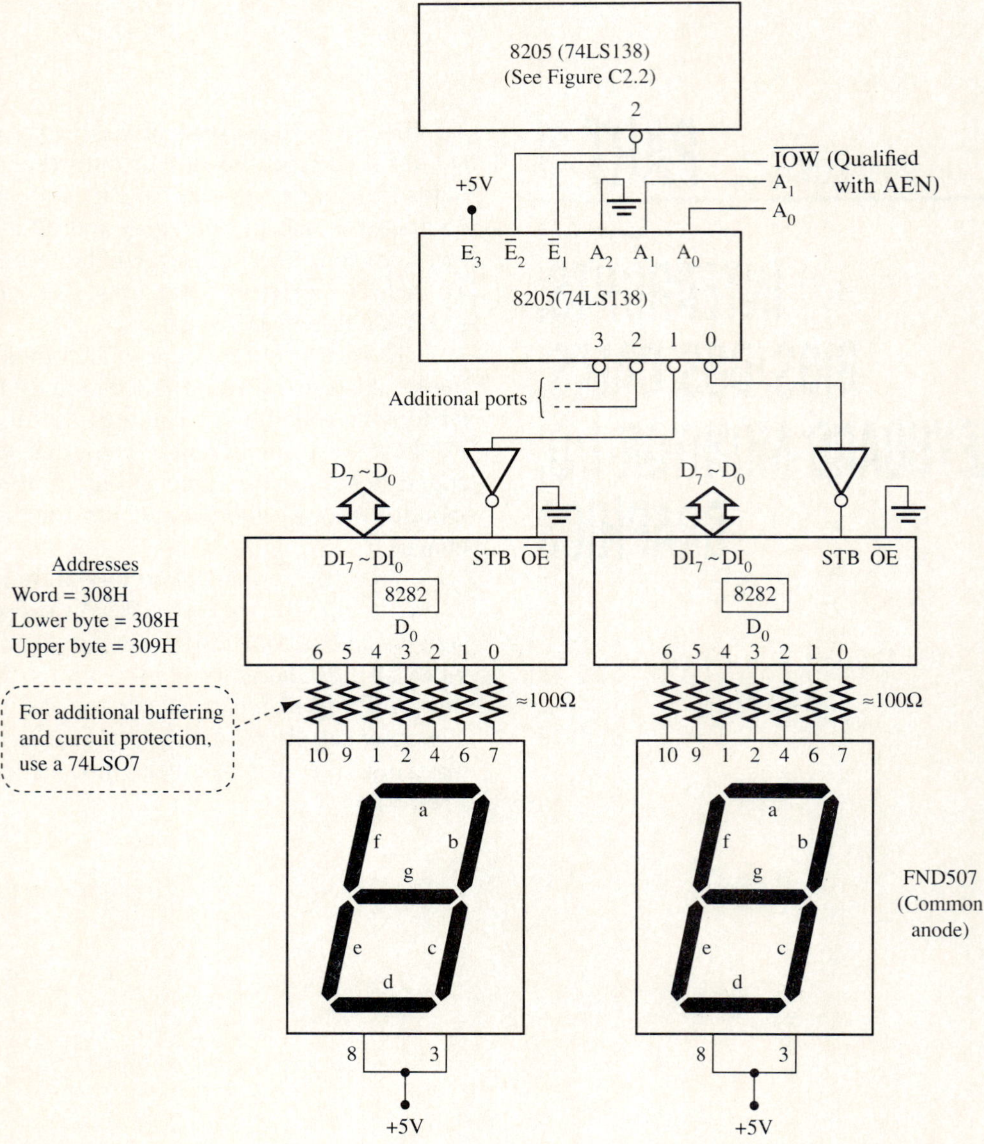

(a) Hardware

FIGURE 1

(continued)

```
; Function OUT7B accepts a hex byte parameter and
; outputs it to the 7-segment displays (at word
; address 308H).  The output value is returned.

NAME         OUT7B

DGROUP GROUP _DATA

_DATA        SEGMENT PUBLIC 'DATA'
  convert  DB  0c0h,0f9h,0a4h,0b0h,99h,92h,82h,0f8h
           DB  80h,98h,88h,83h,0c6h,0a1h,86h,8eh
  upper    DB  ?
  lower    DB  ?
_DATA        ENDS

_TEXT        SEGMENT PUBLIC 'CODE'
             ASSUME CS:_TEXT,DS:DGROUP

  PUBLIC   _out7b

  _out7b PROC NEAR
             push  bp
             mov   bp,sp
             push  bx
             push  cx
             push  dx
             pushf
             mov   bx,OFFSET DGROUP:convert
             mov   al,[bp + 4]
             mov   lower,al
             mov   upper,al
             mov   cl,4
             shr   upper,cl
             and   lower,0fh
             mov   al,lower
             xlat  convert
             mov   lower,al
             mov   al,upper
             xlat  convert
             mov   upper,al
             mov   al,lower
             mov   ah,upper
             mov   dx,308h
             out   dx,ax
             popf
             pop   dx
             pop   cx
             pop   bx
             pop   bp
             ret
  _out7b ENDP

_TEXT        ENDS
             END
```

(b) Library routine _ out7b

ACTIVITY 17

INTERRUPTS

OBJECTIVES

- To process single and multiple interrupts on the IBM PC.
- To use DOS calls to initialize interrupt vectors.

PARTS AND EQUIPMENT

- IBM PC with bus-extender.
- Assembler, debugger, and utilities.
- 2 CD4009 inverters.
- 1 7432 or CD4071 OR gate.
- 2 10K resistors.

DISCUSSION

8086/88 Interrupt Handling

An interrupt is an unpredictable function call, initiated by an external device. We know an interrupt can happen, and we prepare for it—we just don't know when. In computer parlance, this means an interrupt is an *asynchronous* (untimed) event. A subroutine that is processed by an interrupt is called an *interrupt service routine* (ISR). An interrupt is especially useful when an external device requires servicing on an irregular, unpredictable, or emergency basis.

The address of the ISR is obtained when the requesting device supplies a *type* number to the CPU. This type number points to one of the 256 locations in the *interrupt vector table* of Figure 17.1. A double-word address pointer is pulled from the table and "jammed" into the CS:IP registers (performing an indirect FAR call of an ISR).

To request an interrupt, we activate either the NMI (nonmaskable interrupt) or the INTR (interrupt request) pin to the 8086/88. NMI is an edge-sensitive input that cannot be disabled; INTR is a level-sensitive input that is enabled or disabled by the STI (*set interrupt flag*) and CLI (*clear interrupt flag*) instructions. NMI is special because the type number (2) is supplied automatically by the 8086/88—not from external circuitry.

For the more general INTR request, good for all interrupt types from 0 to 255, the following sequence takes place:

1. INTR is activated, requesting an interrupt.
2. The present instruction is allowed to be completed.
3. The CS, IP, and flag registers are automatically pushed onto the stack.
4. $\overline{\text{INTA}}$ (interrupt acknowledge) goes low and external circuitry supplies a type number (0 to 255) by way of the data bus.
5. The type number is automatically multiplied by four within the 8086/88 to give the address of the interrupt vector in the interrupt vector table.
6. The CS:IP address of the ISR is pulled from the interrupt vector table and jammed into the CS:IP registers.
7. The ISR is executed.
8. The special IRET (*interrupt return*) instruction pops the CS:IP return address and the flag register off the stack, and we return to the main program.

The Software Interrupt

Conventional interrupts—those we have covered so far—are triggered by external hardware. However, interrupts may also be triggered by software. We simply place the INT instruction anywhere in our program, and the operand supplies the interrupt type number (i.e., *int 21h*). A software interrupt is often used to test the effects of a hardware interrupt should one occur at a particular program location. They are also used in place of a subroutine call when it is convenient for the operand to be a number rather than a symbol.

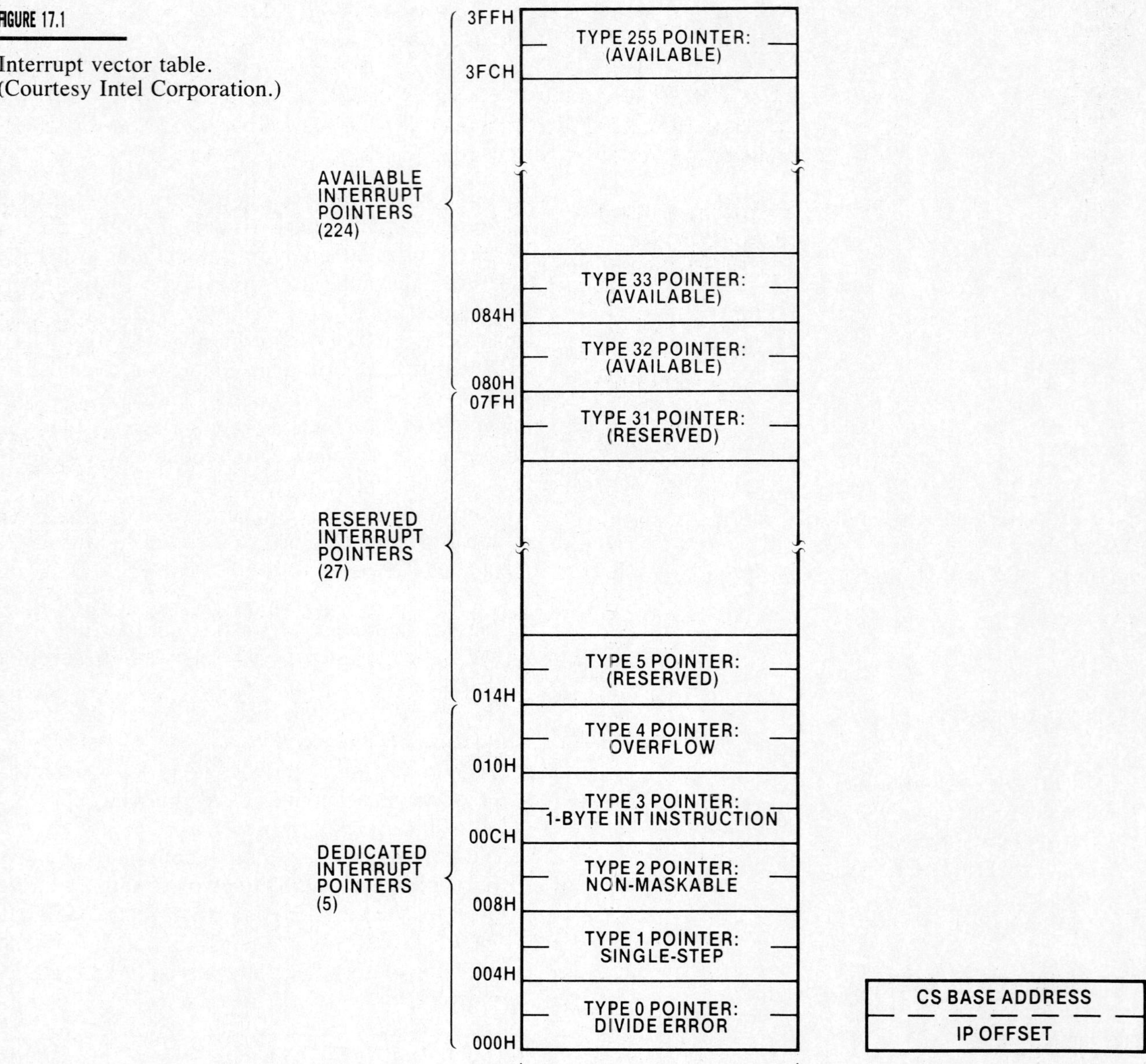

FIGURE 17.1

Interrupt vector table.
(Courtesy Intel Corporation.)

Interrupts on the IBM PC

Interrupts on the IBM PC are handled through the 8259A *priority interrupt controller* of Figure 17.2(a). When an interrupt is requested by activating one of the IR0–IR7 request lines, the 8259A supplies the 8-bit interrupt type number to the 8086/88. The upper 5 bits are determined by programming and the lower 3 bits are determined by the IR0–IR7 external request lines. A variety of modes is set by programming.

The IR2–IR7 inputs to the 8259A are connected directly to the IRQ2–IRQ7 bus system lines. Generally, interrupts IRQ2 (type 10) and IRQ3 (type 11) are available for external use. Because all 8259A interrupt inputs are programmed to be edge triggered, the circuit of Figure 17.2(b) is one way to provide debouncing.

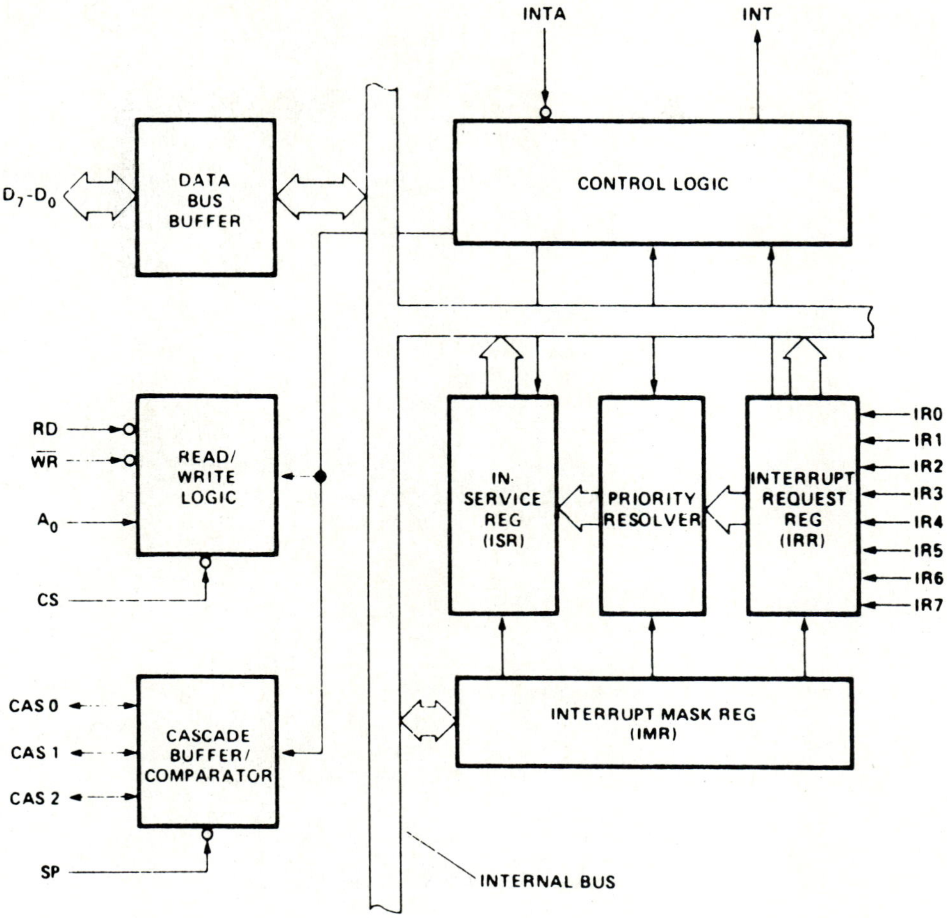

(a) Block diagram

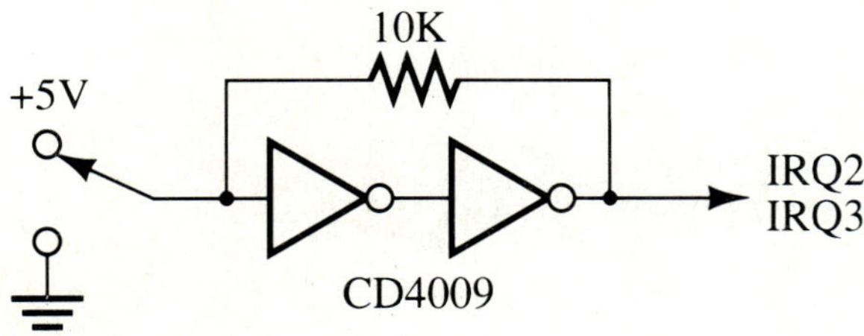

(b) Debouncing the interrupt-request input

FIGURE 17.2

The 8259A priority interrupt controller. (a) Block diagram. (Courtesy Intel Corporation.) (b) Debouncing the interrupt request input.

FIGURE 17.3

Set-interrupt-vector library routine.

```
; Function ISRSET accepts the interrupt type, isr
; segment address, and isr offset address and sets
; the IRQ0 - IRQ7 interrupt vector. (IRQ0 through
; IRQ7 correspond to types 8 through 15.)  Interrupt
; inputs IRQ2 (type 10) and IRQ3 (type 11) are
; generally available.

NAME        ISRSET

DGROUP GROUP _DATA

_DATA       SEGMENT PUBLIC 'DATA'
  convert DB  8 DUP (?)
          DB  0feh,0fdh,0fbh,0f7h,0efh,0dfh,0bfh,7fh
_DATA       ENDS

_TEXT       SEGMENT PUBLIC 'CODE'
            ASSUME CS:_TEXT,DS:DGROUP

  PUBLIC  _isrset

  _isrset PROC NEAR
         push  bp
         mov   bp,sp
         push  ax
         push  bx
         push  dx
         pushf
         push  ds
         mov   ax,[bp + 6]   ; Get ISR segment
         mov   ds,ax         ; Isr seg to ds
         mov   dx,[bp + 4]   ; Get ISR offset to dx
         mov   ah,25h        ; Service 25h
         mov   al,[bp + 8]   ; ISR type
         int   21h           ; Set isr
         pop   ds
         mov   al,[bp + 8]   ; Get ISR type again
         mov   bx,OFFSET DGROUP:convert
         xlat  convert       ; Get mask data
         mov   bl,al         ; Store in bl
         in    al,21h        ; Get present mask
         and   al,bl         ; Unmask
         out   21h,al        ; set new mask
         popf
         pop   dx
         pop   bx
         pop   ax
         pop   bp
         ret
  _isrset ENDP

_TEXT       ENDS
            END
```

The DOS Interrupt Service

When you purchase DOS you also purchase a number of DOS services that are summoned by way of software interrupts. A DOS service of current interest is the *interrupt handling service*. To call this service, we put the service number (25H) into AH and call INT 21H. Registers DS:DX hold the segment:offset ISR address, and register AL holds the interrupt type number. The process is summarized below:

```
DOS (INT 21H), service 25H: Set Interrupt Vector
 AH = 25H
 DS:DX = segment:offset address of ISR
 AL = interrupt type
```

Function ISRSET of Figure 17.3 receives the interrupt type and ISR address as parameters and uses a DOS interrupt service to place this vector at the proper location in the interrupt vector table (00028H–0002BH for type 10 and 0002CH–0002FH for type 11). ISRSET also unmasks the corresponding interrupt input by way of a look-up table.

Demonstration program BINARYCOUNT of Figure 17.4 counts up by one each time the interrupt is requested. ISR COUNTUP increments the LED display, issues an *end-of-interrupt* (EOI) to the 8259A, and returns to the main program. Note the use of a variable mailbox (also known as a *formatted parameter area*) to pass the count parameter from main program to ISR. (Like a regular subroutine, an ISR can be independently assembled and stored in a library.)

FIGURE 17.4

Interrupt demonstration program.

```
; BINARYCOUNT counts up by one each
; time the IRQ3 (type 11) interrupt input
; is cycled.

NAME        BINARYCOUNT

INCLUDE HEADER

_DATA       SEGMENT PUBLIC 'DATA'
  mailbox DB 0
_DATA       ENDS

_TEXT       SEGMENT PUBLIC 'CODE'
            ASSUME CS:_TEXT,DS:DGROUP,SS:DGROUP

  EXTRN _portset:NEAR,_isrset:NEAR

  _isrcount PROC FAR
            mov   dx,304h
            mov   al,mailbox
            out   dx,al
            inc   mailbox
            mov   al,20h
            out   20h,al    ; End-of-interrupt (EOI)
            iret
  _isrcount ENDP

   main:    mov   ax,DGROUP
            mov   ds,ax
            call  _portset
            sti
            mov   ax,11
            push  ax        ; Send type 11
            push  cs        ; Send seg address
            mov   ax,OFFSET _isrcount
            push  ax        ; Send offset address
            call  _isrset ; Set ISR vector
            add   sp,6      ; Clean up stack
   self:    jmp   self      ; Wait for int.

_TEXT       ENDS
            END   main
```

Multiple Interrupts

It is common for several external devices to request service by way of interrupts. This is known as *multiple interrupt* processing. The two major techniques for processing multiple interrupts are the *scanned* (polled) and *vectored* techniques.

The scanned technique

Referring to the scanned technique hardware of Figure 17.5(a), when either of the interrupt request lines is driven high, the ORed output sends an interrupt request to IRQ2 or IRQ3. Within the ISR, we import the interrupt requests and scan (poll) them to see which is requesting service (A or B). The order of polling determines the priority.

Demonstration program UPDOWN_POLLED of Figure 17.5(b) uses the scanned technique to determine if interrupt request A or B is active. Interrupt request A causes the output to increment; interrupt request B causes the output to decrement.

The vectored technique

According to the vectored technique hardware of Figure 17.6(a), each request is assigned its own unique interrupt line. When request A goes active, we request an IRQ2 (type 10) interrupt; when request B is active, an IRQ3 (type 11) interrupt. Priority is determined within the 8259A.

The vectored-technique software solution to task UPDOWN is demonstrated by Figure 17.6(b). Note the two ISRs, one for each interrupt vector.

Multitasking

Multitasking refers to the ability of a single processor to perform multiple tasks by time-sharing. Interrupts are often used in multitasking applications, with each task assigned a unique interrupt type number. To work in a multitasking environment, we may adopt either the polled or vectored technique (or a combination of the two).

PROCEDURE

Single Interrupts

1. Add function ISRSET of Figure 17.3 to library MYLIB.
2. Write program TONE, which sounds a steady tone. Each activation of the interrupt input causes an increase in pitch (frequency).

FIGURE 17.5

Multiple interrupts—scanned (polled) technique. (a) Interfacing and debouncing. (b) Software.

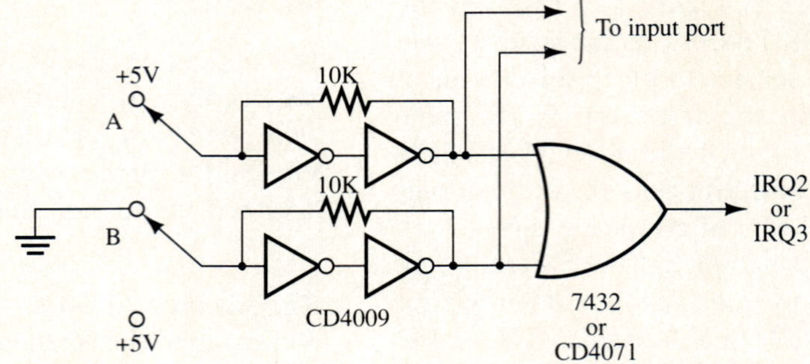

(a) Interfacing and debouncing

```
; This program uses the polled technique
; to determine which interrupt is requesting
; service.  Program uses IRQ3 input (type 11).

NAME        UPDOWN_POLLED

INCLUDE HEADER

_DATA       SEGMENT PUBLIC 'DATA'
  number  DW  0
_DATA       ENDS

_TEXT       SEGMENT PUBLIC 'CODE'
            ASSUME CS:_TEXT,DS:DGROUP,SS:DGROUP

  EXTRN _portset:NEAR,_isrset:NEAR,_ledbl:NEAR
  EXTRN _dipbl:NEAR

  _updown PROC NEAR
            call  _dipbl
            test  al,1        ; Check for A request
            jz    other       ; Jump if not A
            inc   number      ; Count up
            jmp   done
     other: test  al,2        ; Check for B request
            jz    done        ; Not B either
            dec   number      ; Count down
     done:  push  number
            call  _ledbl      ; Display
            add   sp,2
            mov   al,20h
            out   20h,al      ; EOI
            iret
  _updown ENDP

  main:     mov   ax,DGROUP
            mov   ds,ax
            call  _portset
            sti
            mov   ax,11
            push  ax
            push  cs
            mov   ax,OFFSET _updown
            push  ax
            call  _isrset
            add   sp,6
  self:     jmp   self   ; Wait for interrupt
_TEXT       ENDS
            END   main
```

(b) Software

FIGURE 17.6

Multiple interrupts—vectored technique. (a) Interfacing and debouncing. (b) Software.

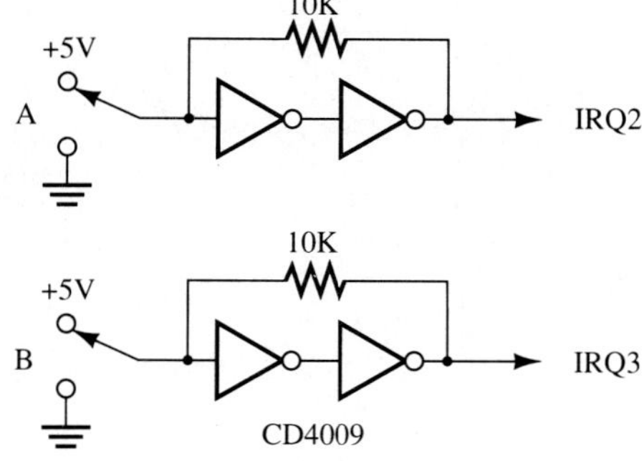

(a) Interfacing and debouncing

```
; This program uses the vectored technique
; to determine which interrupt is requesting
; service.  Program uses IRQ2 (type 10) and
; IRQ3 (type 11).

NAME        UPDOWN_VECTORED

INCLUDE HEADER

_DATA       SEGMENT PUBLIC 'DATA'
  number DW  ?
_DATA       ENDS

_TEXT       SEGMENT PUBLIC 'CODE'
            ASSUME CS:_TEXT,DS:DGROUP,SS:DGROUP

  EXTRN _portset:NEAR,_isrset:NEAR,_ledbl:NEAR

  _up PROC NEAR
            inc    number    ; Count up
            push   number
            call   _ledbl    ; Display
            add    sp,2
            mov    al,20h
            out    20h,al    ; EOI
            iret
  _up ENDP

  _down PROC NEAR
            dec    number     ; Count down
            push   number
            call   _ledbl
            add    sp,2       ; Display
            mov    al,20h
            out    20h,al     ; EOI
            iret
  _down ENDP

  main:     mov    ax,DGROUP
            mov    ds,ax
            call   _portset
            sti
            mov    ax,11
            push   ax
            push   cs
            mov    ax,OFFSET _up
            push   ax
            call   _isrset
            add    sp,6
            mov    ax,10
            push   ax
            push   cs
            mov    ax,OFFSET _down
            push   ax
            call   _isrset
            add    sp,6
   self:    jmp    self
_TEXT       ENDS
            END    main
```

(b) Software

ASSEMBLY-LANGUAGE PROGRAM

Multiple Interrupts

The scanned technique

3. Build the scanned technique interface circuit as shown in Figure 17.5(a).
4. Using the scanned technique, write a program in which the tone generated by the main program increases slightly for each A interrupt request, and decreases slightly for each B interrupt request.

ASSEMBLY-LANGUAGE PROGRAM

5. Does the tone pitch change as expected?

   ____

6. If both interrupt request inputs are activated simultaneously, does the tone increase or decrease?

   increase ____________

   decrease ____________

   Based on your answer, check the interrupt request that has priority:

   A ____________ B ____________

The vectored technique

7. Based on the hardware design of Figure 17.6(a), convert your system over to the vectored technique.
8. Repeat procedure step 4 using the vectored technique.

ASSEMBLY-LANGUAGE PROGRAM

9. Does the tone pitch change as expected?

   ____

10. Activate both interrupt inputs simultaneously and note the results. Why did the system respond in this manner?

Advanced Activity

11. Write program *multitasking* in which three independent tasks are handled simultaneously:
    a. Main-program task TONE, in which a tone is generated whose frequency increases proportionally as the value of an input byte goes down.
    b. Task COUNT, in which a display counts up by one for each activation of interrupt A.
    c. Task EXAMINE, in which the contents of successive memory locations (beginning from label *main* in the _TEXT segment) are displayed for each activation of interrupt B.

Name: ____________________

Date: ____________________

Class: ____________________

QUESTIONS AND PROBLEMS

1. What happens when $\overline{\text{INTA}}$ goes active low?

2. Referring to Figure 17.4, what is the purpose of writing 20h to port 20h?

3. When using the IBM PC, how is the correct interrupt vector placed in the interrupt vector table?

4. Referring to Figure 17.5(a), explain why interrupt A has priority over interrupt B.

5. Theoretically, how many interrupts can be serviced using the scanned technique? the vectored technique?

6. Why is the vectored technique generally faster than the scanned technique?

Advanced Section

7. Explain routine ISRSET of Figure 17.3.

8. What is the *daisy chain* technique of servicing multiple interrupts? How does it differ from the vectored and scanned techniques?

9. Why are software interrupts (rather than conventional calls) used for DOS calls?

10. Rewrite program UPDOWN_POLLED of Figure 17.5(b) so that function UPDOWN is independently assembled and stored in a library.

ACTIVITY 18

BIOS/DOS CALLS, KEYBOARD/VIDEO I/O, AND GRAPHICS

OBJECTIVE

- To use ROM-BIOS and DOS calls to perform keyboard, video, and graphics services.

PARTS AND EQUIPMENT

- IBM PC (bus-extender optional).
- Assembler, debugger, and utilities.

DISCUSSION

ROM-BIOS and DOS Calls

The MS-DOS operating system is composed of three layers: the BIOS (Basic-Input/Output System), the DOS kernel, and the command processor (shell). The most primitive parts of the BIOS are *resident* in ROM, and the remainder of the operating system is *installed* during bootup.

To avoid "reinventing the wheel," we can borrow the services of either the ROM-BIOS or DOS kernel by way of software interrupts. Keep in mind that these services are generally not available in a true embedded system (unless we use Intel's "wildcard" chip).

To call a ROM-BIOS or DOS service, we put the service number into AH and call either INT 10H (ROM_BIOS) or INT 21H (DOS). Depending on the service, additional registers may have to be initialized with parameters prior to the calls. (Activity 17 used DOS service 25H to set an interrupt vector.)

Of the numerous ROM-BIOS and DOS services available, we use the seven listed below for this and all future activities:

- ROM-BIOS (INT 10H), service 1: Set cursor size
  AH = 1H
  CH = top of cursor (0)
  CL = bottom of cursor (13 for monochrome, 7 for color)
- ROM-BIOS (INT 10H), service 2: Set cursor position
  AH = 2H
  DH = row number (0 to 79, top to bottom)
  DL = column number (0 to 24, left to right)
  BH = 0 (page number)
- DOS (INT 21H), service 1: Input ASCII character from keypad (to AL) and echo character to CRT.
  AH = 1 (AH = 8 for no echo)
- DOS (INT 21H), service 2: Display character to CRT.
  AH = 2
  DL = character to display in ASCII
- DOS (INT 21H), service 9: Output string to CRT.
  AH = 9
  DX = offset address of string in data segment
- DOS (INT 21H), service 11: Key pressed? Return 0 to AL if no key pressed; return nonzero otherwise.
  AH = 0BH
- DOS (INT 21H), service 12: Clear keyboard buffer, perform 1, 6, 7, 8, or 10.
  AH = 0CH
  AL = 1, 6, 7, 8, or 10

For a complete listing of the dozens of ROM-BIOS and DOS services that are available, consult the *IBM Disk Operating System Technical Reference Manual* or one of the numerous published books (such as the *Programmer's Guide to the IBM PC*, published by Microsoft Press).

Keyboard/Video I/O Functions

Making use of the seven ROM-BIOS/DOS services mentioned, we can write keyboard/video functions that include any combination of the following:

- Input or output?
- Character, byte, or string?
- Wait for keypress?

FIGURE 18.1

Keyboard/monitor I/O library routines using ROM-BIOS and DOS calls. (a) Procedure NEWLINE. (b) Procedure CLEAR. (c) Procedure SETCUR. (d) Function CURSIZE. (e) Function DUMP. (f) Function ASC2HEX. (g) Function KEYCHAR. (h) Function KEYTEST. (i) Function CRTCHAR. (j) Function KEYBHEX. (k) Function CRTBHEX. (l) Function KEYSTRNG. (m) Function CRTSTRNG. (n) Function KEYDIP. (o) Procedure SETUPSIM. (p) Function DIPBLSIM. (q) Function LEDBLSIM.

```
; Procedure NEWLINE performs a carriage return
; and line feed.  (The cursor is moved to the left
; of the monitor and down one line.)

NAME        NEWLINE

_TEXT       SEGMENT PUBLIC 'CODE'
            ASSUME CS:_TEXT

  PUBLIC _newline

  _newline PROC NEAR
            push  ax
            push  dx
            mov   dl,0dh         ; Ready CR
            mov   ah,2           ; Function 2
            int   21h            ; Carriage return
            mov   dl,0ah
            mov   ah,2
            int   21h            ; Line feed
            pop   dx
            pop   ax
            ret
  _newline  ENDP

_TEXT       ENDS
            END
```

(a) NEWLINE

```
; Procedure CLEAR clears the CRT
; screen by performing 50 line-
; feeds (in case the cursor is at
; the top of the screen).

NAME        CLEAR

_TEXT       SEGMENT PUBLIC 'CODE'
            ASSUME CS:_TEXT

  PUBLIC _clear

   _clear PROC NEAR
         push  ax
         push  cx
         push  dx
         mov   cx,50   ; 50 lines
         mov   ah,2    ; Service 2
         mov   dl,0ah  ; Line feed
  more:  int   21h     ; Clear line
         loop  more    ; 50 times
         pop   dx
         pop   cx
         pop   ax
         ret
   _clear ENDP

_TEXT       ENDS
            END
```

(b) CLEAR

```
; Procedure setcur accepts row and
; column parameters and sets the
; cursor.  (There are 24 rows and 80
; columns; row 0 and column 0 is at
; upper left of screen.)

NAME        SETCUR

_TEXT       SEGMENT PUBLIC 'CODE'
            ASSUME CS:_TEXT

  PUBLIC _setcur

  _setcur PROC NEAR
        push  bp
        mov   bp,sp
        push  ax
        push  bx
        push  dx
        mov   ah,2          ; Service 2
        mov   bh,0          ; Page 0
        mov   dh,[bp + 6]   ; Bring in row
        mov   dl,[bp + 4]   ; Bring in column
        int   10h           ; Move cursor
        pop   dx
        pop   bx
        pop   ax
        pop   bp
        ret
 _setcur  ENDP

_TEXT       ENDS
            END
```

(c) SETCUR

```
; Function CURSIZE sets the size of
; the cursor.  The first parameter sets
; the cursor top, the second the bottom.
; Both numbers are from 0 to 13 (monochrome)
; or 0 to 7 (color graphics).  To blank out
; cursor send both numbers > 7 or 13.

NAME        CURSIZE

DGROUP GROUP _DATA

_DATA       SEGMENT PUBLIC 'DATA'
_DATA       ENDS

_TEXT       SEGMENT PUBLIC 'CODE'
            ASSUME CS:_TEXT,DS:DGROUP

    PUBLIC _cursize

  _cursize PROC NEAR
          push  bp
          mov   bp,sp
          push  cx
          mov   ah,1          ; Service 1
          mov   ch,[bp + 6]   ; Top
          mov   cl,[bp + 4]   ; Bottom
          int   10h
          pop   cx
          pop   bp
          ret
  _cursize ENDP

_TEXT       ENDS
            END
```

(d) CURSIZE

FIGURE 18.1

(continued)

```
; Function DUMP clears the keyboard
; buffer.

NAME        DUMP

DGROUP GROUP _DATA

_DATA       SEGMENT PUBLIC 'DATA'
_DATA       ENDS

_TEXT       SEGMENT PUBLIC 'CODE'
            ASSUME CS:_TEXT,DS:DGROUP

  PUBLIC _dump

  _dump PROC NEAR
            push  ax
            push  dx
            mov   dl,0ffh        ; No output
            mov   ah,12          ; Service 12
            mov   al,6           ; Service 6
            int   21h            ; Input character
            pop   dx
            pop   ax
            ret
  _dump ENDP

_TEXT       ENDS
            END
```

(e) DUMP

```
; Function ASC2HEX accepts an ASCII character
; from 0 to F and returns its hexadecimal
; equivalent.

NAME        ASC2HEX

DGROUP GROUP _DATA

_DATA       SEGMENT PUBLIC 'DATA'
_DATA       ENDS

_TEXT       SEGMENT PUBLIC 'CODE'
            ASSUME CS:_TEXT,DS:DGROUP

  PUBLIC _asc2hex

  _asc2hex PROC NEAR
            push  bp
            mov   bp,sp
            pushf
            mov   al,[bp + 4]    ; Get ASCII char
            test  al,40h         ; Number or letter?
            jz    number         ; Jump if 0 to 9
            add   al,9           ; Convert letter to hex
  number:   and   al,0fh         ; Strip away ASCII
            popf
            pop   bp
            ret                  ; Return in AL
  _asc2hex ENDP

_TEXT       ENDS
            END
```

(f) ASC2HEX

```
; Function KEYCHAR returns a single ASCII
; character, echoes it to the screen, and
; isues a newline.  The function waits
; for a key to be pressed.  Ctrl-break
; is tested.

NAME        KEYCHAR

DGROUP GROUP _DATA

_DATA       SEGMENT PUBLIC 'DATA'
_DATA       ENDS

_TEXT       SEGMENT PUBLIC 'CODE'
            ASSUME CS:_TEXT,DS:DGROUP

  EXTRN _newline:NEAR
  PUBLIC _keychar

  _keychar PROC NEAR
            mov   ah,1           ; Service 1
            int   21h            ; Input character
            call  _newline       ; Newline
            ret                  ; Return in AL
  _keychar ENDP

_TEXT       ENDS
            END
```

(g) KEYCHAR

```
; Function KEYTEST returns zero if no
; keyboard input is available and returns
; non-zero otherwise.  If available, the
; character is not read. Ctrl-Break is
; tested.

NAME        KEYTEST

DGROUP GROUP _DATA

_DATA       SEGMENT PUBLIC 'DATA'
_DATA       ENDS

_TEXT       SEGMENT PUBLIC 'CODE'
            ASSUME CS:_TEXT,DS:DGROUP

  PUBLIC _keytest

  _keytest PROC NEAR
            push  bx             ; Protect BX
            mov   bx,0           ; Clear BX
            mov   ah,11          ; Function 11
            int   21h            ; Character ready?
            pop   bx
            ret
  _keytest ENDP

_TEXT       ENDS
            END
```

(h) KEYTEST

FIGURE 18.1

(continued)

```
; Function CRTCHAR accepts a byte parameter
; consisting of a single ASCII character
; and prints it to the screen at the cursor
; position.  The input character is returned
; (in AL) in case it is needed.

NAME        CRTCHAR

_TEXT       SEGMENT PUBLIC 'CODE'
            ASSUME CS:_TEXT

  PUBLIC _crtchar

  _crtchar PROC NEAR
            push  bp
            mov   bp,sp
            push  dx
            mov   al,[bp + 4]    ; Bring in 4-bit value
            mov   ah,2           ; Function 2
            mov   dl,al
            int   21h            ; Display
            pop   dx
            pop   bp
            ret
  _crtchar ENDP

_TEXT       ENDS
            END
```

(i) CRTCHAR

```
; Function KEYBHEX returns a packed byte consisting
; of two hexadecimal characters entered from the
; keyboard.  The function waits for each key to be
; pressed, with each hex character (0 - F) echoed
; to the screen as it is entered.  The first entry
; goes to the the high-order  bits and the second
; to the low-order bits.  Letter input (A - F) can
; be upper or lower case.  A newline is generated.
; Ctrl-Break is tested.

NAME        KEYBHEX

DGROUP GROUP _DATA

_DATA       SEGMENT PUBLIC 'DATA'
_DATA       ENDS

_TEXT       SEGMENT PUBLIC 'CODE'
            ASSUME CS:_TEXT,DS:DGROUP

  EXTRN _newline:NEAR
  PUBLIC _keybhex

  _keybhex PROC NEAR
            push  bx              ; Protect BX
            push  cx              ; Protect CX
            pushf
            mov   ah,1            ; Service 1
            int   21h             ; Input 1st character
            test  al,40h          ; Number or letter?
            jz    number1         ; Jump if 0 to 9
            add   al,9            ; Convert letter to hex
  number1:  and   al,0fh          ; Strip away ASCII
            mov   cl,4
            shl   al,cl           ; Move to high order
            mov   bl,al           ; Store in BL
            mov   ah,1            ; Service 1
            int   21h             ; Input 2nd character
            test  al,40h          ; Number or letter?
            jz    number2         ; Jump if 0 to 9
            add   al,9
  number2:  and   al,0fh          ; Strip away ASCII
            or    al,bl           ; Combine with 1st
            call  _newline        ; Newline
            popf
            pop   cx
            pop   bx
            ret                   ; Return in AL
  _keybhex ENDP

_TEXT       ENDS
            END
```

(j) KEYBHEX

FIGURE 18.1

(continued)

```
; Function CRTBHEX accepts a byte parameter of
; two packed hexadecimal characters from 0 to FH
; and prints them to the screen (high-order followed
; by low-order).  All letters (A - F) are printed in
; upper case.  The input byte is returned.

NAME        CRTBHEX

_TEXT       SEGMENT PUBLIC 'CODE'
            ASSUME CS:_TEXT

  PUBLIC _crtbhex

  _crtbhex PROC NEAR
            push  bp
            mov   bp,sp
            push  bx            ; Begin protection
            push  cx
            push  dx
            pushf
            mov   al,[bp + 4]   ; Bring in packed byte
            mov   bl,al         ; Copy to BL
            mov   cl,4
            shr   al,cl         ; Prepare upper
            and   bl,0fh        ; Prepare lower
            cmp   al,10         ; Upper number or letter?
            jb    number1       ; Jump if number
            sub   al,9          ; Convert to ASCII
            or    al,40h        ; Convert to ASCII
            jmp   over1
  number1:  or    al,30h        ; Convert to ASCII
  over1:    mov   ah,2          ; Function 2
            mov   dl,al         ; Upper ready
            int   21h           ; Show upper
            cmp   bl,10         ; Lower number or letter?
            jb    number2       ; Jump if number
            sub   bl,9          ; Convert to ASCII
            or    bl,40h        ; Convert to ASCII
            jmp   over2
  number2:  or    bl,30h        ; Convert to ASCII
  over2:    mov   ah,2          ; Function 2
            mov   dl,bl         ; Low-order ready
            int   21h           ; Show low-order
            mov   al,[bp + 4]   ; Return hex value
            popf                ; Begin restore
            pop   dx
            pop   cx
            pop   bx
            pop   bp
            ret
  _crtbhex  ENDP

_TEXT       ENDS
            END
```

(k) CRTBHEX

```
; Function KEYSTRNG accepts the address of a
; string location and places into the string
; a series of ASCII characters entered from
; the keyboard.  The function waits for each
; key to be pressed. When '$' is entered, the
; function returns to the calling routine. All
; characters are echoed to the screen as each
; key is pressed.  A newline is generated.
; Ctrl-break is tested.

NAME        KEYSTRNG

DGROUP GROUP _DATA

_DATA       SEGMENT PUBLIC 'DATA'
_DATA       ENDS

_TEXT       SEGMENT PUBLIC 'CODE'
            ASSUME CS:_TEXT,DS:DGROUP

  EXTRN    _newline:NEAR
  PUBLIC   _keystrng

  _keystrng PROC NEAR
            push  bp
            mov   bp,sp
            push  ax
            push  bx
            pushf
            mov   bx,[bp + 4]   ; Get address
            mov   ah,1          ; Set service
  again:    int   21h
            cmp   al,'$'        ; Done?
            je    over          ; If so, get out
            mov   [bx],al       ; Write to string
            inc   bx            ; Next element
            jmp   again         ; Keep going
  over:     mov   [bx],al       ; Store trailer
            call  _newline      ; Newline
            popf
            pop   bx
            pop   ax
            pop   bp
            ret
  _keystrng ENDP

_TEXT       ENDS
            END
```

(l) KEYSTRNG

FIGURE 18.1

(continued)

```
; Function CRTSTRNG accepts the address
; of an ASCII string and prints it to
; the CRT. The string must be terminated
; by '$'.

NAME        CRTSTRNG

DGROUP GROUP _DATA

_DATA       SEGMENT PUBLIC 'DATA'
_DATA       ENDS

_TEXT       SEGMENT PUBLIC 'CODE'
            ASSUME CS:_TEXT,DS:DGROUP

  PUBLIC    _crtstrng

  _crtstrng PROC NEAR
            push  bp
            mov   bp,sp
            push  ax
            push  dx
            mov   ah,9
            mov   dx,[bp + 4]
            int   21h
            pop   dx
            pop   ax
            pop   bp
            ret
  _crtstrng ENDP

_TEXT       ENDS
            END
```

(m) CRTSTRNG

```
; Function KEYDIP simulates a byte-wide DIP
; switch.   It returns a packed byte consisting
; of two hex characters entered from the keyboard.
; The first entry goes to the high-order bits and
; the second to the low-order bits.  If no keys
; have been pressed it does not wait, but returns
; the last sequence entered.  Letter input (A - F)
; can be upper or lower case.  The input characters
; are not echoed to the screen.  A newline is
; generated.  Ctrl-Break is tested.

NAME        KEYDIP

DGROUP GROUP _DATA

_DATA       SEGMENT PUBLIC 'DATA'
  storage  DB  ?
_DATA       ENDS

_TEXT       SEGMENT PUBLIC 'CODE'
            ASSUME CS:_TEXT,DS:DGROUP

  EXTRN  _newline:NEAR
  PUBLIC _keydip

  _keydip PROC NEAR
            push  bx               ; Protect BX
            push  cx               ; Protect CX
            pushf
            mov   bx,0             ; Clear bx
            mov   ah,11            ; Function 11
            int   21h              ; Character ready?
            or    al,0             ; Test AL
            jz    nochar           ; Jump if no character
            mov   ah,8             ; Function 8
            int   21h              ; Input 1st character
            test  al,40h           ; Number or letter?
            jz    number1          ; Jump if 0 to 9
            add   al,9             ; Convert to hex
  number1:  and   al,0fh           ; Strip away ASCII
            mov   cl,4
            shl   al,cl            ; Move to high order
            mov   bl,al            ; Store in BL
            mov   ah,8             ; Function 8
            int   21h              ; Input 2nd character
            test  al,40h           ; Number or letter?
            jz    number2          ; Jump if 0 to 9
            add   al,9
  number2:  and   al,0fh           ; Strip away ASCII
            or    al,bl            ; Combine with 1st
            mov   storage,al       ; Store away
  nochar:   mov   al,storage       ; Bring back
            call  _newline
            popf
            pop   cx
            pop   bx
            ret
  _keydip ENDP

_TEXT       ENDS
            END
```

(n) KEYDIP

FIGURE 18.1

(continued)

```
; Procedure SETUPSIM clears the screen, prints
; the header and screen-simulated ports, and blanks
; the cursor.  Run CURSIZE to return the cursor.

NAME        SETUPSIM

DGROUP GROUP _DATA

_DATA       SEGMENT PUBLIC 'DATA'
  header DB 'DIP/LED PORT SCREEN SIMULATOR$'
_DATA       ENDS

_TEXT       SEGMENT PUBLIC 'CODE'
            ASSUME CS:_TEXT,DS:DGROUP

  PUBLIC    _setupsim

  _setupsim PROC NEAR
            push  ax
            push  bx
            push  cx
            push  dx
            pushf
; Clear screen
            mov   cx,25
            mov   ah,02h
  more:     mov   dl,0ah    ; line feed
            int   21h
            loop  more
; Set cursor position
            mov   ah,2
            mov   dh,7
            mov   dl,23
            mov   bh,0
            int   10h
; Print header
            mov   ah,9
            mov   dx,OFFSET DGROUP:header
            int   21h
; Blank out cursor
            mov   ah,1
            mov   cl,0fh
            mov   ch,0fh
            int   10h
            popf
            pop   dx
            pop   cx
            pop   bx
            pop   ax
            ret
  _setupsim ENDP

_TEXT       ENDS
            END
```

(o) SETUPSIM

FIGURE 18.1

(*continued*)

```
; Screen simulation function DIPBLSIM allows
; input bits to be toggled according to
; pressing of "home" keys.  Input returned in
; al.  If no keys are pressed, it returns
; the previous value.  Ctrl-Break is tested.
; Pressing ESC restores the cursor.

NAME        DIPBLSIM

DGROUP GROUP _DATA

_DATA       SEGMENT PUBLIC 'DATA'
  dipvalue  db  ?
  d7d0      db  'D7                  D0$'
  portname  db  'DIPBL  $'
_DATA       ENDS

_TEXT       SEGMENT PUBLIC 'CODE'
            ASSUME CS:_TEXT,DS:DGROUP

  PUBLIC _dipblsim

  _dipblsim PROC NEAR
            push  bx
            push  cx
            push  dx
            pushf
; Set cursor position and print D7 to D0
            mov   ah,2
            mov   dh,10   ; row
            mov   dl,15   ; column
            mov   bh,0
            int   10h
            mov   ah,09h
            mov   dx,OFFSET DGROUP:d7d0
            int   21h
; Set cursor position and print DIPBL
            mov   ah,02h
            mov   dh,11
            mov   dl,8
            mov   bh,0
            int   10h
            mov   ah,09h
            mov   dx,offset DGROUP:portname
            int   21h
; Get bit character, if present
            mov   ah,0bh
            int   21h
            cmp   al,0
            je    over
            mov   ah,08h
            int   21h
; Test for restore cursor
            cmp   al,1bh
            jne   try8
            mov   ch,0
            mov   cl,13
            mov   ah,1
            int   10h
            jmp   over
; Set bit to toggle
  try8:     cmp   al,'a'
            jne   try7
            mov   ah,80h
            jmp   toggle
  try7:     cmp   al,'s'
            jne   try6
            mov   ah,40h
            jmp   toggle
  try6:     cmp   al,'d'
            jne   try5
            mov   ah,20h
            jmp   toggle
  try5:     cmp   al,'f'
            jne   try4
            mov   ah,10h
            jmp   toggle
  try4:     cmp   al,'j'
            jne   try3
            mov   ah,08h
            jmp   toggle
  try3:     cmp   al,'k'
            jne   try2
            mov   ah,04h
            jmp   toggle
  try2:     cmp   al,'l'
            jne   try1
            mov   ah,02h
            jmp   toggle
  try1:     cmp   al,';'
            jne   over
            mov   ah,01h
  toggle:   xor   dipvalue,ah
  over:     mov   al,dipvalue
; Display bits to CRT
            mov   cx,8
  more:     rol   al,1
            mov   dl,al
            and   dl,1
            add   dl,30h
            mov   ah,02h
            push  ax
            int   21h
            mov   dl,' '
            int   21h
            int   21h
            pop   ax
            loop  more
            popf
            pop   dx
            pop   cx
            pop   bx
            ret
  _dipblsim ENDP

_TEXT       ENDS
            END
```

(p) DIPBLSIM

FIGURE 18.1

(continued)

```
; Screen simulation function LEDBLSIM
; accepts a byte parameter and displays
; the value on the screen as a simulated
; row of LEDs.  Output value is returned
; in case it is needed.

NAME        LEDBLSIM

DGROUP GROUP _DATA

_DATA       SEGMENT PUBLIC 'DATA'
  D7D0  DB  'D7                  D0$'
  portname  DB  'LEDBL  $'
_DATA       ENDS

_TEXT       SEGMENT PUBLIC 'CODE'
            ASSUME CS:_TEXT,DS:DGROUP

   PUBLIC _ledblsim

   _ledblsim PROC NEAR
            push  bp
            mov   bp,sp
            push  bx
            push  cx
            push  dx
; Set cursor position and print D7 to D0
            mov   ah,2
            mov   dh,15    ; row
            mov   dl,15    ; column
            mov   bh,0
            int   10h
            mov   ah,09h
            mov   dx,OFFSET DGROUP:d7d0
            int   21h
; Set cursor position and print LEDBL string
            mov   ah,2
            mov   dh,16
            mov   dl,8
            mov   bh,0
            int   10h
            mov   ah,09h
            mov   dx,OFFSET DGROUP:portname
            int   21h
; Display bits to CRT
            mov   cx,8
            mov   al,[bp + 4]
   more:    rol   al,1
            mov   dl,al
            and   dl,1
            add   dl,30h
            mov   ah,02h
            push  ax
            int   21h
            mov   dl,' '
            int   21h
            int   21h
            pop   ax
            loop  more
            pop   dx
            pop   cx
            pop   bx
            pop   bp
            ret
  _ledblsim ENDP

_TEXT       ENDS
            END
```

(q) LEDBLSIM

- Hexadecimal, decimal, or ASCII?
- Dump the keyboard buffer?
- Echo to screen?
- Newline?
- Check Ctrl-Break?
- Remember last entry?
- Clear screen?
- Set cursor?
- Change cursor size?

From the hundreds of possibilities, we offer the 17 functions of Figure 18.1. The descriptions that come with each function describe the service performed. Note that the character and string functions process ASCII and the byte functions process hexadecimal. If none of the functions provides the exact service desired, the reader is always free to write new functions. Always remember, given the ability to nest, that new operations can make use of old operations in any way we wish. (Note that several of the functions nest function NEWLINE.)

The three programs of Figure 18.2 demonstrate the use of several of these I/O functions and are based on a simple input/delay/output loop algorithm. Figure 18.3 shows how the special screen-simulation functions [Figures 18.1(o), (p), and (q)] drive the monitor. Demonstration program PAINTBRUSH of Figure 18.4 uses a number of these functions to turn the screen into an artistic medium. (See Activity 16 for a discussion of the INCLUDE HEADER assembler directive.)

Graphics

Graphics refers to the ability to print characters, graphs, pictures, or images to the video display. There are two kinds of graphics display: *character graphics* and *bit-mapped graphics*.

Character graphics divides the screen into a number of rows and columns (typically 80 columns by 25 rows). At each row/column location an ASCII character is printed. Each character location corresponds to a word in video memory.

A bit-mapped graphics display divides the screen into a grid of small picture elements (dots) called *pixels*. For CGA (color graphics adapter) systems there are 320 columns by 200 rows, and for Hercules video systems there are 720 columns by 348 rows. Each column/row location specifies a single pixel, which corresponds to one or more bits in video memory (depending on the number of shades or colors).

To create an image using either method, we write appropriate data to the video memory—either directly, or indirectly by using special DOS or ROM-BIOS calls. The "image" in video memory is continually transferred to the video display by the video adapter, usually at the rate of 60 Hz.

Bit-mapped graphics provides greater resolution and flexibility and is clearly "the wave of the future." However, because bit-mapped graphics is quite complex and because there is no single standard in place for the software or hardware, in this introductory text we restrict ourselves to the simplest mode of operation: character graphics using DOS and ROM-BIOS calls. In a more advanced class, you may use bit-mapped graphics and direct memory access to write programs for use with an operating system that uses a GUI (graphics user interface), such as the popular *Windows* or *OS/2*.

PROCEDURE

1. Add the functions of Figure 18.1 to library MYLIB.
2. Write program DIAGONAL, which prints (as accurately as possible) a diagonal column of x's from upper left to lower right.

   ASSEMBLY-LANGUAGE PROGRAM

3. Modify program DIAGONAL to display a diagonal of whatever character is entered by way of the keypad. (A new diagonal is printed each time a new character is entered.)

   ASSEMBLY-LANGUAGE PROGRAM

FIGURE 18.2

Keyboard/monitor I/O demonstration routines. (a) Hex in, ASCII out. (b) String I/O. (c) Screen-simulation I/O.

```
; Input hex byte using DIP-simulation, delay
; one second, output its ASCII equivalent
; character.

NAME        HEX_TO_ASCII

INCLUDE  HEADER  <-------- See Activity 16

_DATA        SEGMENT PUBLIC 'DATA'
 delay DW 1000
_DATA        ENDS

_TEXT       SEGMENT PUBLIC 'CODE'
            ASSUME CS:_TEXT,DS:DGROUP,SS:DGROUP

    EXTRN _keydip:NEAR,_crtchar:NEAR,_newline:NEAR
    EXTRN _msec:NEAR

  main:     mov   ax,DGROUP
            mov   ds,ax
            nop
    again:  call  _keydip
            mov   bx,ax     ; Msec destroys ax
            push  delay
            call  _msec
            add   sp,2
            push  bx
            call  _crtchar
            add   sp,2
            call  _newline
            jmp   again
_TEXT       ENDS
            END   main
```

(a) Hex in, ASCII out

```
; Input ASCII string of characters (wait for
; each entry), delay one second, output ASCII
; string of characters.

NAME        STRING_IO

INCLUDE  HEADER

_DATA        SEGMENT PUBLIC 'DATA'
 mystring DB 30 DUP(?)
 delay    DW 1000
_DATA        ENDS

_TEXT       SEGMENT PUBLIC 'CODE'
            ASSUME CS:_TEXT,DS:DGROUP,SS:DGROUP

    EXTRN _keystrng:NEAR,_crtstrng:NEAR,_newline:NEAR
    EXTRN _msec:NEAR

  main:     mov   ax,DGROUP
            mov   ds,ax
            nop
    again:  mov   ax,OFFSET DGROUP:mystring
            push  ax
            call  _keystrng
            add   sp,2
            push  delay
            call  _msec
            add   sp,2
            mov   ax,OFFSET DGROUP:mystring
            push  ax
            call  _crtstrng
            add   sp,2
            call  _newline
            jmp   again
_TEXT       ENDS
            END   main
```

(b) String I/O

```
; Input binary byte from screen-simulated DIP,
; delay one second, output binary byte to
; screen-simulated LEDs.

NAME        SCREEN_SIMULATION_IO

INCLUDE  HEADER

_DATA        SEGMENT PUBLIC 'DATA'
 delay DW 1000
_DATA        ENDS

_TEXT       SEGMENT PUBLIC 'CODE'
            ASSUME CS:_TEXT,DS:DGROUP,SS:DGROUP

    EXTRN _setupsim:NEAR,_dipblsim:NEAR,_ledblsim:NEAR
    EXTRN _msec:NEAR

  main:     mov   ax,DGROUP
            mov   ds,ax
            nop
            call  _setupsim
    again:  call  _dipblsim
            mov   bx,ax     ; Msec destroys ax
            push  delay
            call  _msec
            add   sp,2
            push  bx
            call  _ledblsim
            add   sp,2
            jmp   again
_TEXT       ENDS
            END   main
```

(c) Screen-simulation I/O

4. Write a program that says, "Give me a hexadecimal number from 00 to 0FH" and it responds, "Its square is ⟨ ⟩H" (answer represented by brackets).

   ASSEMBLY-LANGUAGE PROGRAM

Advanced Activities

5. By nesting function CRTBHEX (twice), write function CRTWHEX. The output word is returned (in case it is needed).

   Using function CRTWHEX, write a program that inputs two hexadecimal bytes and outputs their hexadecimal product as a word.
6. Using nested loops, write a program that prints a Christmas tree to the screen.
7. Write a program that asks for a string of characters and (after the string is entered) reports the number of spaces in the string.

FIGURE 18.3

Screen simulation of DIP/LED binary ports.

```
                DIP/LED PORT SCREEN SIMULATOR

         D7              D0
DIPBL    0 0 0 1 0 0 1 1

         D7              D0
LEDBL    0 0 0 1 1 0 1 1
```

8. Write a program that emits a continuous series of beeps. The rest period between beeps is changed in real time by way of the keypad. (*Hint:* Make use of functions BEEP, MSEC, and KEYDIP.)
9. Modify program DIAGONAL of procedure step 2 to display continuously a single moving "x" along a diagonal. Each press of the "+" key increases the display speed; each press of the "−" key decreases the display speed. (*Hint:* A character is erased by writing a space to that location.)
10. Using nesting techniques, write library function BOX that draws a square on the screen. Routine BOX accepts parameters *row* and *col* (to position the box), *len* (the length of each side) and *char* (the character used to draw the box).

    Using routine BOX (and others as needed), write a main program that draws a series of boxes diagonally on the screen (one per second). Each new box is slightly larger than the previous box. The first box is drawn with the letter A, the second with B, etc.

    Modify the program to erase the box just before a new one is drawn.

FIGURE 18.4

Demonstration program PAINTBRUSH.

```
; Program PAINTBRUSH continuously asks for
; row and column numbers (in hex) and places
; an * at that location.

NAME        PAINTBRUSH

INCLUDE HEADER

_DATA       SEGMENT PUBLIC 'DATA'
  row       DB 'Give me a row number (2 to 17H): $'
  column    DB 'Now give me a column number (0 to 4FH): $'
  row_value DW ?
  col_value DW ?
_DATA       ENDS

_TEXT       SEGMENT PUBLIC 'CODE'
            ASSUME CS:_TEXT,DS:DGROUP,SS:DGROUP

  EXTRN _clear:NEAR,_newline:NEAR,_setcur:NEAR
  EXTRN _crtstrng:NEAR,_keybhex:NEAR,_crtchar:NEAR

  main:     mov   ax,DGROUP
            mov   ds,ax
            call  _clear     ; Clear screen
  again:    mov   ax,0
            push  ax
            push  ax
            call  _setcur    ; Cursor to upper left
            add   sp,4
            mov   ax,OFFSET DGROUP:row
            push  ax
            call  _crtstrng ; "Give me row"
            add   sp,2
            call  _keybhex
            mov   row_value,ax
            mov   ax,OFFSET DGROUP:column
            push  ax
            call  _crtstrng  ; "Give me column"
            add   sp,2
            call  _keybhex
            mov   col_value,ax
            push  row_value
            push  col_value
            call  _setcur
            add   sp,4
            mov   al,'*'      ; Paint '*'
            push  ax
            call  _crtchar
            add   sp,2
            jmp   again
_TEXT       ENDS
            END   main
```

Name: ______________________

Date: ______________________

Class: ______________________

QUESTIONS AND PROBLEMS

1. What row and column numbers point to approximately the center of the screen?

2. Referring to routine CLEAR of Figure 18.1(b), what does ASCII character 0AH accomplish?

3. What is the advantage of using ROM-BIOS and DOS calls?

Advanced Section

4. Which is at a "higher level," a ROM-BIOS call or a DOS call?

5. By nesting function NEWLINE, write function NEWLINES, which generates any number of newlines (0 to 255) as specified by a byte parameter.

6. By nesting functions KEYTEST and KEYCHAR, write function KYTSTCH, which returns a zero if no character is waiting, but returns the character otherwise. (Will the use of DOS service 6 perform the same function?)

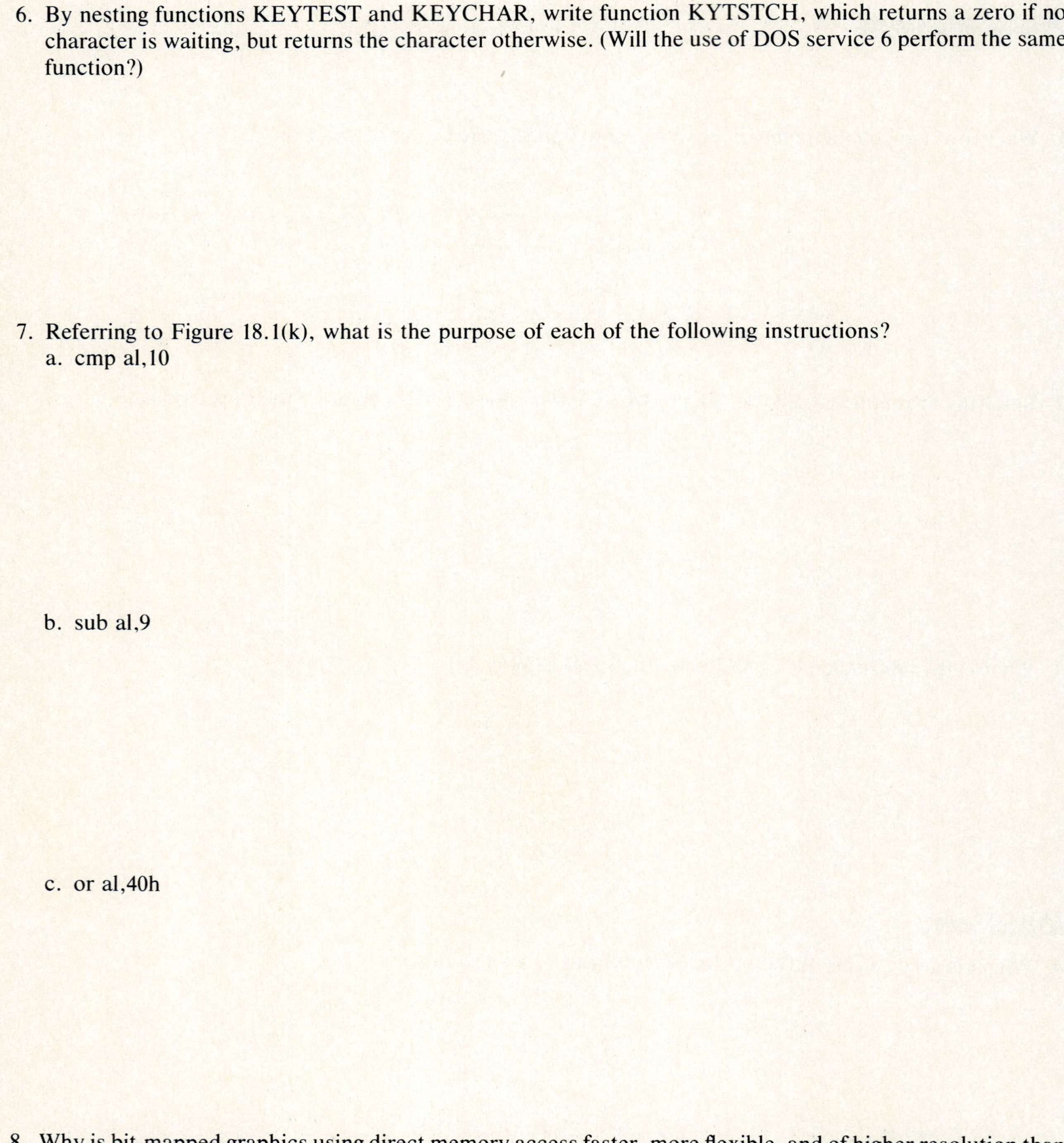

7. Referring to Figure 18.1(k), what is the purpose of each of the following instructions?
   a. cmp al,10

   b. sub al,9

   c. or al,40h

8. Why is bit-mapped graphics using direct memory access faster, more flexible, and of higher resolution than character-mapped graphics using ROM-BIOS/DOS calls?

PART VI

MORE ADVANCED MATHEMATICS

The computer that guided us to the moon had to perform a variety of mathematical operations: Process large distances, manipulate negative and positive velocities, drive decimal readouts, and perform calculations rapidly and accurately. In the four activities of Part VI, we see how the computer fulfills its mission and manipulates numbers in BCD and ASCII, processes large magnitude numbers, makes decisions based on signed numbers, and uses an 8087 math coprocessor to improve computational speed and accuracy drastically.

ACTIVITY 19

BCD AND ASCII ARITHMETIC

OBJECTIVE

- To perform mathematical operations on BCD and ASCII numbers.

PARTS AND EQUIPMENT

- IBM PC (bus-extender optional).
- Assembler, debugger, and utilities.

DISCUSSION

Computers operate on binary bits, while humans prefer decimal numbers and symbolic letters. To satisfy both, *binary coded decimal* (BCD) and *American Standard Code for Information Interchange* (ASCII) were developed. To process BCD and ASCII values, we use the standard arithmetic instructions designed for binary, but *adjust* the values to maintain the BCD or ASCII formats.

The following *adjust* instructions are used in BCD and ASCII arithmetic:

DAA	Decimal adjust for addition
DAS	Decimal adjust for subtraction
AAM	ASCII adjust for multiply
AAD	ASCII adjust for division
AAA	ASCII adjust for addition
AAS	ASCII adjust for subtraction

In all cases, we must take great care to ensure that all numbers are in the correct *packed* or *unpacked* and byte or word format, and that all numbers to be adjusted are in the accumulator.

- A *packed* BCD number contains two decimal digits per byte.
- An *unpacked* BCD or ASCII number contains one decimal digit per byte.

BCD and ASCII Functions

The functions of Figure 19.1 give us the ability to add, subtract, multiply, and divide using BCD numbers. The DAA, DAS, and AAM instructions adjust the result of a binary operation to BCD *after* adding, subtracting, or multiplying; the AAD instruction, on the other hand, is used *before* a binary division to preadjust a BCD number to binary. All the functions return BCD except DIVBCD, which returns a binary number. Note that addition and subtraction use a packed format, while multiplication and division require an unpacked format.

Figure 19.2 shows how the DAA instruction adjusts the binary addition of two BCD numbers back to BCD.

The ASCII numbers range from 30H through 39H and represent the numbers 0 through 9 (see Appendix H). All ASCII numbers are automatically in unpacked format. The functions of Figure 19.3 show us how to add and subtract using ASCII numbers. The AAA and AAS instructions operate on the results of adding and subtracting ASCII numbers, but generate BCD—which is converted back to ASCII by ORing (or adding) the 30H ASCII code bits. To multiply and divide in ASCII, we use BCD methods and simply strip away and add back the ASCII code bits as needed.

PROCEDURE

NOTE: Use the input and display means of your choice. Activity 18 functions KEYBHEX and CRTBHEX can be used for BCD I/O as well as hexadecimal I/O.

BCD

1. Using function ADDBCD, write a program that counts up in BCD from 0 to 95 *by fives* at the rate of approximately 2 Hz.

FIGURE 19.1

The BCD math library routines. (a) Function ADDBCD. (b) Function SUBBCD. (c) Function MULBCD. (d) Function DIVBCD.

```
; Function _addbcd accepts two packed
; BCD bytes as parameters.  After adding,
; the result is adjusted back to BCD with
; DAA.  The answer is returned as a packed
; BCD number in the AL register (AH = 0).
; A carry will set the CF flag.

NAME        ADDBCD

_TEXT       SEGMENT PUBLIC 'CODE'
            ASSUME CS:_TEXT

   PUBLIC _addbcd

   _addbcd PROC NEAR
            push  bp
            mov   bp,sp
            mov   al,[bp + 4]
            add   al,[bp + 6]
            daa
            mov   ah,0
            pop   bp
            ret
    _addbcd ENDP

_TEXT       ENDS
            END
```

(a) ADDBCD.ASM

```
; Function _subbcd accepts two packed BCD bytes
; as parameters.  After subtracting the second
; parameter from the first, the result is adjusted
; back to BCD with DAS. The answer is returned as
; a packed BCD number in the AL register (AH = 0).
; A borrow will set the CF flag.

NAME        SUBBCD

_TEXT       SEGMENT PUBLIC 'CODE'
            ASSUME CS:_TEXT

  PUBLIC _subbcd

  _subbcd PROC NEAR
            push  bp
            mov   bp,sp
            mov   al,[bp + 6] ; Input 1st packed BCD
            sub   al,[bp + 4] ; Subtract 2nd packed BCD
            das               ; Adjust to BCD
            mov   ah,0        ; Clear AH
            pop   bp
            ret               ; Ans packed BCD in AL
  _subbcd ENDP

_TEXT       ENDS
            END
```

(b) SUBBCD.ASM

```
; Function _mulbcd accepts two unpacked BCD bytes as
; parameters. After multiplying, the result goes to
; AH and AL.  The AAM instruction adjusts the
; result back to BCD.  Answer is returned as two
; unpacked BCD digits in AH and AL.  CY and OF flags
; set if product > 255.

NAME        MULBCD

_TEXT       SEGMENT PUBLIC 'CODE'
            ASSUME CS:_TEXT

   PUBLIC _mulbcd

   _mulbcd PROC NEAR
            push  bp
            mov   bp,sp
            mov   al,[bp + 4]          ; Input unpacked BCD
            mul   BYTE PTR[bp + 6]     ; Multiply
            aam                        ; Adjust back to BCD
            pop   bp
            ret                        ; Answer in AH/AL
   _mulbcd ENDP

_TEXT       ENDS
            END
```

(c) MULBCD.ASM

```
; Function _divbcd accepts the first parameter as the
; dividend (two-digit unpacked BCD number in AH and AL),
; and the second parameter (single-digit unpacked BCD)
; as the divisor.  The AAD instruction adjusts the
; dividend to binary.  The single-digit binary unpacked
; quotient will be returned in AL, remainder in AH.

NAME        DIVBCD

_TEXT       SEGMENT PUBLIC 'CODE'
            ASSUME CS:_TEXT

   PUBLIC _divbcd

   _divbcd PROC NEAR
            push  bp
            mov   bp,sp
            pushf
            mov   ax,[bp + 6]          ; Bring in dividend
            aad                        ; Adjust to binary
            div   BYTE PTR[bp + 4]     ; Divide
            popf
            pop   bp
            ret                        ; Answer in AH/AL
   _divbcd ENDP

_TEXT       ENDS
            END
```

(d) DIVBCD.ASM

FIGURE 19.2

Demonstration of the DAA process.

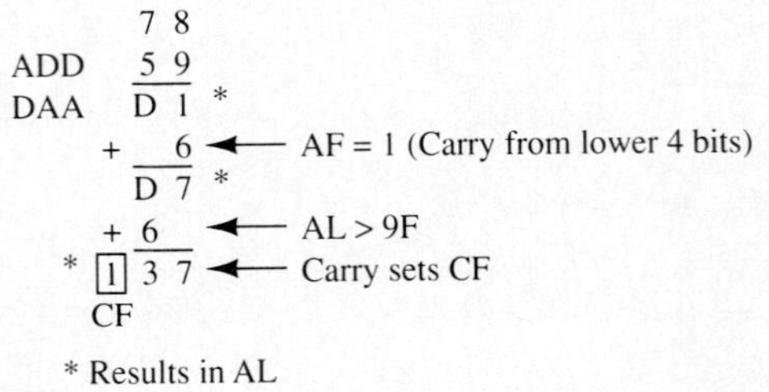

```
         7 8
ADD      5 9
DAA      D 1  *
     +     6  <--- AF = 1 (Carry from lower 4 bits)
         D 7  *
     +   6    <--- AL > 9F
   * [1] 3 7  <--- Carry sets CF
     CF

   * Results in AL
```

FIGURE 19.3

The ASCII math library routines. (a) Function ADDASC. (b) Function SUBASC.

```
; Function _addasc accepts two parameters: a word
; followed by a byte, both in unpacked ASCII format.
; After adding, the result is placed in AX and adjusted
; to BCD with AAA.  AH is incremented if a carry is
; generated.  We OR the result with 3030H to re-generate
; ASCII.  The answer is returned as a word (two unpacked
; ASCII numbers) in AX.

NAME        ADDASC

_TEXT       SEGMENT PUBLIC 'CODE'
            ASSUME CS:_TEXT

  PUBLIC _addasc

  _addasc PROC NEAR
            push  bp
            mov   bp,sp
            mov   ax,[bp + 6] ; 1st unpacked ASCII word
            add   al,[bp + 4] ; Add to 2nd unpacked ASCII
            aaa               ; Adjust to BCD
            or    ax,3030h    ; Return to ASCII
            pop   bp
            ret               ; Two unpacked ASCII in AX
  _addasc ENDP

_TEXT       ENDS
            END
```

(a) ADDASC.ASM

```
; Function _subasc accepts two parameters: a word
; followed by a byte, both in unpacked ASCII format.
; After subtracting the byte from the word, the result
; is placed in AX and adjusted to BCD with AAS.  AH is
; decremented if a borrow is needed.  We OR the result
; with 30H to re-generate ASCII.  The answer is returned
; as a word (two unpacked ASCII numbers) in AX.

NAME        SUBASC

_TEXT       SEGMENT PUBLIC 'CODE'
            ASSUME CS:_TEXT

  PUBLIC _subasc

  _subasc PROC NEAR
            push  bp
            mov   bp,sp
            mov   ax,[bp + 6] ; 1st unpacked ASCII word
            sub   al,[bp + 4] ; Subtract 2nd unpacked ASCII
            aas               ; Adjust to BCD
            or    al,30h      ; Return to ASCII
            pop   bp
            ret               ; Two unpacked ASCII in AX
  _subasc ENDP

_TEXT       ENDS
            END
```

(b) SUBASC.ASM

ASSEMBLY-LANGUAGE PROGRAM

2. Write a program that inputs two BCD bytes (0 to 9) and outputs their product as a word. If the product is ten or greater, a beep is sounded.

ASSEMBLY-LANGUAGE PROGRAM

ASCII

3. Write a program that calculates the sum of the elements of the following ASCII array, *peaches*. The result will be displayed as a two-digit ASCII number.

```
peaches DB 32H, 37H, 33H
        DB 31H, 35H, 39H
```

ASSEMBLY-LANGUAGE PROGRAM

Advanced Activities

4. Write a program that uses the equation given below to calculate the power dissipated in a resistor. The voltage (V) and resistance (R) are input as BCD characters from 0 to 9, and the output is a word BCD character from 0 to 9 (quotient in low-order byte, remainder in high-order byte). Do not divide by zero.

$$P = V^2/R$$

5. Write a program that calculates the *average* value of the elements of the following BCD array, *scores*. The result will be displayed as a BCD number (quotient in low-order, remainder in high-order). (*Remember:* ADDBCD works on packed BCD, and DIVBCD works on unpacked BCD.)

```
scores DB 4, 3, 7, 5, 2, 6
```

6. Write a program that inputs a single-digit ASCII byte (30 to 39) and displays its square as a two-digit ASCII number.

Name: ______________________

Date: ______________________

QUESTIONS AND PROBLEMS

Class: ______________________

1. Using packed BCD, what is the largest BCD number that can be stored in a word location? when using unpacked BCD?

2. BCD number 27 is what in hexadecimal?

3. Assume that BCD number 89 (10001001) is to be subtracted from BCD number 52 (01010010). Following the operation sequence listed below for the DAS instruction, show step by step how the result of the binary subtraction is adjusted back to BCD. (The AF flag detects overflows from bit D3 to D4.)

```
if ((AL) & 0FH) > 9 or (AF) = 1 then
    (AL) = (AL) - 6
    (AF) = 1
if (AL) > 9FH or (CF) = 1 then
    (AL) = (AL) - 60H
    (CF) = 1
```

4. What single instruction would convert an ASCII digit in the AL register to unpacked BCD?

5. Does function DIVBCD return a BCD or a binary number?

Advanced Section

6. Show how to subtract 32 from 87 using the tens-complement (nines complement + 1) process.

ACTIVITY 20

MULTIPLE PRECISION/ CODE CONVERSION

OBJECTIVES

- To perform multiple-precision mathematical operations.
- To convert between binary and BCD.

PARTS AND EQUIPMENT

- IBM PC (bus-extender optional).
- Assembler, debugger, and utilities.

DISCUSSION

Multiple-Precision Addition and Subtraction

Multiple-precision numbers are those requiring more than one word for storage. Using the special add-with-carry (ADC) and subtract-with-borrow (SBB) instructions, we can add and subtract multiprecision numbers.

Looking at the demonstration program of Figure 20.1, we see that multiprecision numbers are arranged as arrays. By processing the arrays from right to left, the numbers can be listed in normal order.

Code Conversions

Code conversion is the process of switching between number systems. To convert between binary (hexadecimal) and decimal (BCD), we write conversion algorithms. For example, function BCD2HEX uses the following equation to convert a packed BCD number to its hexadecimal equivalent:

```
Hexadecimal = (MSD * 10) + (LSD * 1)
```

where MSD = most-significant-digit and LSD = least-significant-digit. Figure 20.2(a) shows the BCD2HEX process in flowchart form.

PROCEDURE

NOTE: Examine memory for answers to multiprecision programs.

Multiple Precision

1. The distance to the moon is 240,000 (03A980H) miles and is stored in array *miles_to_moon*. According to array *miles_traveled,* we have already traveled 154,000 (025990H) miles. Write a program that returns the distance remaining (014FF0H) to array *miles_togo*.

   ASSEMBLY-LANGUAGE PROGRAM

2. By adding a single instruction to the multiprecision subtraction program of procedure step 1 repeat the calculation using BCD numbers (for both input and result).

   ASSEMBLY-LANGUAGE PROGRAM

FIGURE 20.1

Multiprecision addition.

```
; This program adds two multiprecision numbers
; of any byte length.  The numbers are written
; as byte arrays PEACHES and CREAM, with the MSB
; stored first.  The answer is placed in byte
; array DESERT.
;
; Specifically, this program adds the following
; 3-byte multiprecision numbers:

;         309719H
;       + 227681H
;       -----------
;         530D9AH

NAME        MULTI_PRECISION_ADDITION

INCLUDE HEADER

_DATA       SEGMENT PUBLIC 'DATA'
  peaches   DB  30H, 97H, 19H            ; 1st number
  cream     DB  22H, 76H, 81H            ; 2nd number
  desert    DB  3 DUP(?)
_DATA       ENDS

_TEXT       SEGMENT PUBLIC 'CODE'
            ASSUME  CS:_TEXT,DS:DGROUP,SS:DGROUP

  main:     mov   ax,DGROUP
            mov   ds,ax
            mov   cx,3
            mov   bx,cx                  ; Start at right
            dec   bx                     ; Relative to 0
            clc                          ; Clear carry flag
  here:     mov   al,peaches[bx]
            adc   al,cream[bx]           ; Add next bytes
            mov   desert[bx],al          ; Store in DESERT
            dec   bx                     ; Next byte
            loop  here                   ; Done?
            hlt                          ; Answer in DESERT
_TEXT       ENDS
            END   main
```

Code Conversion

3. Using the conversion algorithm given in the discussion [and referring to Figure 20.2(a)], write function BCD2HEX, which receives a packed BCD byte (from 0 to 99) and returns its 8-bit hexadecimal equivalent. (Store in library MYLIB.)

   LIBRARY ROUTINE BCD2HEX

4. Based on the conversion rules listed below [and referring to Figure 20.2(b)], write function HEX2BCD, which receives an 8-bit hexadecimal number and returns its packed BCD equivalent (a byte from 0 to 99). Store in library MYLIB.

   ```
   BCD (high-order) = hexadecimal/10
   BCD (low-order) = remainder
   ```

   LIBRARY ROUTINE HEX2BCD

5. Write a program that performs the following:
   - Inputs two decimal (BCD) bytes.
   - Converts each to hexadecimal.
   - Adds them together.
   - Converts the sum to decimal (BCD).
   - Outputs the result.

   ASSEMBLY-LANGUAGE PROGRAM

6. By nesting functions KEYBHEX and BCD-2HEX, write function KEYBDEC, which inputs a decimal (BCD) byte and returns its value in hexadecimal.

   By nesting functions HEX2BCD and CRT-BHEX, write function CRTBDEC, which accepts a hexadecimal byte parameter and outputs its decimal (BCD) equivalent. The output parameter is returned.

   Using functions KEYBDEC and CRTBDEC, write a program that inputs a decimal (BCD) number from 0 to 15 and outputs its square in decimal.

   ASSEMBLY-LANGUAGE PROGRAM

FIGURE 20.2

Conversion algorithm flowcharts. (a) BCD2HEX. (b) HEX2BCD.

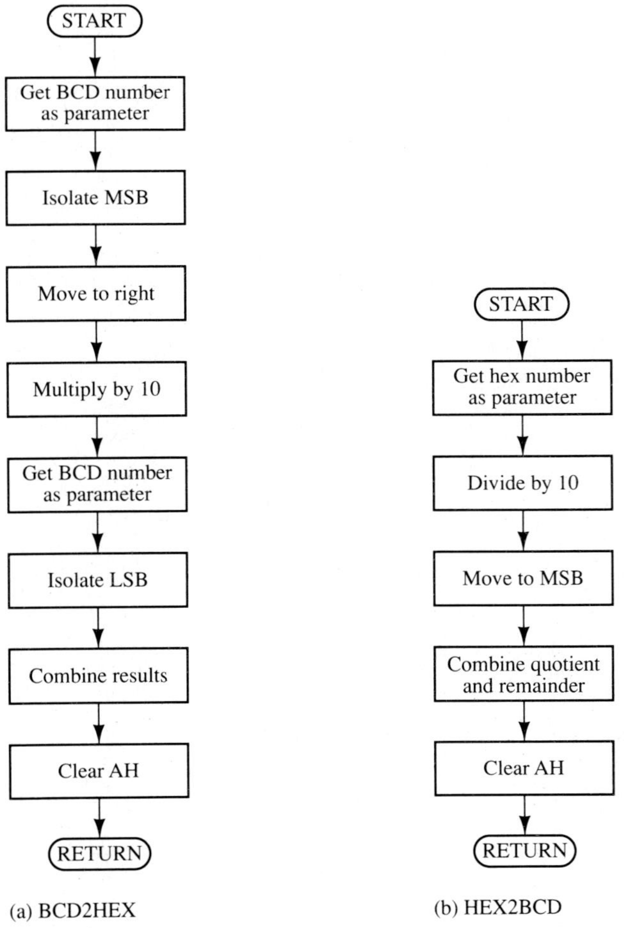

Advanced Activities

7. A museum is buying a number of rare jewels at an auction. BCD array this_jewel holds the cost of a rare diamond ($1,430,600); BCD array *subtotal* holds the total money spent so far ($6,880,720). Making use of the LODS and STOS string instructions, write a program that adds the cost of this_jewel to *subtotal* and generates the new larger *subtotal*. (*Remember:* Array *subtotal* will be in the EXTRA segment.)
8. Write a program that performs the following multiprecision multiplication on byte arrays *multiplicand* (three elements) and *multiplier* (one element). Array *product* (four elements) holds the answer. (All input and output arrays are in hexadecimal.)

multiplicand	013040H	(77,888)
× *multiplier*	0AH	(10)
product	000BE280H	(778,880)

9. Write function HEX2BCDW, which accepts a hexadecimal word parameter and returns its decimal (BCD) equivalent.

   By nesting functions HEX2BCDW and CRTWHEX, write function CRTWDEC, which accepts a word parameter in hexadecimal and outputs its decimal equivalent. The input parameter is returned.

   Using function CRTWDEC, rewrite the program of step 6 to accept numbers from 0 to 255.

Name: ______________________

Date: ______________________

QUESTIONS AND PROBLEMS

Class: ______________________

1. How large can an unsigned triple-precision (3-byte) number be (exclude the CARRY flag)?

2. What changes would enable the program of Figure 20.1 to add word arrays rather than byte arrays?

Advanced Section

3. Why is an 8087 math coprocessor desirable when performing multiprecision multiplication and division? (The 8087 is covered in Activity 22.)

4. What is a *floating point* (real) number?

ACTIVITY 21

ADVANCED SIGNED-NUMBER OPERATIONS

OBJECTIVES

- To write programs using the *integer* multiply and divide instructions.
- To write programs using the signed-number conditional-jump instructions.

PARTS AND EQUIPMENT

- IBM PC (bus-extender optional).
- Assembler, Debugger, and utilities.

DISCUSSION

Integer Multiply and Divide

The *add, subtract,* and *arithmetic shift* instructions work on both signed and unsigned bytes and words. The *multiply* and *divide* instructions do not. To multiply and divide signed numbers, we use the special *integer* instructions (IMUL and IDIV). As always, if the dividend is a byte, it is extended throughout AX by clearing AH if unsigned and using CBW if signed.

Demonstration program REAL_POWER of Figure 21.1 uses the equation

$$P = V^2/4$$

to calculate the power developed in a 4-ohm (Ω) resistor. Since the voltage can be negative as well as positive (a signed number), we must use the special IMUL instruction. (Why can the division be unsigned?)

The Signed-Number Conditional Jumps

The 8086/88 includes the *sign* and *overflow* flags. After an arithmetic or logical operation, the sign flag (SF) is set to the sign bit of the result, and the overflow flag (OF) detects a signed-number overflow. When combined with the conventional flags (CF, AF, and ZF), these five flags tell us about the results of signed-number operations.

The special conditional-jump instructions listed below examine the flag combinations generated by signed-number operations, and branch accordingly.

JG/JNLE	Jump on greater/jump on not less or equal
JGE/JNL	Jump on greater or equal/jump on not less
JL/JNGE	Jump on less/jump on not greater or equal
JLE/JNG	Jump on less or equal/jump on not greater
JNO	Jump on not overflow
JNS	Jump on not sign
JO	Jump on overflow
JS	Jump on sign

The demonstration program of Figure 21.2 samples the outside temperature. If the temperature is below −40, it is considered dangerous and a warning (''DANGER, it's too cold'') is given. Otherwise, the program returns ''Safe to go outside.''

Signed Magnitude Convention

To make the entry and display of signed numbers easier, we can use the *signed-magnitude* convention in which the magnitude is always stored in the true form. The conversion between signed numbers and signed-magnitude numbers is handled by software. Figure 21.3 compares several integers written in both signed and signed-magnitude format.

FIGURE 21.1

Integer multiplication.

```
; Program REAL_POWER inputs the voltage
; as a signed hex byte from -10 to +10 and
; outputs the power across a 4 ohm
; resister as a byte between 0 and 25
; watts.  (The division remainder is
; ignored.)

NAME        REAL_POWER

INCLUDE HEADER

_DATA       SEGMENT PUBLIC 'DATA'
  four  DB  4
_DATA       ENDS

_TEXT       SEGMENT PUBLIC 'CODE'
            ASSUME  CS:_TEXT,DS:DGROUP,SS:DGROUP

  EXTRN  _keybhex:NEAR,_crtbhex:NEAR
  EXTRN  _newline:NEAR

  main:     mov   ax,DGROUP
            mov   ds,ax
  again:    call  _keybhex   ; Input V as signed num
            imul  al         ; P = Vsquared/1
            div   four
            push  ax         ; Send parameter
            call  _crtbhex   ; Display power
            add   sp,2       ; Clean up stock
            call  _newline   ; Newline
            jmp   again
_TEXT       ENDS
            END   main
```

PROCEDURE

Integer Multiply and Divide

1. Using the equation below, write a program that displays the proper Fahrenheit temperature when both positive and negative centigrade temperatures are entered. (Limit the Fahrenheit output to the $-128/+127$ range.)

$$F = 9 * C / 5 + 32$$

ASSEMBLY-LANGUAGE PROGRAM

FIGURE 21.2

Signed-number conditional branching.

```
; For testing purposes, use the following
; relationships:

;    -39 = D9H
;    -40 = D8H     Danger point
;    -41 = D7H

NAME        FROST_BITE_WARNING

INCLUDE HEADER

_DATA       SEGMENT PUBLIC 'DATA'
  enter  DB 'Enter the temperature: $'
  safe   DB 'Safe to go outside$'
  danger DB 'DANGER, it''s too cold$'
_DATA       ENDS

_TEXT       SEGMENT PUBLIC 'CODE'
            ASSUME  CS:_TEXT,DS:DGROUP,SS:DGROUP

  EXTRN  _keybhex:NEAR,_crtstrng:NEAR,_newline:NEAR

  main:     mov   ax,DGROUP
            mov   ds,ax
  again:    call  _newline
            mov   ax,OFFSET DGROUP:enter
            push  ax
            call  _crtstrng
            add   sp,2
            call  _keybhex    ; Get temperature
            cmp   al,-40      ; Too cold?
            jl    over        ; Skip if < -40
            mov   ax,OFFSET DGROUP:safe
            push  ax
            call  _crtstrng
            add   sp,2
            call  _newline
            jmp   again
  over:     mov   ax,OFFSET DGROUP:danger
            push  ax
            call  _crtstrng
            add   sp,2
            call  _newline
            jmp   again
_TEXT       ENDS
            END   main
```

Signed-Number Decision-Making

2. Write a program that scans array *eagle* (shown below) and converts all elements to their absolute values. (All positive elements remain unchanged; all negative elements change sign.)

```
eagle DB 10, -15, 22, -9, -4, 13
```

FIGURE 21.3

The signed-magnitude convention.

Number	Signed	Signed-magnitude
+5	00000101	00000101
-5	11111011	10000101
+7	00000111	00000111
-7	11111001	10000111

ASSEMBLY-LANGUAGE PROGRAM

3. Write a program that scans the elements of word array *checking* (shown below) and displays the number of accounts that are overdrawn by more than 100 dollars.

```
checking DW -100, -180, 1125, -778
         DW -50, 47, -103
```

ASSEMBLY-LANGUAGE PROGRAM

Advanced Activities

4. Using the integer-divide (IDIV) instruction, write a program that gives the Y output for every X input from -128 to $+127$ in the equation below:

$$XY = -100$$

   Using your program, plot a graph of X versus Y. (Do not divide by zero).

5. Write a program that inputs 2 bytes in signed-magnitude convention (-128 to $+127$) and outputs their word product (also a signed-magnitude number).
6. Array *par* holds the par scores for nine holes of golf. Array *score* holds the actual scores for a round of play. Write a program that outputs the number of holes in which we came within one of par (par, par + 1, or par − 1).

Name: ________________

Date: ________________

Class: ________________

QUESTIONS AND PROBLEMS

1. Performing a twos-complement twice in a row has what result?

2. What results if you take the twos-complement of zero?

3. How do we sign a double-precision number?

4. How does the sign flag distinguish between positive and negative numbers?

5. What condition causes the overflow flag (OF) to set?

6. What is an integer?

7. Given the instruction sequence below, what range of bytes in AL will cause a branch?

```
cmp  al,-13
jnle branch
```

8. Given the instruction sequence below, under what conditions will there be a branch?

```
add  al,apples
jno  branch
```

Advanced Section

9. Explain how the Boolean equation below determines the JG (jump on greater) condition:

```
((SF XOR OF) OR ZF) = 0
```

ACTIVITY 22

THE 8087 MATH COPROCESSOR

OBJECTIVE

- To write programs that use the instructions of the 8087 math coprocessor.

PARTS AND EQUIPMENT

- IBM PC with installed 8087 math coprocessor (bus-extender optional).
- Assembler, debugger, and utilities.

DISCUSSION

The 8087 math coprocessor of Figure 22.1 works in tandem with the 8086/88 to perform calculations on integers, real numbers, and BCD numbers many times faster than the 8086/88 alone (see Figure 22.2).

A typical arithmetic calculation follows a three-step sequence:

1. Variables and data are loaded from system memory to internal 8087 registers.
2. The data are processed within the 8087.
3. The result is stored back in memory.

8087 Operation

Both the 8086/88 and the 8087 fetch instructions in parallel, but only one processor will execute a given instruction. As diagrammed by Figure 22.3, the 8087 recognizes its instructions by looking for an "ESC" prefix. Activity between the 8086/88 and 8087 is coordinated by both hardware and software. *Request/grant* handshaking signals arbitrate the use of the bus, and the WAIT instruction monitors the 8087 (via the TEST input) to determine when the result of its calculation is available. (WAIT instructions are automatically inserted before each 8087 instruction by the assembler).

Coprocessor Data Registers

From the programmer's standpoint, the 8087 looks like the 80-bit register set of Figure 22.4. The operation of the eight registers is unconventional because they function like a stack. Data loaded (pushed) onto the stack always go to the top of the stack [the ST(0) position] and previous data are pushed down. When an operation is finished, data are often popped off the ST(0) position and all other data moved up. [Register ST(0) is abbreviated as ST.]

Within the 8087, data are always stored and processed in the 10-byte IEEE *temporary-real* format listed at the bottom of Figure 22.5(a). However, the original data and the result returned to and stored in main memory can be in any of the formats listed. When data are transferred between main memory and 8087 internal stack registers, they are automatically converted to the appropriate format. (Figure 22.5(b) gives the range of each data type.)

As shown in Figure 22.6, the 8087 contains a control register to set the mode of operation and a status register to hold exception (error) flags, condition codes, and interrupt data. In our case, the default values set in the control register are sufficient and this register can be ignored by the programmer.

The 8087 Instruction Set

The 8087 instruction set of Figure 22.7 includes a rich variety of move, arithmetic, control, and comparison instructions. All operations involve signed numbers only. Note that all 8087 instructions begin with an "F."

The comparison and test instructions deserve special mention because they perform decision-making in a highly "cooperative" manner. The process begins with an 8087 comparison or test instruc-

FIGURE 22.1

The 8087 Numeric Data Processor (NDP). (Courtesy Intel Corporation.)
(a) Pinout. (b) Interconnect. (c) Block diagram.

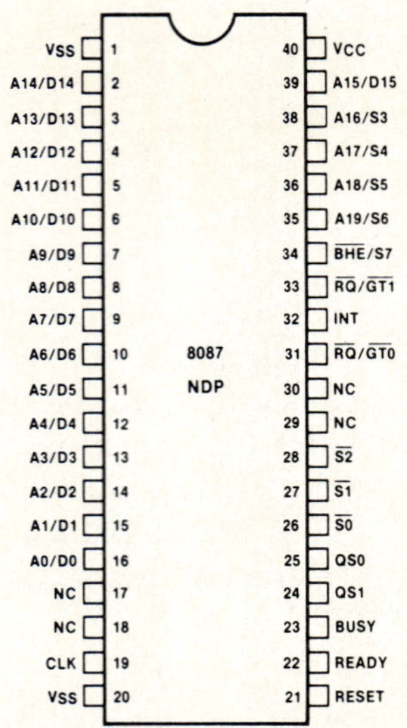

(a) Pin-out

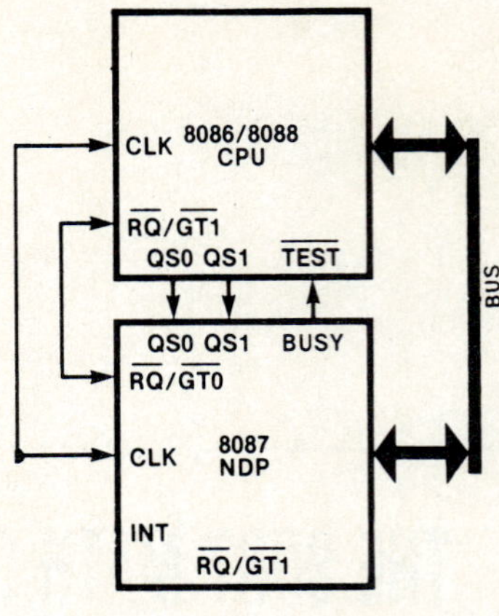

(b) Interconnect

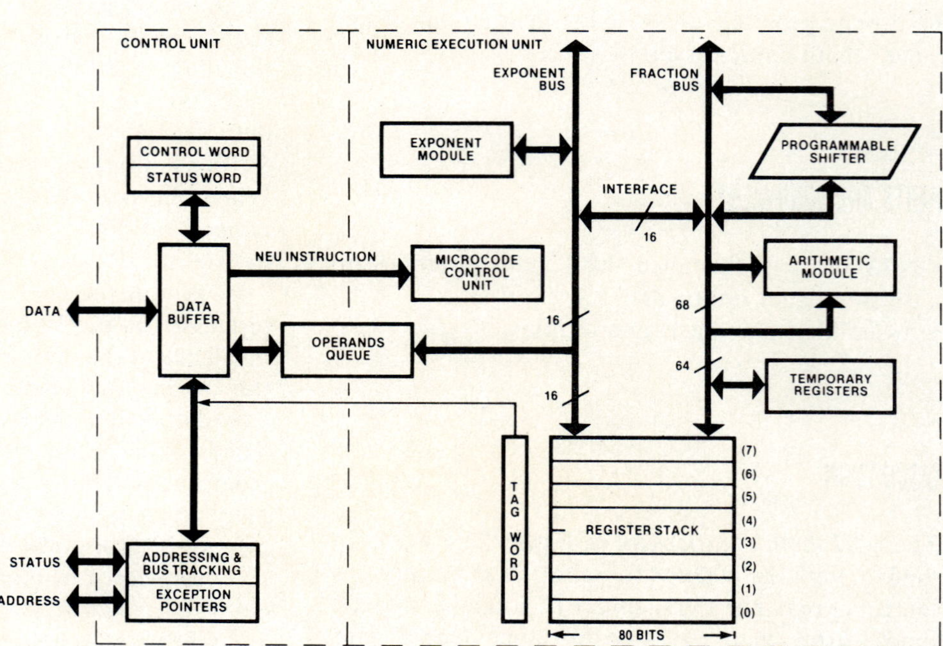

(c) Block diagram

FIGURE 22.2

Speed comparison with and without the 8087. (Courtesy Intel Corporation.)

Instruction	Approximate Execution Time (μs) (5 MHz Clock)	
	8087	8086 Emulation
Multiply (single precision)	19	1,600
Multiply (double precision)	27	2,100
Add	17	1,600
Divide (single precision)	39	3,200
Compare	9	1,300
Load (single precision)	9	1,700
Store (single precision)	18	1,200
Square root	36	19,600
Tangent	90	13,000
Exponentiation	100	17,100

FIGURE 22.3

Using the WAIT instruction to coordinate activity between the 8086/8088 and 8087. (Courtesy Intel Corporation.)

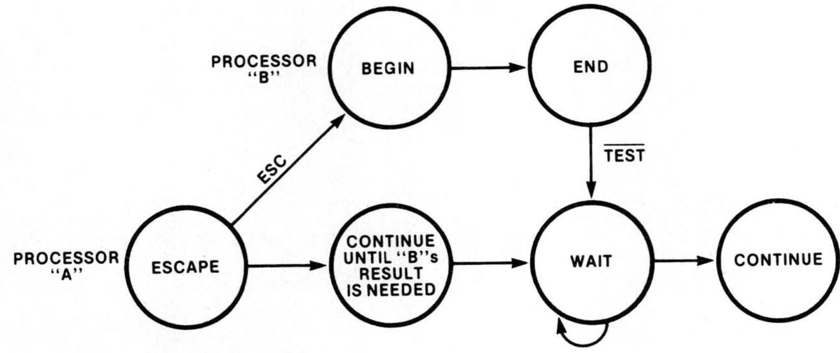

FIGURE 22.4

The 8087 data registers.

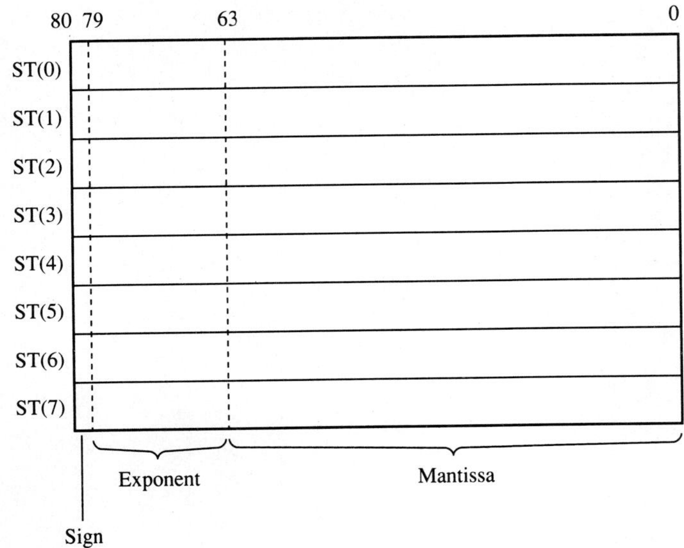

FIGURE 22.5

The 8087 data types. (Courtesy Intel Corporation.) (a) Format. (b) Range.

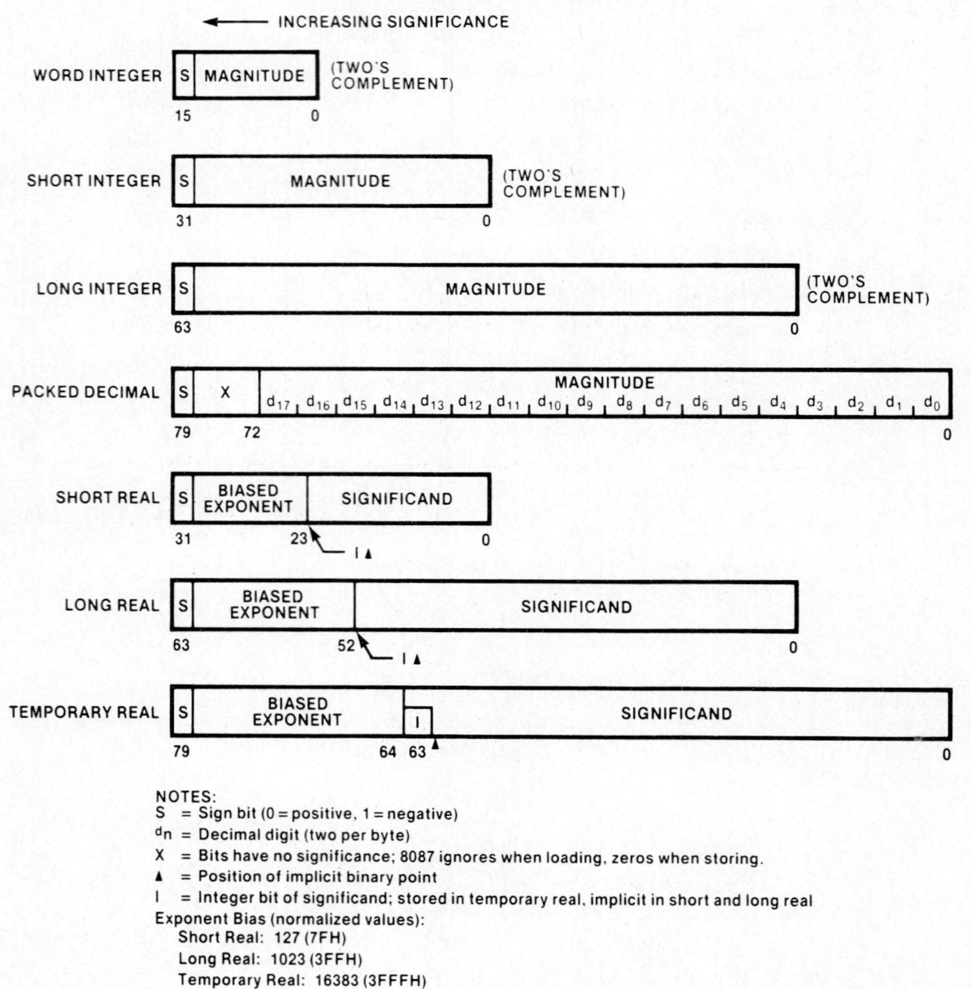

(a) Format

Data Type	Bits	Significant Digits (Decimal)	Approximate Range (Decimal)
Word integer	16	4	$-32,768 \leqslant X \leqslant +32,767$
Short integer	32	9	$-2\text{x}10^9 \leqslant X \leqslant +2\text{x}10^9$
Long integer	64	18	$-9\text{x}10^{18} \leqslant X \leqslant +9\text{x}10^{18}$
Packed decimal	80	18	$-99...99 \leqslant X \leqslant +99...99$ (18 digits)
Short real*	32	6-7	$8.43\text{x}10^{-37} \leqslant \|X\| \leqslant 3.37\text{x}10^{38}$
Long real*	64	15-16	$4.19\text{x}10^{-307} \leqslant \|X\| \leqslant 1.67\text{x}10^{308}$
Temporary real	80	19	$3.4\text{x}10^{-4932} \leqslant \|X\| \leqslant 1.2\text{x}10^{4932}$

(b) Range

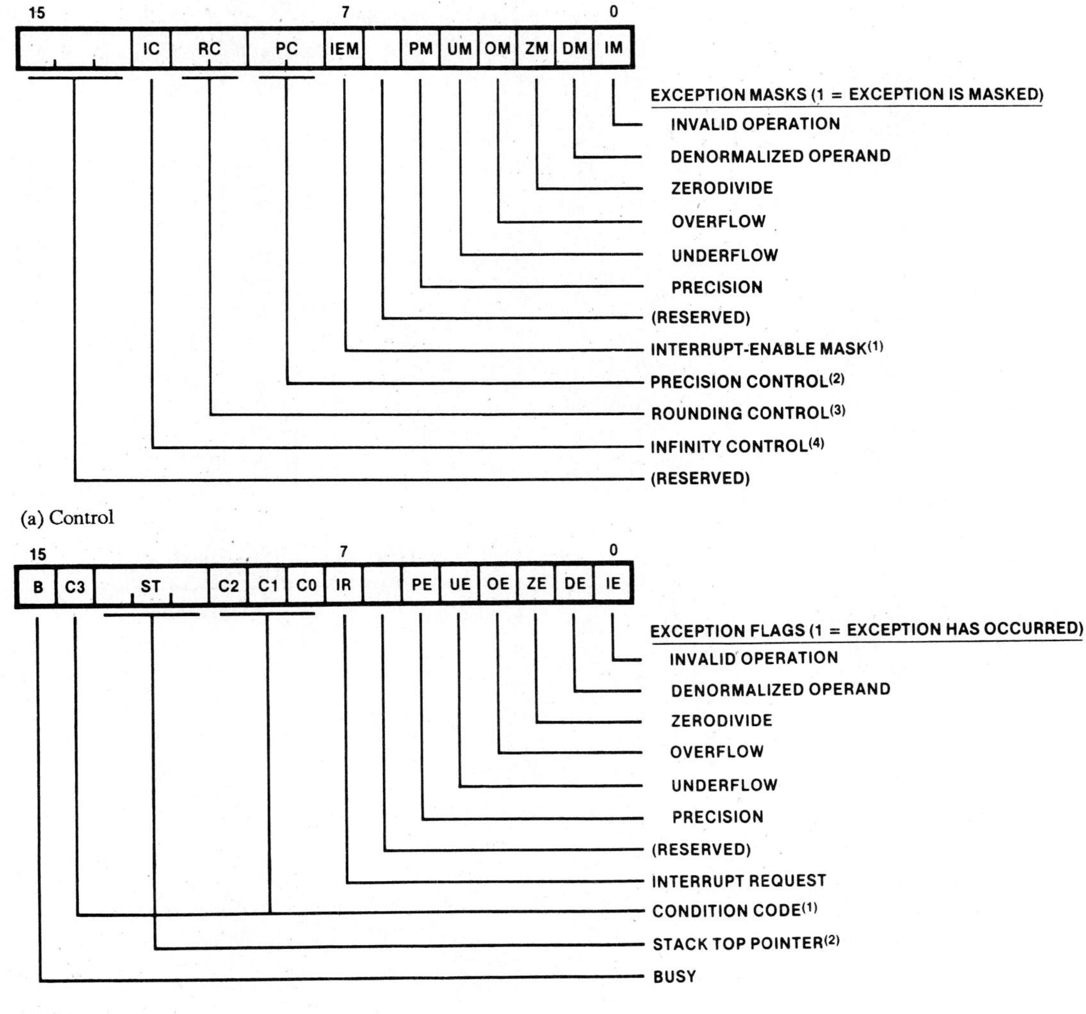

FIGURE 22.6

The 8087 control and status registers. (Courtesy Intel Corporation.) (a) Control. (b) Status.

tion setting the condition flags within the status register according to Figure 22.8(a). With the help of the special FSTSW (store status word) instruction, the flags of the 8087 are transferred to the 8086/88, where they overwrite the comparable flags as shown in Figure 22.8(b). The conditional jump instructions of the 8086/88 test the flags and jump if the condition is true.

Addressing Modes

Like the 8086/88, the 8087 determines the addressing mode of each instruction by examining the operand structure. As given by the examples below, there are four from which to choose. (If no operands are listed, it defaults to the *classical stack* form.)

ADDRESSING MODE	EXAMPLE	OPERATION
Classical stack	`fmul`	`ST = ST(1) * ST (Both operands are destroyed by ''popping.'')`
Memory	`fadd apples[bx]`	`ST = ST + apples[bx]`
Register	`fsub st,st(3)`	`ST = ST - ST(3)`
Register pop	`faddp st(4),st`	`ST(3) = ST(4) + ST (Both operands are destroyed by ''popping.'')`

FIGURE 22.7

The 8087 instruction set. (Courtesy Intel Corporation.)

Real Transfers	
FLD	Load real
FST	Store real
FSTP	Store real and pop
FXCH	Exchange registers
Integer Transfers	
FILD	Integer load
FIST	Integer store
FISTP	Integer store and pop
Packed Decimal Transfers	
FBLD	Packed decimal (BCD) load
FBSTP	Packed decimal (BCD) store and pop

Data transfer

Addition	
FADD	Add real
FADDP	Add real and pop
FIADD	Integer add
Subtraction	
FSUB	Subtract real
FSUBP	Subtract real and pop
FISUB	Integer subtract
FSUBR	Subtract real reversed
FSUBRP	Subtract real reversed and pop
FISUBR	Integer subtract reversed
Multiplication	
FMUL	Multiply real
FMULP	Multiply real and pop
FIMUL	Integer multiply
Division	
FDIV	Divide real
FDIVP	Divide real and pop
FIDIV	Integer divide
FDIVR	Divide real reversed
FDIVRP	Divide real reversed and pop
FIDIVR	Integer divide reversed
Other Operations	
FSQRT	Square root
FSCALE	Scale
FPREM	Partial remainder
FRNDINT	Round to integer
FXTRACT	Extract exponent and significand
FABS	Absolute value
FCHS	Change sign

Arithmetic

FPTAN	Partial tangent
FPATAN	Partial arctangent
F2XM1	2^X-1
FYL2X	$Y \bullet \log_2 X$
FYL2XP1	$Y \bullet \log_2(X+1)$

Transcendental

FCOM	Compare real
FCOMP	Compare real and pop
FCOMPP	Compare real and pop twice
FICOM	Integer compare
FICOMP	Integer compare and pop
FTST	Test
FXAM	Examine

Comparison

FLDZ	Load +0.0
FLD1	Load +1.0
FLDPI	Load π
FLDL2T	Load $\log_2 10$
FLDL2E	Load $\log_2 e$
FLDLG2	Load $\log_{10} 2$
FLDLN2	Load $\log_e 2$

Constant

FINIT/FNINIT	Initialize processor
FDISI/FNDISI	Disable interrupts
FENI/FNENI	Enable interrupts
FLDCW	Load control word
FSTCW/FNSTCW	Store control word
FSTSW/FNSTSW	Store status word
FCLEX/FNCLEX	Clear exceptions
FSTENV/FNSTENV	Store environment
FLDENV	Load environment
FSAVE/FNSAVE	Save state
FRSTOR	Restore state
FINCSTP	Increment stack pointer
FDECSTP	Decrement stack pointer
FFREE	Free register
FNOP	No operation
FWAIT	CPU wait

Processor control

The register pop mode is used only with operands of the form ST(num),ST. The following two instructions compare the regular with the "pop" modes.

```
Regular:   fadd  st(3),st ; ST(3) = ST(3) + ST
Pop:       faddp st(3),st ; ST(2) = ST(3) + ST
```

In both cases, ST(3) is added to ST and the result placed in ST(3). However, the "pop" mode goes one step further and pops the stack, with ST moving off the stack and ST(3) moving to ST(2).

An "r" after any instruction reverses the order of the operands, but not the location of the result. For example:

```
fdiv  st(2),st   ; ST(2)  =  ST(2)/ST
fdivr st(2),st   ; ST(2)  =  ST/ST(2)
```

Demonstration Programs

Continuing with our "learn-by-example" approach, let's briefly review the five demonstration programs of Figure 22.9.

The first program [Figure 22.9(a)] adds variables *checking* and *savings* and places the answer in variable *total.* Note that all three variables are stored as word integers (DW). For larger numbers, we can use 4-byte short integers (DQ) or 10-byte long integers (DT). (Single-byte integers ae not allowed.)

The calculation begins with an integer load (the FILD instruction) of variable *checking,* which is automatically converted to temporary-real format and placed in ST. The integer add instruction (FIADD) adds byte variable *savings* (converted to temporary-real format) to ST and places the answer back in ST (also in temporary-real format). The integer store instruction (FIST) copies the answer in ST to variable *distance,* automatically converting from temporary real to integer word.

The second demonstration program [Figure 22.9(b)] is the same as the first, except we use the 10-byte BCD format instead of the integer format. Because we are using BCD, all mathematical processing within the 8087 must be done on numbers stored in registers.

Our next demonstration program [Figure 22.9(c)] is one often seen in the literature: the calculation of the area of a circle. This time, all variables are in the real format. Note the special instruction provided (FLDPI) for loading the value of pi. Because we used the "non-POP" form of the final store instruction (FST), the answer also remains in ST.

The program of Figure 22.9(d) shows how to perform a trigonometric calculation using short real numbers. The purpose of the program is to convert an angle in degrees to its tangent. The first five 8087 instructions perform the operation pi * 30/180 to convert the angle in degrees (30) to radians and place in register ST. The tangent instruction (FPTAN) operates on the radian value and leaves the *X* and *Y* result in ST(1) and ST. These *X* and *Y* values represent the sides of a right triangle and can be processed to generate the *sine, cos,* and *tangent* of the angle. Since we seek the tangent value, we divide *X* by *Y* and store the answer in variable *tangent.*

Our last demonstration program [Figure 22.9(e)] shows that 8086/88 and 8087 instructions can be mixed in any appropriate order. The purpose of the program is to place into variable *count* the number of elements in ten-word array *scores* that are greater than −1000 (−999 is greater than −1000). The decision-making step shows the cooperation between the 8086/88 and 8087: The 8087 sets the flags with the FICOM instruction, they are transferred to the 8086 via memory, and the 8086/88 performs the conditional jump.

FIGURE 22.8

The 8087 flag operation. (a) The 8087 flags after a compare or test. (b) Overwriting the 8086/8088 flags.

After FCOM	After FTEST	C_3	C_0
ST > source	ST is positive	0	0
ST < source	ST is negative	0	1
ST = source	ST = 0	1	0

(a) The 8087 flags after a compare or test

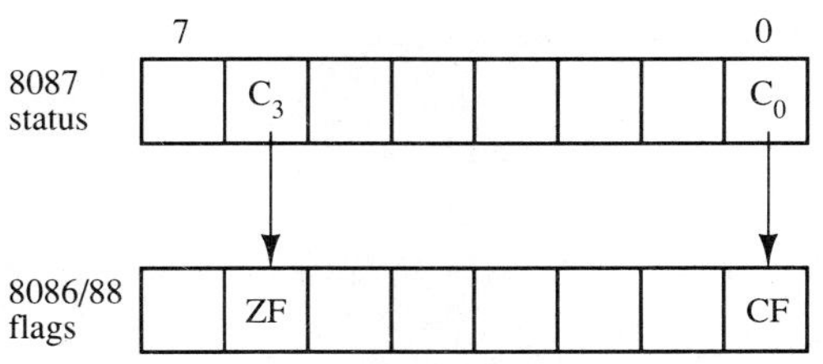

(b) Overwriting the 8086/88 flags

FIGURE 22.9

8087 demonstration programs. (a) Addition using integers. (b) Addition using BCD. (c) Finding the area of a circle using real numbers. (d) Evaluating the tangent of an angle using real numbers. (e) Determining the number of elements in integer array *scores* that are above −1000.

```
NAME        MONEY

DGROUP GROUP _DATA

_DATA       SEGMENT
  checking  DW  -8765
  savings   DW  10500
  total     DW  ?
_DATA       ENDS

_TEXT       SEGMENT
            ASSUME CS:_TEXT,DS:DGROUP
  start:    mov   ax,DGROUP
            mov   ds,ax
            fild  checking      ; Load checking to ST(0)
            fiadd savings       ; ST(0) = ST(0) + savings
            fist  total         ; ST(0) to total
            hlt
_TEXT       ENDS
            END   start
```

(a) Addition using integers

```
NAME        MONEY_BCD

DGROUP GROUP _DATA

_DATA       SEGMENT
  checking  DT  -8765
  savings   DT  10500
  total     DT  ?
_DATA       ENDS

_TEXT       SEGMENT
            ASSUME CS:_TEXT,DS:DGROUP
  start:    mov   ax,DGROUP
            mov   ds,ax
            fbld  checking      ; Push checking to ST(0)
            fbld  savings       ; Push savings to ST(0), checking to ST(1)
            fadd                ; ST(0) = ST(0) + ST(1)
            fbstp total         ; Pop ST(0) to total
            hlt
_TEXT       ENDS
            END   start
```

(b) Addition using BCD

```
NAME        AREA_OF_CIRCLE

DGROUP GROUP _DATA

_DATA       SEGMENT
  radius    DD  2.0E1           ; Short (4 bytes)
  area      DQ  ?               ; Long (8 bytes)
_DATA       ENDS

_TEXT       SEGMENT
            ASSUME CS:_TEXT,DS:DGROUP
  start:    mov   ax,DGROUP
            mov   ds,ax
            fld   radius        ; Load radius to ST(0)
            fmul  ST,ST         ; ST(0) = ST(0) * ST(0)
            fldpi               ; 3.14 to ST(0), r squ to ST(1)
            fmul                ; ST = ST(1) (r squ) * ST (pi)
            fst   area          ; Store ST in area
            hlt
_TEXT       ENDS
            END   start
```

(c) Finding the area of a circle using real numbers

FIGURE 22.9

(continued)

```
NAME      TANGENT

DGROUP GROUP _DATA

_DATA     SEGMENT
  angle       DD  30.0
  semicircle  DD  180.0
  tangent     DD   ?
_DATA     ENDS

_TEXT     SEGMENT
          ASSUME CS:_TEXT,DS:DGROUP
  start:  mov   ax,DGROUP
          mov   ds,ax
          fld  semicircle ; Load 180 degrees to ST
          fld  angle      ; 180 to ST(1),angle to ST
          fdivr           ; ST (angle/180) = ST/ST(1)
          fldpi           ; Pi to ST,angle/180 to ST(1)
          fmul            ; ST (angle in radians) = ST(1) * ST
          fptan           ; Y in ST and X in ST(1)
          fdiv            ; ST (tangent) = ST(1)/ST (X/Y)
          fst   tangent   ; Store tangent in real form
          hlt
_TEXT     ENDS
          END   start
```

(d) Evaluating the tangent of an angle using real numbers

```
NAME         GREATER_THAN_MINUS_1000

DGROUP GROUP _DATA

_DATA        SEGMENT PUBLIC 'DATA'
  scores     DW  -1203, 345, -29, 10444,-31000
             DW  -3228, 17, 24602, 4338, -998
  count      DW  0
  minus1000  DW -1000
  flags      DW  ?
_DATA        ENDS

_TEXT        SEGMENT PUBLIC 'CODE'
             ASSUME CS:_TEXT,DS:DGROUP,SS:DGROUP
  main:      mov   ax,DGROUP
             mov   ds,ax
             mov   bx,0              ; Point to 1st element
             fild  minus1000         ; -1000 to ST
             mov   cx,10             ; Ten iterations
  back:      ficom scores[bx]        ; Compares array element to ST
             fstsw flags             ; Status register to memory
             mov   ax,flags          ; flags to ax
             sahf                    ; AH to low byte of flags word
             jae   over              ; Skip count if <= -1000
             inc   count             ; > -1000 so count
   over:     add   bx,TYPE scores    ; Next array element
             loop  back              ; If not done, loop
             hlt
 _TEXT       ENDS
             END   main
```

(e) Determing the number of elements in integer arrow *scores* that are above -1000

FIGURE 22.10

Using library routines for 8087-based calculations. (a) Library routine SQRTINT. (b) Main program.

```
; Library routine _sqrtint accepts a word
; integer parameter from mailbox number
; and returns its square root back to number.

NAME        SQUARE_ROOT_WORD_INTEGER

DGROUP GROUP _DATA

_DATA       SEGMENT PUBLIC 'DATA'
  EXTRN number:WORD
_DATA       ENDS

_TEXT       SEGMENT PUBLIC 'CODE'
            ASSUME CS:_TEXT,DS:DGROUP

     PUBLIC _sqrtint

    _sqrtint PROC NEAR
          fild  number     ; Number to ST(0)
          fsqrt            ; Squrt of ST(0) to ST(0)
          fistp number     ; ST(0) to number
          ret
    _sqrtint ENDP

_TEXT       ENDS
            END
```

(a) Library routine _ sqrtint

```
NAME        SQUAREROOT_TEST

DGROUP GROUP _DATA,STACK

STACK       SEGMENT STACK 'STACK'
            DW  100h DUP(?)
STACK       ENDS

_DATA        SEGMENT PUBLIC 'DATA'
  number  DW  24688
  PUBLIC number
_DATA        ENDS

_TEXT       SEGMENT PUBLIC 'CODE'
            ASSUME CS:_TEXT,DS:DGROUP,SS:DGROUP

    EXTRN _sqrtint:NEAR

 main:      mov   ax,DGROUP
            mov   ds,ax
            call  _sqrtint
            hlt
_TEXT       ENDS
            END   main
```

(b) Main program

8087-Based Functions

The program of Figure 22.10 shows that functions can contain 8087 instructions as well as main programs. Function SQRTINT accepts a word integer and returns its square root. Although we could pass parameters on the stack (especially for word integers), the expanded data types used with the 8087 are more appropriate for the mailbox technique.

In this activity, we have covered only the basic operation and programming of the 8087. For a more detailed discussion, consult the appropriate Intel literature.

PROCEDURE

NOTE: Unless otherwise indicated, store all input values and all solutions in memory using the data types indicated. To display/enter real or BCD numbers under Codeview, use DS/ES (short), DL/EL (long), and DT/ET (10-byte) as needed. To view 8087 registers, enter "7."

1. Make sure your computer has an installed 8087.
2. If the earth is approximately 250,000,000 miles from the sun, and light travels at 286,000 miles/second, write a program that calculates how many *minutes* it takes for light to travel from the sun to the earth. Use long (8-byte) integers for all variables.

   ASSEMBLY-LANGUAGE PROGRAM

3. Repeat the problem of procedure step 2 using BCD for all variables.

   ASSEMBLY-LANGUAGE PROGRAM

4. If the earth has a radius of approximately 4000 miles, write a program that calculates its volume in cubic miles. Use the equation below with short real numbers for all variables.

$$V = 4/3\pi R^3$$

ASSEMBLY-LANGUAGE PROGRAM

Advanced Activities

5. Using the data type of your choice, write a program that calculates the hypotenuse of a right triangle, given variables *side1* and *side2*.
6. Using library routine SQRTINT of Figure 22.10(a) (and additional functions as needed), write a program that inputs signed words and outputs their square root. Whenever an illegal negative number is entered, the calculation is skipped, and the display is cleared. (*Hint:* Because we are using words, we can use 8086/88 instructions to test for negative numbers.)

Name: ____________________

Date: ____________________

Class: ____________________

QUESTIONS AND PROBLEMS

1. List the allowed 8087 types for each of the following:
   a. Integer
   b. BCD
   c. Real
2. State in your own words what is accomplished by each of the following instructions:
   a. *fiadd apples*
   b. *fmul*
   c. *fdivr*
   d. *fsubp* st(2),st
3. How does the 8087 recognize that certain instructions are for it rather than the 8086/88?

4. We load two numbers from memory, add them together, and store the result back to yet another memory location. Can all three numbers be of different types? How is this possible?

5. When must we include an "i" or a "b" in an 8087 instruction?

Advanced Section

6. Using 8087 instructions, how is the sine of an angle determined?

7. Referring to the program of Figure 22.9(e), we compare *signed* numbers, but use the *unsigned* conditional-jump instruction *jump above* (JAE) to perform the conditional branch. Explain how this is possible.

PART VII

THE C HIGH-LEVEL LANGUAGE / MIXED-LANGUAGE PROGRAMMING

After Part VII our ability to develop and test the hardware/software system of our choice (to mix and match) will be complete. We use the C high-level language for more efficient programming, we combine assembly-language and C for *mixed-language programming,* and we gain access to the C-language *run-time library*.

Compared to assembly-language, programs written in a high-level language are easier to write, understand, and modify. However, the price we pay is less control over our code, resulting in less efficient programs that require more memory and run more slowly. We conclude that there is a strong need for both levels of programming, depending on the application at hand. This is the reason why mixed-language programming is so powerful.

For compatibility with assembly-generated routines, our C code conforms to the SMALL model of segmentation. All demonstration programs use the ANSI standard format.

Troubleshooting C programs under a debugger is similar to troubleshooting assembly-language programs. Codeview, for example, automatically senses which language was used to write the source file, and all commands are identical for both assembly-language and C.

For further information on the C language, consult your compiler's Users Guide, any appropriate text, or refer to the "bible" of C programming: *The C Programming Language,* 2nd ed., by B. W. Kernighan and D. M. Ritchie (Prentice Hall, 1988).

ACTIVITY 23

THE C LANGUAGE

OBJECTIVES

- To write programs in C that emphasize control flow.
- To define and declare variables.

PARTS AND EQUIPMENT

- IBM PC (bus-extender optional).
- C compiler, debugger, and utilities.

DISCUSSION

The C programming language is a general-purpose high-level structured language. It has become the language of choice for professionals because it is versatile, elegant, terse, and places few restrictions on the programmer.

In this introductory activity, we write programs that emphasize control flow: using nested combinations of the three basic patterns of Figure 23.1. We carry out *selection* by means of the IF, IF/ELSE, and SWITCH statements, and we carry out *repetition* by means of the WHILE, DO/WHILE, and FOR statements.

C Program Format

Looking over the three programs of Figure 23.2, we see that all are named *main* and all are "delimited" (opened and closed) by braces. The parentheses after the function name (*main*) appear after all functions and are used for parameter passing. The body of a program consists of a sequence of *statements* (rather than the simple *instructions* of assembly-language). Comments are placed anywhere in the program by using the delimiters /* and */.

Data Types

The C language supports a number of data types. The *fundamental* types are listed in Figure 23.3, along with their storage requirements and range of values.

Of the many data types available, the four integral types listed below are the most commonly used within this text because they are so closely related to the two fundamental data types of assembly language (DB and DW).

Data Type	*Value*
char	signed byte
unsigned char	unsigned byte
short (int)	signed word
unsigned short	unsigned word

The signed data types assume signed numbers and automatically force the use of signed number operations (for example, the use of IMUL); the unsigned data types assume unsigned numbers and automatically force the use of unsigned number operations (for example, the use of MUL).

Operators

The *operators* used in the C-language programs of this text are from the complete list of Figure 23.4(a). Looking over the list, we note the following:

- They are listed in order of priority, from top to bottom.
- All but the unary and assignment operators are evaluated from left to right.
- The *bitwise* operators (~, ^, &, and ¦) perform bit manipulation and masking operations on individual bits. The *logical* operators (!, &&, ¦¦, ==, !=, <, and >) are most often used to logically connect relational expressions, and they result in a true/false (nonzero/zero) situation.
- A single equal sign (=) means "assigned," and a double equal sign (==) means "equal to."

When a single variable is to be updated by an operation, we can use the shorthand *compound operators* of Figure 23.4(b). For example $i = i + 4$ can be shortened to i += 4.

FIGURE 23.1

The three basic control-flow patterns of structured programming.

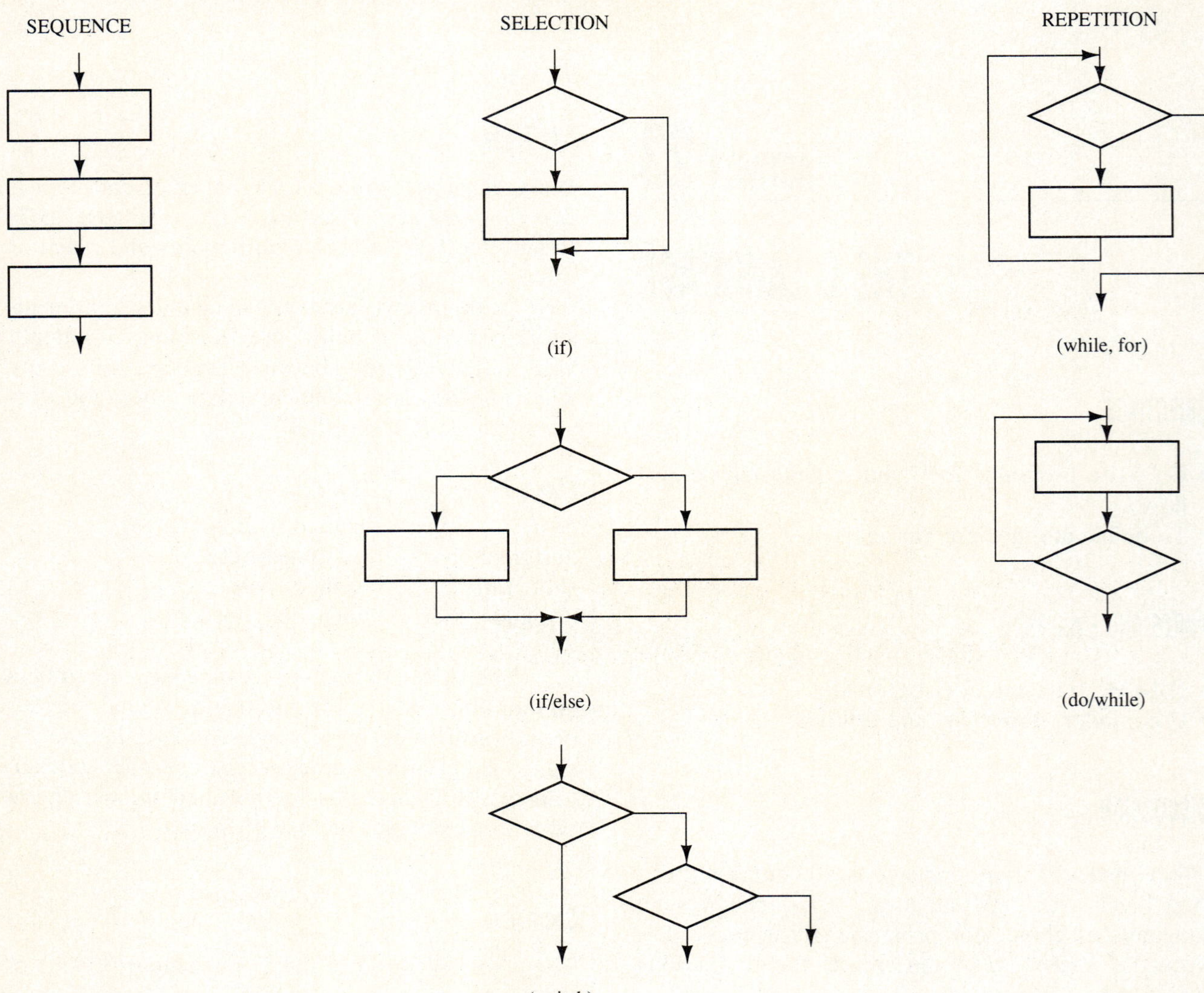

Selection

Returning to Figure 23.2, the three programs listed demonstrate the *selection* pattern. Turning first to Figure 23.2(a), *if* the *conditional expression* within the parentheses evaluates to *true* (*pay* is greater than $1000), the statement that follows is performed and your pay is added evenly to both your checking and savings accounts. Else, if not true, all your pay is deposited into checking. (If *pay* is an odd number greater than $1000, what happens to the "leftover" 50 cents that should be placed into each account?)

As with assembly-language, note that variables *pay, checking,* and *savings* are defined (or declared) as *unsigned short* (0 to 65,535) before they are used.

Because two or more statements follow *if,* they are *compound* and must be set off (delimited) by braces. Because only a single statement follows *else,* the braces are optional.

Multiple-pathway decision-making is achieved by nesting IF or IF/ELSE statements, as demonstrated by the egg-sorting program of Figure 23.2(b). An egg is placed into one of three categories (1, 2, or 3) depending on its weight.

For certain types of programs, the SWITCH statement of Figure 23.2(c) handles multiple-pathway decision-making more efficiently than nesting. As shown, if the value of expression *character* matches ASCII *case constants* 'M' or 'm', we multiply variables *apples* and *peaches*; if 'D' or 'd', we divide. If no match is found the DEFAULT state-

FIGURE 23.2

Control flow (selection). (a) IF/ELSE. (b) Nested IF/ELSE. (c) SWITCH.

```
/* This program demonstrates IF/ELSE
   and compound statements.  If pay
   is greater than $1,000, add half to
   checking and half to savings.
   Otherwise add all to checking.  */
main()
{
     unsigned short pay,checking,savings;

     if (pay > 1000){
          checking += pay / 2;
          savings  += pay / 2;
     }
     else
          checking += pay;
}
```

(a) If/else

```
/* This program uses nested if
   statements to place variable
   eggweight into one of three
   categories.  */
main()
{
     unsigned char eggweight,size;

     if (eggweight > 100)
          size = 1;
     else
          if (eggweight > 50)
               size = 2;
          else
               size = 3;
}
```

(b) Nested if/else

```
/* This program uses the SWITCH statement to
   multiply variables apples and peaches if
   variable character is 'M' or 'm' and to
   divide if character is 'D' or 'd'. */
main()
{
     unsigned char apples = 3;
     unsigned char peaches = 6;
     unsigned char character;
     unsigned short answer;

     switch(character){
          case 'M':
          case 'm': answer = apples * peaches;
                    break;
          case 'D':
          case 'd': answer = peaches / apples;
                    break;
          default : answer = 0;
     }
}
```

(c) Switch

ment is performed. (If no match is found and the default statement is not present, no action is taken.) The BREAK statement forces an exit from the entire SWITCH statement. (If a break is not present,

FIGURE 23.3

Common data types and their storage.

	Type	Storage	Range
Integral types	Char	1 byte	-128 to -127
	short, int*	2 bytes	-32,768 to 32,767
	long	4 bytes	-2,147,483,648 to 2,147,483,647
	unsigned char	1 byte	0 to 255
	unsigned short, unsigned int*	2 bytes	0 to 65,535
	unsigned long	4 bytes	0 to 4,294,967,295
Floating point types	float	4 bytes	3.4e-38 to 3.4e+38
	double	8 bytes	1.7e-308 to 1.7e+308

* On 16-bit machines, short and int are the same; on 32-bit machines int is long (4 bytes).

all statements following the entry point to the next break or to the end of the switch statement are executed.) As demonstrated by this program, variables may be initialized in the definition.

Repetition

Repetition is demonstrated by the programs of Figure 23.5, which determine the sum of all integers from 1 to (and including) *n*. Starting with the WHILE statement of Figure 23.5(a), the body of the statement (*answer* += *i*) is continually executed as long as (while) the conditional expression within the parentheses is true. When it turns false, we exit the statement.

The double plus sign (++) in the conditional expression of Figure 23.5(a) means *increment.* If placed before a variable (as shown), the variable is incremented before it is used. If placed after a variable (*i*++), the variable is used before it is incremented. The same holds true for the *decrement* operator (−−). If ++*i* appears alone as a single statement, the position of the "++" does not matter.

The DO/WHILE statement of Figure 23.5(b) is similar, except the body of the statement is performed before the condition is tested. This means the body of the statement is performed at least once.

The FOR statement of Figure 23.5(c) is the most complex and versatile of the three because the expression within the parentheses contains three *fields* separated by semicolons. The first field (the *initialization expression*) is evaluated once upon entry to the statement. As shown, multiple statements within a field are separated by commas. If the second field (the *conditional expression*) evaluates *true,* the body of the statement is executed and the third field (the *loop expression*) is performed. The process repeats with the evaluation of the *conditional expression.* When the *conditional expression* evaluates false, execution of the FOR statement terminates.

FIGURE 23.4

The C operators. (a) Precedence. (b) Using the compound operator to shorten assignment statements.

```
()              Parenthesis
~ - ! ++ --     Unary   (1s   complement,   minus,   Logical-NOT,
                increment, decrement)
* / %           Multiply, divide, modulus (remainder)
+ -             Add, subtract
<< >>           Shift-left, shift-right
< > <= >=       Less-than, greater-than, less-than-or-equal,
                Greater-than-or-equal
== !=           Equal, not-equal
&               Bitwise AND
^               Bitwise-exclusive OR
|               Bitwise OR
&&              Logical AND
||              Logical OR
?:              Conditional expression
=               Assignment (including compound assignment)
,               Comma
```

(a) Precedence

```
Compound
Operator     Operation                Example        Equivalent to

  +=         Plus assign              y += a          y = y + a
  -=         Minus assign             y -= a          y = y - a
  *=         Times assign             y *= a          y = y * a
  /=         Divide assign            y /= a          y = y / a
  %=         Modulus assign           y %= a          y = y % a
  <<=        Left shift assign        y <<= a         y = y << a
  >>=        Right shift assign       y >>= a         y = y >> a
  &=         Bitwise and equals       y &= a          y = y & a
  ^=         Bitwise exc OR equals    y ^= a          y = y ^ a
  |=         Bitwise or equals        y |= a          y = y | a
```

(b) Using the compound operator to shorten assignment statements

Type Conversions

The C programming language allows for a limited mixing of data types. When a *lower* type is converted to a *higher* type, it is called *promotion*; when the reverse is true, it is called *demotion*. The ranking of data types from lowest to highest is as follows:

char
short
unsigned short
int
unsigned int
long
unsigned long
float
double

Promotion and demotion can occur when using many of the operators of Figure 23.4.

As a case in point we turn back to Figure 23.2(c). Note that variables *apples* and *peaches* are both unsigned char, and variable *answer* is unsigned short. During the assignment statements, the unsigned char data type on the right is *promoted* to unsigned short on the left.

We will see other examples of type conversions in the activities to follow. (For a complete discussion of promotion and demotion, see *The C Programming Language,* 2nd ed., Appendix A. See page 233 for a complete citation.)

BREAK and CONTINUE

The BREAK statement terminates the execution of any loop statement, and a CONTINUE statement passes control to the next iteration of any loop statement. For example, the program of Figure 23.6 uses the CONTINUE and BREAK statements to determine the sum of all numbers from 1 to *n*, as did the programs of Figure 23.5. However, if we compare the programs of Figure 23.5 with Figure 23.6, we see that the BREAK and CONTINUE statements often lead to inefficient programming and should be used sparingly. Because "false" is represented in C by zero and "true" by nonzero, "while(1)" means to loop forever (except when a BREAK is executed).

The Conditional Operator

An IF/ELSE statement is often called on to assign one of two values to a variable. For example, vari-

FIGURE 23.5

Control flow (repetition). (a) WHILE. (b) DO/WHILE. (c) FOR.

```
/* This program uses the WHILE statement
   to determine the sum of all numbers
   from 1 to n.  (n < 23). */

main()
{
    unsigned char n,i,answer;

    answer = 0;
    i = 0;
    while(++i < (n + 1))
        answer += i;
}
```

(a) WHILE

```
/* This program uses the DO/WHILE statement
   to determine the sum of all numbers
   from 1 to n.  (n < 23) */

main()
{
    unsigned char n,i,answer;

    answer = 0;
    i = 0;
    do
        answer += i;
    while(++i < (n + 1));
}
```

(b) DO/WHILE

```
/* This program uses the FOR statement
   to determine the sum of all numbers
   from 1 to n.  (n < 23) */

main()
{
    unsigned char n,i,answer;

    for(i = 0,answer = 0;i < (n + 1);++i)
        answer += i;
}
```

(c) FOR

able *biggest* is assigned the larger of variables *a* and *b* as follows:

```
if (a > b)
    biggest = a;
else
    biggest = b;
```

Using the conditional operator (?:), we express the same decision in shorthand form:

```
biggest = (a > b) ? (a) : (b);
```

FIGURE 23.6

Using the BREAK and CONTINUE statements.

```
/* This program uses the WHILE(1) statement
   and break and continue to determine the
   sum of all numbers from 1 to n.  (n < 23
   to avoid overflow). */

main()
{
    unsigned char n,i,answer;

    answer = 0;
    i = 0;
    while(1)
        if (++i < (n + 1)){
            answer += i;
            continue;
        }
        else
            break;
}
```

A Demonstration Program

The demonstration program of Figure 23.7(b) summarizes the major elements of control flow. It adds all the signed integers from −12 to +10 that have a "1" in bit position D2. The result is placed in variable *answer*. Data type *int,* storing integers from −32K to +32K, is probably the most commonly used data type in C. As shown, decimal numbers are written directly, and hexadecimal numbers begin with "0x".

The flowchart of Figure 23.7(a) is called a *structured* flowchart, and it shows the form of structured programs: single-entry/single-exit nested combinations of the three basic patterns of Figure 23.1.

PROCEDURE

NOTE: Unless specified by the problem, for each variable defined in the steps below select the integer data type that seems most appropriate: *char, unsigned char, int, unsigned short.* For most variables, more than one data type is appropriate.

1. Set up your system for C operation by referring to the development package update of Figure 23.8. [The disk storage section of Figure 23.8(a) lists those files to be *added* to the existing files.] Make the necessary changes if using software other than Microsoft software or different development system techniques (such as QuickC's "environment").

FIGURE 23.7

Demonstration program ADD. (a) Flowchart. (b) Program.

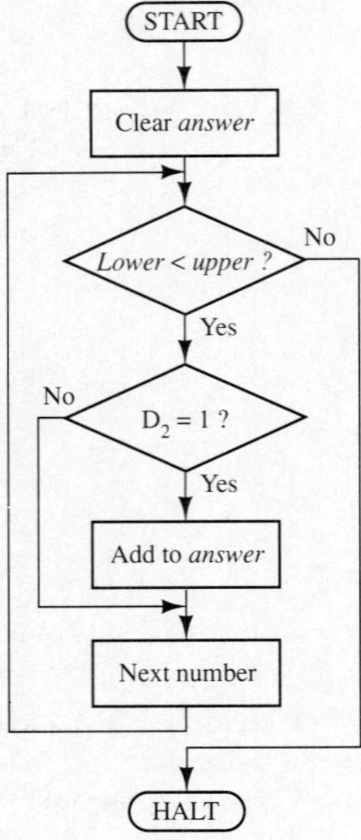

(a) Flowchart

```
/* This demonstration program uses nested
   combinations of sequence, selection,
   and repetition to determine the sum of
   all signed numbers from lower to upper
   that have a "1" in bit position D2. */

main()
{
    int answer;
    int lower = -12;
    int upper = 0xa;

    answer = 0;
    while(lower < upper){
        if((lower & 4) == 4)
            answer += lower;
        ++lower;
    }
}
```

(b) Program

FIGURE 23.8

Development package for C programming. (a) Disk storage (files to *add* to disk). (b) Template (.C). (c) Batch file (.BAT).

```
template  (.C)
QC.EXE
QCL.EXE
SLIBCE.LIB  (Use SETUP to create)
```

(a) Disk storage (Items to add to existing files.)

```
main()
{
}
```

(b) Template (.c)

```
:BEGIN
ED %1.C
QCL /c /AS /Gs /Zi %1.C
IF ERRORLEVEL 1 GOTO STOP
LINK /CO %1,,,SLIBCE;
CV /B /W %1
ERASE %1.OBJ
ERASE %1.EXE
ERASE %1.MAP
GOTO END
:STOP
REM Error found, reenter editor
GOTO BEGIN
:END
```

(c) Batch file (.BAT)

2. Using an IF/IF/ELSE sequence, write program GIFT, which adds $100 to the smaller of integer variables *visa* and *mastercard*, but only if both variables are negative.

   STRUCTURED FLOWCHART C PROGRAM

3. Repeat procedure step 2 using the conditional operator for the IF/ELSE statement.

   STRUCTURED FLOWCHART C PROGRAM

4. Using nested IF/ELSE statements, write a program that places into variable *answer* the largest of three variables. (Use variable names and initial values of your choice.)

   STRUCTURED FLOWCHART C PROGRAM

5. Using the WHILE statement, write program COUNT_ONES that places into variable *answer* the number of ones (1's) contained in word variable *serial*. For example, if *serial* holds 1001000111010111B, 9 is reported. [*Hint:* Use the shift (>>) operator.]

   STRUCTURED FLOWCHART C PROGRAM

6. Rewrite program COUNT_ONES of procedure step 5 using the FOR statement.

   STRUCTURED FLOWCHART C PROGRAM

7. Using the SWITCH statement, write program CRAPS, which pays $1000 (places $1000 into variable *payoff*) if variable *dice* holds the integers 7 or 11, pays $100 if *dice* holds 3 or 5, and pays zero otherwise.

   STRUCTURED FLOWCHART C PROGRAM

Advanced Activities

8. Write a program that adds all the bytes from variable *lower* to (and including) variable *upper* that are odd *and* have at least three ones.
9. Write program MATCH, which compares two variables and places into variable *answer* the number of bit positions that are the same. [*Hint:* Use the bitwise exclusive-OR operator (^).]
10. Write program PRIME, which determines if the value in variable *number* is prime (can only be divided evenly by itself or 1, such as 2, 3, 5, 7, etc.). If prime, it is assigned to variable *answer*; otherwise, zero is assigned to *answer*. [*Hint:* Make use of the MOD operator (%).]

Name: ______________________

Date: ______________________

Class: ______________________

QUESTIONS AND PROBLEMS

1. What are the C symbols for each of the following:
   a. add
   b. increment
   c. AND (logical)
   d. NOT equal to
   e. OR (bitwise)
2. In C, what does *while*(1) accomplish?

3. Are the following two conditional expressions equivalent? Explain your answer.

   a. `(a > 2 ¦¦ a < 10)`
   b. `((a > 2) ¦¦ (a <10))`
4. In each of the following, make any necessary corrections in the use of the bitwise and logical operators:

   a. `apples = peaches && 4;`
   b. `if(apples > 2 ¦ apples < 10)......`
   c. `if((apples && 0xf) == 7¦¦ (apples && 0xf0) == 16)..`
5. What is the difference between the operators "=" and "=="?

6. If x is 1 and y is 4, what is the result of each of the following?

   a. `x & y`
   b. `x && y`   (True or false?)

7. If $n = 3$, what is in x after each of the following?

   a. `x = ++n;`
   b. `x = n++`
   c. `x = n + 1;`

8. Which of the following operators guarantees that the loop operation will be performed at least once?
   a. WHILE
   b. DO/WHILE
   c. FOR
9. By evaluating the effects of the BREAK and CONTINUE commands, give the sequence of numbers that would appear in variable *answer* from start to end of program execution for the program at the top of page 244.

```
main()
{
     unsigned char answer = 0;

     while (1){
          if ((answer & 1) == 1){
               answer = answer + 3;
               continue;
          }
          if (answer < 11){
               answer++;
               continue;
          }
          break;
     }
}
```

10. What is the "long form" of the *answer* += *i* statement (found in the programs of Figure 23.5)?

Advanced Section

11. A conditional expression evaluates *true* or *false*. At the assembly-language level, how are the true or false conditions determined for each of the following?
    a. When the expression is a simple variable (i.e., *peaches*).

    b. When the expression is a condition (i.e., *apples* > *peaches*).

12. What is in variable *number* at the completion of each of the following?

a.
```
number = 0;
while(number < 5)
    ++number;
```

b.
```
number = 0;
while(number < 5)
    number++;
```

c.
```
number = 0;
while(++number < 5)
    ;
```

d.
```
number = 0
while(number++ < 5)
    ;
```

13. What are in variables *number* and *count* at the completion of each of the following? (*Count* gives the number of iterations.)

a.
```
for(number = 0,count = 0;number < 5;++number)
    count++;
```

b.
```
for(number = 0,count = 0;++number < 5;++number)
    count++;
```

c.
```
for(number = 0,count = 0;number++ < 5;++number)
    count++;
```

14. What data types are available in C?

15. Does C have a rotate operator?

16. When programming EPROMs, how do the variable initialization values get into RAM?

17. Using the C programming method of your choice, carry out the following deductive logic (from a Sherlock Holmes adventure):

```
If the moon is out OR lightning is flashing, AND the dog
did NOT bark, then the suspect is nearby.
```

(Assume *moon* = 1 if out and 0 if not, etc.)

18. How could we modify the program of Figure 23.2(a) to save the dollar lost when the pay is an odd number?

19. Referring to the program of question 9, why is the conditional expression (*answer & 1*) == *1* the same as simply *answer & 1*?

20. Referring to the third line of the batch file of Figure 23.8(c), what is the purpose of each of the "controls": */c, /AS, /Gs, /Zi*?

21. Why is the *demotion* process more dangerous than the *promotion* process?

ACTIVITY 24

ARRAYS, TABLES, AND STRUCTURES IN C

OBJECTIVE

- To process arrays, tables, and structures using C.

PARTS AND EQUIPMENT

- IBM PC (bus-extender optional).
- C compiler, debugger, and utilities.

DISCUSSION

Arrays

In a high-level language such as C, arrays are processed using subscripted variables and a loop construct. As a typical example of array processing, program COUNT_CARDS of Figure 24.1(a) scans seven-element array *pokerhand* and outputs the number of eights found. If the array had not been initialized in the definition, then the *dimension number* (7) would be required, as shown below:

```
unsigned char pokerhand[7];
```

A look-up table is a special form of an array in which the subscript number is logically related to the contents of the corresponding array element. The demonstration program of Figure 24.1(b) uses a look-up table to determine the square of all integers from 0 to 9. The integer value in variable *input* is used as an index value to array *square,* and the value of the corresponding element (the square of the element number) is placed in variable *output*.

Structures

A *structure* is a collection of related variables and arrays grouped together under a single name. Unlike an array, the various *members* of the structure can be any mix of data types. Structures may even be nested.

Turning to Figure 24.2(a), we first declare structure *grade* (its *tag*) to have two *members*: *final* (an integer) and *quiz[5]* (a five-element array of type char). We then define variable *mary* to be of structure type grade, and we initialize the variable according to the structure format. Finally, using structure variables (such as *mary.quiz[i]*), we add Mary's quiz and final scores and report the sum (461) to variable *total*.

Figure 24.2(b) takes us one step further by defining an array of structure type grade. Using vari-

FIGURE 24.1

Array demonstration programs. (a) Array. (b) Look-up table.

```
unsigned char pokerhand[] = {8,3,10,8,8,2,8};

/* Program COUNT_CARDS */
main()
{
    unsigned char i,answer;
    unsigned char number = 0;

    for(i = 0;i != 7;++i){
        if (pokerhand[i] == 8)
            ++number;
        }
    answer = number;
}
```

(a) Array

```
unsigned char square[] = {0,1,4,9,16,25,36,49,64,81};

/* Using a look-up table to convert byte
   variable input (from -9 to 9) to its
   square and place in byte variable
   output.  */

main()
{
    char input;
    unsigned char output;

    output = square[input];
}
```

(b) Lookup table

FIGURE 24.2

Structure demonstration programs. (a) Standard structure. (b) Array of structures.

```
struct grade {
    char quiz[3];
    int  final;
}
struct grade mary = {61,76,54,
                     270};
/* Program STRUCTURE. */
main()
{
    int i,total = 0;

    for (i = 0;i < 3;i++)
        total += mary.quiz[i];
    total += mary.final;
}
```

(a) Standard structure

```
struct grade {
    char quiz[3];
    int  final;
}
struct grade student[3] = {61,76,54,270,
                           60,98,87,285,
                           88,54,71,197};
/* Program ARRAY_OF_STRUCTURES. */
main()
{
    int j,i,student_number = 0,total = 0,
        previous = 0;

    for (j = 0;j < 3;j++){
        for (i = 0;i < 3;i++)
            total += student[j].quiz[i];
        total += student[j].final;
        if (total > previous)
            student_number = j;
        previous = total;
        total = 0;
    }
}
```

(b) Structure of arrays

ables such as *student[j].quiz[i]*, we process the data and write to variable *student number* the number of the student (0, 1, or 2) with the highest total grade (student 1).

Aggregate Types

Arrays and structures are known as *aggregate types*. When aggregate types are initialized, most C compilers (such as QuickC) place restrictions on their definitions. As shown by the programs of Figures 24.1 and 24.2, one allowed technique is to initialize them "globally" (outside the body of the program).

PROCEDURE

NOTE: Unless specified by the problem, for each variable select the data type that seems most appropriate.

Arrays

1. Write program TOP_GUN, which searches for and places into variable *answer* the largest value in an array of five elements.

HIGH-LEVEL LANGUAGE PROGRAM

Look-Up Tables

2. Using look-up table techniques, write a program that takes the centigrade temperature (from 0 to 9) in variable *c* and places its corresponding Fahrenheit temperature in variable *f*.

HIGH-LEVEL LANGUAGE PROGRAM

Structures

3. Declaring structure *pay*, with members *payrate, hours-per-day[5]*, and *weekly-bonus*, write a program that reports John's total pay for the week to variable *check*.

HIGH-LEVEL LANGUAGE PROGRAM

Advanced Activities

4. Array *suspectprint* holds five elements of data describing a fingerprint. Array *printfile* holds the five-element fingerprint data of an individual in the police files. Write a program that reports the number of elements that match to variable *answer*.
5. Write program CENSORED, which scans a string (such as that listed below) and reports to variable *answer* the number of four-letter words found.

   'Oh darn and heck and damn and nuts.'

6. Use the bubble sort technique to arrange the five elements of array *grades* from highest to lowest.
7. Using an array of structures, modify the program of step 3 to process the data for three employees and report the day of the week (0–4) with the highest total payroll. (No bonus is involved.)
8. Write a program that scans the seven elements of array *pokerhand* (which holds numbers from 1 to 10) and reports to variable *answer* the value of any four-of-a-kind found. (For example, if the hand contains 4 fives, 5 is reported; if 4 sevens, 7 is reported.)

Name: ____________________

Date: ____________________

QUESTIONS AND PROBLEMS

Class: ____________________

1. Show how char array *apples* is initialized with 2, 3, 5, and 1.

2. Give an example of a subscripted variable; a structure variable.

3. In C, is the subscript of the first element in an array a 0 or a 1?

Advanced Section

4. Give an example of a typical variable in C when using a *structure of arrays*. An *array of structures*.

5. How are variables and arrays initialized when writing code for ROM?

6. What is the difference between a *structure* and a *union*?

ACTIVITY 25

FUNCTIONS AND PARAMETERS IN C

OBJECTIVE

- To write programs in C that involve functions and parameters.

PARTS AND EQUIPMENT

- IBM PC (bus-extender optional).
- C compiler, debugger, and utilities.

DISCUSSION

A function in C is similar to a subroutine in assembly-language—both are the primary means of carrying out top-down design. Using functions, we break up a large program into smaller "bite-sized" modules. As with subroutines, functions help to shield the detailed implementation from the overall concepts—much like the details contained in the chapters of a book are shielded by the more conceptual table of contents.

Based on the assembly-level techniques of Activity 14, any number of parameters may be passed to a function. If no value is returned, it is known as a *void* function; if a value is returned, it is often called a *typed* function.

Demonstration Programs

The three demonstration programs of Figure 25.1 show how functions are defined and parameters are passed for both void and typed functions.

The program of Figure 25.1(a) consists of two modules: calling function MAIN and called function DELAY. As shown, DELAY is called by simply writing its name in the main program. The parentheses after the function name tells the compiler that DELAY is a function rather than a variable. Because no parameters are passed, the parentheses are empty.

The function itself is defined by writing its name (*delay*), followed by the body of the function (a simple delay loop) within braces. Because function DELAY does not receive or return parameters. the parentheses after the function name and the "return type" (before the function name) are both "void." We use data type *unsigned short* (or *unsigned int*) for variable *i* to allow delay numbers up to 65,535.

As we learned when developing functions in assembly-language, a function that generates a single delay is not very useful. To generate a wide range of delay times, we send *actual parameter* (argument) *time* to function DELAY by way of *formal parameter t* [see Figure 25.1(b)]. Because the function still does not return a value, it retains the "void" return type.

A function that returns a value (a *typed* function) is demonstrated by Figure 25.1(c). Byte variables *first* and *second* are sent to function *product* as actual parameters. They are received by formal parameters *one* and *two,* multiplied together, returned to *main* (using the RETURN statement), and assigned to word variable *answer*. The use of data types *char* and *int* allows all variables to be signed numbers.

Note that the void function name (*delay*) of Figures 25.1(a) and (b) stands alone as a single statement. The typed function name (*product*) of Figure 25.1(c), on the other hand, does not stand alone because the returned value must be "picked up" and used. (A type function name can stand alone if the returned value is ignored.)

Function Definitions and Declarations

As with variables, all functions are *declared* before they are used. The declarations are either *defining declarations* or *referencing declarations*.

Returning to the programs of Figure 25.1, functions DELAY and PRODUCT are *defined* when they are written: by writing the function name, the formal parameters (including types), the return type, and the function body.

These functions are *declared* by writing their *function prototype* external to all functions—usually near the beginning of the program. The function prototype includes the function name, return type, and formal parameters—but not the function body. Furthermore, it is terminated by a semicolon and the formal parameter names need not be listed (only

FIGURE 25.1

Void and typed functions. (a) A void function that accepts no parameters. (b) A void function that accepts parameters. (c) A typed function that accepts parameters.

```
/* Function main calls function delay.
   No parameters are sent and no
   information is returned. */

void delay(void);  <-- Function prototype (declaration)

main()
{
    delay();  <-- Function call
}

Return type --> void delay(void)  <-- Function definition
{
    unsigned short i;

    for(i = 0;i < 0xffff;i++)
        ;
}
```

(a) Void function that accepts no parameters

```
/* To create a range of delay times, a
   parameter is sent to function delay. */

void delay(unsigned short);

main()
{
    unsigned short time;

    delay(time);    Actual parameter (argument)
}

void delay(unsigned short t)    Formal parameter
{
    unsigned short i;

    for(i = 0;i < t;i++)
        ;
}
```

(b) Void function that accepts parameters

```
/* This typed function accepts two signed
   integer byte variables and returns
   their product as a signed word integer. */

int product(char,char);

main()
{
    char first,second;    Multiple arguments
    int answer;

    answer = product(first,second);
}

Return type --> int product(char one,char two)
{
Return statement --> return(one * two);
}
```

(c) Typed function that accepts parameters

their types). The use of function prototypes is optional—if missing, the compiler constructs its own. However, they are highly recommended, especially when functions are external library routines (Activity 26).

The Binary I/O Port Functions

Available to QuickC programmers are a number of predefined (built-in) functions that access external (bus-extender) I/O ports:

FIGURE 25.2

Three major ways of using the return value of a typed function. (a) Assigning the return value. (b) As a parameter to another function. (c) Within a conditional expression.

```
#include <conio.h>

char average(char num1,char num2);

/* GET_AVERAGE
This program demonstrates the assignment
method of retrieving a returned value.
Two signed byte integers are input and
their average value is output. */
main()
{
    char result;

    while(1){
        result = average(inp(0),inp(1));
        outp(2,result);
    }
}

char average(char num1,char num2)
{
    return((num1 + num2) / 2);
}
```

(a) Assigning the return value

```
#include <conio.h>

char average(char num1,char num2);

/* GET_AVERAGE
This program uses the parameter nesting
method to retrieve a returned value.  Two
byte integers are input and their average
value is output.  */
main()
{
    while(1)
        outp(2,average(inp(0),inp(1)));
}

char average(char num1,char num2)
{
    return((num1 + num2) / 2);
}
```

(b) As a parameter to another function

```
#include <conio.h>

char average(char num1,char num2);

/* GET_AVERAGE
Using the conditional expression method to retrieve
a returned value.  If the average of two input byte
integers is greater than 10, 0xff is output.
Otherwise, 00 is output. */
main()
{
    while(1)
        if(average(inp(0),inp(1)) > 10)
            outp(2,0xff);
        else
            outp(2,0);
}

char average(char num1,char num2)
{
    return((num1 + num2) / 2);
}
```

(c) Within a conditional expression

inp( )	input byte
outp( )	output byte
inpw( )	input word
outpw( )	output word

The three programs of Figure 25.2, which output the average of two input byte values, demonstrate their use. (Include file *conio.h* holds the QuickC prototypes for the port I/O functions.) As an added bonus, these three programs summarize the three major methods of "picking up" and using the returned value from a typed function: (a) assigning the return value to a variable, (b) passing the return value to another function as a parameter (nesting functions), and (c) using the return value within a conditional expression.

The Internal Speaker

Using the I/O port functions, and the same techniques as Activity 8, the following statement performs a toggle/output of the IBM PC internal speaker:

```
outp(0x61,(inp(0x61) ^ 2) & 0xfe);
```

Recursion

As an advanced topic, a recursive function is one that calls itself. Recursion is useful for performing repetitive calculations, such as that demonstrated by function ODDSUM of Figure 25.3(a). Function ODDSUM accepts a byte parameter representing the first "*n*" odd numbers and returns their sum. For example, if $n = 3$, we expect to have 9 returned $(1 + 3 + 5)$. During recursion we go deeper and deeper into the nesting level; when a certain condition is met, we reverse the process and return. The actual calculations are done during the return process.

Suppose function ODDSUM is sent the number 3. Since the value is not 0, the first statement executed is *oddsum(n−1)*. The function calls itself, sending itself the parameter 2. The process repeats for parameters 1 and 0. However, upon receiving 0, *return(0)* is executed and we backtrack out of the nesting levels. The following summarizes the steps involved:

Call *oddsum* from *main* and send 3
Call self and send 2
Call self and send 1
Call self and send 0
Return 0 to self
Calculate $2*1-1 + 0 = 1$ and return 1 to self
Calculate $2*2-1 + 1 = 4$ and return 4 to self
Calculate $2*3-1 + 4 = 9$ and return 9 to main

Of course, the same result can be obtained with a simple loop, as shown by Figure 25.3(b). However, for certain types of problems, recursion is often easier to write.

FIGURE 25.3

Comparing recursion and loops when determining the sum of the first *n* odd numbers. (a) Using recursion. (b) Using loops.

```
/* Function oddsum uses recursion to
   return the sum of the first n odd
   numbers. */

unsigned short oddsum(unsigned char n)
{
    if(n == 0)
        return(0);
    else
        return(2*n-1 + oddsum(n-1));
}
```

```
/* Function oddsum uses loops to return
   the sum of the first n odd numbers */

unsigned short oddsum(unsigned char n)
{
    unsigned short i;
    for(i = 0;n>0;n--)
        i += 2*n-1;
    return(i);
}
```
(b) Using loops

Pointers

As another advanced topic, a *pointer* type refers to a variable that contains the address of another variable. One use of pointers is to enable a function to return more than one result back to the calling function.

Turning to Figure 25.4, function EXCHANGE swaps the values of two variables. First, the addresses of the two main-program variables (*x* and *y*) are sent as parameters (using the "&" operator). The parameters are received in variables *p1* and *p2*, where the "*" indicates that *p1* and *p2* hold pointers (to variables *x* and *y*). Using these pointers, the values of *x* and *y* (in main) are exchanged.

Pointers are especially useful when passing an array to a function. Instead of passing the array's data, we pass its address. The C language has made it easy, for whenever an array name is listed as a parameter, its address is automatically passed. Re-

FIGURE 25.4

Passing pointers to access local variables and to return multiple values.

```
void exchange(unsigned char *,unsigned char *);

/* POINTER DEMONSTRATION
Function exchange swaps the values
of two parameters.  It uses pointers to
return two variables. */
main()
{
    unsigned char x,y;

    exchange(&x,&y);
}

void exchange(unsigned char *p1,unsigned char *p2)
{
    unsigned char temp;

    temp = *p1;  /* x to temp */
    *p1 = *p2;   /* y to x */
    *p2 = temp;  /* temp to y */
}
```

ferring to program COUNT_EIGHTS of Figure 25.5, function COUNTCARDS accepts the address of array *pokerhand* (and the number of cards) and returns the number of eights.

Within function COUNTCARDS, the term $*(p+i)$ means "the element of array *pokerhand* pointed to by the sum of p (the address of the first element) plus i (the element number)." We could have used conventional array notation (p[i]) instead; however, the use of pointer notation often makes it easier to process addresses mathematically.

Call by Value Versus Call by Reference

In the C language, if the function arguments are simple numbers or variables, they are passed "by value." That is, the values of the parameters are sent to a function. The major advantage of "call by value" is that the called function cannot alter the original argument in the calling function. All the programs in this activity that do not use pointers are based on call by value.

The alternative to "call by value" is "call by reference," in which the *address* of the variable (a pointer) is passed rather than its value. All the "pointer" programs of this activity use call by reference.

PROCEDURE

NOTE: As always, unless otherwise specified, select the data type for each variable that seems most appropriate.

1. QuickC users add "#include <conio.h>" to your source program template and place file *conio.h* on your disk.

Void Functions

2. Write program WARBLE, in which a tone steadily increases in frequency, drops back to a low frequency (when a delay value underflows), and continuously repeats the process. The changing delay values are sent to function DELAY via parameter *freq*. (Use the internal speaker if desired.)

FIGURE 25.5

Using a pointer to pass an array to a function.

```
unsigned char countcards(unsigned char *,unsigned char);
unsigned char pokerhand[] = {8,3,4,8,8,9,8};

/* Program COUNT_EIGHTS
The number of eights in array pokerhand is
placed in variable answer. An array name is
passed as an address.  */
main()
{
    unsigned char answer;

    answer = countcards(pokerhand,7);
}

unsigned char countcards(unsigned char *p, unsigned char c)
{
    unsigned char i,j;

    j = 0;
    for(i = 0; i < c; i++)
        if(*(p+i) == 8)
            j++;
    return(j);
}
```

C PROGRAM

Typed Functions

3. Write a program that sends initialized variables *hours, pay rate,* and *bonus* to function WAGES, which returns the total pay for storage in variable *answer*.

C PROGRAM

Advanced Activities

4. By writing and using C functions NOTE (receives *frequency* and *duration* parameters) and REST (receives *duration* parameter), write a program that generates a continuous NOTE/REST sequence. (See Activity 9.)
5. Modify the program of step 4 so the NOTE/REST sequence is controlled by an array of structures. (*Hint:* Use three structure elements corresponding to: frequency of note, duration of note, and duration of rest.)
6. By writing and using C functions SQUARE and MULTIPLY, write a program that outputs in real time the distance traveled from time zero when an object is in free-fall. (Use bus-extender, if available.) The equation relating distance and time is:

$$D = 16 * T^2$$

where D = distance traveled and T = time elapsed.
7. The seven card values of array *pokerhand* (varying from 1 to 10) are stored as a global array. Within the main program we pass the array name (as a pointer) and a card value from 1 to 10 to function COUNT, which returns the number of cards with that value to byte variable *answer*.
8. Using recursion, write a C-language routine that returns $N!$ (N factorial) for any N from 1 to 8. Repeat using a loop.
9. Using a debugger, view the assembly-level code for any of the programs of Figure 25.2 and note the method of passing and returning parameters. (Is it the same as that learned in Activity 14?)

Name: ______________________

Date: ______________________

QUESTIONS AND PROBLEMS

Class: ______________________

1. Write "void" or "typed" before each statement:

   a. ______________ Returns a value.

   b. ______________ Stands alone as a single statement.

   c. ______________ Used anywhere a variable is used.

2. If a typed function is used in the manner of a void function (stands alone as a single statement), what happens to the returned value?

3. The source parameter is known as the "actual parameter" (or *argument*) and the destination parameter is known as the "formal parameter." In the program of Figure 25.2(c), what are the *actual* parameters and what are the *formal* parameters?

4. Why must functions that return a value be typed?

5. At the assembly-language level, how does C return byte and word values from a typed function?

6. Do the actual and formal parameters have to be of the same type? Do multiple actual and formal parameters have to be listed in the same order?

7. What is a *pointer variable*?

8. When calling *by value*, can the called function change local variables within the calling function? when calling *by reference*?

9. What is the purpose of a function declaration (*prototype*)?

10. What are the three major ways in which typed functions (those that return a value) can be used in C programs?

Advanced Section

11. For analysis purposes, we can consider a typed function name to be a memory "container" that receives the returned value. Does the function name represent an *actual* memory location? Give reasons for your answer.

12. If *apples* is the name of an array, what is contained in variable *crate* for each of the following?
    a. crate = apples
    b. crate = *(apples + i)
13. What is a *linked list* and how are pointers used to implement a linked list?

ACTIVITY 26

C LIBRARY ROUTINES/MIXED-LANGUAGE PROGRAMMING

OBJECTIVES

- To combine (link) modules written in C and ASM.
- To write programs that nest functions.

PARTS AND EQUIPMENT

- IBM PC (bus-extender optional).
- Assembler, C compiler, debugger, and utilities.

DISCUSSION

In this key activity, we take three giant steps toward more efficient top-down design: our C functions are independently compiled and placed in a library (the same library that holds our assembly-generated subroutines), C and assembly-generated functions are combined in the same program (*mixed-language programming*), and functions are nested as deeply as we wish.

C Library Routines

Demonstration program GET_AVERAGE of Figure 26.1 is identical to that of the previous activity [Figure 25.2(b)]—except that function MAIN and function AVERAGE are written and compiled as separate files. Unlike assembly-language, no PUBLIC/EXTERN directives are required for the functions. (All C functions are automatically public, and all function calls are tagged external by default.)

FIGURE 26.1

Demonstration program GET_AVERAGE using independently compiled modules. (a) Main module. (b) Library function AVERAGE.

```
#include <conio.h>

char average(char,char);

/* GET_AVERAGE
   Library routine AVERAGE was written in C,
   separately compiled, and stored in MYLIB. */
main()
{
     while(1)
          outp(2,average(inp(0),inp(1)));
}
```

(a) Main module

```
char average(char num1,char num2)
{
     return((num1 + num2) / 2);
}
```

(b) Library function *average*

After compilation, function AVERAGE is stored in library MYLIB.LIB (overwriting that created in Activity 15) and linked to MAIN during the batch process.

Mixed-Language Programming

A *mixed-language program* is one that contains modules written in more than one language. For example, the main program of Figure 26.2 performs the same function as GET_AVERAGE of Figure 26.1. However, instead of using the built-in C functions for external port I/O, we borrowed several

FIGURE 26.2

Mixed-language programming.

```
char average(char,char);
char keybhex(void),crtbhex(char);
void newline(void);

/* GET_AVERAGE_MIXED
   Library function AVERAGE was written in C
   and library functions KEYBHEX, CRTBHEX,
   and NEWLINE were written in assembly-
   language.  */
main()
{
     while(1){
          crtbhex(average(keybhex(),keybhex()));
          newline();
     }
}
```

familiar keyboard/monitor library routines previously written in assembly-language (see Activity 18).

The mixed-language program works because all modules—both assembly and C—are compatible. That is, all assembly-language modules obey C-language syntax and C-language parameter-passing techniques. Just remember that when passing multiple parameters from a C main program to an assembly-generated library routine, the parameters are passed in reverse order. (The last parameter listed is the first one pushed.)

Nesting Library Routines

Nesting gives us the ability to call any function (except MAIN) at any time, regardless of the language in which either was written. It follows that there is no limit to how deep functions can be nested.

The program of Figure 26.3 demonstrates the nesting of functions. The main program inputs and passes a number to high-level library routine SOUNDOFF, which emits a number of beeps equal to the passed value. Routine SOUNDOFF in turn calls low-level nested library routines MSEC and BEEP. All modules—regardless of nesting level—are placed into the library, and all are properly combined at link time.

Library routine nesting is a very powerful and commonly used technique. Because most of the standard programs in this manual are small, nesting is not always necessary for efficient programming. However, for the more complex "advanced activities" and the projects of Activity 43, nesting is a very powerful tool and should be used to maximum advantage.

FIGURE 26.3

Nesting demonstration program. (a) Main. (b) High-level library routine SOUNDOFF.

```
/* This program demonstrates function
   nesting.  The main program calls
   high-level library routine SOUNDOFF,
   sending it a parameter value input in
   decimal. */

void soundoff(unsigned char);
unsigned char keybdec(void);

main()
{
    while(1)
        soundoff(keybdec());
}
```

(a) Main

```
/* This high-level library routine accepts a
   byte parameter and sounds that number of
   beeps.  It in turn calls lower level library
   routines MSEC and BEEP.  */

void msec(unsigned short),beep(void);

void soundoff(unsigned char n)
{
    unsigned char i;

    for (i = 0; i < n; ++i){
        msec(500);
        beep();
    }
}
```

(b) High-level library routine SOUND_OFF

A Milestone Demonstration Program

The program of Figure 26.4 summarizes a great deal of the purpose and intent of this lab/text manual. Briefly, this milestone program inputs a string of up to 20 digits. Then, every 3 s, a series of beeps is generated equal to the square of each successive string value. We note the following:

1. The indirection operator (*) in the CRTSTRNG and KEYSTRNG function prototypes indicates that the function arguments are pointers (array addresses) to the character elements of the array.
2. The ASCII numbers from 0 to 9 are converted to decimal by ANDing with 0xf.

FIGURE 26.4

A milestone program.

```
/* A MILESTONE PROGRAM
   A string of digits (0 - 9) is asked for and
   input.  Every three seconds a series of beeps
   is generated equal to the square of each
   successive string value. (Be sure to terminate
   the input string with $.)*/

void soundoff(unsigned char),msec(unsigned short);
void crtstrng(char *),keystrng(char *);
unsigned short square(unsigned char);

char ask[] = {"Give me some numbers (0 - 9): $"};
char numbers[20];

main()
{
    unsigned char i;

    crtstrng(ask);
    keystrng(numbers);
    for (i = 0; numbers[i] != '$';i++){
        msec(3000);
        soundoff(square(numbers[i] & 0xf));
    }
}
```

This milestone program combines the structure theorem (control-flow), libraries, mixed-language programming, function nesting, keyboard-monitor I/O, ASCII, strings, and masking. It is concise, powerful, and fast; and it is easy to write, read, and troubleshoot. Most important, it demonstrates the concept of top-down-programming, as we go from the more conceptual main program at the top down to the more detailed MSEC and BEEP functions at the bottom.

Given the advantages of top-down programming, we can concentrate on what human beings do best: solving problems. From this point on, expect programming to be more of an art than a science.

Storage Class Specifiers

A function or variable declaration must include a *storage class specifier*. These specifiers control the "visibility" of a function or variable (where are they valid?) and the "lifetime" of a function or variable (when are they valid?). We have five to choose from:

auto
register
static
extern
none (default, or no specifier given)

Because we have not as yet seen any of the first four specifiers, the default case must be the most commonly used. A storage class specifier must appear with all functions, local variables, and global variables. Let's examine each case separately by referring to Figure 26.5, which performs the following calculation:

```
output = first+second+first+third.
```

FIGURE 26.5

The most often used storage class specifiers. (a) Main program source file. (b) Library routine source file.

```
/* This main program defines global
   variable first and local variable
   second. */

void crtwdec(int);
int myfunction(int);

int first = 1;
main()
{
    int second = 2;

    crtwdec(myfunction(first+second));
}
```

(a) Main program source file

```
/* This function declares global
   variable first and defines local
   variable third. */

extern int first;

int myfunction(int subtotal)
{
    int third = 3;

    return(subtotal+first+third);
}
```

(b) Library routine source file

Functions

As shown in Figure 26.5, all functions carry the *extern* specifier by default. This means that all functions are defined at the "external level." No function can appear within another function, and any function can call any other function (except main) at any time. Furthermore, all functions have "global lifetimes" (they are permanent) and are "visible" (valid) throughout all the source files that make up the program.

A function declared to be *static* has all the characteristics of *extern,* except it is visible only within the source file in which it is defined.

Local variables

Remaining with Figure 26.5, variables *second* and *third* carry the *auto* (automatic) storage class specifier by default. This is because these variables are declared at the "local level" (within functions MAIN and MYFUNCTION). They are visible only within the module in which they are defined, and they have "local lifetimes." (They are created on the stack when we enter the function and are destroyed when we leave the function.) Automatic variables may be initialized in the definition.

A local variable declared with the *register* storage class specifier has all the characteristics of *auto,* except the variable is stored in an internal register—*if one is available*. Register variables speed access and reduce code size.

A local variable declared with the *static* specifier has all the characteristics of *auto,* except it has a "global lifetime." (It is permanently stored in the data segment rather than temporarily on the stack.) When tagged static, an aggregate type (such as an array) can be initialized locally.

Global variables

Referring to function MAIN of Figure 26.5(a), variable *first* is declared at the "external level." It carries no storage class specifier and is initialized. Therefore, according to the rules of the C language, the declaration is a *defining declaration* and space is allocated in memory. Variable *first* has a "global lifetime'' and is visible throughout the rest of the main program.

Referring to function MYFUNCTION of Figure 26.5(b), variable *first* carries the *extern* storage class specifier. Therefore, the declaration is a *referencing declaration,* which tells the compiler that *first* is *defined* in another source file. This makes the definition of variable *first* (in function MAIN) visible to function MYFUNCTION.

An external variable given the *static* storage class specifier is visible only within its own source file.

To avoid the obvious confusion inherent in the subject of storage class specifiers, just remember two things: the default case is used most of the time, and global variables must be tagged *extern* if they are used by the present module but defined in another module.

A Recommendation

The choice of assembly-language or C for any given module depends on the application. For many applications, we recommend that the higher-level modules (such as main) be written in C and the lower-level library routines (such as MSEC) be written in assembly-language. The reasons are basic: Because the lower-level routines will be used over and over, and because most of the computing time is spent within them, we can afford to spend the extra time required to write compact and efficient routines in assembly-language.

Each higher-level module, on the other hand, is likely to be written only once for each application and accounts for only a small fraction of computing time. Therefore, we choose a high-level language to help us work at the conceptual level, to speed the product to market, and to write programs that are self-documenting.

Calling C Routines from Assembly-Language Programs

Any library routine written in C assumes that a certain initialization code has been executed previously. This implies that we cannot call a C library routine from an assembly-language main program. For example, the main program of Figure 26.6(a) cannot call module AVERAGE, because module AVERAGE was written in C.

We solve the problem by writing the assembly-language main program as a procedure and calling it from a ''startup'' C module. For example, the startup C module of Figure 26.6(b) calls module MAINASM of Figure 26.6(c) (now a procedure), which in turn is now able to call C-generated module AVERAGE.

PROCEDURE

NOTE: ''Mix-and-match'' I/O methods in any way you wish. Use C for all main programs.

1. Microsoft users add library MYLIB to the link command in your batch file, as shown in Figure 26.7. Make the necessary changes if using software other than from Microsoft.
2. Using C, write independently compiled function TRIANGLE, which accepts two unsigned char parameters representing the base and altitude of a right triangle, and returns the area of the triangle as an unsigned short.

FUNCTION TRI

3. Compile function TRIANGLE and add to library MYLIB.

NOTE: To compile a C library routine, we use the third line of the batch file, as shown below for QuickC:

```
QCL/c/AS/Gs/Zi filename.C <E>
```

4. Write a main program in C that inputs variables *base* and *altitude* (unsigned char), passes them as parameters to function TRIANGLE, and outputs the returned area (unsigned short).

MAIN-PROGRAM DISPLAY_AREA

FIGURE 26.6

Calling C routines from assembly-language modules. (a) Assembly-language main program cannot call C-generated routine AVERAGE. (b) C-level startup routine calls assembly-language main program as a procedure. (c) Assembly-level main module written as a procedure.

```
; Main program MIMIC_AVERAGE written
; in assembly-language.

NAME        MIMIC_AVERAGE

INCLUDE HEADER

_DATA       SEGMENT PUBLIC 'DATA'
_DATA       ENDS

_TEXT       SEGMENT PUBLIC 'CODE'
            ASSUME CS:_TEXT,DS:DGROUP,SS:DGROUP

     EXTRN  _keybdec:NEAR, _crtbdec:NEAR
     EXTRN  _newline:NEAR, _average:NEAR

    main:   mov    ax,DGROUP
            mov    ds,ax
    again:  call   _keybdec
            push   ax
            call   _keybdec
            push   ax
            call   _average
            add    sp,4
            push   ax
            call   _crtbdec
            add    sp,2
            call   _newline
            jmp    again
_TEXT       ENDS
            END    main
```

(a) Assembly-language main program cannot call C-generated routine AVERAGE

```
/* This start-up routine is required
   if any library routine written in
   C is called from any assembly-language
   routine.  */

void mainasm(void);

main()
{
    mainasm();
}
```

(b) C-level start-up routine

```
; This assembly-language main module is
; called from a C startup routine because
; library routine _average was written in
; C.

NAME        MAINASM

INCLUDE HEADER

_DATA       SEGMENT PUBLIC 'DATA'
_DATA       ENDS

_TEXT       SEGMENT PUBLIC 'CODE'
            ASSUME CS:_TEXT,DS:DGROUP

      PUBLIC _mainasm

      EXTRN  _keybdec:NEAR,_crtbdec:NEAR
      EXTRN  _newline:NEAR,_average:NEAR

  _mainasm  PROC NEAR
    again:  call   _keybdec
            push   ax
            call   _keybdec
            push   ax
            call   _average
            add    sp,4
            push   ax
            call   _crtbdec
            add    sp,2
            call   _newline
            jmp    again
            ret
  _mainasm  ENDP

_TEXT       ENDS
            END
```

(c) Assembly-level main module as a procedure

FIGURE 26.7

Adding our "homemade" library (MYLIB.LIB) to the link command.

```
LINK /CO %1,,,MYLIB SLIBCE;
```

5. Run your batch file and test your program. Is the area properly calculated? ____________
6. Using assembly-generated library routine SQUARE, write a loop program that inputs unsigned bytes and outputs their square (unsigned short).

MAIN-PROGRAM MIMIC_SQUARE

7. Using assembly-generated library routines SQUARE, MSEC, and BEEP, write a program that sounds four beeps in a row spaced 1, 4, 9, and 16 s apart. (Routine PORTSET is required if BEEP uses the external speaker.)

MAIN-PROGRAM BEEP_SQUARE

8. Arrays *base* and *altitude* each hold ten elements. Write a program that reads in each base/altitude pair at the rate of one every 5 s, displays each area, and beeps whenever the area is greater than 100. The program halts when all ten elements are read.

MAIN PROGRAM

Advanced Activities

9. Using nesting techniques, write library routine SPOT, which accepts character, column, and row parameters, and prints to the screen the specified character at the specified position.

   Using routine SPOT, write a main program that prints "HAPPY NEW YEAR" to the screen in a diagonal format.
10. Write a combination lock program that emits a beep every 4 s. After each beep, a number is entered. When the correct combination is entered in sequence (such as 7, 12, and 2), OPEN is displayed.

MAIN-PROGRAM COMBINATION

11. Using assembly-language, write library routine BEEPF, in which the sound frequency is controlled by a byte parameter. The parameter is returned.

    Making use of routine BEEPF, write program PROGRAMMABLE_MUSIC, which first accepts five input frequency values, then plays back the information in the form of a continuous series of five beeps at the frequencies corresponding to the input values.

Name: ______________________

Date: ______________________

Class: ______________________

QUESTIONS AND PROBLEMS

1. Why are library routines often written in assembly-language and main programs often written in a high-level language?

2. How do we know from this experiment (without looking at any assembly-level code) that the C compiler must use the C method of passing parameters introduced in Activity 14? (*Hint:* Would mixed-language programming work if this were not true?)

3. Referring to Figure 26.2, does function/parameter nesting on one line improve readability?

4. Why don't we include *conio.h* in the program of Figure 26.2?

5. Function CRTBHEX was written to return the output value. What happens to the returned value in the program of Figure 26.2?

Advanced Section

6. When writing a function prototype, the parameter variable names can be different from those in the function definition (and, in fact, are optional). Why is this vital when using library routines in C programs?

7. Considering functions and global variables in C, what is the difference between a *definition* and a *declaration*?

8. Why are the PUBLIC/EXTERN directives not needed when linking functions written in C?

9. When is a variable given the *extern* storage class specifier?

ACTIVITY 27

THE C RUN-TIME LIBRARIES

OBJECTIVE

- To perform a variety of operations, including keyboard/video I/O, using C run-time functions.

PARTS AND EQUIPMENT

- IBM PC (bus-extender optional).
- Assembler, C compiler, debugger, and utilities

DISCUSSION

When you purchase a C compiler, you also purchase a number of "run-time" library functions that provide more than 200 predefined (built-in) functions and macros. QuickC users, for example, have already been using run-time library SLIBCE.LIB for needed "start-up" routines and for binary port I/O.

The function declarations for the run-time functions are contained in a number of "h" files. They are highly recommended to prevent improper use of functions and to uncover errors, but they are not required. (Within this text, all "h" file categories are based on QuickC.)

In this activity, we make use of the following run-time functions:

Character I/O

getch( ) Waits for a key to be pressed; inputs and returns a single ASCII character from the keyboard. [getche( ) echoes the character to the monitor and moves the cursor one space to the right.] Function declared in *conio.h*.

putch( ) Prints a single ASCII character to the monitor and moves the cursor one space to the right. Returns the character written, or EOF (end of file) if error. Function declared in *conio.h*.

Numeric I/O

scanf( ) Inputs one or more *fields* (sequences of characters) from the keyboard, and stores in one or more argument locations. In its simplest form, it inputs a single field and terminates when a "newline" is performed. The cursor moves to a new line. Data can be entered from the keyboard in a number of types (hexadecimal, decimal, floating point, etc.). Function may require conversion specifier *lf* when inputting values of type *double*. All input values are echoed to the screen. Returns the number of fields assigned. Function declared in *stdio.h*.

printf( ) Prints any combination of numeric values and strings to the screen. The type of the numeric value (hexadecimal, decimal, character, etc.) is specified by the function. A newline is performed whenever the "\n" character is encountered in the string. Returns the number of characters printed. Function declared in *stdio.h*.

String I/O

gets( ) Inputs a sequence of characters (a string) until a newline is encountered. The characters are echoed to the screen and stored in an array of type char. The last character entered (newline) is replaced by NULL ('\0'). The cursor moves to a new line. Returns its argument. Function declared in *stdio.h*. [Function scanf( ) also performs string input to an array with automatic NULL termination.]

puts( ) Outputs the string stored in an array to the screen, followed by newline. Returns zero if successful; nonzero if not. Function declared in *stdio.h*.

[Function printf( ) also performs string output from an array that is terminated by NULL.]

Stream I/O

fopen( ) Opens a file and specifies a type of access: "r" for read, "w" for write, "r+" for read/write of existing file, "w+" for read/write of new file, "a" to append, and "a+" to read and append. Returns a pointer to the open file; returns NULL if error. Function declared in *stdio.h*.

fclose( ) Flushes all buffers and closes a file. Returns 0 if successful; EOF if not. Function declared in *stdio.h*.

fgetc( ) Returns single character (as int) from input stream and points to next character. All streams are terminated with EOF. Function declared in *stdio.h*.

fputc( ) Writes a single character to the output stream and points to next position. All streams are terminated with EOF. Stream name *stdout* directs characters to screen. Function declared in *stdio.h*.

String manipulation

strcmpi( ) Compares two strings and returns a zero if they are equal. The comparison is made without regard to case. Function declared in *string.h*.

Math

rand( ) Returns a pseudorandom number from 0 to 32,787. Function declared in *stdlib.h*. [To generate a random number from 0 to $x - 1$, use rand( )%x.]

srand( ) Sets the starting point for generation of random numbers by function rand( ). Function declared in *stdlib.h*.

sin( ), cos( ), tan( ) Returns the indicated trig value for any input angle in radians from 0 to 2π. Function declared in *math.h*. Uses data type *double*.

log10( ) Returns the value of the common logarithm. Function declared in *math.h*. Uses data type *double*.

sqrt( ) Returns the square root. Function declared in *math.h*. Uses data type *double*.

pow( ) Returns x raised to the y power. Function declared in *math.h*. Uses data type *double*.

abs( ) Returns the absolute value of integer argument. Function declared in *stdlib.h*.

The string, math, and stream functions and macros are from the complete sets of Figure 27.1, and all are available to us. For a complete description of these and other run-time functions, refer to the appropriate literature (such as Microsoft's *Run-Time Library Reference*).

Character Constants and Escape Sequences

Several of the run-time functions listed in Figure 27.1 recognize *character constants*. A character constant is one character within single quotes, such as 'A'. Its value is the ASCII equivalent of the character (in this case 41H). When programming in C, we find it convenient to represent certain characters by *escape sequences* (backslash followed by one or more characters). These escape sequences are also valid within strings.

The following list gives a variety of character constants, most using escape sequences to represent the character:

CHARACTER CONSTANT	ASCII EQUIVALENT
'A' (Capital A)	41H
'\n' (Newline/Linefeed)	0AH
'\0' (NULL or zero)	00H
'3' (Three)	33H
'\a' (Bell)	07H
'\b' (Backspace)	08H
'\r' (Carriage return)	0DH
'*' (Asterisk)	2AH
'\\' (Print backslash)	5CH

In many cases, when writing programs, you may use either the character constant or its ASCII equivalent. For example, all of the following cause a carriage return:

```
putch('\r');
putch(0xd);
putch(13);
```

Newline

Newline stands for the combination of *linefeed* (0AH) and *carriage return* (0DH). Therefore, looking over the list of character constants from the previous section, does character \n stand for a newline or does it stand for line feed? The answer is, it could stand for either. In the first case below, \n generates a line feed, and in the second case it generates a newline (linefeed and carriage return in sequence). It all depends on how the function interprets the character constant or its ASCII equivalent.

putch('\n') (Linefeed)
printf("\n"); (Newline)

FIGURE 27.1

Several run-time library groups. (a) The string manipulation functions. (b) The math functions. (c) The stream (file) I/O functions.

GROUP	FUNCTION	RETURNS
Compare	strcmp	Compares two strings
	strcmpi	Compares two strings (case insensitive)
	strncmp	Compares characters of two strings
	strnicmp	Compares characters of two strings (case insensitive)
Find	strchr	Finds first occurrence of character in string
	strcspn	Finds first occurrence of a character from given character set in string
	strlen	Finds length of string
	strpbrk	Finds first occurrence of character from one string in another
	strrchr	Finds last occurrence of given character in string
	strspn	Finds first substring from given character set in string
	strstr	Finds first occurrence of given string in another string
	strtok	Finds next token in string
Copy/append	strcat	Appends a string
	strcpy	Copies one string to another
	strdup	Duplicates string
	strncat	Appends characters of string
	strncpy	Copies characters of one string to another
Convert	strlwr	Converts string to lowercase
	strupr	Converts string to uppercase
Set	strnset	Sets characters of string to given character
	strset	Sets all characters of string to given character
Other	strerror	Saves error message
	strrev	Reverses string

(a) The string manipulation run-time functions

GROUP	FUNCTION	RETURNS
Arithmetic	ceil(x)	The nearest whole number above x
	fabs(x)	The absolute value of x
	floor(x)	The nearest whole number below x
	pow(x,y)	x raised to y power
	sqrt(x)	The square root of x
Trigonometric	acos(x)	The arc cosine of x
	asin(x)	The arc sine of x
	atan(x)	The arc tangent of x
	atan2(y,x)	The arc tangent of y/x
	cos(x)	The cosine of x
	cosh(x)	The hyperbolic cosine of x
	sin(x)	The sine of x
	sinh(x)	The hyperbolic sine of x
	tan(x)	The tangent of x
	tanh(x)	The hyperbolic tangent of x
Logarithmic	exp(x)	The value of the exponential e
	log(x)	The value of the natural logarithm of x
	log10(x)	The value of the common logarithm of x
Random numbers	frand(x)	A pseudo random number between 0.0 and 1.0
	rand(x)	A pseudo random whole number from 0 to 32,767
	srand(x)	Reseeds the random generator with a value of x

(b) The math run-time functions

FIGURE 27.1 (*continued*)

GROUP	FUNCTION	RETURNS
Open/close	fopen	Opens file for access
	fclose	Closes a file
	freopen	Closes file and opens another
Read	getc	Reads a character from file
	fgetc	Reads a character from file
	fgets	Reads a string from file
	fscanf	Reads data from file
	fread	Reads n items from file
	ungetc	Pushes character back into file
Write	putc	Writes a character to file
	fputc	Writes a character to file
	fputs	Writes a string to file
	fprintf	Writes data to file
	fwrite	Writes n items to file
	fflush	Writes buffer to file
Pointer	fseek	Locates file pointer
	rewind	Sets file pointer to beginning of file
	ftell	Gets current position of file pointer
Error	clearerr	Clears errors
	ferror	Detects read/write error
	perror	Prints error message
Other	rename	Renames a file
	setbuf	Assigns buffer
	feof	Detects end of file

(c) The stream I/O run-time functions

The same problem can arise when you press 'Enter'' from the keypad. The ''Enter'' key inputs the code for carriage return (0DH). If the programmer wishes this to generate a new line, the code for linefeed (0AH) must be added.

EOF

Several of the functions of Figure 27.1 use EOF (*end-of-file*) to indicate the end of a file or an error. In the C programming language, EOF is defined in *stdio.h* as an integer of value −1 (FFFFH). EOF is typed as an integer because no character can have that value. Although a char value for EOF (FFH) would be unique for the ASCII code range (00 to 7FH), as soon as we add parity bits and allow for extended code, we require an integer-value EOF.

Therefore, when using any function that recognizes or returns EOF, it's best to type all appropriate variables as *int*.

Keyboard/Monitor/Stream I/O

The programs of Figure 27.2 use the simple input/delay/output loop algorithm to demonstrate the use of the I/O run-time functions.

The character I/O functions of Figure 27.2(a) are straightforward. A single ASCII character is input from the keyboard and output to the monitor.

The string I/O functions of Figure 27.2(b) input sequences of characters (strings) from the keyboard and write them to the monitor. All strings are terminated with NULL.

Moving to Figure 27.2(c), we use SCANF to input a decimal number from the keyboard (as a sequence of pressed keys terminated by *newline*) and store them as a single unit in variable *temp*. (The ''&'' is an operator that returns the address of variable *temp* and is required by the SCANF function when inputting to a variable.) Using function PRINTF, we display the input value. Within PRINTF, the quotes ('' '') indicate the string to be printed, and the %d ''place marker'' (conversion specifier) indicates where the input value from variable *number* is to appear within the string. The ''d'' tells the system to print the input value to the screen as a decimal number, and the \n *escape sequence* commands a newline. Any number of conversion specifiers and their corresponding expressions can be used. Other conversion specifiers include: %x (hexadecimal), %u (unsigned), %f (floating point), %e (scientific notation), %c (character), and %s (string).

The stream I/O functions of Figure 27.2(d) are useful for storing large amounts of data in a floppy or hard disk file. We first define variable *stream* as a file pointer. We open file ''myfile'' and return to *stream* the file's location. We use GETCHE to input characters from the keypad and we use FPUTC to write them to the file. When a carriage return is entered (ASCII 13), we exit and close the file (automatically appending EOF to the end of the file). After a 1-s delay, we open the same file and use FGETC to read characters from the file and FPUTC to write them to the monitor. When EOF is reached, we exit the loop and close the file.

FIGURE 27.2

Simple I/O loops using the run-time functions. (a) Character I/O using GETCH and PUTCH. (b) String I/O using GETS and PUTS. (c) Numeric I/O using SCANF and PRINTF. (d) Stream I/O using FGETC and FPUTC.

```
#include <conio.h>
unsigned short msec(unsigned short);
/* Character I/O using run-time functions
   GETCH and PUTCH. */
main()
{
    char temp;

    while(1){
        temp = getch();
        msec(1000);
        putch(temp);
    }
}
```

(a) Character I/O using GETCH and PUTCH

```
#include <stdio.h>
unsigned short msec(unsigned short);
/* String I/O using run-time functions
   GETS and PUTS. */
main()
{
    char name[20];

    while(1){
        puts("What is your name?");
        gets(name);
        msec(1000);
        puts("Is this your name?");
        puts(name);
    }
}
```

(b) String I/O using GETS and PUTS

```
#include <stdio.h>
unsigned short msec(unsigned short);
/* Numeric I/O using run-time functions
   PRINTF and SCANF. */
main()
{
    int temp;

    while(1){
        printf("Input a number: ");
        scanf("%d",&temp);
        msec(1000);
        printf("The input is %d.\n",temp);
    }
}
```

(c) Numeric I/O using SCANF and PRINTF

```
#include <stdio.h>
unsigned short msec(unsigned short);
main()
{
    FILE *stream;
    int c;

    clear();
    stream = fopen("myfile", "w");
    while ((c = getche()) != 13)
        fputc(c,stream);
    fclose(stream);
    newline();
    msec(1000);
    stream = fopen("myfile","r");
    while ((c = fgetc(stream)) != EOF)
        fputc(c,stdout);
    fclose(stream);
}
```

(d) Stream I/O using FGETC and FPUTC

FIGURE 27.3

Run-time demonstration programs. (a) Count letters. (b) Random shots. (c) Security. (d) Sine wave. (e) Seismograph.

```
/* This program first inputs a string.  It then inputs a
   letter, reporting how many of that letter are in the
   string.  We enter other letters until ESC is entered,
   which allows entry of another string and repeat of the
   process.  */
#include <conio.h>
#include <stdio.h>
main()
{
    char string[80],letter;
    int i,count;

    while(1){
        puts("Give me a string:");
        gets(string);
        do{
            puts("Give me a letter.");
            puts("(Press ESC to get another string.)");
            letter = getch();
            for (i = 0,count = 0;string[i] != '\0';i++)
                if (string[i] == letter)
                    count++;
            printf("The string contains %d %c's\n\n",count,letter);
        }while (letter != 27);
    }
}
```

(a) Count letters

```
/* This program asks the player to bet from 1 to 100
   dollars.  Using three vertical lines, it divides the
   screen into four sections.  "Shots" (asterisks) are
   fired at random locations at the rate of 4/s.  Each
   shot that lands in the left-most section pays $3.  When
   the game is over, your winnings are reported. */
#include <conio.h>
#include <stdio.h>
unsigned short msec(unsigned short);
void clear(void),beep(void);
void setcur(unsigned char,unsigned char);
main()
{
    int  c,seed,i,j,wager,winnings = 0;

    clear();
    printf("Give me seed value: ");
    scanf("%d",&seed);
    srand(seed);
    printf("\nHow much do you want to bet? ");
    scanf("%d",&wager);
    clear();
    for (i = 20;i<80;i += 20)
        for (j = 0;j<25;j++){
            setcur(i,j);
            putch('|');
        }
    for (i = 0;i<wager;i++){
        msec(250);
        setcur(c = rand()%80,rand()%25);
        putch('*');
        if (c < 20){
            beep();
            winnings += 3;
        }
    }
    setcur(5,5);
    printf("You bet %d and won %d",wager,winnings);
}
```

(b) Random shots

FIGURE 27.3

(continued)

```
/* Program SECURITY_CLEARANCE asks your
   name and age.  After thinking for
   several seconds, it passes you if your
   name is John and your age is 35. */
#include <stdio.h>
#include <string.h>
#include <conio.h>
void clear(void);
unsigned short msec(unsigned short);
main()
{
    char name[20];
    int  age,i;

    clear();
    while(1){
        printf("What is your name? ");
        scanf("%s",name);
        printf("how old are you? ");
        scanf("%d",&age);
        puts("I'm thinking");
        for (i = 0;i < 10;++i){
            putch('*');
            msec(500);
        }
        if ((strcmpi(name,"John\0") == 0) && (age == 35))
            printf("\nYOU MAY PASS!\n\n");
        else
            printf("\n%s, who is %d, you may NOT pass\n\n",name,age);
    }
}
```

(c) Security

```
/*This program draws a sine wave and x axis
  on the screen.*/
#include <conio.h>
#include <math.h>
void clear(void);
void setcur(unsigned char, unsigned char);
main()
{
    double pi = 3.1415926;
    int x,y,i,degrees;

    clear();
    for (degrees = 0,x = 0,y = 12;degrees <= 360;degrees += 5){
        setcur(x,y);
        putch('*');
        x++;
        y = 12 - (int)12*sin(degrees*pi/180);
    }
    for (i = 0;i < 80;i++){
        y = 12;
        setcur(i,y);
        putch('-');
    }
}
```

(d) Sine wave

```
/* This program reads "seismic" data from file
   myfile and prints it to the screen as a
   graph.  Whenever the plot changes by more
   that 10 units, a beep is sounded. */
#include <stdio.h>
#include <conio.h>
unsigned short msec(unsigned short);
void setcur(unsigned char,unsigned char);
void beep(void),clear(void);
main()
{
    FILE *stream;
    int c,pre = 10,col = 0;

    clear();
    stream = fopen("myfile", "r");
    while ((c = fgetc(stream)) != EOF){
        c = (c & 0xf)*2;
        setcur(col++,c+3);
        putch('*');
        if (abs(pre-c) > 10)
            beep();
        pre = c;
        msec(300);
        if (col > 79){
            col = 0;
            clear();
        }
    }
    fclose(stream);
}
```

(e) Sysmigraph

Run-Time Demonstration Programs

The demonstration programs of Figure 27.3 make use of a variety of run-time functions to carry out various tasks. The program of Figure 27.3(a) uses a number of I/O functions to count the number of selected letters in a sentence. The program of Figure 27.3(b) highlights the RAND function, which is used to generate random "shots" on the screen. Program SECURITY_CLEARANCE of Figure 27.3(c) focuses on function STRCMPI to verify a person's name before granting access. The program of Figure 27.3(d) is built around trig function SIN, and makes it easy for us to draw a sine wave on the

FIGURE 27.4

Modulation of program RANDOM SHOTS. (a) Library routines. (b) Main program. (c) Structure chart.

```
/* Library routine SEEDME asks for
   a seed value and randomizes the
   RAND function.   */

#include <stdio.h>
void seedme(void)
{
    int seed;

    printf("Give me seed value: ");
    scanf("%d",&seed);
    srand(seed);
}
```

SEEDME

```
/* Library routine GETBET asks for a wager
   (0 to 64,000) and returns the value. */

#include <stdio.h>
int getbet()
{
    unsigned int  wager;

    printf("\nHow much do you want to bet? ");
    scanf("%d",&wager);
    return(wager);
}
```

GETBET

```
/* Library routine LINES divides the
   screen into four equal parts by
   drawing three vertical lines. */

#include <stdio.h>
void setcur(unsigned char,unsigned char);
void lines(void)
{
    char i,j;

    for (i = 20;i<80;i += 20)
        for (j = 0;j<25;j++){
            setcur(i,j);
            putch('|');
        }
}
```

LINES

```
/* Library routine SHOOT accepts the wager
   as a parameter and prints that many
   astericks ("shots") to the screen at
   random locations at the rate of 4/s.
   Whenever a shot lands in the left-
   most quadrant, a beep sounds and $3
   is added to winnings.  After all shots
   are fired, the total winnings are
   returned.  */

#include <conio.h>
#include <stdio.h>
#include <stdlib.h>
unsigned short msec(unsigned short);
void beep(void);
void setcur(unsigned char,unsigned char);
int shoot(int wager)
{
    int  i,j,c,winnings = 0;

    for (i = 0;i<wager;i++){
        msec(250);
        setcur(c = rand()%80,rand()%25);
        putch('*');
        if (c < 20){
            beep();
            winnings += 3;
        }
    }
    return(winnings);
}
```

SHOOT

```
/* Library routine GIVEWIN accepts both
   the original wager and the winnings as
   parameters and prints them to the
   screen.  */

#include <stdio.h>
void setcur(unsigned char,unsigned char);
void givewin(int bet,int win)
{
    setcur(0,5);
    printf("You bet %d and won %d",bet,win);
}
```

GIVEWIN

(a) Library routines

```
/* Main program highly modularized. */
void seedme(void),lines(void);
int getbet(void);
int shoot(int);
void givewin(int,int),clear(void);
#include <stdio.h>
main()
{
    char c;
    int bet;

    do{
        clear();
        seedme();
        bet = getbet();
        clear();
        lines();
        givewin(bet,shoot(bet));
        printf("\n\nPlay again? ");
    }while(((c = getche()) == 'y') || (c == 'Y'));
}
```

(b) Main program

FIGURE 27.4

(continued)

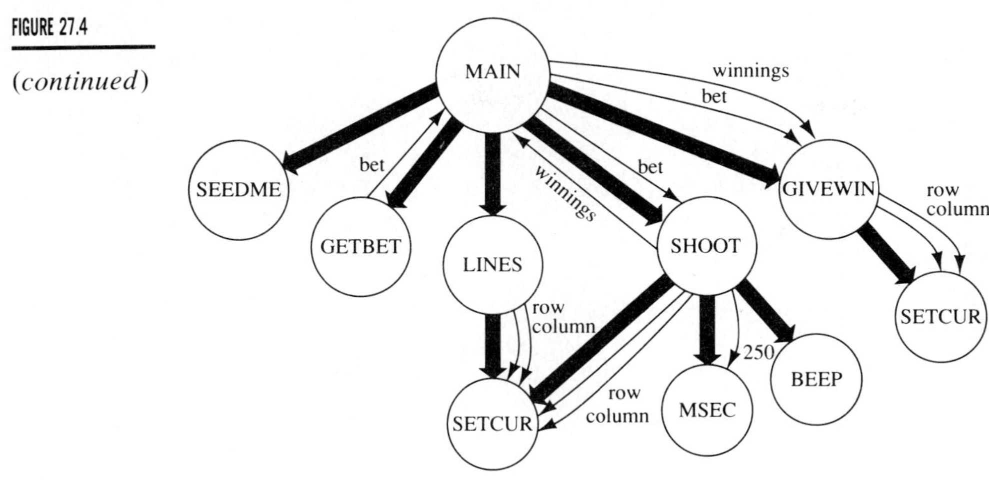

(c) Structure chart

monitor. The last demonstration program of Figure 27.3(e) reads a sequence of "seismic data" (ASCII numbers from 0 to 9) from a file of unlimited length and prints them to the screen in graphic form.

A careful study of all the demonstration programs will help you perform the procedure steps.

Type Conversions Revisited

To see another example of promotion and demotion, turn to Figure 27.3(d). Function *sin* operates only upon data type *double*. As shown, the parameter expression *degrees*pi/180* involves one factor of type *double* (pi) and two of type *int* (*degrees* and 180). Following the general rule first given in Activity 23, the integer (lower type) is promoted to double (higher type) and the result is double.

Therefore, when using those math functions that require type *double*, make sure that at least one of the factors in the parameter expression is of type *double*.

The *cast* operator forces a type conversion. In Figure 27.3(d) the *(int) type cast* demotes the result of the *sin* expression to type *integer*. This is done to avoid further unnecessary, time-consuming mathematical processing at the *double* level.

Always remember that the choice of data types and the use of promotion and demotion ultimately rest on the requirements of each specific application.

Modularization

The code of program RANDOM SHOTS of Figure 27.3(b) is really too large to belong to a single module. By breaking up the program into the five modules (library functions) of Figure 27.4(a), the main program of Figure 27.4(b) is much simpler to write, read, modify, and analyze. We even took the opportunity to add an additional feature (repeat play).

A good rule of thumb is that any given module should fill no more than a single screen.

The structure chart of Figure 27.4(c) shows the relationship between the modules and all parameters that are passed. As we learned in Activity 15, a structure chart is often the first step in program design. (For simplicity, the run-time functions are not shown.) Prior to coding (writing the programs), flowcharts or *pseudocode* (introduced in Activity 29) are often written for the more complex modules.

A Word About Efficiency

In our "bag of tricks" (libraries MYLIB and SLIBCE), we now have a variety of useful functions. In many cases, more than one function will do the job. The rule is: use the simplest function available. For example, when outputting a single byte of hexadecimal data to the screen, use *crtbhex( )* rather than *printf( )*.

In some cases (such as inputting a string), it might be more efficient to write a customized function that uses *getche( )* in a loop rather than the highly complex (but popular) *scanf( )*.

Such careful use of functions yields programs that require less memory and execute faster.

PROCEDURE

NOTE: For all programs make maximum use of library routines. For all I/O, use the functions that seem most appropriate.

1. Make sure the appropriate include files (such as *stdio.h* and *math.h*) are on your disk, and that

the appropriate include statements are in uour source file. (The include statements are highly recommended, but are not required.)

2. Write a program that inputs unsigned bytes and then prints to the screen: "The square of ⟨input value⟩ is ⟨value squared⟩." (Use assembly-generated function SQUARE.)

C PROGRAM

3. Write program COMBINATION LOCK in which "Enter a digit" appears on the screen (and the system waits for an entry). The operator enters a digit from 1 to 99. If the digit value equals the number of entries up to that time, the system prints "OPEN." (For example, if "6" is the sixth digit entered, the "combination" is found and OPEN is printed.)

C PROGRAM

4. Write a program that inputs from the monitor an angle in degrees and the character "s" (for sine), "c" (for cosine), or "t" (for tangent) and displays the corresponding value.

C PROGRAM

5. Write a program that accepts an output voltage and an input voltage and prints its gain in decibels (dB). [The DB gain = 20log10(Vout/Vin).]

C PROGRAM

6. Write a program that asks for a number of coin tosses and prints the odds of that many heads in a row. (Odds = 1 in 2^n.)

C PROGRAM

7. Write a program that asks for a distance in feet and prints the time in seconds it takes to free-fall that distance. ($D = 16t^2$.)

C PROGRAM

8. By modifying the program of Figure 27.3(d), use the following to write an amplitude modulated sine wave to the screen.

$$A(t) = [1+\cos(2\text{pi}f(m)t)]\sin(2\text{pi}f(c)t]$$

where *f(m)* is the modulation frequency and *f(c)* is the carrier frequency. A ratio of *f(c)/f(m)* of approximately 8 to 1 gives good results. (Note: the maximum value of *[1+cos(x)]sin(y)* is 2.)

C PROGRAM

9. Write a program that continuously asks, "Who was the 16th president of the U.S.?" When answered correctly, it prints "THAT'S RIGHT!" (*Hint:* Make use of function STRCMPI.)

C PROGRAM

10. Write a program that inputs a series of names and reports the number of names in the list.

C PROGRAM

11. Write a program that inputs a word and outputs the same word. However, if the word contains four letters, it is censored (all letters replaced with x's).

C PROGRAM

12. Write a program that reports the amount of money earned after one month if we start with a penny and double it every day.

C PROGRAM

13. Write a program that inputs a phrase and outputs the same phrase but with all numbers blanked out.

C PROGRAM

14. First write the following "tools" (library routines):

SECRET: Asks the "moderator" for a number from 1 to 100. Returns the number.
GETNUM: Asks the "contestant" to enter a number from 1 to 100. Returns the number.
EVALUATE: Accepts the "secret" number and the guessed number. Prints "Too high," "Too low," or "THAT'S RIGHT." Returns 1 if guessed number equals target, and 0 otherwise.

Using these tools, write main-program GUESS in which the "moderator" enters a secret number. The screen is cleared. The "contestant" enters numbers and notices the clues (too high or too low). When the correct number is entered, the number of tries is reported.

Advanced Activities

15. As suggested in the discussion, write customized string I/O functions *mygets( )* and *myputs( )* that use *getche( )* and *putch( )* in loops to perform the same operations as *gets( )* and *puts( )*. (Note: It is not necessary for the new functions to return values.)

    Using the new functions, write a main program that inputs a sentence from the keyboard (echoes it to the screen), and outputs the same sentence to the screen five times at one-second intervals.
16. Write a gambling program in which the "player" starts with \$25. The system asks for a number from 1 to 10 and generates a random number from 1 to 10. If the same, \$8 is added; otherwise \$1 is subtracted. The amount of money is continuously displayed. The game is over when the player loses or doubles the original stake.
17. Write program VOWEL in which "Enter a sentence:" is written to the screen (and the system waits for an entry). A sentence of any length is entered from the keyboard and echoed to the screen. When ⟨CR⟩ is pressed (ASCII 13), the screen prints "That sentence contains ⟨number⟩ vowels."
18. Using the formulas below, write a program that inputs the amount invested (principal), the interest rate (0 to 100%), and the time in years. The total amount earned is printed for both yearly and daily compounding. (*Note:* In the following formulas, *R* varies from 0.0 to 1.0.)

YEARLY COMPOUND	DAILY COMPOUND
$E = P(1 + R^T)$	$E = P(1 + R/365)^{T*365}$

19. Write a program that inputs the real and imaginary components of a vector (such as voltage) in rectangular form and outputs the value in polar form (amplitude and phase angle).
20. Making use of function STRCMNPI (string compare), write program GUESS PHRASE, in which "Enter a phrase:" is written to the screen. The "moderator" enters a phrase of any length (which, of course, is not echoed to the screen). One character at a time, the phrase is printed to the screen from left to right. After each letter appears, the "contestant" has two tries to guess the phrase. After guessing cor-

rectly, the following is printed to the screen: "That's right! You got it after ⟨ ⟩ letters."

21. Using at least two library routines, modularize the program of procedure step 20.
22. Write a program that prints to the monitor the RC curve in the time domain of a single RC low-pass filter. Draw a vertical line at the RC time constant point (63% rise).
23. Write a program that prints to the monitor the RC curve in the frequency domain (Bode plot) of the same RC low-pass filter of procedure step 22. At the 3-dB down point, a vertical line is drawn and the break frequency reported.
24. By modifying program SINE_WAVE of Figure 27.3(d), a single moving asterisk will continuously trace out the sine wave. The phase angle is printed out in real time. At the 0, 90, 180, and 270 degree points, a beep is sounded.

Name: ______________________

Date: ______________________

QUESTIONS AND PROBLEMS

Class: ______________________

1. What is the purpose of the "h" files (such as *stdio.h*)?

2. Theoretically, could any of the library functions within the run-time library (SLIBCE.LIB for QuickC) be written in assembly-language?

3. Within a PRINTF command, what is the purpose of "%u"? of "\n"?

4. When a zero ("0") is input from the keyboard, why does function GETCH return a 48?

5. What numerical values are represented by NULL and EOF?

6. What range of values is stored by data type *double*?

Advanced Section

7. What hardware is required in order to use the *graphics* run-time functions and macros?

8. Referring to Figure 27.3(d), why did we not type cast the *sin* expression in the following way?

```
12*(int)sin(degres*pi/180)
```

9. Again referring to Figure 27.3(d), if we had not used the *int* type cast, when would the demotion to integer have taken place?

ACTIVITY 28

INTERRUPTS IN C

OBJECTIVE

- To process interrupts in C.

PARTS AND EQUIPMENT

- IBM PC (bus-extender required).
- Assembler, C compiler, debugger, and utilities.

DISCUSSION

In Activity 17 we covered the basic theory of 8086/88 interrupts and how they are processed in assembly-language. In this activity we process interrupts in C.

To turn an ordinary C function into an *interrupt service routine* (ISR), we use the keyword INTERRUPT. This causes the compiler to generate push/pop pairs automatically for all the registers and flags and to end the program with *iret*.

To demonstrate interrupts, we turn to program COUNT (Figure 28.1). Each activation of the interrupt request causes the display to count up by one. Library routine ISRSET comes from Activity 17, and ENABLE is a run-time library routine that enables the interrupt system.

FIGURE 28.1

Interrupt demonstration program using C.

```
#include <conio.h>
#include <dos.h>

unsigned char mailbox = 0;
void interrupt far isrcount(void);
void isrset (void far *,unsigned char);
void portset(void),ledbl(unsigned char n);
unsigned char dipbl(void);

/*INTERRUPT TYPE 11
  Using the IRQ3 bus input and routine
   _isrset() from Activity 17. */
main()
{
    portset();
    isrset(isrcount,11);
    _enable();
    while(1)
        ;
}

void interrupt far isrcount(void)
{
    mailbox++;
    ledbl(mailbox);
    outp(0x20,0x20);  /* End-of-interrupt */
}
```

PROCEDURE

NOTE: Refer to Activity 17 as needed. Keyboard/screen I/O and internal speaker may be substituted for bus-extender ports where possible.

1. QuickC users should place include file *dos.h* on your USER disk. Those using software other than QuickC should make sure that the ENABLE function is available and its prototype included.
2. By modifying the program of Figure 28.1, write a main program that generates a steady tone. Each interrupt request causes a slightly higher pitch (frequency). (Eventually, the delay number will decrease to zero and underflow, repeating the cycle.)

C PROGRAM

Multiple Interrupts (Scanned)

3. Begin with the tone-generation main program of procedure step 2. Using the scanned technique, write a program that increases the pitch when interrupt A is activated and decreases the pitch when interrupt B is activated.

C PROGRAM

Multiple Interrupts (Vectored)

4. Repeat procedure step 3 using the vectored technique.

C PROGRAM

Advanced Activities

5. Design a stop watch that counts in BCD at 0.10-s increments. Each interrupt request alternately clears, starts, and stops the count. (*Hint:* Use the SWITCH statement).

Name: ______________________

Date: ______________________

Class: ______________________

QUESTIONS AND PROBLEMS

1. When using C, what is the difference between a regular function and an ISR?

2. On the 8086/88, what is the difference between NMI and INTR?

3. How many interrupts can be serviced using the scanned technique? the vectored technique?

4. What changes does the compiler make on a function when the keyword INTERRUPT is used?

5. For the QuickC program of Figure 28.1, why is the include file *dos.h* recommended?

Advanced Section

6. Why must we use the ''mailbox'' technique (global variables) to pass parameters between the main program and ISR (rather than the stack)?

7. Referring to Figure 28.1, under what conditions would we have to associate the following declaration with function ISRCOUNT?

```
extern unsigned char mailbox;
```

PART VIII

INTERFACING AND APPLICATIONS

The end product of computer evolution will be a machine that closely simulates the actions and responses of a human. Such a machine must communicate easily with its human creators, and it must perform useful tasks. Our computer will do this during the 14 interfacing and applications activities of Part VIII. For these activities, consider the following comments and suggestions:

- Make maximum use of a mix-and-match environment. Use the best combination of assembly-language, C, and mixed-language programming; and use the best combination of keyboard/monitor I/O, bus-extender, and simulated binary port I/O.
- Make maximum use of nested library routines. Following the suggestions of Activity 26, we recommend that all main programs be written in C and most library routines in assembly-language.
- Where appropriate, write new library routines. For example, C offers no built-in rotate commands. As shown in Figure 1, writing your own routines is simple and straightforward.

FIGURE 1

Library routine ROTR.

```
; Function ROTR accepts two byte parameters:  The
; first is the variable to be rotated, and the second
; the number of rotations.  The result is returned in
; AL.  AH is cleared. The CF and OF flags are affected.

NAME        ROTR

_TEXT       SEGMENT PUBLIC 'CODE'
            ASSUME CS:_TEXT

  PUBLIC  _rotr

  _rotr PROC NEAR
            push  bp
            mov   bp,sp
            push  cx
            pushf
            mov   al,[bp + 6]     ; Input variable
            mov   cl,[bp + 4]     ; Input factor
            ror   al,cl           ; Perform rotation
            mov   ah,0
            popf
            pop   cx
            pop   bp
            ret
  _rotr ENDP

_TEXT       ENDS
            END
```

FIGURE 2

Include file *myheader.h.*

```
void speakint(void),speakext(void),portset(void),beep(void);
void isrset(unsigned short,unsigned short,unsigned char);
void clear(void),setcur(unsigned char,unsigned char);
void newline(void),keystrng(char *),dump(void);
void crtstrng(char *),soundoff(unsigned char);
char average(char,char),keytest(void);
char crtbhex(char),keybhex(void);
unsigned char dipbl(void),dipbh(void),ledbl(unsigned char);
unsigned char ledbh(unsigned char);
unsigned char crtchar(char);
unsigned char crtbdec(unsigned char),keybdec(void);
unsigned char keydip(void);
unsigned char asc2hex(unsigned char);
unsigned char out7b(unsigned char);
unsigned char hex2bcd(unsigned char),bcd2hex(unsigned char);
unsigned char addbcd(unsigned char,unsigned char);
unsigned char subbcd(unsigned char,unsigned char);
unsigned char addascii(unsigned char),subascii(unsigned char);
unsigned short crtwdec(unsigned short),keywdec(void);
unsigned short dipw(void),ledw(unsigned short);
unsigned short mulbcd(unsigned char,unsigned char);
unsigned short divbcd(unsigned char,unsigned short);
unsigned short hex2bcdw(unsigned short),msec(unsigned short);
unsigned short triangle(unsigned char,unsigned char);
unsigned short square(unsigned char);
int crtwhex(int),keywhex(int);
```

- To further simplify future C programs, place the function prototypes for all past and future "home-made" library routines into include file *my-header.h*, as shown in Figure 2. At the head of all modules that use any of these functions, place *#include ⟨myheader.h⟩*.
- Modify any of the activities and projects to lead to a more beneficial and challenging experience.

Above all, this is your opportunity to concentrate on creativity, problem-solving, and critical thinking. Use the power of the development system, the structure theorem, top-down programming, and the mix-and-match environment to free you from the low-level details and menial tasks. In Part VIII, your imagination is your prime development tool!

ACTIVITY 29

HARDWARE/SOFTWARE DESIGN

OBJECTIVE

- To demonstrate design techniques appropriate for the interfacing and applications experiments of Part VIII.

PARTS AND EQUIPMENT

- IBM PC (bus-extender optional).
- Assembler, C compiler, debugger, and utilities.

DISCUSSION

Experience shows that hardware/software design follows five distinct phases:

1. Problem specification
2. Solution development
3. Hardware/software design
4. Testing, troubleshooting, and hardware/software integration
5. Maintenance

Throughout the design we are guided by the principles of *top-down structured design*. Many techniques have been developed to aid the top-down structured design process. Two of the most popular are the *structure chart* (introduced earlier) and *pseudocode*.

A Demonstration Problem

To demonstrate the five phases of design, we borrow a problem from Activity 25: task FREE_FALL.

FIGURE 29.1

Task FREE_FALL system design. (a) Structure chart. (Alternative format using "square-shaped modules). (b) Pseudocode for main program.

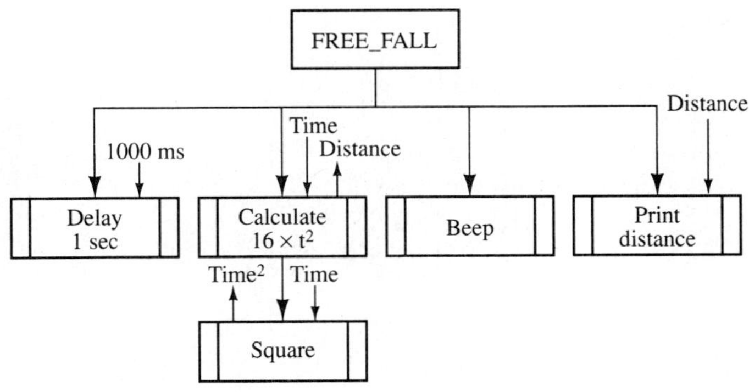

(a) Structure chart (Alternative format using "square-shaped" modules).

```
MAIN_MODULE FREEFALL
  DO FROM 0 TO 63 SECONDS
    DISTANCE = 16 × T²
    IF DISTANCE > 5,000
       BEEP
    DISPLAY DISTANCE
    DELAY ONE SECOND
  END
END
```

(b) Pseudocode for main program

1. *Specification:* The system will output every second in real time the distance traveled from time zero when an object is in free-fall. From 5000 feet on, a beep will be heard every second.
2. *Solution development:* We search the literature and find that the equation relating distance and time in free-fall is:

$$D = 16 * T^2$$

Using a *structure chart,* we subdivide the program into the modules shown in Figure 29.1(a).
3. *Hardware/software design:* Since the hardware is already developed, this step will involve only software design. Looking to Figure 29.1(b), we use *pseudocode* and structured-design techniques to combine the blocks in the structure chart with the *sequence, alternation,* and *repetition* patterns of structured programming. (Pseudocode is similar to a high-level language code, but is more "English-like" and does not require the strict rules of syntax.) Choosing the PRINTF function for output, we generate the functions of Figure 29.2. (To save time, we wrote function CALCULATE in C.)
4. *Testing, troubleshooting, and hardware/software integration:* We test our program and find that the time between displayed values is slightly greater than 1 s. We experimentally adjust the parameter value (currently 1000) to give an overall time delay as close as possible to 1 s. For hardware/software troubleshooting, an *in-circuit emulator* is a useful tool.
5. *Maintenance:* This important step deals with repairing design defects and modifying the program to meet new needs. In our case, we use graphic techniques to display the more complex ballistic trajectory of an object in real-time free-fall (Figure 29.3).

FIGURE 29.2

Task FREE_FALL software. (a) Main program. (b) Library function CALCULATE.

```
#include <myheader.h>
#include <stdio.h>

unsigned short calculate(unsigned char);

/* FREE_FALL
   This program determines the distance traveled
   during free-fall.  The distance overflows at
   64 seconds.  From 5000 feet on, a beep is
   heard every second. */
main()
{
    unsigned char time;
    unsigned short distance;

    for (time = 0;time < 64;++time)
    {
        printf("\n%u",distance = calculate(time));
        if (distance > 5000)
            beep();
        msec(1000);
    }
}
```

(a) Main program

```
#include <myheader.h>

/* Library function calculate uses function
   square to accept the time and return
   the distance. */
unsigned short calculate(unsigned char t)
{
    return(16 * square(t));
}
```

(b) Library routine *calculate*

PROCEDURE

1. Using our five phases of design, solve task SKEET_SHOOT:
   a. *Specification:* After a several-second delay, a beep sounds and the target ("clay pigeon") moves across the screen from left to right. As quickly as possible you fire a shot (press any key) and momentarily freeze the target at its shot location. The faster you are, the higher your score (0 to 80). After 10 shots, the game is over and your total score is displayed. (*Hint:* Make use of functions DUMP and KEYTEST from Activity 18.)
   b. *Solution development:* Show structure chart.
   c. *Hardware/software design:* Show pseudocode, library functions, and main program.
   d. *Testing, troubleshooting, and hardware/software integration:* Indicate results of testing and summarize any troubleshooting required.
   e. *Maintenance:* Modify program SKEET_SHOOT so the waiting period between shots and the speed of the target are pseudorandom. (*Hint:* Make use of run-time function RAND.)

Advanced Activities

2. Research the literature and become familiar with the *Warnier-Orr diagram.* Using a Warnier-Orr diagram, show task SKEET_SHOOT. Is a Warnier-Orr diagram more like a structure chart or more like pseudocode?

FIGURE 29.3

Modifying task FREE_FALL to include a real-time graphic display.

```
#include <myheader.h>
#include <stdio.h>

unsigned short calculate(unsigned char);

/* FREE-FALL
   This modified program shows the ballistic trajectory
   of an object on a small moon with a gravitational
   acceleration of 2 ft/sec/sec.  The initial horizontal
   and vertical velocity components are 8 ft/s.  All
   distances and velocities are displayed at the top of
   the screen.  Beeps are heard every second on the
   downward trajectory.  The object hits the ground in
   8 sec.  The equations are:

                 2
      y  = 8t - t
      x  = 8t
      Vy = 8 - 2t
      Vx = 8
*/
main()
{
    int t,x,y;

    clear();
    for (t = 0;t < 9;++t)
    {
        x = 8 * t;
        y = 24 - (8*t - t*t);
        setcur(x,y);
        putch('*');
        if (x >= 32)
            beep();
        setcur(0,0);
        printf("TIME = %d seconds.\n",t);
        printf("DISTANCE: x = %d and y = %d\n",x,8*t - t*t);
        printf("VELOCITY: Vx = %d and Vy = %d",8,8 - 2*t);
        msec(1000);
    }
}
```

Name: ______________________

Date: ______________________

Class: ______________________

QUESTIONS AND PROBLEMS

1. When using a high-level language, why can we often skip the pseudocode step and go right to program coding?

2. Using pseudocode, describe the Indianapolis 500 race. (The track is a one-mile oval.)

3. Library routines we know we will need are often written before the main program. Why is this *tool-building* phase often called *bottom-up programming*?

4. Referring to routine CALCULATE of Figure 29.2(b), we called nested routine SQUARE for learning value. Would it be just as easy and efficient in this case to stick to the high-level solution [i.e., return(16 * t * t)]?

Advanced Section

5. Why is structured programming also known as *GOTO-less programming*?

ACTIVITY 30

COMPUTER GAMES
Sumo Wrestling

OBJECTIVE

- To develop a computer game based on the sport of Sumo wrestling.

PARTS AND EQUIPMENT

- IBM PC (bus-extender optional).
- Assembler, C compiler, debugger, and utilities.

DISCUSSION

Sumo wrestling is perhaps the oldest and most popular sport in Japan. The rules are quaintly simple: Two corpulent, well-fed giants meet head on in the center of the mat and attempt to push each other off. The Sumo wrestling game board is laid out as shown in Figure 30.1. (The ports can be real or simulated.)

When the program is executed, the two center LEDs (D3 and D4) go on. Each LED represents a Sumo wrestler belonging to player A or player B. After several seconds delay, the two lights go off. Whichever player is then able to throw the corresponding input port switch high first is the winner, and the two "wrestlers" will reappear and both move over one notch in the appropriate direction. The two switches are returned to the OFF position and the players again wait for the LEDs to go out. The process continues until one wrestler is "pushed off the mat" and the game is over.

PROCEDURE

1. Based on the flowchart of Figure 30.2, develop the Sumo wrestling program. (If bus-extender ports are not available, consider use of the screen-simulation I/O routines of Activity 18, but be sure to include means for the players to return "switches" D0 and D7 to zero before beginning each round.)
2. Play the game of Sumo wrestling. Is the program working properly? ____________

Advanced Activities

3. To the basic Sumo wrestling program of procedure step 1, add any of the following options.
   a. An option that produces a semirandom delay time.
   b. An option that automatically returns the wrestlers to the center of the mat when a player wins a game (pushes the other player off the mat). As an added attraction, a beep is sounded each time a player wins a game.
   c. An option that keeps score.
   d. An option that penalizes a player one position (and beeps twice) for jumping the gun.

FIGURE 30.1

The Sumo wrestler game board. (Courtesy Intel Corporation.)

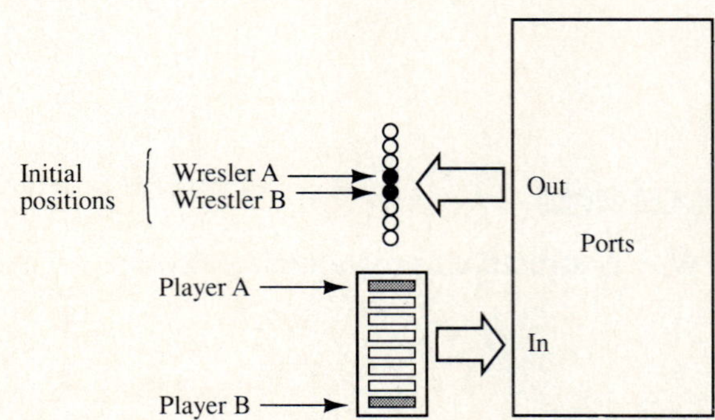

FIGURE 30.2

SUMO_WRESTLER solution. (a) Flowchart. Reproduced with permission of the Glencoe Division of Macmillan/McGraw-Hill Publishing Company. (b) Program.

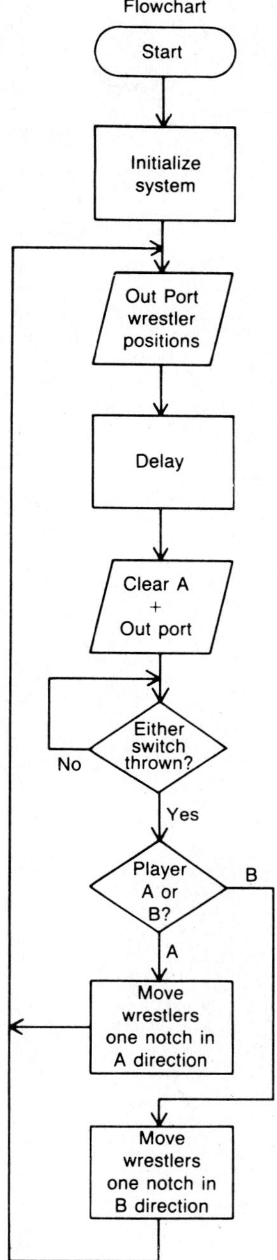

(a) Flowchart

(b) Program

Name: ______________________

Date: ______________________

Class: ______________________

QUESTIONS AND PROBLEMS

1. When using bus-extender DIP input, why is debouncing of the switches not required?

2. How could human reaction time be used to generate a semirandom delay?

Advanced Section

3. Why is a tie a very rare occurrence?

ACTIVITY 31

COMPUTER MUSIC

OBJECTIVE

- To generate a melody (a sequence of notes).

PARTS AND EQUIPMENT

- IBM PC (bus-extender optional).
- Assembler, C compiler, debugger, and utilities.

DISCUSSION

A melody is a sequence of notes, each with its own frequency and duration parameters. These parameters are stored in memory as arrays or structures and are retrieved as the melody progresses.

PROCEDURE

1. Building on Activity 9, write assembly-language library routine NOTE, which accepts frequency and duration parameters (both bytes) and generates the corresponding note. (Choose parameter values that will give appropriate frequency and duration ranges.)
2. Using routine NOTE, write a main program that continuously generates a note/rest sequence. The frequency and duration of the note can be changed in real-time by input byte parameters.
3. Using your note/rest program, determine parameter values that generate the note-of-A (440 Hz) for four beats (1 to 2 s).

   Note-of-A frequency value: ____________

   Four-beat duration value: ____________
4. Using simple ratios, fill in the frequency values next to each note on the musical scale of Figure 31.1(a). Again using simple ratios, fill in the "duration number" column in the table of Figure 31.1(b).
5. Using the routines and data developed, write a program that continuously generates in sequence the three notes of the chord of C (C, E, and G) of durations 1, 2, and 4 beats, respectively.
6. Beside each note of the musical score "2001: A Space Odyssey" of Figure 31.2, write the frequency and duration values.
7. Write a program that continuously plays the theme from "2001: A Space Odyssey."

Advanced Activities

8. Modify any of your music programs so the letter designation of each note is displayed in real time. (If using the seven-segment bus-extender port, use nine for "g.")
9. Write program PIANO in which keys A through G sound the corresponding note. Pressing "+" or "−" increases or decreases (doubles or halves) the octave range. (*Hint:* Make use of routine KEYTEST of Activity 18 and the fact that ASCII A–G is 41H–47H and a–g is 61H–67H.)
10. Write program SPACE ODYSSEY using an array of structures.
11. Add a color organ option to program SPACE ODYSSEY. (Use red LED for high-frequency notes, orange for medium-frequency, and green for low-frequency.)

FIGURE 31.1

Musical data. (a) Frequency and note information. (b) Note duration table. Reproduced with permission of the Glencoe Division of Macmillan/McGraw-Hill Publishing Company.

STANDARD FREQUENCIES FOR THE 12-NOTE EQUALLY TEMPERED MUSICAL SCALE

Octave Number	Note C	C♯	D	D♯	E	F
0*	16.352	17.324	18.354	19.445	20.602	21.827
1	32.703	34.648	36.708	38.891	41.203	43.654
2	65.406	69.296	73.416	77.782	82.407	87.307
3	130.81	138.59	146.83	155.56	164.81	174.61
4	261.63	277.18	293.66	311.13	329.63	349.23
5	523.25	554.37	587.33	622.25	659.26	698.46
6	1046.5	1108.7	1174.7	1244.5	1318.5	1396.9
7	2093.0	2217.5	2349.3	2489.0	2637.0	2793.8
8	4186.0	4434.9	4698.6	4978.0	5274.0	5587.7

Octave Number	Note F♯	G	G♯	A	A♯	B
0*	23.125	24.500	25.957	27.500	29.135	30.868
1	46.249	48.999	51.913	55.000	58.270	61.735
2	92.499	97.999	103.83	110.00	116.54	123.47
3	185.00	196.00	207.65	220.00	233.08	246.94
4	369.99	392.00	415.30	440.00	466.16	493.88
5	739.99	783.99	830.61	880.00	932.33	987.77
6	1480.0	1568.0	1661.2	1760.0	1864.7	1975.5
7	2960.0	3136.0	3322.4	3520.0	3729.3	3951.1
8	5919.9	6271.9	6644.9	7040.0	7458.6	7902.1

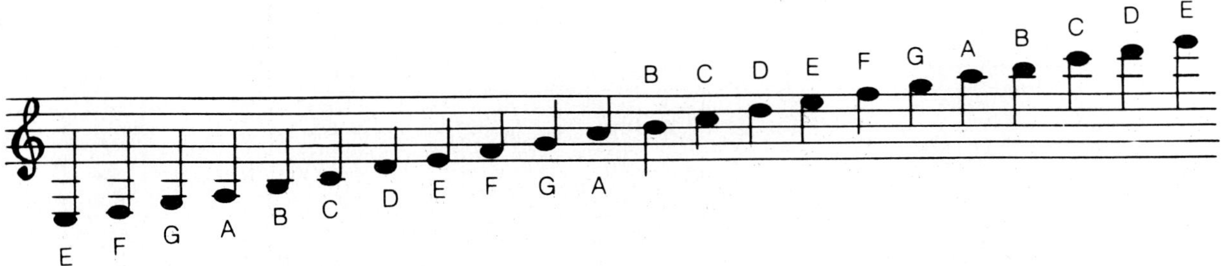

(a) Frequency and note information

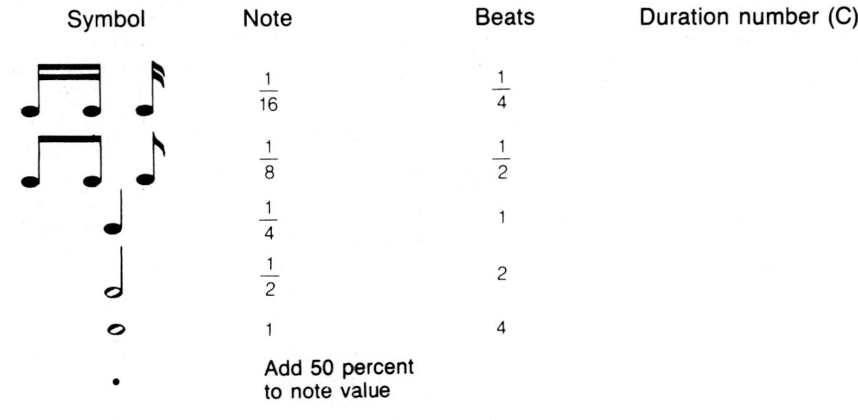

Symbol	Note	Beats	Duration number (C)
	1/16	1/4	
	1/8	1/2	
	1/4	1	
	1/2	2	
	1	4	
•	Add 50 percent to note value		

(b) Note duration table

FIGURE 31.2

Musical score from "2001: A Space Odyssey." Reproduced with permission of the Glencoe Division of Macmillan/McGraw-Hill Publishing Company.

Name: ______________________

Date: ______________________

QUESTIONS AND PROBLEMS

Class: ______________________

1. Looking over the standard frequencies for the equally tempered musical scale of Figure 31.1(a), why is it unavoidable that the majority of notes produced by the music program of this experiment will be to some degree flat or sharp?

2. To ''sharpen'' a note (raise its frequency), should you increase or decrease the frequency number?

3. For a complex music program that includes frequency, duration, letter, and color organ options, why would a *record* be a good way of storing the information?

Advanced Section

4. How might you modify the hardware and software to play chords rather than single notes?

ACTIVITY 32

DIGITAL-TO-ANALOG CONVERSION
Waveform Generation

OBJECTIVE

- To generate repetitive waveforms using a digital-to-analog converter (DAC).

PARTS AND EQUIPMENT

- IBM PC with bus extender.
- Assembler, C compiler, debugger, and utilities.
- Three 10K and five 20K resistors (or single-chip DAC, such as the AD558).
- Oscilloscope.

DISCUSSION

The simplest digital-to-analog converter is the ladder network of Figure 32.1(a). Output binary numbers from 0 to FH will generate analog voltage levels proportional to the size of the number. With 16 steps and assuming 4-volt (V) outputs, we achieve a resolution of approximately 0.25 V.

For greater accuracy and convenience, choose from a number of single-chip DACs—such as the AD558 of Figure 32.1(b). Using 8 bits and a 4-V output peak, the resolution increases to approximately 0.016 V.

As shown in Figure 32.1(c) a variety of buffers, scalers, and filters can protect the DAC from loading, scale the output voltage range, and smooth out the sharp edges.

FIGURE 32.1

The digital-to-analog hardware. (a) Resistor ladder. (b) Single-chip DAC. (c) Optional buffers, scalers, and filters.

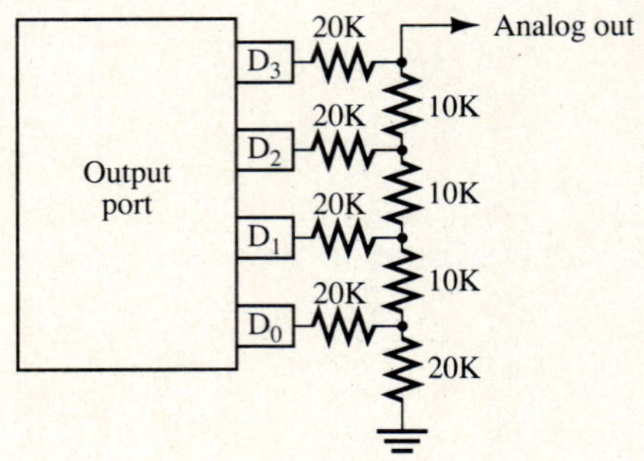

(a) Resistor ladder

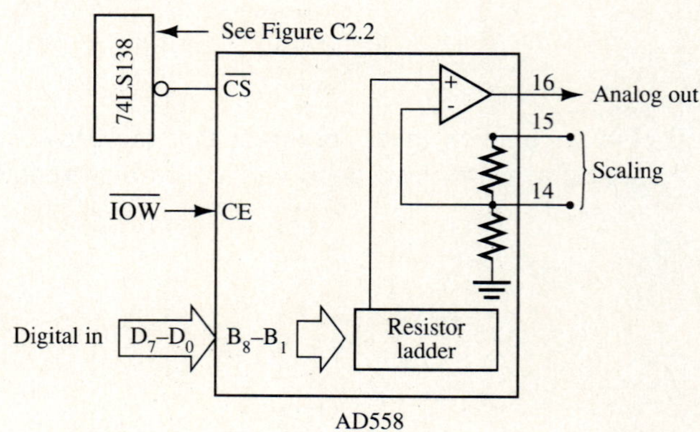

(b) Single-chip DAC

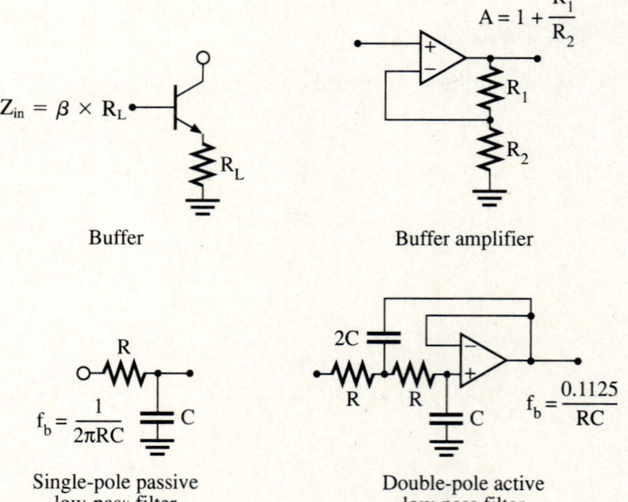

(c) Optional buffers, scalers, and filters.

PROCEDURE

1. Install either the resistor ladder or single-chip DAC of Figure 32.1. (It is not necessary to buffer, scale, or filter the output.)
2. Write a program that generates a repetitive exponential curve on the oscilloscope. (An exponential curve is one in which the amplitude doubles during each time span.)
3. By adding ''intelligence'' (alternation or repetition), generate a triangular waveform in which the number of steps is controlled from the keypad.

Advanced Activities

4. Using the sin function, generate a sine wave on the oscilloscope.
5. Smooth out the triangular or sine wave waveforms with a low-pass filter of your design [see Figure 32.1(c)]. Sketch the result for various break frequencies.
6. To provide volume control, attach a buffered speaker to the output of the DAC. Modify library routine NOTE of Activity 31 to include programmable volume. Using frequency, duration, and volume parameters, generate the ''Space Odyssey'' melody of Activity 31. (*Hint:* Assign each note a volume number from 0 to 7, with each complemented to generate eight levels of volume.)

Name: ______________________

Date: ______________________

Class: ______________________

QUESTIONS AND PROBLEMS

1. Based on theory or experiment, how do the waveforms of procedure step 2 compare when switching from the resistor ladder network [Figure 32.1(a)] to the single-chip DAC [Figure 32.1(b)]?

2. A 12-bit DAC is able to pinpoint the voltage level to what percent of accuracy?

3. Why is digital-to-analog conversion an especially fast process?

4. Regarding a DAC, define *resolution*.

Advanced Section

5. Theoretically, can a DAC/filter combination generate a *perfect* sine wave (one with no harmonic overtones)? Explain your answer.

ACTIVITY 33

ANALOG-TO-DIGITAL CONVERSION A Digital Voltmeter

OBJECTIVES

- To perform several techniques for converting analog to digital.
- To design a digital voltmeter.

PARTS AND EQUIPMENT

- IBM PC with bus-extender.
- Assembler, C compiler, debugger, and utilities.
- Four-bit DAC resistor ladder.
- LM311 comparator or equivalent.
- A 1K to 50K potentiometer.
- Oscilloscope.

DISCUSSION

A digital voltmeter is an analog-to-digital (A/D) converter that is accurately calibrated. To convert analog voltages to digital values, we have two popular methods at our disposal:

1. Counter method
2. Successive approximation.

Turning first to the counter technique, the computer increments the output to a DAC, compares the staircase signal to the analog input, and stops when a match is made. The digital number to the DAC represents the answer when the match occurs.

Although the counter method is simpler, the more popular *successive approximation* technique accomplishes the A/D conversion much quicker and makes use of the same hardware.

Successive approximation is a trial-and-error process. Beginning with the most significant bit (MSB), each successive bit position is set high and the resulting value is compared to the input. If the test voltage is higher than the input voltage, the logic 1 test bit is masked out; if lower, the bit is retained. Successive approximation homes in on the answer by successively cutting in half the space where the answer lies.

PROCEDURE

NOTE: Use the display method of your choice.

Counter Method

1. Install the A/D hardware as shown in Figure 33.1. Calibration is via the input potentiometer.
2. Write program VOLTMETER using the counter method of A/D conversion.
3. Run your program and adjust the calibration potentiometer until the output corresponds to the analog input voltage levels. Does the digital output properly track the analog input? ______________
4. As you vary the input analog voltage, measure the DAC output using an oscilloscope. Do the waveforms resemble those of Figure 33.2(a)? ______________

FIGURE 33.1

Analog-to-digital hardware.

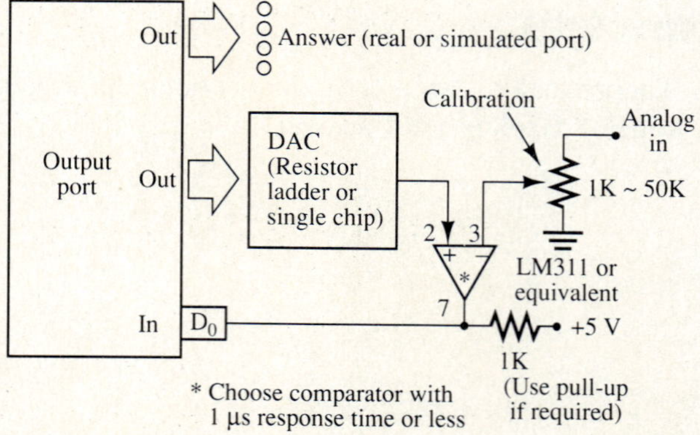

FIGURE 33.2

DAC output waveforms during analog-to-digital conversion. (a) Counter technique. (b) Successive approximation technique.

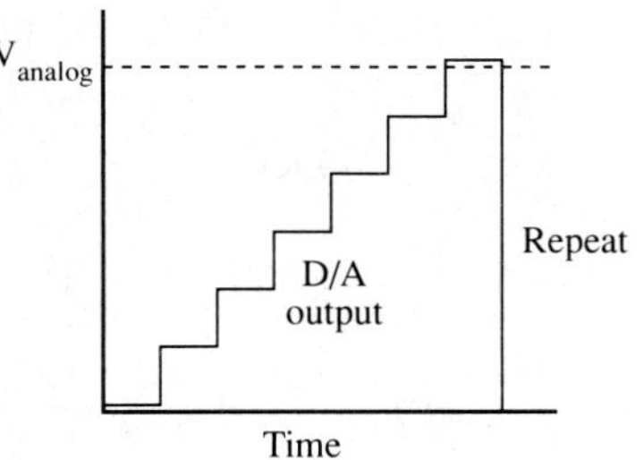

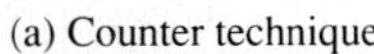

(a) Counter technique

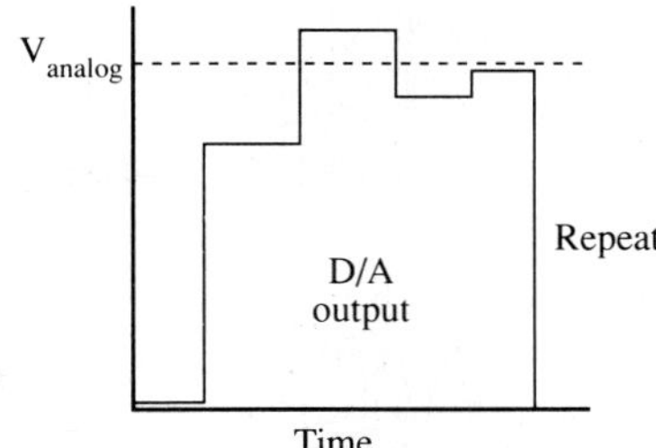

(b) Successive-approximation technique

FIGURE 33.3

Single-chip A/D conversion. (a) AD574 interfacing. (b) Conversion and read timing.

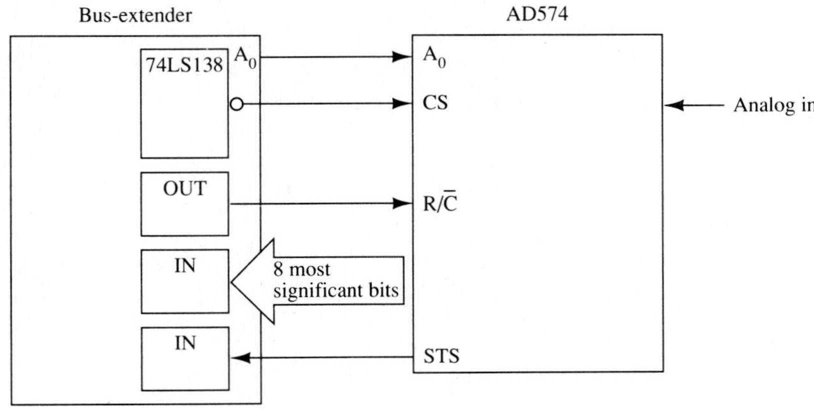

(a) AD574 interfacing

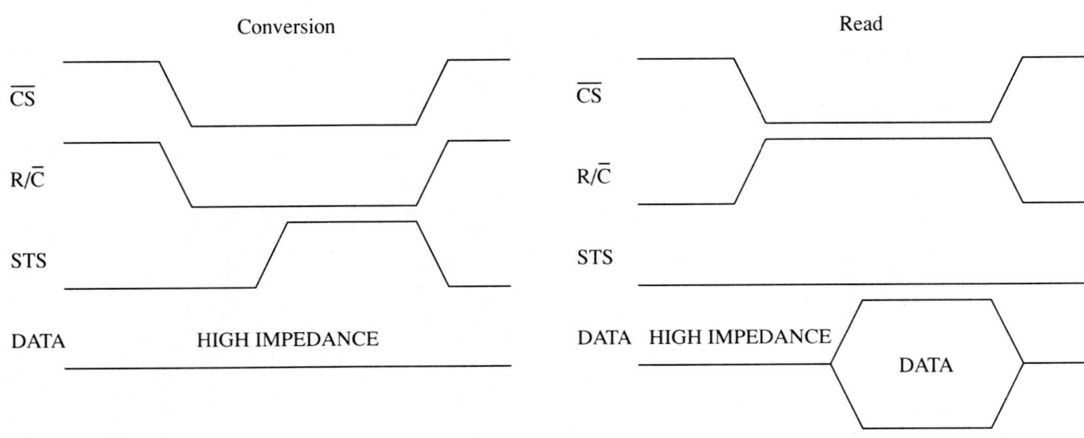

(b) Conversion and read timing

Successive Approximation Method

5. Write program VOLTMETER using the successive approximation method of A/D conversion.
6. Run your program and adjust the calibration potentiometer until the output corresponds to the analog input voltage levels. Does the output properly track the analog input? ______________
7. As you vary the input analog voltage, measure the DAC output using an oscilloscope. Do the waveforms resemble those of Figure 33.2(b)? ______________

Advanced Activities

8. If using a bus-extender output port, modify the successive approximation program of procedure step 5 so the voltage output will be converted to BCD and displayed on seven-segment displays.
9. Write library function A2D, which uses the successive approximation method to return a single digital equivalent (0 to 0FH) of an analog input voltage each time it is called. Using function A2D, design a storage oscilloscope in which a portion of an analog signal is sampled, converted to digital, and stored in RAM. The digital signals are immediately played back continuously through a DAC and viewed on an oscilloscope. (An input frequency in the range of 50 Hz for 256 storage locations yields satisfactory resolution.)
10. Repeat procedure step 9, but play back the waveform on the computer screen. (*Note:* Playback on the screen is one-time-only.)
11. Test one of the integrated A/D chips that are currently available (such as the AD574 of Figure 33.3).

Name: ______________________

Date: ______________________

QUESTIONS AND PROBLEMS

Class: ______________________

1. Using the counter technique, why is the time required to process one A/D conversion approximately proportional to the size of the analog voltage?

2. When using a 4-bit DAC in the circuitry, and assuming that the maximum output voltage is 5 V, what is the resolution of an A/D converter?

3. Why is the successive approximation method generally faster than the counter method?

Advanced Section

4. Why should the speed of the comparator (LM 311) used in Figure 33.1 be 1 μs or faster?

5. Why is the *flash* technique an unusually fast method of A/D conversion?

ACTIVITY 34

THE GAME OF ROULETTE

OBJECTIVE

• To simulate the game of roulette on a computer.

PARTS AND EQUIPMENT

• IBM PC with bus-extender.
• Assembler, C compiler, debugger, and utilities.

DISCUSSION

Roulette is one of the oldest games of chance. A bet is placed on a number and the wheel spins. If the spinning ball lands on the same number as the bet, the player wins a multiple of the bet; otherwise, the player loses the bet. To give the "house" an advantage, the payoff upon winning is less than the mathematical odds would indicate.

By playing several numbers, the chance of winning is increased, but the payoff is proportionately reduced.

PROCEDURE

1. Write program ROULETTE, in which $25 is displayed, and the "ball" (the digits from 0 to 9) appear in sequence (too fast for the eye to catch). When a single bet is placed from the keyboard, the display stops at a single number. If the display number matches the bet number, 8 is added to the total score; otherwise, 1 is subtracted from the total score. The process is repeated until the money is doubled or gone.
2. Improve program ROULETTE of procedure step 1 by having the "ball" gradually slow down when a bet is placed.

Advanced Activities

3. Modify the program of procedure step 2 to display the "ball" on the screen as a rotating asterisk inside a circle of the numbers from 0 to 9. For added realism, show the "ball" moving at a visible speed, but slowing down at a pseudorandom rate (to avoid anticipating where the ball will land).

Name: ______________________

Date: ______________________

Class: ______________________

QUESTIONS AND PROBLEMS

1. Based on the program of procedure step 1, what advantage in odds does the "house" enjoy?

2. When the "ball" stops, why is it reasonable to expect that its position is random?

Advanced Section

3. Based on the odds of question 1, how many spins would be required before the player would expect to lose half of the initial $25? (Assume that $1 is bet each spin.)

4. In general terms, how would you modify the program of procedure step 3 to allow for multiple bets (more than one number is bet at a time), with corresponding reduction in payoff?

ACTIVITY 35

THE SCANNED KEYBOARD
An Electronic Organ

OBJECTIVE

- To design a four-note electronic organ that is activated by a scanned keyboard.

PARTS AND EQUIPMENT

- IBM PC with bus-extender.
- Assembler, C compiler, debugger, and utilities.
- Two 10K resistors.

DISCUSSION

The simplest method of interfacing keys to a computer system is to assign each key to a port bit. However, when large numbers of keys are interfaced to a computer system, the *scanned* method greatly reduces the hardware requirements. When using the scanned method, a key is located by coincident selection—by specifying its row and column address.

In this activity, we set up a simple 2 × 2 scanned keyboard as a four-key electronic organ and piano.

PROCEDURE

1. Interface the scanned keyboard as shown in Figure 35.1. Label each key A, B, C, and D. (Using bare wires and making contact by hand can simulate the pressing of keys.)
2. Write program ORGAN, which sounds a different tone for each keypress. (The tone sounds as long as the key is pressed; it stops when the key is released.)
3. Modify the program of procedure step 2 so "A," "B," "C," or "D" is displayed as each note corresponding to key A, B, C, or D is pressed. (Display is cleared when tone stops.)

Advanced Activities

4. Write program PIANO, in which each of the four keys (labeled A, B, C, and D) generates the corresponding tone and letter display *for a set duration*. (*Suggestion:* Use library procedure NOTE from Activity 31.)

FIGURE 35.1

The scanned keypad technique.

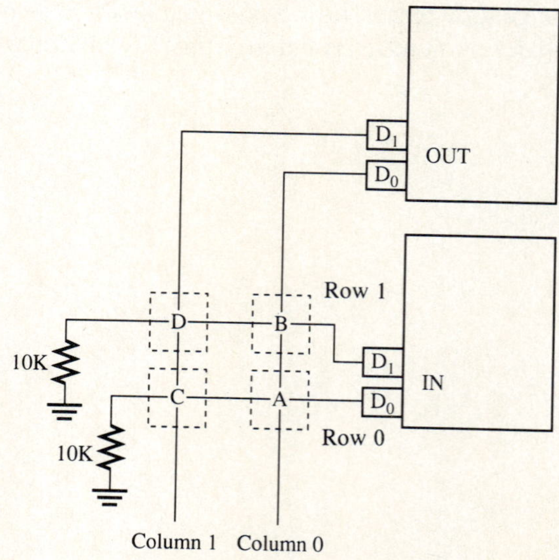

Name: ______________________

Date: ______________________

Class: ______________________

QUESTIONS AND PROBLEMS

1. Using the scanned technique, how many keys can a system with one 8-bit input port and one 8-bit output port service?

2. Why is debouncing of the keys not required for the electronic organ?

Advanced Section

3. Why does the IBM PC use interrupt I/O for keyboard interfacing?

ACTIVITY 36

HANDSHAKING
The 8255A PPI and the Centronics Interface Standard

OBJECTIVES

- To interface a printer using MODE 0 and MODE 1 of the 8255A Programmable Peripheral Interface (PPI).
- To use the handshaking signals of the Centronics parallel interface standard.
- To use both programmed I/O and interrupt I/O to transfer characters.

PARTS AND EQUIPMENT

- IBM PC with bus-extender.
- Assembler, C compiler, debugger, and utilities.
- Centronics standard parallel printer and cable.
- One CD4009A inverter.

DISCUSSION

The 8255A PPI of Figure 36.1 is a general-purpose programmable I/O device offering three ports and three major modes of operation.

In this activity, we illustrate the 8255A and its modes of operation by providing a physical interface and device driver for a Centronics interface printer. The handshaking scheme must match the Centronics printer interface standard of Figure 36.2. We configure the 8255A for MODE 0 (normal) and MODE 1 (automatic handshaking), using both programmed and interrupt I/O.

Figures 36.3 and 36.4 summarize the MODE 0 and MODE 1 designs. In both cases, we are sending the letter "A" to the printer continuously.

- The MODE 0 designs make use of the level-active BUSY signal to indicate when the printer is ready for the next character. Briefly, the sequence is as follows:
  1. The printer issues a BUSY signal, indicating it is ready for the next character. The BUSY signal is either polled or issues an interrupt.
  2. The computer outputs the next character and issues a STROBE to the printer, which sets BUSY high.
  3. The cycle is repeated.
- The MODE 1 designs make use of the $\overline{\text{ACK}}$ pulse to indicate when the printer is ready for the next character. Briefly, the sequence is as follows:
  1. The printer issues an $\overline{\text{ACK}}$ pulse, indicating it is ready for the next character. The $\overline{\text{ACK}}$ pulse sets $\overline{\text{OBF}}$ (for polled operation) or INTR (for interrupt I/O operation).
  2. The computer outputs the next character and issues a STROBE to the printer, which resets $\overline{\text{OBF}}$ and INTR.
  3. The cycle is repeated.

PROCEDURE

NOTE: Consider concentrating on just one or two of the following procedure sections.

Mode 0

Programmed I/O operation

1. Interface your printer to the computer as shown in Figure 36.3(a).
2. Based on the flowchart of Figure 36.3(a), write a program that continuously sends the character "A" (41H in ASCII) to the printer.

Interrupt I/O operation

3. Interface your printer to the computer as shown in Figure 36.3(b).
4. Based on the flowchart of Figure 36.3(b), write a program that continuously sends the character "A" to the printer.

FIGURE 36.1

The 8255A Programmable Peripheral Interface. (Courtesy Intel Corporation.) (a) Pinout and block diagram. (b) Mode definitions and bus interface. (c) Mode definition format. (d) Bit set/reset format.

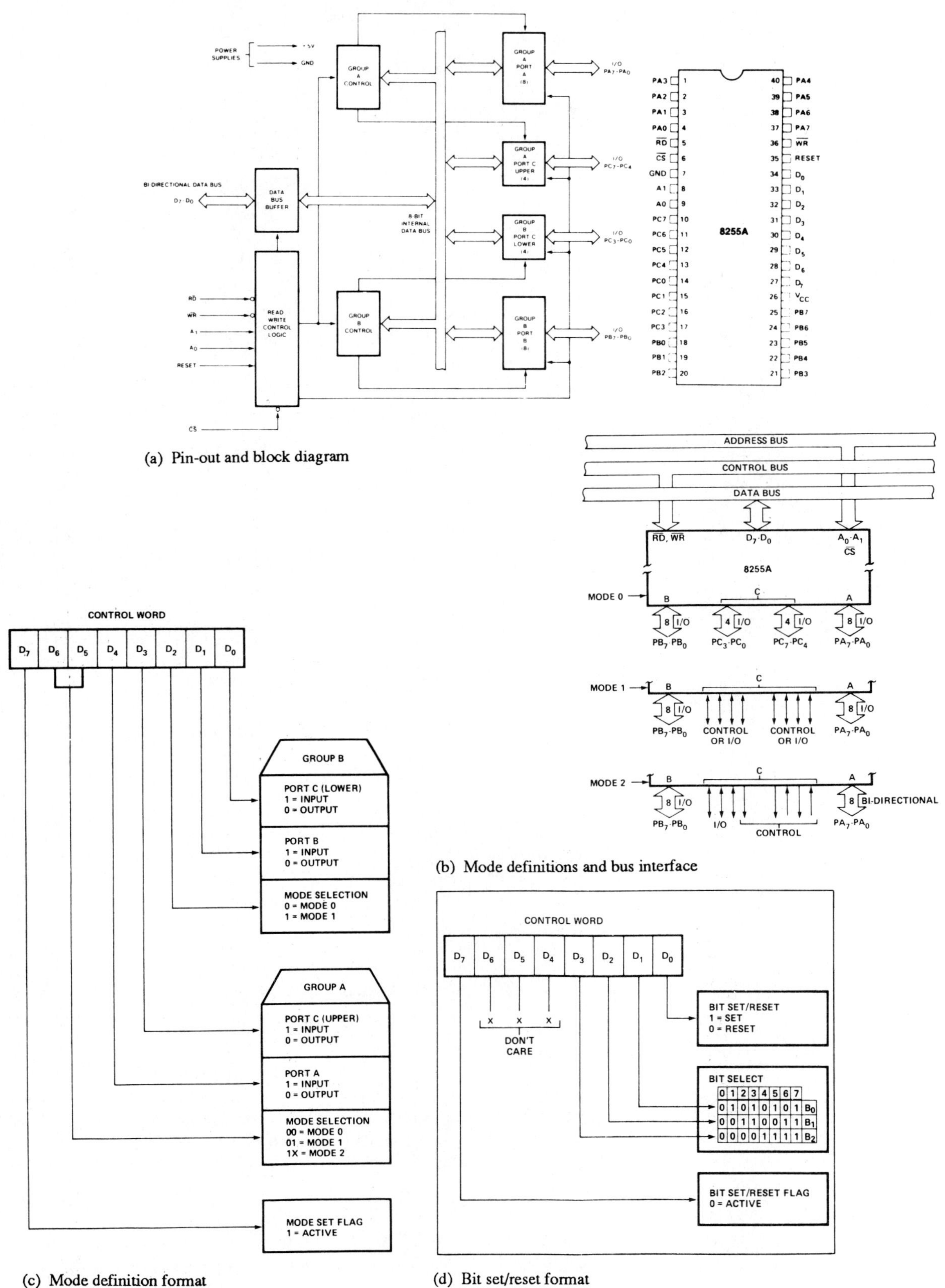

(a) Pin-out and block diagram

(b) Mode definitions and bus interface

(c) Mode definition format

(d) Bit set/reset format

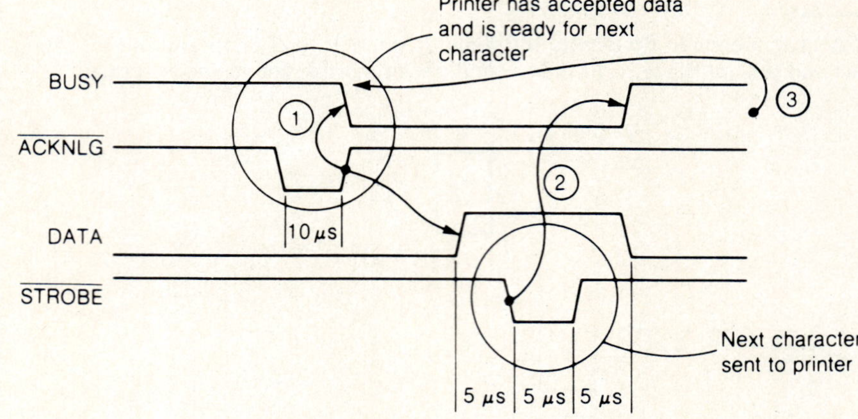

FIGURE 36.2

The Centronics printer interface standard. Reproduced with permission of the Glencoe Division of Macmillan/McGraw-Hill Publishing Company.

Mode 1

Programmed I/O operation

5. Interface your printer to the computer as shown in Figure 36.4(a).
6. Based on the flowchart of Figure 36.4(a), write a program that continuously sends the character "A" to the printer.

Interrupt I/O operation

7. Interface your printer to the computer as shown in Figure 36.4(b).
8. Based on the flowchart of Figure 36.4(b), write a program that continuously sends the character "A" to the printer.

Advanced Activities

9. Using the MODE 0 polled method [Figure 36.3(a)], write library function OUTPRINT, which accepts an ASCII character as a parameter and transmits it to the printer. (The character is returned from the function in case it is needed.)
10. Using function OUTPRINT, write a program that continuously prints whatever ASCII character is typed on the keyboard. [*Note:* When the program detects a carriage return (0x0d), it should append a line feed (0x0a).] On many printers, characters entered fill up the buffer and are printed only upon receiving a *line feed* or the buffer fills.
11. Write a program that continuously prints:

    Roses are red
    Violets are blue

12. Write a program that prints one of four phrases, depending on whether a 0, 1, 2, or 3 is entered. (*Hint:* Use the SWITCH statement.)

FIGURE 36.3

MODE 0 printer interface. (a) Programmed I/O. (b) Interrupt I/O.

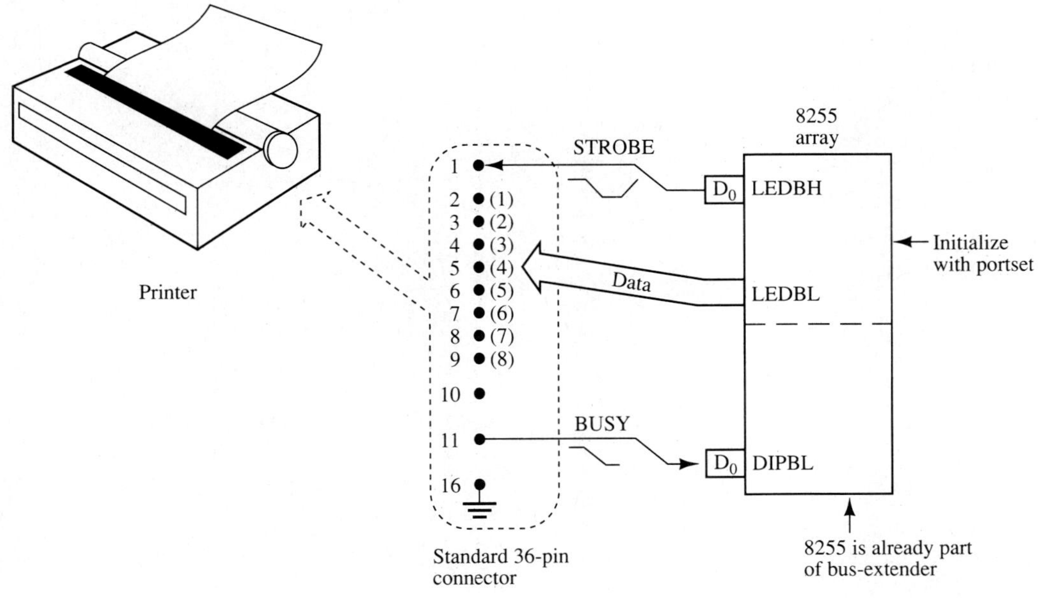

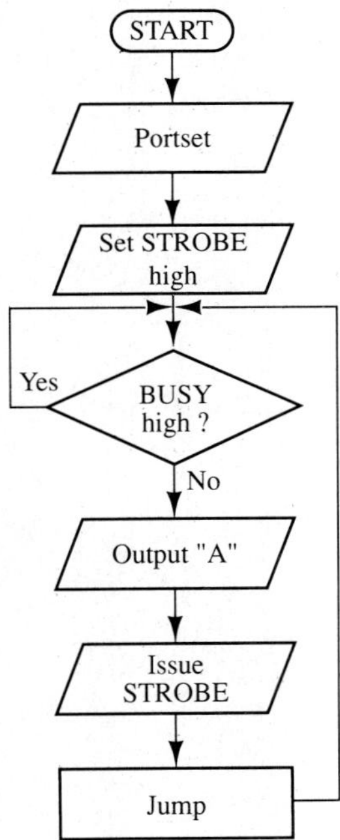

(a) Programmed I/O

FIGURE 36.3

(*continued*)

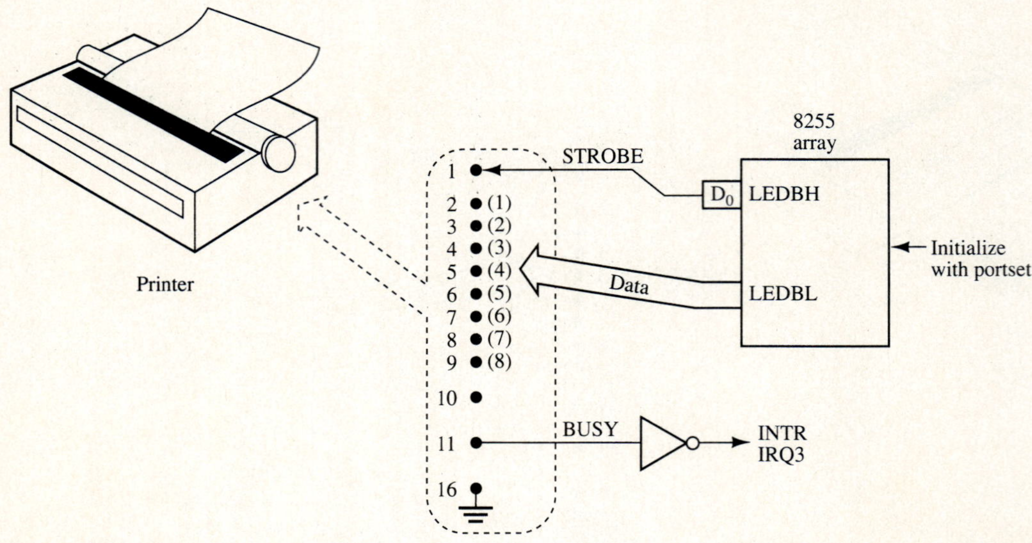

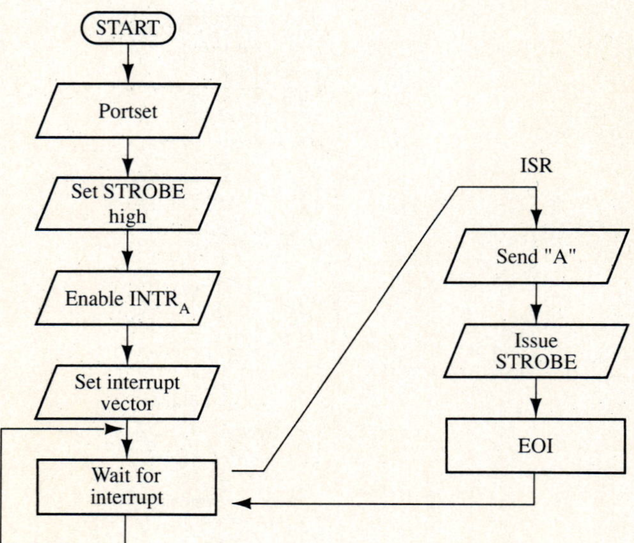

(b) Interrupt I/O

FIGURE 36.4

MODE 1 printer interface. (a) Programmed I/O. (b) Interrupt I/O.

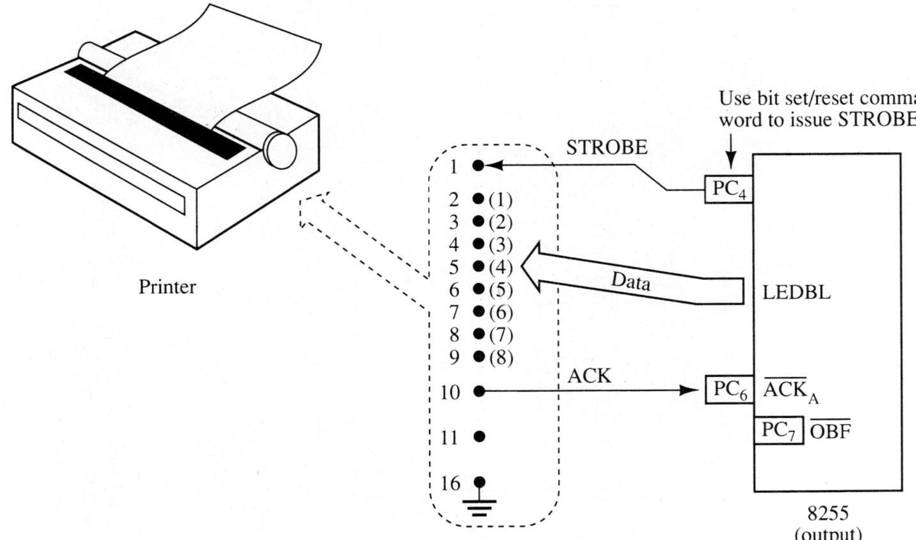

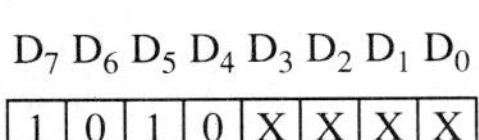

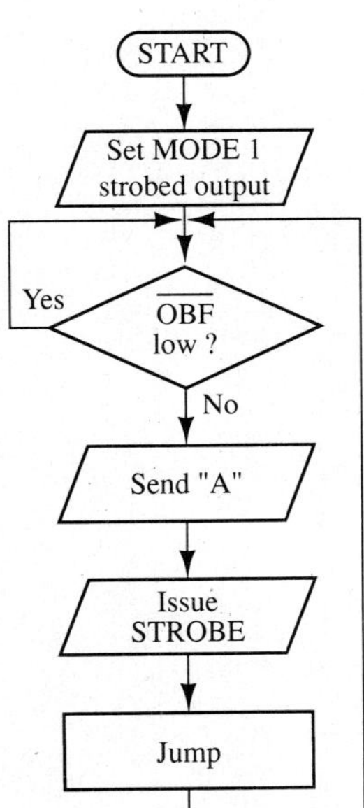

(a) Programmed I/O

FIGURE 36.4

(*continued*)

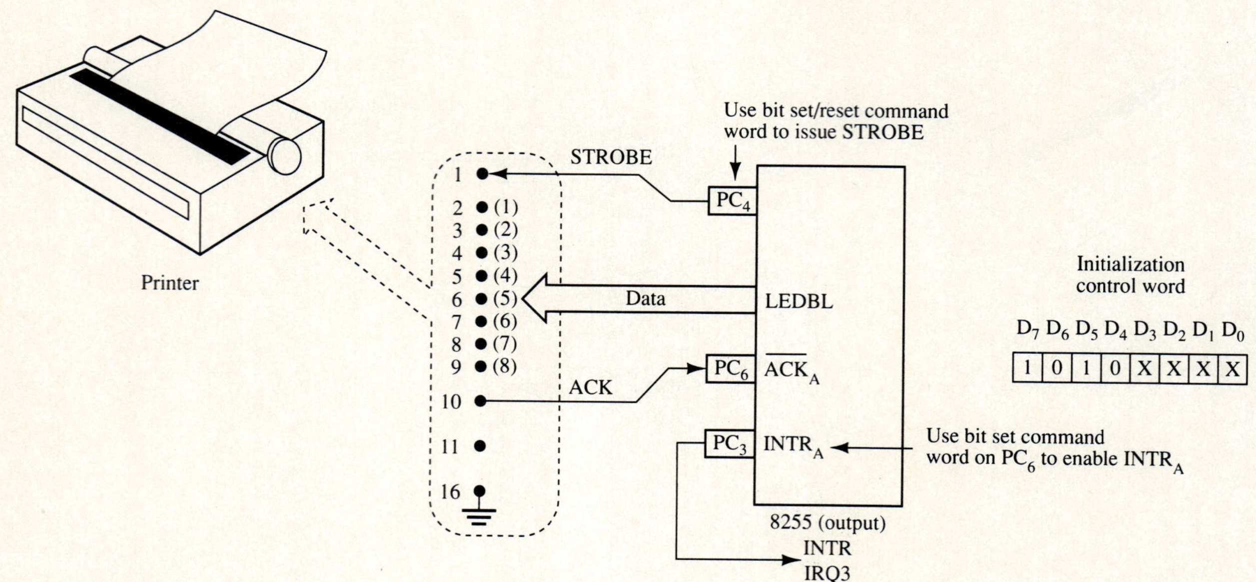

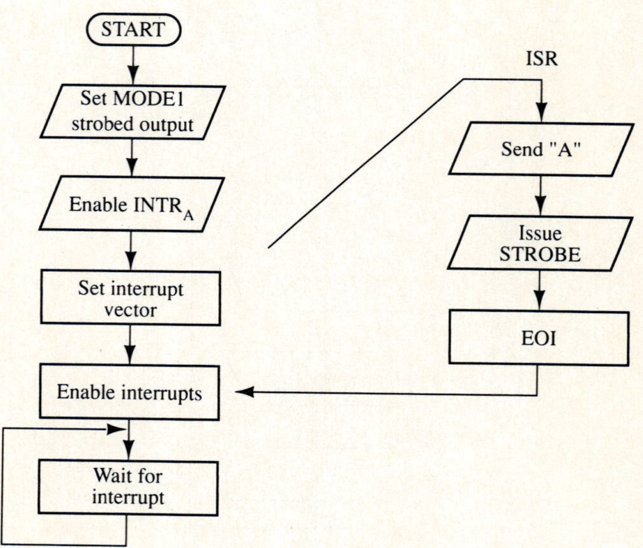

(b) Interrupt I/O

Name: ______________________

Date: ______________________

QUESTIONS AND PROBLEMS

Class: ______________________

1. Handshaking consists of a *request/acknowledge* sequence. Is STROBE a *request* signal or an *acknowledge* signal?

2. Why is handshaking normally not required when transferring data between the CPU and a RAM chip?

Advanced Section

3. Chances are that the programmed I/O and interrupt I/O printing speeds from the procedure section were approximately the same. Why should this be so?

4. Why can we use either BUSY or $\overline{\text{ACK}}$ to request the MODE 0 interrupt I/O of Figure 36.3(b)? Why must we use only BUSY in the MODE 0 polled circuit of Figure 36.3(a)?

5. What does "graphics capability" refer to when discussing a printer?

ACTIVITY 37

THE 8253 PROGRAMMABLE INTERVAL TIMER

OBJECTIVES

- To interface the 8253 programmable timer.
- To write programs that use the 8253.

PARTS AND EQUIPMENT

- IBM PC with bus-extender.
- Assembler, C compiler, debugger, and utilities.
- 8253 programmable timer.
- Dual-channel oscilloscope.

DISCUSSION

The 8253 Architecture and Modes

The 8253 programmable interval timer of Figure 37.1(a) contains three 16-bit counters that are independently programmed to operate in one of six modes [see Figure 37.1(b)].

As shown in Figure 37.2(a), programming each counter is a two-step process. First, the mode-control word of Figure 37.2(b) is written to the mode-control register of a particular counter. Next, one or two count value bytes are written to the counter registers.

Information is steered to the proper counter or mode-control register by way of address pins A0 and A1 according to the chart of Figure 37.2(c).

8253 Interfacing

Based on the suggested bus-extender circuitry of Figure C2.2, the 8253 timer is interfaced as shown in Figure 37.3. The GATE input enables each timer output. (Use a divider circuit that gives a clock signal to the 8253 not above 2.6 MHz.)

Representative Modes of Operation

In this experiment we work with MODES 3 and 4, as representative of the six modes of operation of the 8253. Referring to Figure 37.1(b), MODE 3 is used to generate continuous waveforms of varying frequency. MODE 4 generates an active-low strobe after a programmed span of time.

Sound Generation Using the Internal 8253

As a convenient option, we can use the *internal* 8253 and speaker within the IBM PC to generate sound. The block diagram of Figure 37.4(a) gives the port addresses, and the demonstration program of Figure 37.4(b) generates a note/rest sequence for the note-of-C (261.63 Hz).

PROCEDURE

NOTE: Procedure steps 2, 6, 7, and 8 can use the internal 8253.

Mode Three

1. Interface an 8253 to your bus-extender as suggested in Figure 37.3.
2. Using MODE 3, write a program that generates a frequency of precisely 1000 Hz.
3. By using all three counters programmed for MODE 3, design a system that generates tone bursts. (For example, a 1-kHz tone is turned on and off at a 1-s rate.)

FIGURE 37.1

8253 architecture and modes of operation. (Courtesy Intel Corporation.) (a) Block diagram and pinout. (b) Timing diagrams.

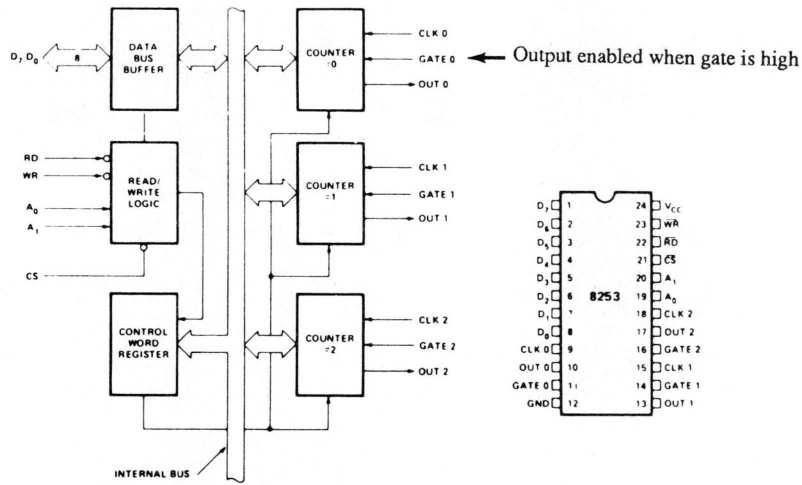

(a) Block diagram and pin-out

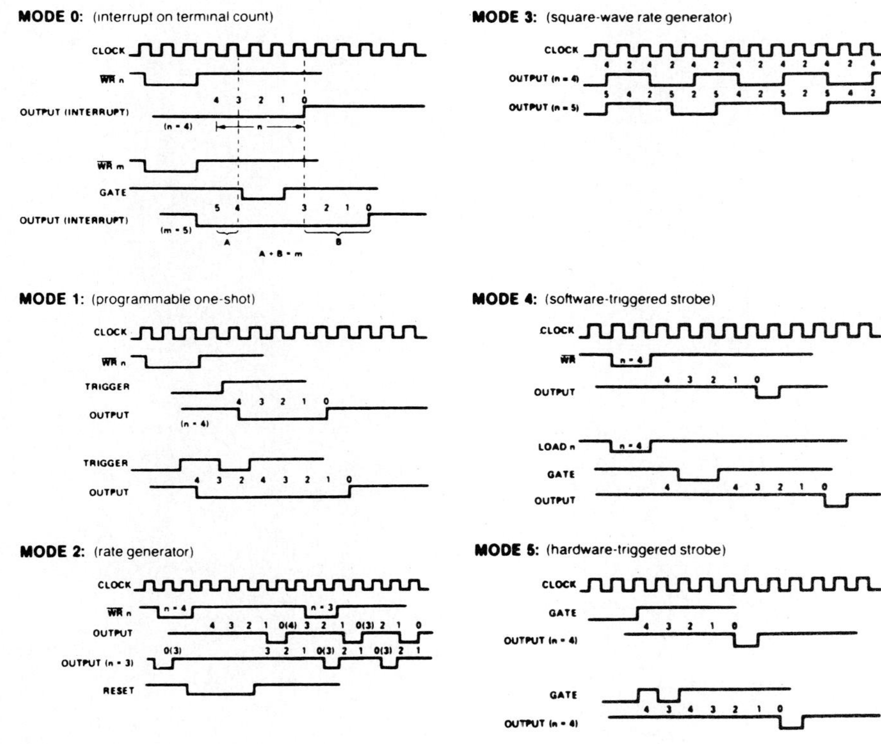

(b) Timing diagrams

Mode Four

4. Write a MODE 4 (software-triggered strobe) program in which the distance between the $\overline{WR}$ signal and the output strobe is equal to an input number.
5. Place $\overline{WR}$ into channel A of your oscilloscope (and trigger off channel A). Place the counter 0 output into channel B. Set the sweep frequency to 1 μs. Input a variety of numbers and note the change on the oscilloscope. Sketch and label several waveforms.

Advanced Activities

6. Using arrays, modify the program of Figure 37.4(b) to generate continuously in sequence the

FIGURE 37.2

Programming the 8253. (Courtesy Intel Corporation.) (a) Two-step process for programming each counter. (b) Mode-control format. (c) Register addressing.

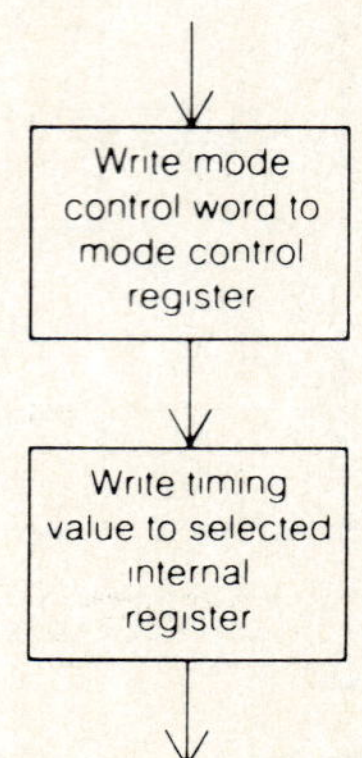

(a) Two-step process for programming each counter

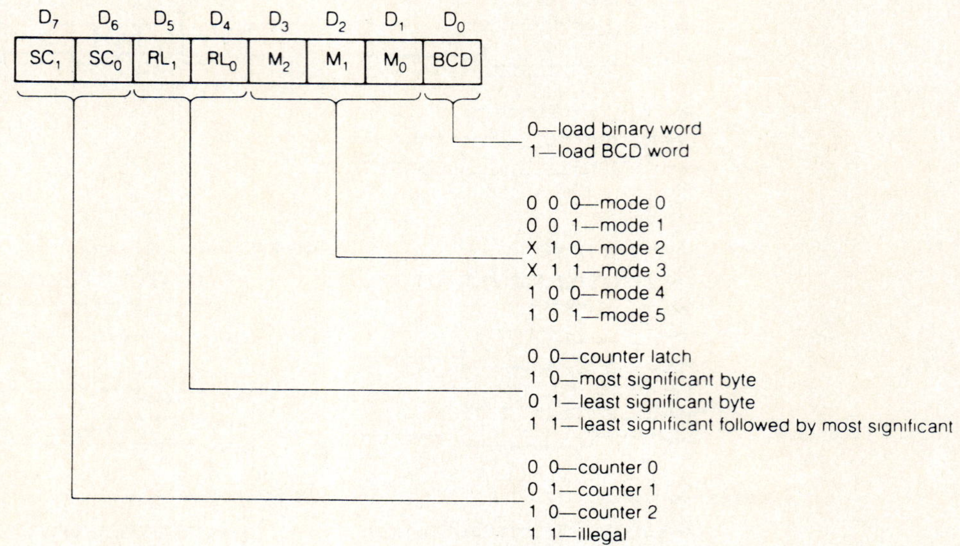

(b) Mode-control format

A_1	A_0	
0	0	Counter 0
0	1	Counter 1
1	0	Counter 2
1	1	Mode-control register

(c) Register addressing

FIGURE 37.3

8253 interfacing (port addresses 30CH, 30DH, 30EH, 30FH).

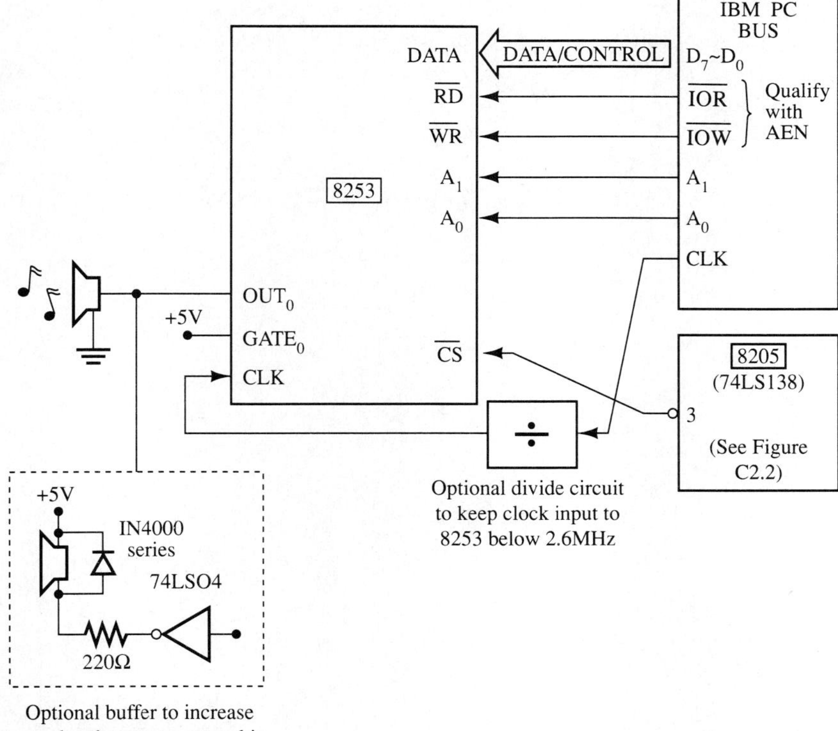

FIGURE 37.4

Internal timer chip and speaker control. (a) Block diagram and port addresses. (b) Program for note-of-C.

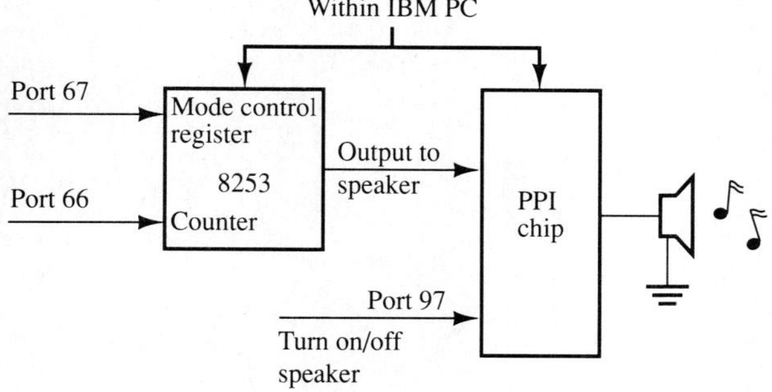

(a) Block diagram and port addresses

```
#include <conio.h>
#include <myheader.h>

main()
{
    outp(67,0xb7);      /* Counter 2, word data, mode 3, BCD.*/
    outp(66,0x72);      /* Load least significant.*/
    outp(66,0x45);      /* Load most significant.*/
    while(1){
        outp(97,(inp(97) | 3));     /* Turn on speaker. */
        msec(500);
        outp(97,(inp(97) & 0xfc)); /* Turn off speaker. */
        msec(500);
    }
}
```

(b) Program for note of C

three notes of the *chord* of C (C, E, and G). Each tone will be approximately 2 beats (1 s) in duration, and the letter designation of each note will be displayed as each is heard. (C = 261.63, E = 329.63, G = 392.00.)

7. Write program HEARING_TEST, in which tones increase in 20 steps from 1K to 20 kHz at the rate of once each 2 s. At each step, the corresponding frequency (in thousands of hertz) is displayed. What is the highest tone you can hear (assuming the speaker can generate these high frequencies)?
8. Based on the internal sound system of Figure 37.4(a), write a program that displays the following on the screen: Enter a sequence of 10 notes using any sequence of "C," "E," and "G." Each entry will be echoed to the screen. When all 10 notes have been entered, the system continuously plays them back in the same sequence.

Name: ______________________

Date: ______________________

Class: ______________________

QUESTIONS AND PROBLEMS

1. Grounding the GATE input to an 8253 counter has what result?

2. What is the difference between MODE 4 and MODE 5?

3. By cascading all three counters in MODE 3, what is the lowest frequency that can be generated? (Assume a 1-MHz clock.)

4. How does the 8253 distinguish data from control information?

Advanced Section

5. Can the 8253 be interfaced in the *memory-mapped* configuration? List some of the advantages and disadvantages of memory-mapped I/O compared to isolated I/O.

ACTIVITY 38

CONTROLLERS
A Flight Control System

OBJECTIVES

- To introduce the computer as a feedback control system.
- To design and test a flight control simulator.

PARTS AND EQUIPMENT

- IBM PC with bus-extender.
- Assembler, C compiler, debugger, and utilities.
- A 1K resistor.
- A 2-μF capacitor.
- A 5K potentiometer.
- VOM (analog volt-ohm meter).
- DAC resistor network.

DISCUSSION

A *controller* is a negative-feedback cybernetics system that manages, regulates, or directs a real-life system. (*Cybernetics* is the science of communication and control.) In simple terms, as shown in Figure 38.1, a feedback control system compares *where you want to be* with *where you are* and sends out an error signal with the purpose of driving *where you are* to *where you want to be* (reducing the error to zero). The autopilot system of an aircraft is a well-known application of a negative-feedback cybernetics system.

Referring to Figure 38.2(a), the aircraft pitch is simulated by a simple RC circuit. The signal into the RC circuit simulates the elevator position (full up or full down), and the flow of charge into the capacitor simulates the response of the aircraft. The actual aircraft pitch is represented by the voltage across the capacitor, and the desired pitch is entered into an internal variable. A potentiometer simulates external wind forces.

Briefly, this is how the system works:

1. An internal (guidance) variable is loaded with the desired pitch angle.
2. With the autopilot running, the actual aircraft pitch (feedback signal) is sampled via the A/D converter and compared to the desired pitch.
3. If the aircraft pitch is above the desired value, a logic 0 error signal (elevators full down) is produced and the capacitor discharges. If the aircraft pitch is below the desired value, a logic 1 error signal (elevators full up) is produced and the capacitor charges.
4. The routine is placed in a loop and the actual pitch angle (average capacitor voltage) is maintained at the desired level.
5. If the external potentiometer voltage (gusty wind simulator) attempts to drive the system off course, the autopilot system produces a net charge (elevators up) or net discharge (elevators down) error signal and brings the plane back on course (unless the wind is too strong).

PROCEDURE

1. Based on Figure 38.2(a), interface the autopilot system hardware.
2. When the autopilot is off, the plane is at the mercy of the wind. To simulate this condition,

FIGURE 38.1

Feedback control system block diagram.

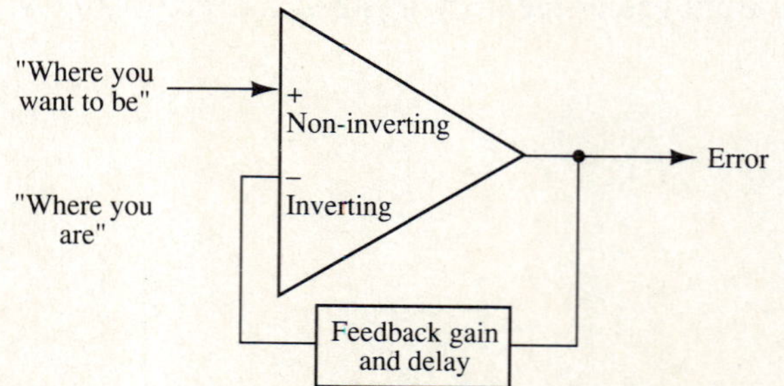

FIGURE 38.2

Flight control simulator. (a) Circuit configuration. (b) Pitch angle in terms of analog and digital values.

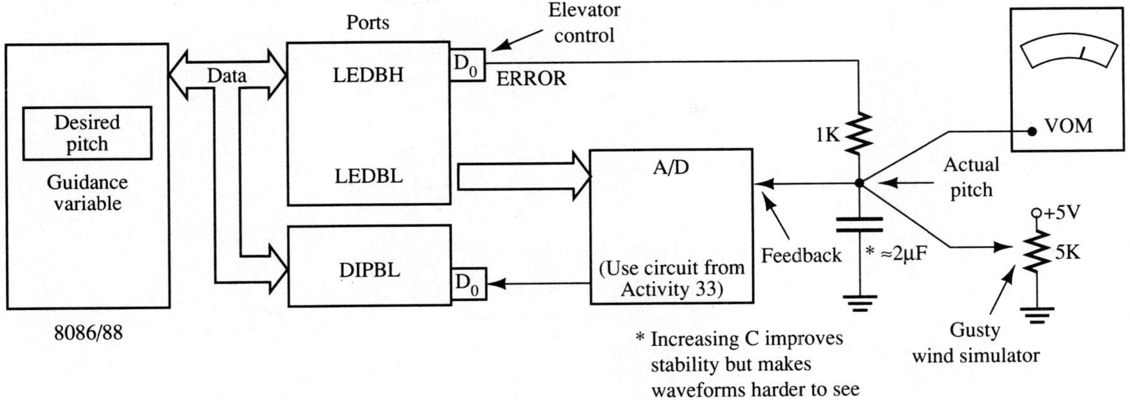

(a) Circuit configuration

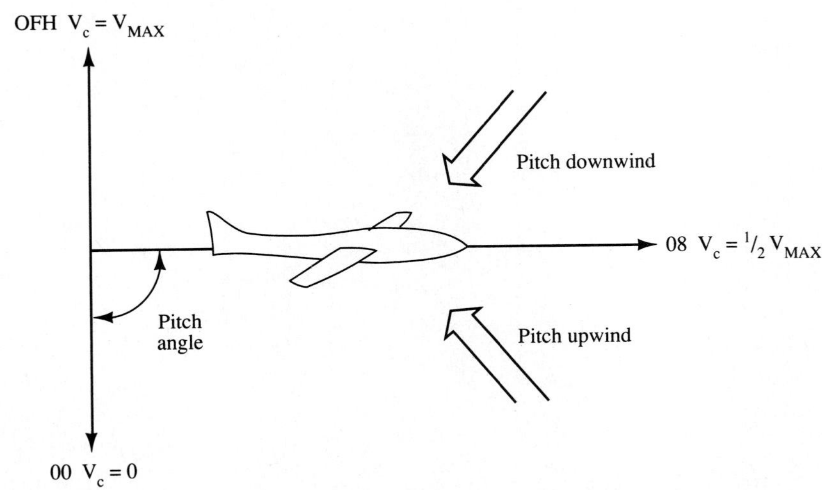

(b) Pitch angle in terms of analog and digital values

FIGURE 38.3

Effect of autopilot on pitch angle under changing wind conditions.

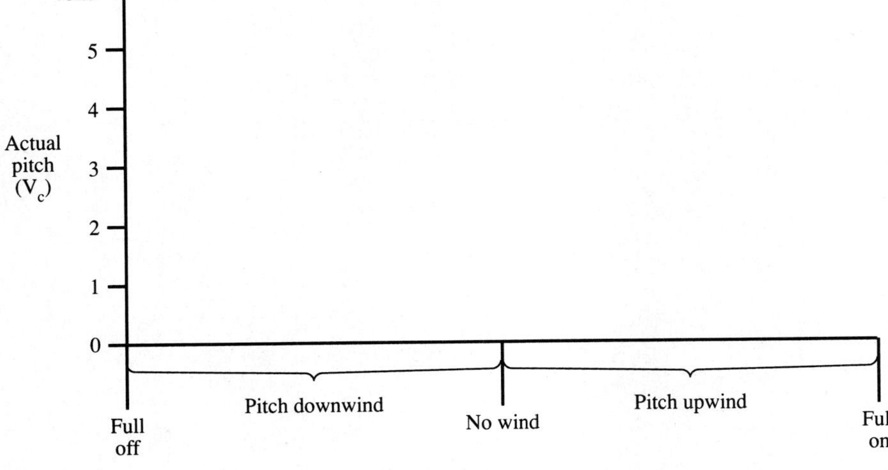

FIGURE 38.4

Flight control flowchart and program. Reproduced with permission of the Glencoe Division of Macmillan/McGraw-Hill Publishing Company.

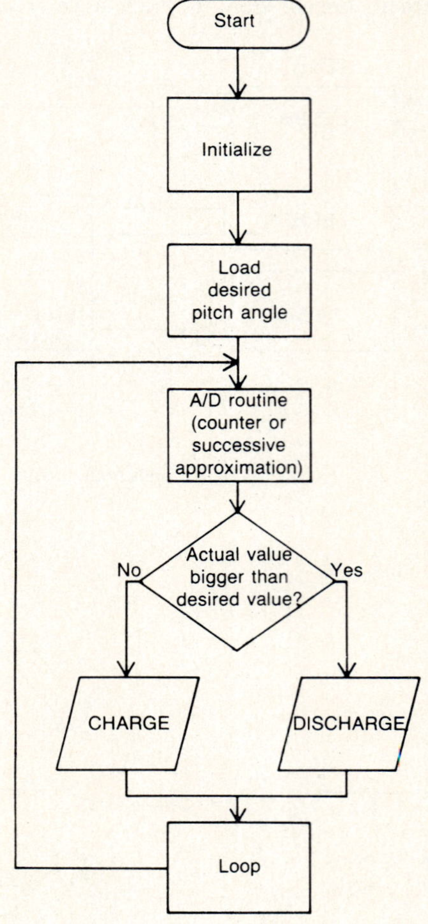

FIGURE 38.5

Autopilot simulator waveforms. Reproduced with permission of the Glencoe Division of Macmillan/McGraw-Hill Publishing Company.

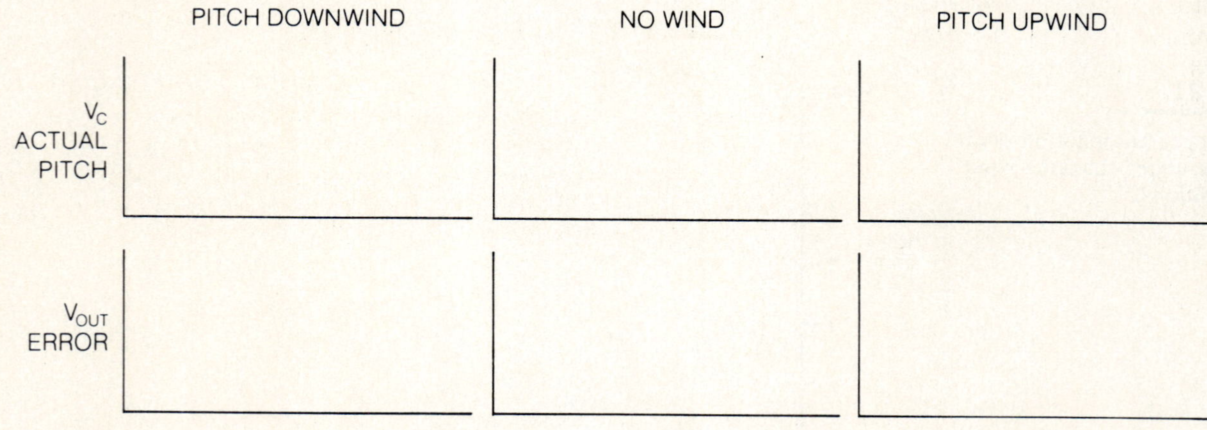

FIGURE 38.6

Op amp circuit for greater precision and control.

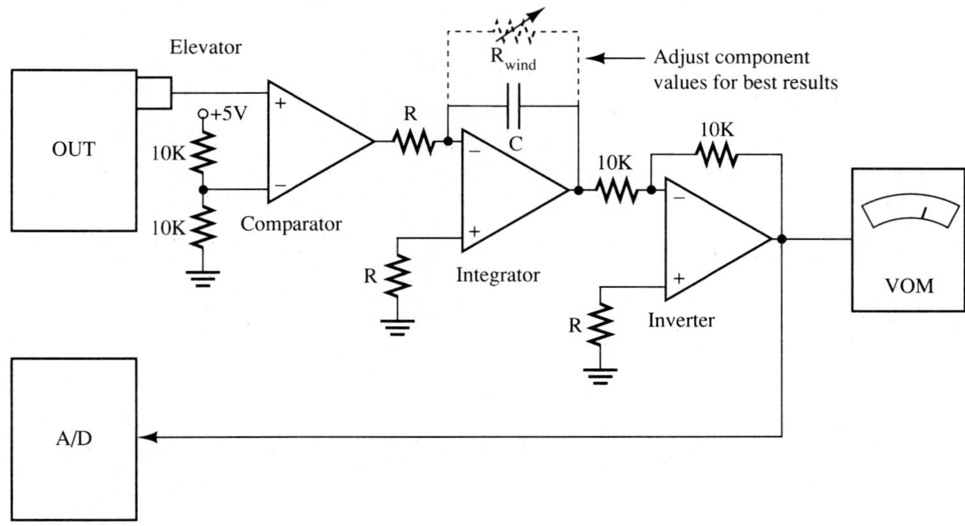

disconnect the elevator control (error signal line) to the RC network. On the graph of Figure 38.3, plot a curve of pitch angle versus wind force (capacitor voltage versus potentiometer position). (*Hint:* The curve should be a straight line at an angle.)

3. Guided by the flowchart of Figure 38.4, write the simulator program. To command horizontal flight, load a pitch value of 7 or 8 into the guidance variable. (A pitch value of 7 or 8 is halfway between 0 and 15 for a 4-bit A/D system.)
4. To activate the autopilot, load and execute the software. Using a VOM (analog volt-ohm meter) to measure average capacitor voltage (actual pitch angle), plot another graph of pitch angle versus wind (potentiometer position) on Figure 38.3. Did the autopilot "lock on" to the desired pitch over a range of wind strengths and directions? ____________
5. By viewing the pitch and error signals on your oscilloscope, fill in the graphs of Figure 38.5 for the "pitch downwind," "no wind," and "pitch upwind" cases. (*Note:* Triggering ease varies with exact potentiometer position.)

Advanced Activities

6. Modify the program of procedure step 3 so that the desired pitch angle can be changed in real time by way of input values. Does the system "lock on" to each new input value over a range of wind strengths? ____________
7. Add programmed guidance to the flight control system by changing the desired pitch register in real time (one change per second) according to a predetermined flight path specified as an array.
8. Modify the program of step 7 to allow the programmed flight path values to first be entered from the keyboard. Then, as the system is running continuously, plot both the desired values from guidance and the real values from flight control as a real-time graph. Be sure to operate the wind simulator and note the results.
9. For greater simulation accuracy, substitute various op amp configurations for the simple RC circuit used thus far. (Example given in Figure 38.6.)

Name: ____________________

Date: ____________________

QUESTIONS AND PROBLEMS

Class: ____________________

1. What is the difference between a closed-loop and an open-loop system?

2. How do the RC values of Figure 38.2 affect the control speed of the cybernetics system?

3. Why did the autopilot system lose control when the pitch upwind or pitch downwind became too great?

Advanced Section

4. Name at least one feedback control system that is operating in the human body.

5. To what does the term *process control* refer?

6. Related to computer processing, to what does the term *real time* refer? (Is the present autopilot system a real-time system?)

7. How could you modify the error signal output of Figure 38.2 to give *proportional* control, rather than pulse-width control? (*Note:* In proportional control, the error signal equals the difference between the desired and actual values.)

8. What electronic component added to the output would simulate inertia? How could we simulate damping to offset the effects of inertia?

9. Is a phase-locked-loop a cybernetic system? Explain.

ACTIVITY 39

ROBOTICS
The Stepper Motor

OBJECTIVES

- To introduce robotics as a specialized control system.
- To use the stepper motor to provide computer-controlled motion.

PARTS AND EQUIPMENT

- IBM PC with bus-extender.
- Assembler, C compiler, debugger, and utilities.
- Four-phase stepper motor.
- 100-ohm (Ω) resistor.
- 8216 buffer (or equivalent).

DISCUSSION

A stepper motor provides controlled rotation in precise increments. Referring to Figure 39.1(a), if the grounds presently on windings W_1 and W_4 are rotated to W_4 and W_2, the rotor will turn clockwise 90 deg. Due to its internal construction, each rotation step of a commercial motor is typically less than 10 deg.

When the rotating pattern of grounds is diagrammed as in Figure 39.1(b), we see that each step is the result of a rotating bit pattern—a pattern easily generated by a computer.

A library function that accepts one or more input parameters and generates a basic elemental movement is known as a *robotics instruction*. A collection of basic movement instructions becomes a robotics language.

PROCEDURE

1. Interface a four-phase stepper motor to an output port according to the diagram of Figure 39.2. (A wide variety of buffers can be used if the motor is small and rotation speeds are limited.)
2. Write assembly-language library routines STEPR and STEPL. Each routine accepts a byte value as a parameter and returns the value rotated one step in the appropriate direction.

FIGURE 39.1

Stepper motor control. (a) Mechanical design. (b) Shift-register pattern of four-phase rotation. Reproduced with permission of the Glencoe Division of Macmillan/McGraw-Hill Publishing Company.

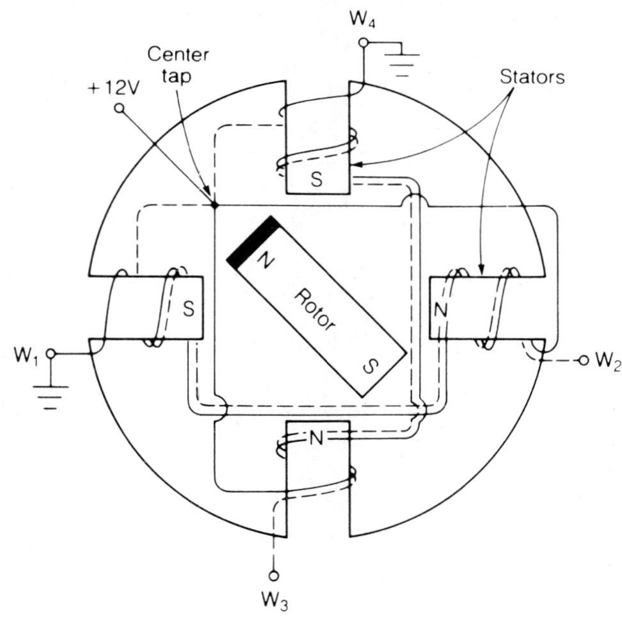

(a) Mechanical design

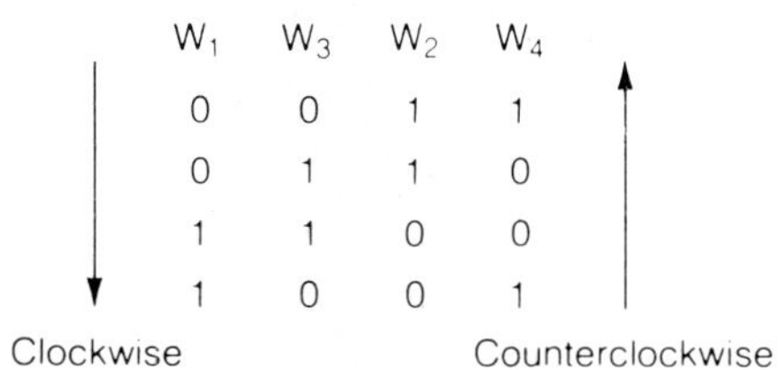

W_1	W_3	W_2	W_4
0	0	1	1
0	1	1	0
1	1	0	0
1	0	0	1

Clockwise ↓ Counterclockwise ↑

(b) Shift-register pattern of four-phase rotation

FIGURE 39.2

Stepper motor interface.

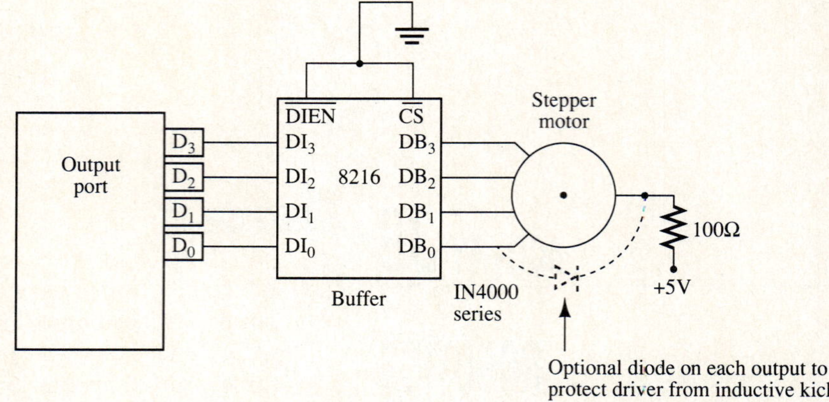

3. Using routines STEPR and STEPL, write program BACK_AND_FORTH, which causes the stepper motor to rotate continuously right five steps followed by left five steps. Each step should occur approximately 0.5-s apart.
4. By greatly modifying routines STEPR and STEPL, write robotic library functions SPINR and SPINL. Each routine accepts three byte parameters. The first is the present position of the motor, the second gives the number of steps, and the third specifies the speed (delay between steps). Both routines return the new motor position.
5. Using routines SPINR and SPINL, write program SCAN, which steps left and right continuously, with the number of steps and speed of stepping controlled from the keyboard or bus-extender ports.

Advanced Activities

6. Write a program that accepts character commands from the keyboard: R causes continuous right rotation, L causes continuous left rotation, S causes a stop, "−" slows down the motor, "+" speeds up the motor, and Q quits the program. The state of the motion (direction and speed) are printed to the screen in real time.
7. Using robotics instructions SPINR and SPINL, write program DRUMROLL in which the stepper motor rotates back and forth at ever smaller angles and ever faster speeds. When the angle and speed reach reasonable limits, the cycle repeats. For added realism, a beep sounds at each hit of the drum.
8. Keyboard commands "R" and "L" cause a single right or single left step. At the rate of approximately 2/s, the keyboard is read and a series of Rs or Ls is read into a file. "N" (for *no operation*) is placed into the file if an R or L is not in the buffer. After this "learning" process is done, the commands are played back at the same rate and the motor performs the programmed sequence without human intervention.
9. Modify any of the programs of this activity so that an asterisk (*) spins on the screen at the same direction and speed as the motor.

Name: ____________________

Date: ____________________

QUESTIONS AND PROBLEMS

Class: ____________________

1. Why is feedback not necessary when driving a stepper motor? What danger is there when feedback is not used?

2. What is the resolution of a stepper motor that requires 120 steps to complete one revolution?

3. A robotics language consists of instructions that perform specific primitive motions. What instructions make up the robotics language of this activity?

Advanced Section

4. Devise a method for rotating the stepper motor using only C statements. (Do not use external functions written in assembly-language.)

5. Regarding a stepper motor, what is the ''half-step'' mode and how is it implemented?

ACTIVITY **40**

SERIAL COMMUNICATIONS The 8251A Serial Communications Interface

OBJECTIVE

- To perform serial data communications using the 8251A Serial Communications Interface.

PARTS AND EQUIPMENT

- IBM PC with bus-extender.
- Assembler, C compiler, debugger, and utilities.
- 8251A Serial Communications Interface.

DISCUSSION

The 8251A Serial Communications Interface of Figure 40.1 is used to simplify serial communication and to reduce the software overhead. Also known as a *universal synchronous/asynchronous receiver/transmitter* (USART), the 8251A is a serial-to-parallel and parallel-to-serial converter in which all serial data conform to standard asynchronous or synchronous protocols.

The 8251A Architecture and Modes of Operation

Programming the mode of operation is handled by the control and status words of Figure 40.2. When C/$\bar{D}$ (control/data) is high, the *mode, command* or *status* register is accessed; when low, the parallel data buffer is accessed. (The CPU differentiates between a mode word and a command word by the order in which they are written. After system reset, the next input to the 8251A must be a mode word. All control words written after that will automatically be interpreted as command words.)

FIGURE 40.1

8251A architecture. (Courtesy Intel Corporation.)

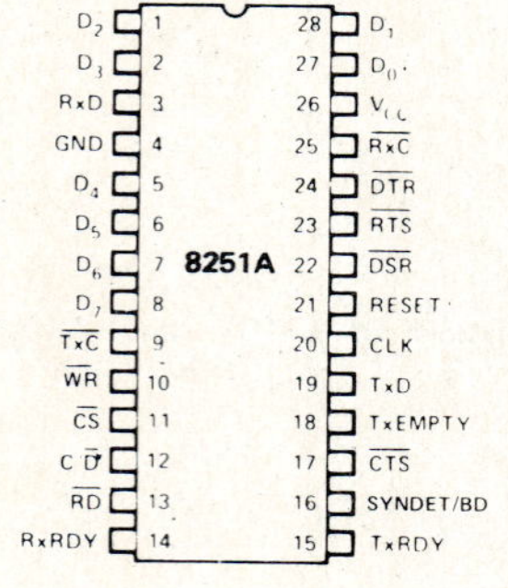

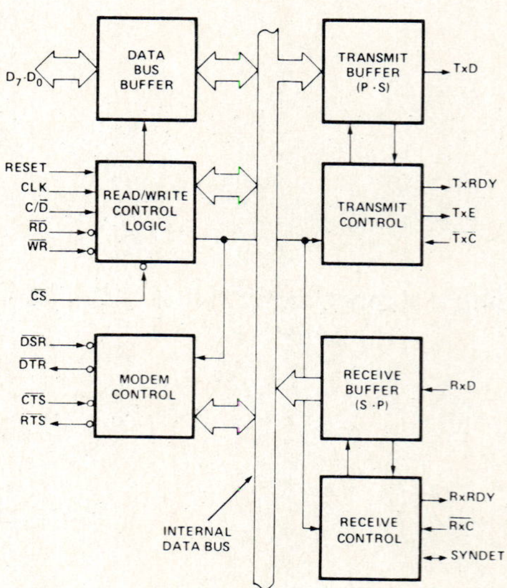

FIGURE 40.2

8251A programming. (Courtesy Intel Corporation.) (a) Control. (b) Status.

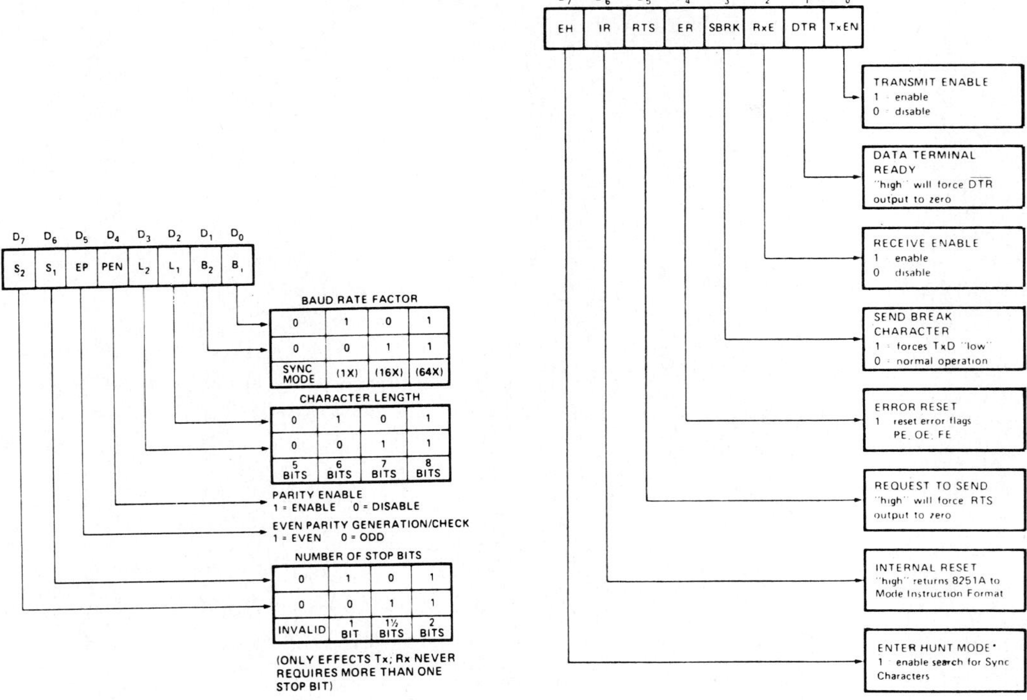

(a) Control

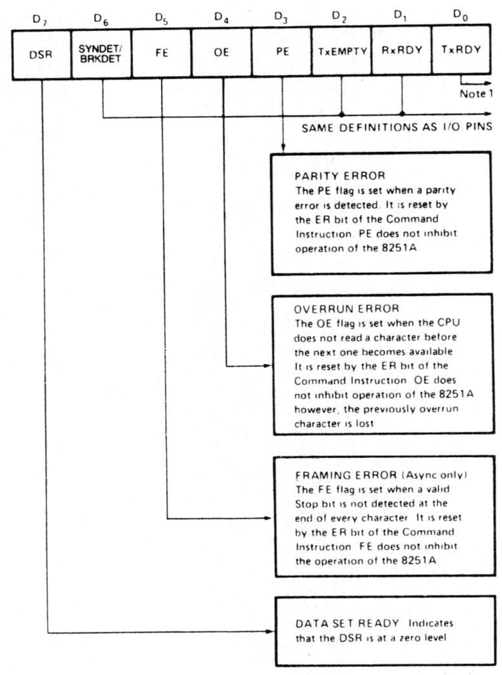

(b) Status

FIGURE 40.3

Asynchronous data transmission format.

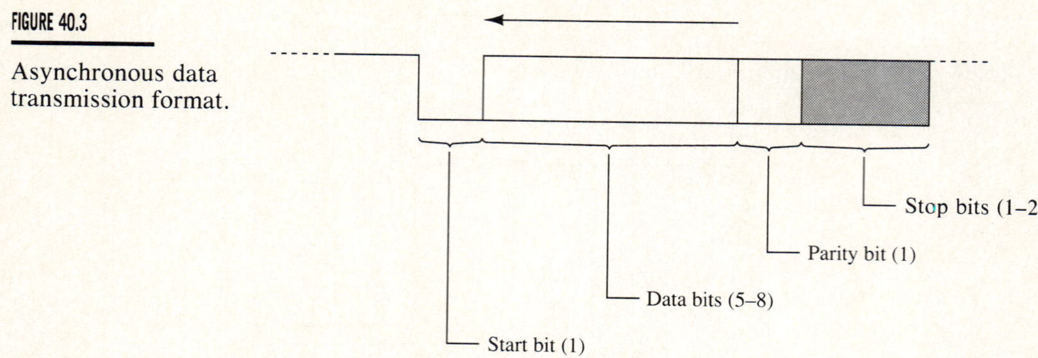

Synchronous Versus Asynchronous

The 8251A operates in either the *asynchronous* or *synchronous* modes. As shown in Figure 40.3, the asynchronous (unclocked) mode sends data as individual characters, with each character surrounded by start and stop bits. Because the receiver clocks are reset at the arrival of each active-low start bit, the clocks of the receiver and transmitter can be slightly different (skewed). Furthermore, the data characters can come at irregular intervals.

The more complex and higher speed synchronous (clocked) mode sends data in groups (or *packets*), with each packet surrounded by synchronization and error-checking characters. Because data flow continuously, the clocks of the receiver and transmitter must be perfectly matched (often accomplished with a phase-locked loop).

In this activity, we work exclusively with the asynchronous mode, and transmit data following the format of Figure 40.3.

8251A Asynchronous Operation

Briefly, the 8251A operates in the asynchronous mode as follows:

- During transmission, data are walked out the TxD (transmit data) pin at the baud rate (bits per second) set by the $\overline{\text{TxC}}$ (transmit clock) input. When the serial buffer empties, the information in the parallel buffer is immediately transferred to the serial buffer and start, stop, and parity bits are automatically added. The TxRDY (transmit ready) pin (for interrupt I/O) and the TxRDY status bit (for programmed I/O) go active, notifying the CPU to write the next piece of parallel information into the parallel buffer—which automatically resets TxRDY.
- During reception, data are walked into the RxD pin at the baud rate set by the $\overline{\text{RxC}}$ (receive clock) input. When the serial buffer fills, the information is stripped of its start, stop, and parity bits and automatically transferred to the parallel buffer. The CPU is notified by way of the RxRDY (receive ready) pin (interrupt I/O) or the RxRDY status bit (programmed I/O), and the information read into the CPU.

PROCEDURE

NOTE: If experiencing difficulty with serial transmission, hardware reset the 8251A prior to program execution.

Programmed I/O

1. Interface the 8251A by referring to Figure 40.4. (C/$\overline{\text{D}}$ goes to a low-level address line.)
2. Referring to Figure 40.2, determine the mode and command words required to set up the following parameters:
   - Asynchronous mode
   - Baud rate factor of 64
   - Eight-bit character length
   - Disable parity
   - Two stop bits
   - Enable transmit
3. Based on the flowchart of Figure 40.5(a), write a programmed I/O routine that continuously transmits in serial a byte of information that is input.
4. Load and run the program. Triggering off $\overline{\text{WR}}$, view the serial data on an oscilloscope. Change the input data and note the change on the oscilloscope.

FIGURE 40.4

8251A interfacing.

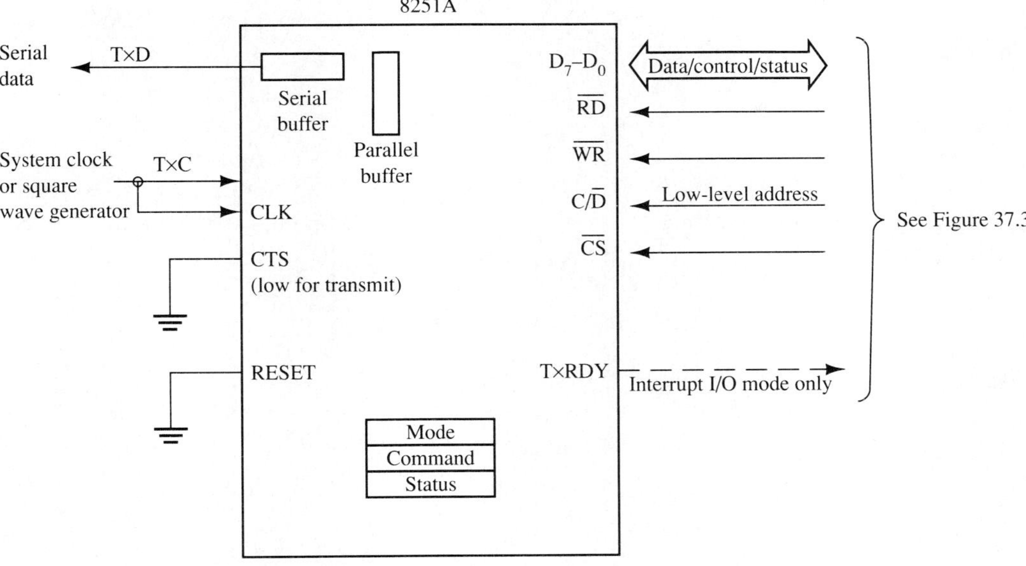

FIGURE 40.5

USART transmission sequence. (a) Programmed I/O. (b) Interrupt I/O.

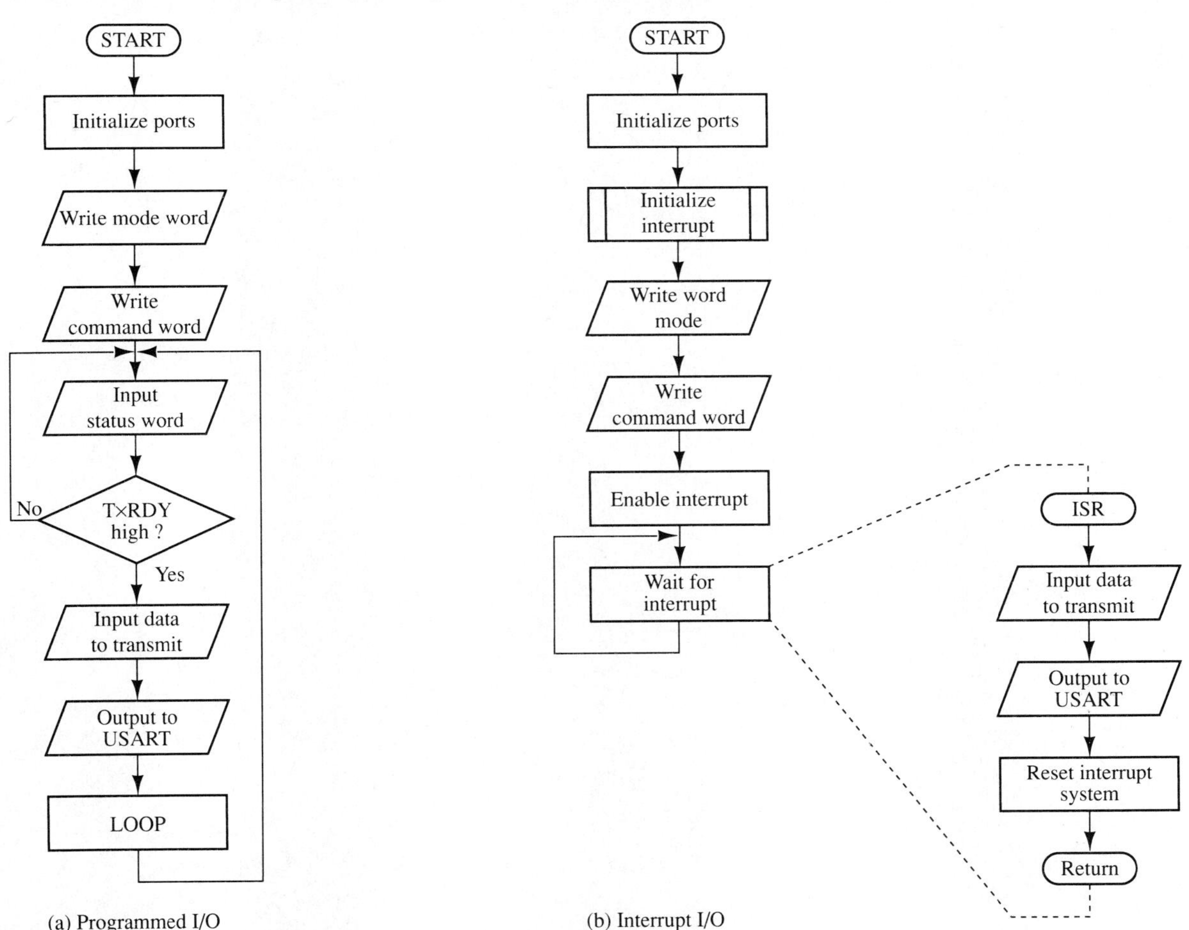

(a) Programmed I/O (b) Interrupt I/O

5. Repeat the serial transmission process using interrupt I/O. [Refer to Figure 40.5(b).]

Advanced Activities

NOTE: All advanced activities will use programmed I/O.

6. Write the following two library routines:
   a. INITS to initialize the 8251A for serial transmission.
   b. OUTS to accept a byte parameter and write it to the 8251A for serial transmission.
7. Making use of routines INITS and OUTS, write a program in which the serial data (displayed on the oscilloscope screen) count up in binary at approximately 1 Hz.
8. Write program VIEW_STEPPER in which the following two tasks take place simultaneously:
   a. A stepper motor scans back and forth in eight-position (seven-step) increments at a rate controlled by an input byte.
   b. The position of the motor is viewed on the oscilloscope screen as a bar graph of serial information transmitted from the 8251A.

Name: ____________________

Date: ____________________

QUESTIONS AND PROBLEMS

Class: ____________________

1. When using a USART, what is the advantage of using interrupt I/O over programmed I/O?

2. What is the purpose of the active-low start bit in the asynchronous serial transmission format? of one or more stop bits?

3. How does the 8251A differentiate between a mode word and a command word? between a mode/command word and a status word?

4. When does TxRDY go active?

5. What is the *baud rate factor*?

Advanced Section

6. What is the purpose of the $\overline{DTR}$, $\overline{RTS}$, $\overline{DSR}$, and $\overline{CTS}$ pins on the 8251A?

7. What is a *framing error* and how is it indicated? [See Figure 40.2(b).]

8. What change takes place in the transmitted information when the parity bit is enabled?

9. When sending an 11-character word (8 data, 1 start, 2 stop), by how much can the transmitting and receiving clocks differ before transmission loss occurs?

ACTIVITY 41

ADVANCED MATHEMATICS
Calculus and Spectral Analysis

OBJECTIVES

- To perform integration and differentiation using digital computer techniques.
- To plot the frequency-domain components of a time-domain waveform.

PARTS AND EQUIPMENT

- IBM PC with bus-extender.
- Assembler, C compiler, debugger, and utilities.

DISCUSSION

If a baseball travels at the speed of 50 mph for 2 s, how far has it traveled? Conversely, if a baseball travels 100 ft in 2 s, how fast is it going? Because the velocity is a *constant,* we can use the well-known *multiply* and *divide* operators.

However, suppose we drop the baseball over a cliff. In this case, we cannot simply multiply and divide because the velocity is not constant—it is in fact a *variable* (a *function* of time). The question is, how do we "multiply" and "divide" variables? (A question Isaac Newton must also have asked.) The answer is, we use the methods that Isaac Newton invented: integral and differential calculus.

Integration

If asked to find the area of a rectangle, such as that of Figure 41.1(a), we simply multiply height times width. The process works because both height and width are *constants*.

However, to find the area of a circle, such as that shown in Figure 41.1(b), we cannot multiply because the circumference is a function of the radius $[c(r) = 2\pi r]$.

Using integration to calculate the area of a circle, we start by dividing the circle into concentric sections, as shown in Figure 41.1(c). Because each section is given *approximately* by $2\pi r\Delta r$, the total area is approximately equal to the sum of all the sections:

$$\sum_{1}^{R/\Delta r} 2\pi r\Delta r$$

Using this formula on a circle of three sections, Figure 41.1(c) generates an approximate area of 12π units.

Clearly, if we subdivide the circle into smaller and smaller sections, the summation will be more and more accurate. In fact, in the limit as Δr approaches zero, we have:

$$\sum_{\substack{1 \\ \lim \Delta r\to 0}}^{R/\Delta r} 2\pi r\Delta r = \int_0^R 2\pi r \, \mathrm{d}r = \pi R^2$$

which is a specific application of the *fundamental theorem of calculus:*

$$\sum_{\substack{1 \\ \lim \Delta x\to 0}}^{(X_2-X_1)/\Delta x} f(x)\Delta x = \int_{X_1}^{X_2} f(x)\,\mathrm{d}x = f(x_2) - f(x_1)$$

Using these methods, as shown in Figure 41.1(d), we now obtain the correct answer.

When using a digital computer to find the area of a circle, we must use the approximate summation method because we cannot take Δr to zero—but we can make Δr as small as our data type allows us.

The demonstration program of Figure 41.1(e) uses the summation of 100 sections to calculate the area of a circle of any radius.

Differentiation

Returning to our baseball example, Figure 41.2(a) shows that for a ball thrown horizontally, we simply divide 100 ft by 2 s to obtain the speed (50 ft/s). It works because we assume the velocity is a constant.

However, as shown in Figure 41.2(b), it's a different "ballgame" when we drop the baseball over a cliff. For example, if dropped over a 100-ft cliff, what is the ball's velocity when it hits the ground 2.5 s later? Dividing 100 by 2.5 does not work because we merely obtain the average velocity. To obtain the *instantaneous* velocity at the bottom, we must *differentiate* using functions.

The following equation gives the functional distance of an object in free-fall. (Distance is the *dependent* variable and time is the *independent* variable.)

FIGURE 41.1

The process of integration. (a) Finding the area of a rectangle by using the multiply operator. (b) To find the area of a circle, we cannot multiply because the circumference is a function. (c) Approximating the area of a circle by dividing into sections. (d) Finding the exact area of a circle from the limit as Δr approaches zero. (e) Program to find the area of a circle by summation of 100 sections.

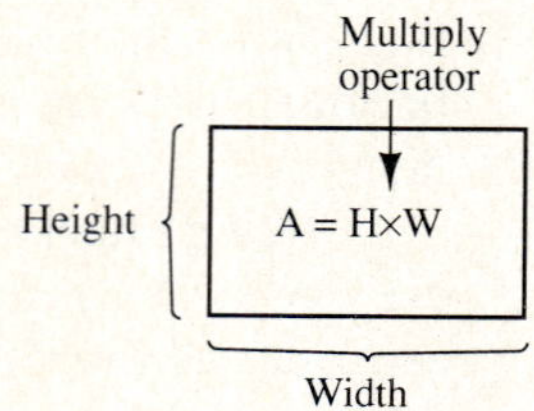

(a) Finding the area of a rectangle by using the multiply operator

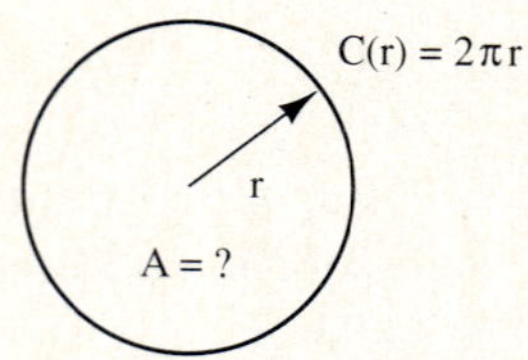

(b) To find the area of a circle, we cannot multiply because the circumference is a function

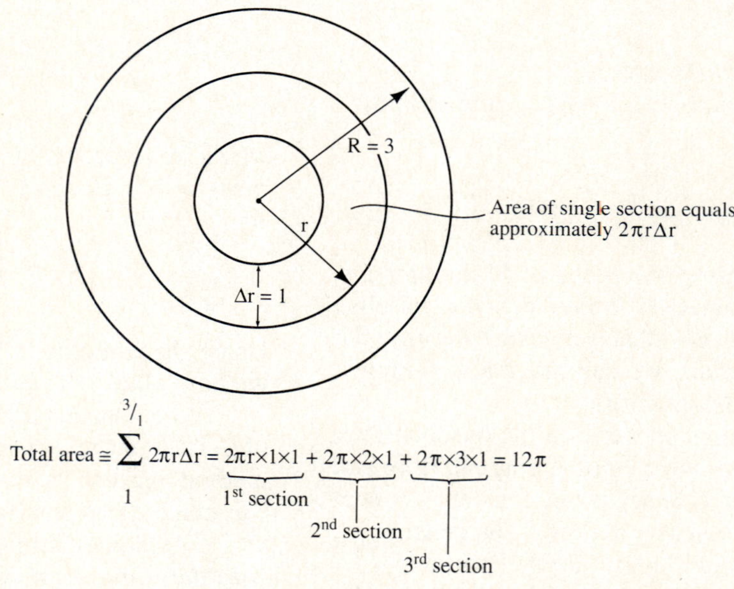

(c) Approximating the area of a circle by dividing into sections

$$\text{Total area} = \sum_{1}^{3/\Delta r} 2\pi r \Delta r = \int_{0}^{3} 2\pi r\, dr = \pi r^2 \Big]_{0}^{3} = 9\pi$$

LIMIT $\Delta r \to 0$

(d) Finding the exact area of a circle from the limit as Δr approaches 0

FIGURE 41.1

(continued)

```
/* Using integration to find the area
   of a circle. */
#include <stdio.h>
#include <math.h>
#define  PI  3.14159265
main()
{
    double radius,r,dr,area;

    while(1){
        printf("\n\nGive me a radius: ");
        scanf("%lf",&radius);
        dr = radius/100.0;
        for(r = 0.0,area = 0.0;r < radius;r += dr)
            area += 2.0 * r * PI * dr;
        printf("\nIf radius = %f, area = %f",radius,area);
    }
}
```

(e) Program to find area of circle by summation of 100 sections

$d(t) = 16 \times t^2 \quad (d = \text{distance and } t = \text{time})$

How do we "divide" distance by time to obtain velocity when distance is a function? We differentiate!

As before, let's begin with an approximation. We determine the *approximate* velocity at any time by calculating the *change* in distance divided by a small *change* in time. The calculation becomes:

$$V(t) = \frac{16(t + \Delta t)^2 - 16t^2}{\Delta t}$$

Using this formula on a 0.5-s interval at the 100-ft (2.5 s) point, Figure 41.2(c) determines a velocity of 88 ft/s. We note from the triangle that our result is the approximate *slope* of the curve at the desired point.

Clearly, if we move the two points closer and closer together, the calculation will be more and more accurate, and the approximate slope will approach a true tangent to the curve. In fact, in the limit as Δt approaches zero, we have:

$$\underset{\lim \Delta t \to 0}{V(t)} = \frac{16(t + \Delta t)^2 - 16t^2}{\Delta t} = \frac{d16t^2}{dt} = 32t$$

which again is a specific application of the *fundamental theorem of calculus* (differential form):

$$\underset{\lim \Delta x \to 0}{F'(x)} = \frac{F(x + \Delta x) - F(x)}{\Delta x} = \frac{dF(x)}{dx}$$

Using these methods, as shown in Figure 41.2(d), we now obtain the right answer.

When using a digital computer to find the velocity, we must use the approximate (increment) method because we cannot take Δt to zero—but again we can make Δt as small as our data type allows us.

The demonstration program of Figure 42.1(e) uses time increments of 1% to calculate the free-fall velocity at any time.

Spectral Analysis

Any time-domain function may be converted into its equivalent frequency-domain representation by use of the *continuous Fourier transform* (CFT):

$$X(j\omega t) = \int_{-\infty}^{\infty} x(t)e^{-j\omega t}\, dt = \int_{-\infty}^{\infty} x(t)\,(\cos(\omega t) - j\sin(\omega t))\, dt$$

However, we know that an integral can be approximated by a summation (appropriate for computer analysis), and we know that we can convert from rectangular to polar form (square root of the squares) if we are interested in only the amplitude of each frequency component (not the phase). The result is:

$$X(f) = \frac{1}{N}\left\{\left[\sum_{t=0}^{N-1} x(t)\cos(2\pi \text{ft}/N)\right]^2 + \left[\sum_{t=0}^{N-1} x(t)\sin(2\pi \text{ft}/N)\right]^2\right\}^{1/2}$$

The larger the number of sampling points (N), the more accurate the result.

As a demonstration of its use, let's obtain the frequency spectrum of the time-domain waveform of Figure 41.3(a). As shown, the waveform is a simple summation of two sine waves of the amplitudes and frequencies shown.

FIGURE 41.2

The process of differentiation. (a) Finding velocity using the division operator. (b) To find the instantaneous velocity at the bottom, we cannot divide because distance is a function. (c) Approximating the velocity from small changes in distance and time. (d) Finding the exact velocity at 2.5 s from the limit as Δt approaches zero. (e) Program to find velocity at any free-fall time by dividing 1% increments.

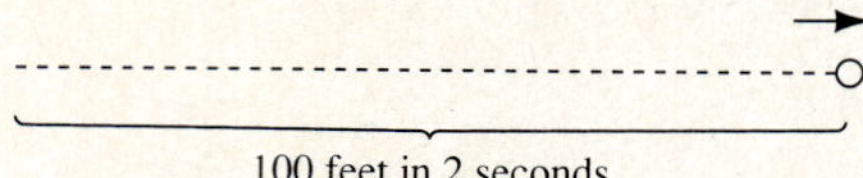

Velocity = distance/time = 100 ft/2 sec = 50 ft/sec

Division operator

(a) Finding velocity using the division operator

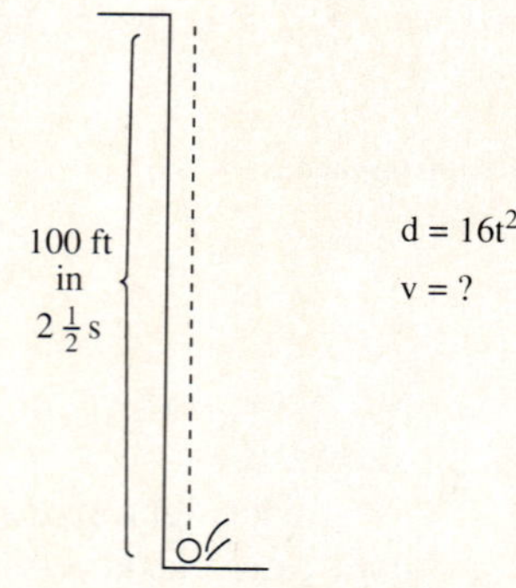

(b) To find the instantaneous velocity at the bottom, we cannot divide because distance is a function

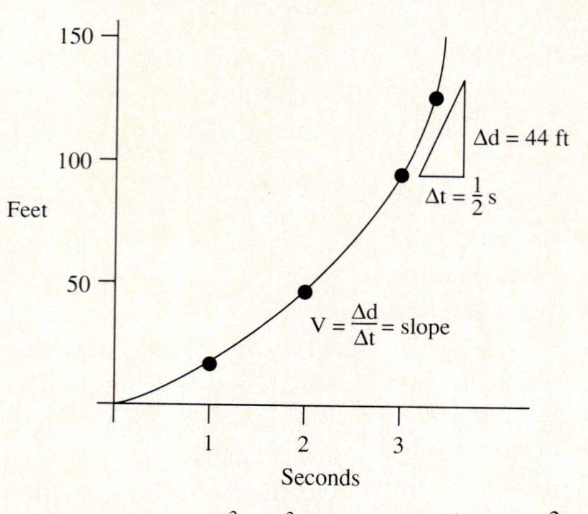

$$\text{Velocity} \cong \frac{16\,(t + \Delta t)^2 - 16t^2}{\Delta t} = \frac{16\,(2.5 + 1/2)^2 - 16(2.5)^2}{1/2} = 88\text{ft/s}$$

(c) Approximating the velocity from small changes in distance and time

$$\text{Velocity} = \lim_{\Delta t \to 0} \frac{16\,(t + \Delta t)^2 - 16t^2}{\Delta t} = \left.\frac{d\,16t^2}{dt}\right|_{t=2.5} = 32t = 80\text{ft/s}$$

(d) Finding the exact velocity at 2.5 seconds from the limit as Δt approaches zero

FIGURE 41.2

(continued)

```
/* Using differentiation to find velocty
   from free-fall distance equation. */
#include <stdio.h>
#include <math.h>
main()
{
    double time,dt,velocity;

    while(1){
        printf("\n\nGive me a time: ");
        scanf("%lf",&time);
        dt = time / 100.0;
        velocity = (16*(time+dt)*(time+dt) - 16*time*time)/dt;
        printf("If time = %f, velocity = %f",time,velocity);
    }
}
```

(c) Program to find velocity at any free fall time by dividing one percent increments

FIGURE 41.3

Spectral analysis. (a) Time-domain waveform. (b) Program to plot the frequency spectrum of the time-domain waveform.

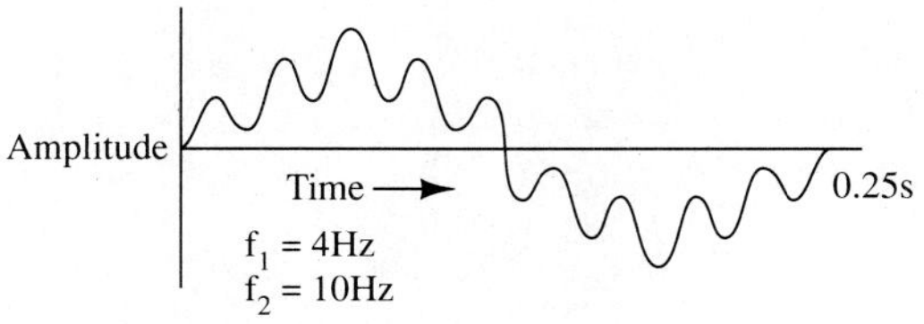

Amplitude

Time ⟶

0.25s

$f_1 = 4Hz$
$f_2 = 10Hz$

$A(t) = \sin(2\pi f_1 t) + 0.5 \sin(2\pi f_2 t)$

(a) Time domain waveform

```
/* Using a discrete Fourier transform to
   find the spectral components of two sine
   waves added together. */
#include <stdio.h>
#include <math.h>
#include <myheader.h>
#define TPI 6.283185307
main()
{
    double realc,imagc;
    int    j,t,k,fcomp;

    clear();
    for (j = 0;j < 20;j++){
        realc =0.0;
        imagc = 0.0;
        for (t = 0;t < 40;t++){
            realc += ((sin(TPI*t/10.0)+0.5*sin(TPI*t/4.0))*cos(t*j*TPI/40.0));
            imagc += ((sin(TPI*t/10.0)+0.5*sin(TPI*t/4.0))*sin(t*j*TPI/40.0));
        }
        fcomp = sqrt(realc*realc + imagc*imagc);
        for (k = 0;k<fcomp;k++){
            setcur(4*j,24-k);
            putch('*');
        }
        setcur(1,1);
        printf("The frequency is %dHz.",j);
    }
}
```

(b) Program to plot frequency spectrum of time-domain waveform

The program of Figure 41.3(b) uses 40 sampling points to determine the frequency spectrum of the time-domain waveform of Figure 41.3(a) and print it to the screen as a graph.

In essence, the transform compares (by multiplying) a sine and cos waveform pair to the time-domain waveform. If for a given frequency the correlation is high, a great deal of constructive interference results over the 40 sampling points, and the amplitude of that frequency component is large. If the correlation is low, a great deal of destructive interference results and the amplitude is low. If the process is repeated over the complete range of frequencies from 0 to π rad/s and the results are plotted on a graph, we generate the frequency-domain spectrum of the time-domain waveform.

PROCEDURE

Integration

1. Modify the program of Figure 41.1(e) so that the number of Δr increments (presently 100) can be input from the keyboard.

C PROGRAM

2. Is the answer more accurate as the number of increments increases (Δr gets smaller)? What does the limit (as Δr approaches zero) appear to be for a radius of 10? Is this limit the correct answer?

3. Using integration techniques, calculate the volume of a sphere for any input radius and any number of Δr increments. (Surface area of a sphere $= 4\pi r^2$.)

C PROGRAM

Differentiation

4. Modify the program of Figure 41.2(e) so that the time increment "divisor" (presently 100) can be input from the keyboard.

C PROGRAM

5. For a given time, does the velocity become more accurate as Δt gets smaller? As Δt approaches zero, what does the limit appear to be for a time of 2.5 s? Is this limit the correct answer?

6. If current varies as $4t^3$, write a program that reports the voltage across an inductor for any input time and inductance value.

C PROGRAM

Advanced Activities

7. Based on the program of Figure 41.3(b), plot a graph of the frequency-domain spectrum of the amplitude-modulated sine wave given below:

$$f(t) = \{1 + \cos[2\pi f(m)t]\} \sin[2\pi f(c)t]$$

where $f(m)$ is the modulation frequency and $f(c)$ is the carrier frequency. [Suggest $f(m) = 4$ Hz and $f(c) = 10$ Hz.]

Name: ______________________

Date: ______________________

QUESTIONS AND PROBLEMS

Class: ______________________

1. Demonstrate how to find the area of a circle using the "area under the curve" method of integration. (*Hint:* Find the area under a semicircle by dividing it into a number of small vertical strips, then double the answer.)

2. What is the difference between *multiplication* and *integration*? Why is multiplication a subset of integration?

3. What is the difference between *division* and *differentiation*? Why is division a subset of differentiation?

4. When we take the *limit* as Δt approaches zero of the change in distance divided by the change in time, is the resulting velocity still an approximation?

Advanced Section

5. Why did Isaac Newton require calculus to determine the energy needed to travel to the moon? (*Note:* When force is a constant, energy = force × distance.)

6. Comparing the program of Figure 41.3(b) with the transform equation given in the discussion, why did we not divide *fcomp* by 40 (the number of sampling points)?

ACTIVITY 42

WHEEL OF FORTUNE

OBJECTIVES

- To write a program that plays the popular television show "Wheel of Fortune."
- To introduce the projects of Activity 43.

PARTS AND EQUIPMENT

- IBM PC.
- Assembler, C compiler, debugger, and utilities.

DISCUSSION

The game "Wheel of Fortune" is played as follows: The moderator enters a phrase that the player is not allowed to see. The player guesses a letter. If the letter appears in the phrase, it is shown at the correct locations. The player guesses the phrase. If incorrect, another letter is guessed. Play continues until the unknown phrase is entered correctly.

When we add multiple players and scorekeeping for added realism, we are at the project level of Activity 43.

PROCEDURE

1. Review the suggested structure chart (Figure 42.1) for program "Wheel of Fortune." (Note that all intermodular communication is by way of global variables.) Each function is briefly described below:
   - MAIN: Displays a menu. Calls functions MOD or PLAYER, depending on selection.
   - SELECT: Displays the menu.
   - MOD (for "moderator"): Clears the screen and inputs the phrase to be guessed by the player.
   - PLAYER: Clears the screen and shows a series of dashes corresponding to the letter locations in the phrase. It asks for a letter and replaces the dashes at the proper places. After each letter it asks the player to guess the phrase. Play continues until the guess is correct.

FIGURE 42.1

Structure chart for task "Wheel of Fortune."

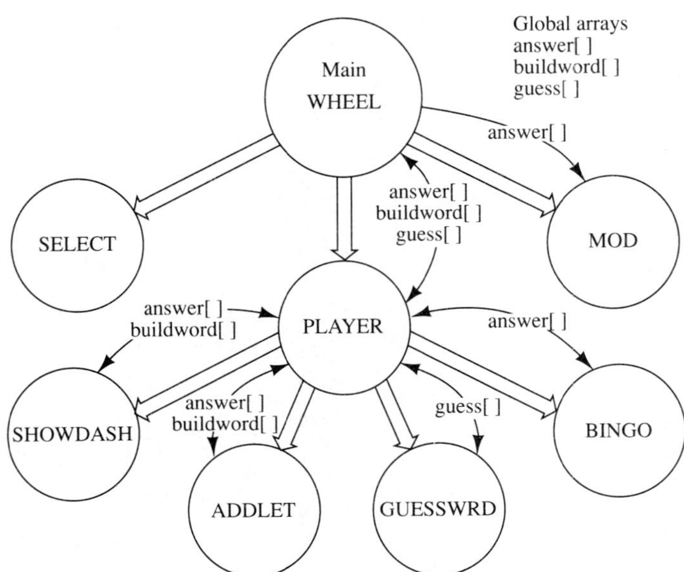

FIGURE 42.2

Pseudocode for function PLAYER.

```
VOID PLAYER(VOID)

CLEAR( )
SHOWDASH( )
WHILE(1)
    ADDLET( )
    GUESSWRD( )
    IF (ANSWER IS RIGHT)
      BREAK
    BEEP( )
    PRINT(NOPE That's not it).
END
CLEAR( )
BINGO( )
MSEC(5000)
```

- SHOWDASH: Displays dashes on the screen at locations corresponding to the phrase.
- ADDLET: Asks for a letter and places the letter at all the proper places, beeping each time.
- GUESSWRD: Asks for and receives the trial phrase from the player.
- BINGO: Says "You Got It!" and displays the correct phrase.

2. Write pseudocode as needed for any of the functions. For example, Figure 42.2 shows pseudocode for function PLAYER.
3. Write the main program and functions. Add the functions to your library.
4. Play the game and make modifications as needed.

Advanced Activities

5. See project 23 of Activity 43 for suggestions on how to improve the software developed in this activity.

Name: ______________________

Date: ______________________

Class: ______________________

QUESTIONS AND PROBLEMS

1. How does the term ''tool building'' apply to most of the functions of Figure 42.1?

2. How many times may a global array be *defined* (as opposed to *declared*)?

Advanced Section

3. How do you know when a function is too large and should be modularized (broken down into additional functions)?

ACTIVITY 43

PROJECTS

OBJECTIVE

- To apply the knowledge and skills gained to projects of greater depth and scope.

PARTS AND EQUIPMENT

- IBM PC with bus-extender (as required).
- Assembler, C compiler, debugger, and utilities.
- Other circuits and components as required.

DISCUSSION

In learning the game of chess, in mastering a new gymnastics routine, or in programming a computer, *practice* is the key to success. To learn quickly and to acquire new skills, it is also important to accept continually problems of greater difficulty and challenge.

The projects listed in this activity are designed to put your knowledge and skills to the test. Very few hints, suggestions, and details have been provided because the true test of learning is individual accomplishment.

For all projects, you should make maximum use of the design techniques of Activity 29.

PROCEDURE

1. *Digital circuit tester:* Using the I/O ports, design a program that exercises a JK flip-flop and displays the results on the monitor.
2. *Traffic light controller:* Design a four-way traffic light system using green, red, and yellow LEDs. Be sure to control the intersection the way it is controlled at a real corner.
3. *Combination lock:* Write a program that displays OPEN when the correct four numbers are entered in sequence via the keypad. Otherwise, it displays CLOSED. If more than four incorrect attempts are made, the system shuts down.
4. *Capacitance meter:* Design a computerized capacitance meter. (*Hint:* Use an op amp integrator and measure the charge time.)
5. *EPROM programmer:* Design a system to program EPROMs.
6. *Math tutor:* Design a system that displays a set of five math problems. The student has three tries for each and gets five points for being correct on the first try, three on the second, and one on the third. The cumulative score is displayed.
7. *Automatic teller machine:* Write program ATM (automatic teller machine). First, you enter your secret number. If correct, you are instructed to select an option (''V'' for view account, ''D'' for deposit, or ''W'' for withdraw). After the ''D'' and ''W'' options, you enter the desired amount. ''Q'' quits the program.
8. *Stop watch:* Design a stop watch that counts from 00.0 to 99.9 s. Each activation of an interrupt (or front panel key) alternately clears, starts, and stops the display.
9. *Bubble sort:* Write a program that takes in 25 consecutive inputs from the keypad and then bubble sorts them in descending order. After the numbers are sorted, they are displayed in order.
10. *Pokerhand:* Write a program that analyzes the seven cards of a poker hand (2 through 10, J, Q, K, and A). The program determines the best hand.
11. *Fingerprint:* Five arrays of ten bytes each represent the fingerprint profile of five people stored in the FBI ''file.'' A suspect fingerprint (of ten bytes) is entered via the keypad and the best match is displayed as a percentage.
12. *Low-pass filter:* Using an A/D input and D/A output, design a single-pole, low-pass filter using digital processing.
13. *Lissajous:* Using two 4-bit DACs and the ability to produce sine waves, generate lissajous figures on the CRT screen.
14. *Digital voltmeter:* Design a digital voltmeter using a commercially available A/D chip.

15. *RADAR:* Using a stepper motor and phototransistor, design a light detection system in which a "beep" sounds when the scanner detects a light. The position of the light appears as a bar graph on the scope. (Use the 8251A to send information to the scope.)
16. *Data acquisition:* Using the CD4016 analog switch, design a data acquisition system using a temperature sensor (thermistor) and a light sensor (photocell). Data will be input from the sensors by time multiplexing and will be displayed simultaneously.
17. *Music from 8253:* Using the 8253 timer, write a program that plays a song of at least 10 notes. Include a method of varying the duration of each note, and control the basic tempo via input data.
18. *dc motor control:* Using tachometer feedback (light source/photocell modulated by motor), control the speed of a dc motor under varying load conditions.
19. *Digital thermometer:* Using the temperature characteristics of a transistor, design a computerized digital thermometer.
20. *Moon-landing simulator:* A lunar-landing vehicle (LLV) is controlled by a stepper motor, and a potentiometer controls the thrust. Design the software to simulate the LLV under the pull of gravity.
21. *Music display:* A musical staff is written to the screen. As a song plays, the notes appear in the staff at the proper vertical scale and horizontal position. The notes will assume the shape of the conventional quarter, half, and whole notes.
22. *Advanced music:* Modify project *Music display* so notes can be entered and changed from the keyboard.
23. *Modified Wheel of Fortune:* Add multiple players and score-keeping to the design of Activity 42. To simulate a spinning wheel, use the techniques of Activity 34.

APPENDIX A

MAJOR DOS COMMANDS

We assume all commands are listed after the drive A prompt (A>). Each command is initiated with an "enter" (carriage return).

COMMAND	EXAMPLES	
Directory	DIR	Lists files on default drive A.
	DIR B:/W	Lists files on drive B in horizontal format.
	DIR *.ASM	Lists all files on default drive A with "ASM" extension. ("*" is a wild card.)
Copy	COPY B:TEST.ASM PROG.ASM	Copies file TEST.ASM on drive B to default drive A and renames it PROG.ASM.
	COPY *.ASM B:	Copies all files on default drive A with ASM extension to drive B. File names remain unchanged.
	COPY B:\P\PROG.ASM	Copies file PROG.ASM in *subdirectory* P on drive B to default drive A.
Print	COPY TEST.ASM PRN	Prints file TEST.ASM on default drive A.
Diskcopy	DISKCOPY A: B:	Copies disk A to disk B (format if necessary).
Rename	RENAME PROG.ASM TEST.ASM	Renames file PROG.ASM to TEST.ASM. Both files are on default drive A.
Format	FORMAT /S	Formats disk in default drive A and makes it a system disk (copies DOS to A).
Display	TYPE PROG.LST	Displays file PROG.LST on default drive A to screen. (Ctrl/S will control scrolling on screen.)
Run	TEST	Executes file TEST.EXE on default drive A.

APPENDIX B

THE PC-WRITE EDITOR

- *Entering PC-Write*
  - To edit old file: ED ⟨file name⟩ ESC
  - To create new file: ED ⟨file name⟩ F9
- *Positioning the cursor*
  - Move cursor: arrows
  - Cursor to bottom: + Shift
  - Cursor to top: − Shift
- *Editing*
  - Erase letters and words: Del
  - Erase lines: Ctrl Enter
  - Create new line: Cursor at left, Enter
- *Block activities*
  - F3 to mark blocks (beginning and end)
  - F6 to move marked block to cursor position
  - F5 to unmark
- *Saving files*
  - F1/F2 to save and exit
  - F1/F3 to save but not exit
  - F9 to unsave
- *Help*
  - F1 to enter help screens for information on all commands

NOTE: Most Wordstar commands are accepted by PC-Write.

APPENDIX C

CODEVIEW SUMMARY

Function Keys

F2 Toggle register display.
F3 Switch among source, list, and mixed format.
F4 Toggle between output and codeview screen.
F5 Execute or execute to F9 breakpoint (Ctrl/C return).
F6 Toggle cursor between window and dialog box.
F7 Execute and break at cursor.
F8 Single-step.
F9 Set and clear breakpoint.
F10 Step over calls.

Window Menus

Alt W To set watch value.
Alt F To exit to DOS.
Alt R To reset to beginning of program.

Dialog Box (bottom of screen)

R Display or set register.
DB DW Display bytes or words of memory.
EB EW Enter bytes or words in memory.
A Assemble instructions into program.

APPENDIX D

BUS-EXTENDER HARDWARE

The following companies offer bus-extender hardware that is suitable for use with the activities in this book.

*1. Global Specialties, P.O. Box 1405, New Haven, CT 06505; phone (800)345-6251.

The PC-88/4 offers a protoboard array that is connected to the PC bus via a ribbon cable and buffered plug-in card. It offers a large prototyping area and convenient access to all bus signals.

* The PB-88/4 by Global Specialties was the system used by the author.

2. Royer Associates, 206 Santa Margarita Avenue, Menlo Park, CA 94025.

The IT-10 "Interfacing Tutor" is a ready-to-go single-board device that offers a number of interfacing ICs on a board. They are connected to the IBM PC via a ribbon cable and buffer card that fits in a short slot. Also included are a number of advanced interfacing experiments that go beyond those given in this manual.

3. ABC Inc., 57 Dover Street, Lowell, MA 01851; phone (617)452-6120.

The CID-700 is similar to the PC-88. It contains a built-in power supply.

4. Advantech Company, 6969 Dal Bon Court, San Jose, CA 95119; phone (408)224-6456.

The PC-LabCard series offers a number of inexpensive plug-in boards. All bus lines are buffered and can be extended to the outside. Promised for the future is a plug-in buffered board with ribbon cable included.

APPENDIX E

THE INSTRUCTION SET

MCS-86™ Assembly Language Reference Guide

8086 REGISTER MODEL

AX	AH	AL	ACCUMULATOR	GENERAL REGISTER FILE
BX	BH	BL	BASE	
CX	CH	CL	COUNT	
DX	DH	DL	DATA	
	SP		STACK POINTER	
	BP		BASE POINTER	
	SI		SOURCE INDEX	
	DI		DESTINATION INDEX	
	IP		INSTRUCTION POINTER	
	FLAGS$_H$	FLAGS$_L$	STATUS FLAGS	
	CS		CODE SEGMENT	SEGMENT REGISTER FILE
	DS		DATA SEGMENT	
	SS		STACK SEGMENT	
	ES		EXTRA SEGMENT	

Instructions which reference the flag register file as a 16-bit object use the symbol FLAGS to represent the file:

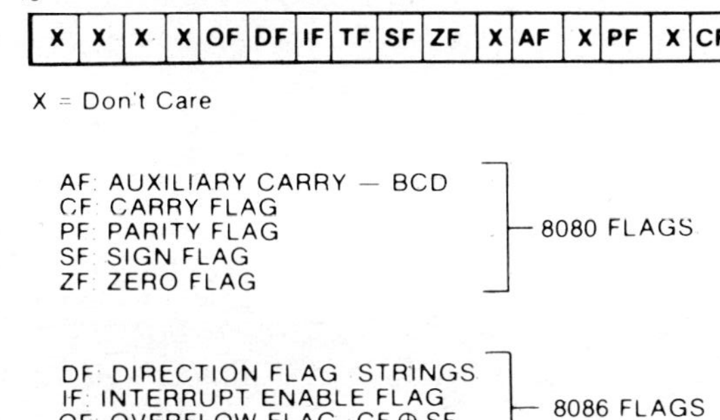

X = Don't Care

AF: AUXILIARY CARRY — BCD
CF: CARRY FLAG
PF: PARITY FLAG
SF: SIGN FLAG
ZF: ZERO FLAG
— 8080 FLAGS

DF: DIRECTION FLAG (STRINGS)
IF: INTERRUPT ENABLE FLAG
OF: OVERFLOW FLAG (CF ⊕ SF)
TF: TRAP — SINGLE STEP FLAG
— 8086 FLAGS

(Courtesy Intel Corporation. ©1978.)

OPERAND SUMMARY

"reg" field Bit Assignments:

16-Bit (w = 1)	8-Bit (w = 0)	Segment
000 AX	000 AL	00 ES
001 CX	001 CL	01 CS
010 DX	010 DL	10 SS
011 BX	011 BL	11 DS
100 SP	100 AH	
101 BP	101 CH	
110 SI	110 DH	
111 DI	111 BH	

SECOND INSTRUCTION BYTE SUMMARY

mod	xxx	r/m

mod	Displacement
00	DISP = 0*, disp-low and disp-high are absent
01	DISP = disp-low sign-extended to 16-bits, disp-high is absent
10	DISP = disp-high: disp-low
11	r/m is treated as a "reg" field

r/m	Operand Address
000	(BX) + (SI) + DISP
001	(BX) + (DI) + DISP
010	(BP) + (SI) + DISP
011	(BP) + (DI) + DISP
100	(SI) + DISP
101	(DI) + DISP
110	(BP) + DISP*
111	(BX) + DISP

DISP follows 2nd byte of instruction (before data if required).

*except if mod = 00 and r/m = 110 then EA = disp-high: disp-low

Operand Address (EA) Timing (clocks):

Add 4 clocks for word operands at ODD ADDRESSES.
Immed Offset = 6
Base (BX, BP, SI, DI) = 5
Base + DISP = 9
Base + Index (BP + DI, BX + SI) = 7
Base + Index (BP + SI, BX + DI) = 8
Base + Index (BP + DI, BX + SI) + DISP = 11
Base + Index (BP + SI, BX + DI) + DISP = 12

MEMORY SEGMENTATION MODEL

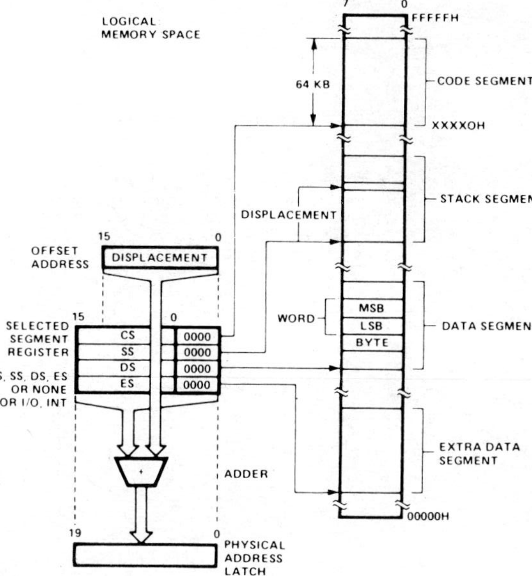

SEGMENT OVERRIDE PREFIX

0 0 1 reg 1 1 0

Timing: 2 clocks

USE OF SEGMENT OVERRIDE

Operand Register	Default	With Override Prefix
IP (code address)	CS	Never
SP (stack address)	SS	Never
BP (stack address or stack marker)	SS	BP + DS or ES, or CS
SI or DI (not incl. strings)	DS	ES, SS, or CS
SI (implicit source addr for strings)	DS	ES, SS, or CS
DI (implicit dest addr for strings)	ES	Never

DATA TRANSFER

MOV = Move
Register/memory to/from register

1 0 0 0 1 0 d w	mod reg r/m

Timing (clocks): register to register 2; memory to register 8+EA; register to memory 9+EA

Immediate to register/memory

1 1 0 0 0 1 1 w	mod 0 0 0 r/m	data	data if w=1

Timing: 10+EA clocks

Immediate to register

1 0 1 1 w reg	data	data if w=1

Timing: 4 clocks

Memory to accumulator

1 0 1 0 0 0 0 w	addr-low	addr-high

Timing: 10 clocks

Accumulator to memory

1 0 1 0 0 0 1 w	addr-low	addr-high

Timing: 10 clocks

Register/memory to segment register

1 0 0 0 1 1 1 0	mod 0 reg r/m

Timing (clocks): register to register 2; memory to register 8+EA

Segment register to register/memory

1 0 0 0 1 1 0 0	mod 0 reg r/m

Timing (clocks): register to register 2; register to memory 9+EA

PUSH = Push
Register/memory

1 1 1 1 1 1 1 1	mod 1 1 0 r/m

Timing (clocks): register 10; memory 16+EA

Register

0 1 0 1 0 reg

Timing: 10 clocks

Segment register

0 0 0 reg 1 1 0

Timing: 10 clocks

POP = Pop
Register/memory

1 0 0 0 1 1 1 1	mod 0 0 0 r/m

Timing (clocks): register 8; memory 17+EA

Register

0 1 0 1 1 reg

Timing: 8 clocks

Segment register

0 0 0 reg 1 1 1

Timing: 8 clocks

XCHG = Exchange
Register/memory with register

1 0 0 0 0 1 1 w	mod reg r/m

Timing (clocks): register with register 4; memory with register 17+EA

Register with accumulator

1 0 0 1 0 reg

Timing: 3 clocks

IN = Input to AL/AX from
Fixed port

1 1 1 0 0 1 0 w	port

Timing: 10 clocks

Variable port (DX)

1 1 1 0 1 1 0 w

Timing: 8 clocks

OUT = Output from AL/AX to
Fixed port

1 1 1 0 0 1 1 w	port

Timing: 10 clocks

Variable port (DX)

1 1 1 0 1 1 1 w

Timing: 8 clocks

XLAT = Translate byte to AL

1 1 0 1 0 1 1 1

Timing: 11 clocks

LEA = Load EA to register

1 0 0 0 1 1 0 1	mod reg r/m

Timing: 2+EA clocks

LDS = Load pointer to DS

1 1 0 0 0 1 0 1	mod reg r/m

Timing: 16+EA clocks

LES = Load pointer to ES

1 1 0 0 0 1 0 0	mod reg r/m

Timing: 16+EA clocks

LAHF = Load AH with flags

1 0 0 1 1 1 1 1

Timing: 4 clocks

SAHF = Store AH into flags

1 0 0 1 1 1 1 0

Timing: 4 clocks

PUSHF = Push flags

1 0 0 1 1 1 0 0

Timing: 10 clocks

POPF = Pop flags

1 0 0 1 1 1 0 1

Timing: 8 clocks

ARITHMETIC

ADD = Add
Reg./memory with register to either

0 0 0 0 0 0 d w	mod reg r/m

Timing (clocks): register to register 3; memory to register 9+EA; register to memory 16+EA

Immediate to register/memory

1 0 0 0 0 0 s w	mod 0 0 0 r/m	data	data if s:w=01

Timing (clocks): immediate to register 4; immediate to memory 17+EA

(Continued on following page)

Immediate to accumulator

0 0 0 0 0 1 0 w	data	data if w=1

Timing: 4 clocks

ADC = Add with carry
Reg./memory with register to either

0 0 0 1 0 0 d w	mod reg r/m

Timing (clocks): register to register 3
memory to register 9+EA
register to memory 16+EA

Immediate to register/memory

1 0 0 0 0 0 s w	mod 0 1 0 r/m	data	data if s:w=01

Timing (clocks): immediate to register 4
immediate to memory 17+EA

Immediate to accumulator

0 0 0 1 0 1 0 w	data	data if w=1

Timing: 4 clocks

INC = Increment
Register/memory

1 1 1 1 1 1 1 w	mod 0 0 0 r/m

Timing (clocks): register 2
memory 15+EA

Register

0 1 0 0 0 reg

Timing: 2 clocks

AAA = ASCII adjust for add

0 0 1 1 0 1 1 1

Timing: 4 clocks

DAA = Decimal adjust for add

0 0 1 0 0 1 1 1

Timing: 4 clocks

SUB = Subtract
Reg./memory and register to either

0 0 1 0 1 0 d w	mod reg r/m

Timing (clocks): register from register 3
memory from register 9+EA
register from memory 16+EA

Mnemonics © Intel, 1978.

Immediate

1 0 0 0 0 0 s w	mod 1 0 1 r/m	data	data if s:w=01

Timing (clocks): immediate from register 4
immediate from memory 17+EA

Immediate from accumulator

0 0 1 0 1 1 0 w	data	data if w=1

Timing: 4 clocks

SBB = Subtract with borrow
Reg./memory and register to either

0 0 0 1 1 0 d w	mod reg r/m

Timing (clocks): register from register 3
memory from register 9+EA
register from memory 16+EA

Immediate from register/memory

1 0 0 0 0 0 s w	mod 0 1 1 r/m	data	data if s:w=01

Timing (clocks): immediate from register 4
immediate from memory 17+EA

Immediate from accumulator

0 0 0 1 1 1 0 w	data	data if w=1

Timing: 4 clocks

DEC = Decrement
Register/memory

1 1 1 1 1 1 1 w	mod 0 0 1 r/m

Timing (clocks): register 2
memory 15+EA

Register

0 1 0 0 1 reg

Timing: 2 clocks

NEG = Change sign

1 1 1 1 0 1 1 w	mod 0 1 1 r/m

Timing (clocks): register 3
memory 16+EA

CMP = Compare
Register/memory and register

0 0 1 1 1 0 d w	mod reg r/m

Timing (clocks): register with register 3
memory with register 9+EA
register with memory 9+EA

Mnemonics © Intel, 1978.

Immediate with register/memory

1 0 0 0 0 0 s w	mod 1 1 1 r/m	data	data if s:w=01

Timing (clocks): immediate with register 4
immediate with memory 17+EA

Immediate with accumulator

0 0 1 1 1 1 0 w	data	data if w=1

Timing: 4 clocks

AAS = ASCII adjust for subtract

0 0 1 1 1 1 1 1

Timing: 4 clocks

DAS = Decimal adjust for subtract

0 0 1 0 1 1 1 1

Timing: 4 clocks

MUL = Multiply (unsigned)

1 1 1 1 0 1 1 w	mod 1 0 0 r/m

Timing (clocks): 8-bit 71+EA
16-bit 124+EA

IMUL = Integer multiply (signed)

1 1 1 1 0 1 1 w	mod 1 0 1 r/m

Timing (clocks): 8-bit 90+EA
16-bit 144+EA

AAM = ASCII adjust for multiply

1 1 0 1 0 1 0 0	0 0 0 0 1 0 1 0

Timing: 83 clocks

DIV = Divide (unsigned)

1 1 1 1 0 1 1 w	mod 1 1 0 r/m

Timing (clocks): 8-bit 90+EA
16-bit 155+EA

IDIV = Integer divide (signed)

1 1 1 1 0 1 1 w	mod 1 1 1 r/m

Timing (clocks): 8-bit 112+EA
16-bit 177+EA

AAD = ASCII adjust for divide

1 1 0 1 0 1 0 1	0 0 0 0 1 0 1 0

Timing: 60 clocks

Mnemonics © Intel, 1978.

CBW = Convert byte to word

1 0 0 1 1 0 0 0

Timing: 2 clocks

CWD = Convert word to double word

1 0 0 1 1 0 0 1

Timing: 5 clocks

LOGIC

NOT = Invert

1 1 1 1 0 1 1 w	mod 0 1 0 r/m

Timing (clocks):	register	3
	memory	16+EA

SHL/SAL = Shift logical/arithmetic left

1 1 0 1 0 0 v w	mod 1 0 0 r/m

Timing (clocks):	single-bit register	2
	single-bit memory	15+EA
	variable-bit register	8+4/bit
	variable-bit memory	20+EA+4/bit

SHR = Shift logical right

1 1 0 1 0 0 v w	mod 1 0 1 r/m

Timing (clocks):	single-bit register	2
	single-bit memory	15+EA
	variable-bit register	8+4/bit
	variable-bit memory	20+EA+4/bit

SAR = Shift arithmetic right

1 1 0 1 0 0 v w	mod 1 1 1 r/m

Timing (clocks):	single-bit register	2
	single-bit memory	15+EA
	variable-bit register	8+4/bit
	variable-bit memory	20+EA+4/bit

ROL = Rotate left

1 1 0 1 0 0 v w	mod 0 0 0 r/m

Timing (clocks):	single-bit register	2
	single-bit memory	15+EA
	variable-bit register	8+4/bit
	variable-bit memory	20+EA+4/bit

ROR = Rotate right

1 1 0 1 0 0 v w	mod 0 0 1 r/m

Timing (clocks):	single-bit register	2
	single-bit memory	15+EA
	variable-bit register	8+4/bit
	variable-bit memory	20+EA+4/bit

RCL = Rotate through carry left

1 1 0 1 0 0 v w	mod 0 1 0 r/m

Timing (clocks):	single-bit register	2
	single-bit memory	15+EA
	variable-bit register	8+4/bit
	variable-bit memory	20+EA+4/bit

RCR = Rotate through carry right

1 1 0 1 0 0 v w	mod 0 1 1 r/m

Timing (clocks):	single-bit register	2
	single-bit memory	15+EA
	variable-bit register	8+4/bit
	variable-bit memory	20+EA+4/bit

AND = And
Reg./memory and register to either

0 0 1 0 0 0 d w	mod reg r/m

Timing (clocks):	register to register	3
	memory to register	9+EA
	register to memory	16+EA

Immediate to register/memory

1 0 0 0 0 0 0 w	mod 1 0 0 r/m	data	data if w=1

Timing (clocks):	immediate to register	4
	immediate to memory	17+EA

Immediate to accumulator

0 0 1 0 0 1 0 w	data	data if w=1

Timing: 4 clocks

TEST = And function to flags, no result
Register/memory and register

1 0 0 0 0 1 0 w	mod reg r/m

Timing (clocks):	register to register	3
	register with memory	9+EA

Mnemonics © Intel, 1978.

Immediate data and register/memory

1 1 1 1 0 1 1 w	mod 0 0 0 r/m	data	data if s:w=1

Timing (clocks):	immediate with register	4
	immediate with memory	10+EA

Immediate data and accumulator

1 0 1 0 1 0 0 w	data	data if w=1

Timing: 4 clocks

OR = Or
Reg./memory and register to either

0 0 0 0 1 0 d w	mod reg r/m

Timing (clocks):	register to register	3
	memory to register	9+EA
	register to memory	16+EA

Immediate to register/memory

1 0 0 0 0 0 0 w	mod 0 0 1 r/m	data	data if w=1

Timing (clocks):	immediate to register	4
	immediate to memory	17+EA

Immediate to accumulator

0 0 0 0 1 1 0 w	data	data if w=1

Timing: 4 clocks

XOR = Exclusive or
Reg./memory and register to either

0 0 1 1 0 0 d w	mod reg r/m

Timing (clocks):	register to register	3
	memory to register	9+EA
	register to memory	16+EA

Immediate to register/memory

1 0 0 0 0 0 0 w	mod 1 1 0 r/m	data	data if w=1

Timing (clocks):	immediate to register	4
	immediate to memory	17+EA

Immediate to accumulator

0 0 1 1 0 1 0 w	data	data if w=1

Timing: 4 clocks

STRING MANIPULATION

REP = Repeat

1 1 1 1 0 0 1 z

Timing: 6 clocks/loop

Mnemonics © Intel, 1978.

MOVS = Move String

1 0 1 0 0 1 0 w

Timing: 17 clocks

CMPS = Compare String

1 0 1 0 0 1 1 w

Timing: 22 clocks

SCAS = Scan String

1 0 1 0 1 1 1 w

Timing: 15 clocks

LODS = Load String

1 0 1 0 1 1 0 w

Timing: 12 clocks

STOS = Store String

1 0 1 0 1 0 1 w

Timing: 10 clocks

CONTROL TRANSFER

NOTE: Queue reinitialization is not included in the timing information for transfer operations. To account for instruction loading, add 8 clocks to timing numbers.

CALL = Call

Direct within segment

1 1 1 0 1 0 0 0	disp-low	disp-high

Timing: 11 clocks

Indirect within segment

1 1 1 1 1 1 1 1	mod 0 1 0 r/m

Timing: 13+EA clocks

Direct intersegment

1 0 0 1 1 0 1 0	offset-low	offset-high
	seg-low	seg-high

Timing: 20 clocks

Indirect intersegment

1 1 1 1 1 1 1 1	mod 0 1 1 r/m

Timing: 29+EA clocks

JMP = Unconditional Jump

Direct within segment

1 1 1 0 1 0 0 1	disp-low	disp-high

Timing: 7 clocks

Direct within segment-short

1 1 1 0 1 0 1 1	disp

Timing: 7 clocks

Indirect within segment

1 1 1 1 1 1 1 1	mod 1 0 0 r/m

Timing: 7+EA clocks

Direct intersegment

1 1 1 0 1 0 1 0	offset-low	offset-high
	seg-low	seg-high

Timing: 7 clocks

Indirect intersegment

1 1 1 1 1 1 1 1	mod 1 0 1 r/m

Timing: 16+EA clocks

RET = Return from CALL

Within segment

1 1 0 0 0 0 1 1

Timing: 8 clocks

Within seg. adding immed to SP

1 1 0 0 0 0 1 0	data-low	data-high

Timing: 12 clocks

Intersegment

1 1 0 0 1 0 1 1

Timing: 18 clocks

Intersegment, adding immediate to SP

1 1 0 0 1 0 1 0	data-low	data-high

Timing: 17 clocks

JE/JZ = Jump on equal/zero

0 1 1 1 0 1 0 0	disp

Timing (clocks): Jump is taken 8
Jump is not taken 4

JL/JNGE = Jump on less/not greater or equal

0 1 1 1 1 1 0 0	disp

Timing (clocks): Jump is taken 8
Jump is not taken 4

JLE/JNG = Jump on less or equal/not greater

0 1 1 1 1 1 1 0	disp

Timing (clocks): Jump is taken 8
Jump is not taken 4

JB/JNAE = Jump on below/ not above or equal

0 1 1 1 0 0 1 0	disp

Timing (clocks): Jump is taken 8
Jump is not taken 4

JBE/JNA = Jump on below or equal/not above

0 1 1 1 0 1 1 0	disp

Timing (clocks): Jump is taken 8
Jump is not taken 4

JP/JPE = Jump on parity/parity even

0 1 1 1 1 0 1 0	disp

Timing (clocks): Jump is taken 8
Jump is not taken 4

JO = Jump on overflow

0 1 1 1 0 0 0 0	disp

Timing (clocks): Jump is taken 8
Jump is not taken 4

JS = Jump on sign

0 1 1 1 1 0 0 0	disp

Timing (clocks): Jump is taken 8
Jump is not taken 4

JNE/JNZ = Jump on not equal/not zero

0 1 1 1 0 1 0 1	disp

Timing (clocks): Jump is taken 8
Jump is not taken 4

JNL/JGE = Jump on not less/greater or equal

0 1 1 1 1 1 0 1	disp

Timing (clocks): Jump is taken 8
Jump is not taken 4

(Continued on following page)

JNLE/JG = Jump on not less or equal/greater

0 1 1 1 1 1 1 1	disp

Timing (clocks): Jump is taken 8
Jump is not taken 4

JNB/JAE = Jump on not below/above or equal

0 1 1 1 0 0 1 1	disp

Timing (clocks): Jump is taken 8
Jump is not taken 4

JNBE/JA = Jump on not below or equal/above

0 1 1 1 0 1 1 1	disp

Timing (clocks): Jump is taken 8
Jump is not taken 4

JNP/JPO = Jump on not parity/parity odd

0 1 1 1 1 0 1 1	disp

Timing (clocks): Jump is taken 8
Jump is not taken 4

JNO = Jump on not overflow

0 1 1 1 0 0 0 1	disp

Timing (clocks): Jump is taken 8
Jump is not taken 4

JNS = Jump on not sign

0 1 1 1 1 0 0 1	disp

Timing (clocks): Jump is taken 8
Jump is not taken 4

LOOP = Loop CX times

1 1 1 0 0 0 1 0	disp

Timing (clocks): Jump is taken 9
Jump is not taken 5

LOOPZ/LOOPE = Loop while zero/equal

1 1 1 0 0 0 0 1	disp

Timing (clocks): Jump is taken 11
Jump is not taken 5

LOOPNZ/LOOPNE = Loop while not zero/ not equal

1 1 1 0 0 0 0 0	disp

Timing (clocks): Jump is taken 11
Jump is not taken 5

JCXZ = Jump on CX zero

1 1 1 0 0 0 1 1	disp

Timing (clocks): Jump is taken 9
Jump is not taken 5

8086 CONDITIONAL TRANSFER OPERATIONS

Instruction	Condition	Interpretation
JE or JZ	ZF = 1	"equal" or "zero"
JL or JNGE	(SF xor OF) = 1	"less" or "not greater or equal"
JLE or JNG	((SP xor OF) or ZF) = 1	"less or equal" or "not greater"
JB or JNAE	CF = 1	"below" or "not above or equal"
JBE or JNA	(CF or ZF) = 1	"below or equal" or "not above"
JP or JPE	PF = 1	"parity" or "parity even"
J0	OF = 1	"overflow"
JS	SF = 1	"sign"
JNE or JNZ	ZF = 0	"not equal" or "not zero"
JNL or JGE	(SF xor OF) = 0	"not less" or "greater or equal"
JNLE or JG	((SF xor OF) or ZF) = 0	"not less or equal" or "greater"
JNB or JAE	CF = 0	"not below" or "above or equal"
JNBE or JA	(CF or ZF) = 0	"not below or equal" or "above"
JNP or JPO	PF = 0	"not parity" or "parity odd"
JNO	OF = 0	"not overflow"
JNS	SF = 0	"not sign"

*"Above" and "below" refer to the relation between two unsigned values, while "greater" and "less" refer to the relation between two signed values

INT = Interrupt
Type specified

1 1 0 0 1 1 0 1	type

Timing: 50 clocks

Type 3

1 1 0 0 1 1 0 0

Timing: 51 clocks

INTO = Interrupt on overflow

1 1 0 0 1 1 1 0

Timing: 52 clocks if pass   4 clocks if fail

IRET = Interrupt return

1 1 0 0 1 1 1 1

Timing: 24 clocks

PROCESSOR CONTROL

CLC = Clear carry

1 1 1 1 1 0 0 0

Timing: 2 clocks

CMC = Complement carry

1 1 1 1 0 1 0 1

Timing: 2 clocks

CLD = Clear direction

1 1 1 1 1 1 0 0

Timing: 2 clocks

CLI = Clear interrupt

1 1 1 1 1 0 1 0

Timing: 2 clocks

HLT = Halt

1 1 1 1 0 1 0 0

Timing: 2 clocks

LOCK = Bus lock prefix

1 1 1 1 0 0 0 0

Timing: 2 clocks

STC = Set carry

1 1 1 1 1 0 0 1

Timing: 2 clocks

NOP = No operation

1 0 0 1 0 0 0 0

Timing: 3 clocks

STD = Set direction

1 1 1 1 1 1 0 1

Timing: 2 clocks

STI = Set interrupt

1 1 1 1 1 0 1 1

Timing: 2 clocks

WAIT = Wait

1 0 0 1 1 0 1 1

Timing: 3 clocks

ESC = Escape (to external device)

1 1 0 1 1 x x x	mod x x x r/m

Timing: 7+EA clocks

Footnotes:
if d = 1 then "to"; if d = 0 then "from"
if w = 1 then word instruction; if w = 0 then byte instruction
if s:w = 01 then 16 bits of immediate data form the operand
if s:w = 11 then an immediate data byte is sign extended to form the 16-bit operand
if v = 0 then "count" = 1; if v = 1 then "count" in (CL)
x = don't care
z is used for some string primitives to compare with ZF FLAG

AL = 8-bit accumulator
AX = 16-bit accumulator
CX = Count register
DS = Data segment
DX = Variable port register
ES = Extra segment
Above/below refers to unsigned value
Greater = more positive;
Less = less positive (more negative) signed values
See page 1 for Operand Summary.
See page 2 for Segment Override Summary.

ASSEMBLER DIRECTIVES

Symbol Definition:
- EQU
- LABEL
- PURGE

Memory Reservation and Data Definition:
- DB
- DW
- DD
- RECORD

Location Counter and Segmentation Control:
- SEGMENT/ENDS
- ORG
- GROUP
- ASSUME
- PROC/ENDP
- CODEMACRO/ENDM

Program Linkage:
- NAME
- PUBLIC
- EXTRN
- END

PROCESSOR RESET REGISTER INITIALIZATION

Flags = OOOOH (to disable interrupts and single-stepping)

CS = FFFFH
IP = OOOOH (to begin execution at FFFFOH)

DS = OOOOH
SS = OOOOH
ES = OOOOH

No other registers are acted upon during reset.

MCS-86™ RESERVED LOCATIONS

Reserved Memory Locations

Intel Corporation reserves the use of memory locations FFFFOH through FFFFFH (with the exception of FFFFOH - FFFF5H for JMP instr.) for Intel hardware and software products. If you use these locations for some other purpose, you may preclude compatibility of your system with certain of these products.

Reserved Input/Output Locations

Intel Corporation reserves the use of input/output locations F8H through FFH for Intel hardware and software products. Users who wish to maintain compatibility with present and future Intel products should not use these locations.

Reserved Interrupt Locations

Intel Corporation reserves the use of interrupts 0-31 (locations 00H through 7FH) for Intel hardware and software products. Users who wish to maintain compatibility with present and future Intel products should not use these locations.

Interrupts 0 through 4 (00H-13H) currently have dedicated hardware functions as defined below.

Interrupt	Location	Function
0	00H-03H	Divide by zero
1	04H-07H	Single step
2	08H-0BH	Non-maskable interrupt
3	0CH-0FH	One-byte interrupt instruction
4	10H-13H	Interrupt on overflow

INTERRUPT POINTER TABLE

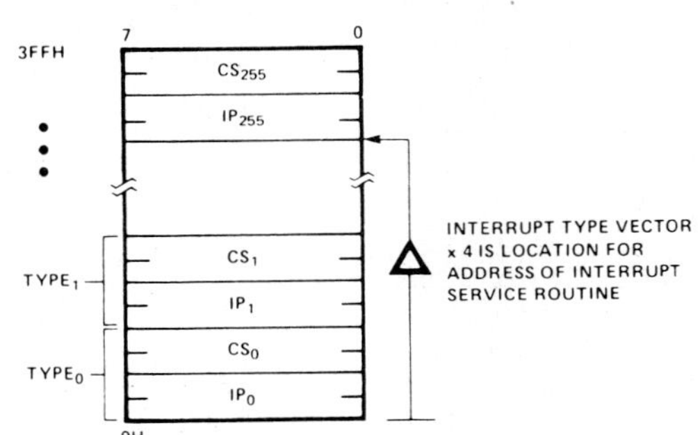

8086 INSTRUCTION SET MATRIX

Hi \ Lo	0	1	2	3	4	5	6	7
0	ADD b,f,r/m	ADD w,f,r/m	ADD b,t,r/m	ADD w,t,r/m	ADD b,ia	ADD w,ia	PUSH ES	POP ES
1	ADC b,f,r/m	ADC w,f,r/m	ADC b,t,r/m	ADC w,t,r/m	ADC b,i	ADC w,i	PUSH SS	POP SS
2	AND b,f,r/m	AND w,f,r/m	AND b,t,r/m	AND w,t,r/m	AND b,i	AND w,i	SEG =ES	DAA
3	XOR b,f,r/m	XOR w,f,r/m	XOR b,t,r/m	XOR w,t,r/m	XOR b,i	XOR w,i	SEG =SS	AAA
4	INC AX	INC CX	INC DX	INC BX	INC SP	INC BP	INC SI	INC DI
5	PUSH AX	PUSH CX	PUSH DX	PUSH BX	PUSH SP	PUSH BP	PUSH SI	PUSH DI
6								
7	JO	JNO	JB/ JNAE	JNB/ JAE	JE/ JZ	JNE/ JNZ	JBE/ JNA	JNBE/ JA
8	Immed b,r/m	Immed w,r/m	Immed b,r/m	Immed is,r/m	TEST b,r/m	TEST w,r/m	XCHG b,r/m	XCHG w,r/m
9	NOP	XCHG CX	XCHG DX	XCHG BX	XCHG SP	XCHG BP	XCHG SI	XCHG DI
A	MOV m → AL	MOV m → AX	MOV AL → m	MOV AX → m	MOVS b	MOVS w	CMPS b	CMPS w
B	MOV i → AL	MOV i → CL	MOV i → DL	MOV i → BL	MOV i → AH	MOV i → CH	MOV i → DH	MOV i → BH
C			RET, (i+SP)	RET	LES	LDS	MOV b,i,r/m	MOV w,i,r/m
D	Shift b	Shift w	Shift b,v	Shift w,v	AAM	AAD		XLAT
E	LOOPNZ/ LOOPNE	LOOPZ/ LOOPE	LOOP	JCXZ	IN b	IN w	OUT b	OUT w
F	LOCK		REP	REP z	HLT	CMC	Grp1 b,r/m	Grp1 w,r/m

Hi \ Lo	8	9	A	B	C	D	E	F
0	OR b,f,r/m	OR w,f,r/m	OR b,t,r/m	OR w,t,r/m	OR b,i	OR w,i	PUSH CS	
1	SBB b,f,r/m	SBB w,f,r/m	SBB b,t,r/m	SBB w,t,r/m	SBB b,i	SBB w,i	PUSH DS	POP DS
2	SUB b,f,r/m	SUB w,f,r/m	SUB b,t,r/m	SUB w,t,r/m	SUB b,i	SUB w,i	SEG CS	DAS
3	CMP b,f,r/m	CMP w,f,r/m	CMP b,t,r/m	CMP w,t,r/m	CMP b,i	CMP w,i	SEG DS	AAS
4	DEC AX	DEC CX	DEC DX	DEC BX	DEC SP	DEC BP	DEC SI	DEC DI
5	POP AX	POP CX	POP DX	POP BX	POP SP	POP BP	POP SI	POP DI
6								
7	JS	JNS	JP/ JPE	JNP/ JPO	JL/ JNGE	JNL/ JGE	JLE/ JNG	JNLE/ JG
8	MOV b,f,r/m	MOV w,f,r/m	MOV b,t,r/m	MOV w,t,r/m	MOV sr,t,r/m	LEA	MOV sr,f,r/m	POP r/m
9	CBW	CWD	CALL l,d	WAIT	PUSHF	POPF	SAHF	LAHF
A	TEST b,i	TEST w,i	STOS b	STOS w	LODS b	LODS w	SCAS b	SCAS w
B	MOV i → AX	MOV i → CX	MOV i → DX	MOV i → BX	MOV i → SP	MOV i → BP	MOV i → SI	MOV i → DI
C			RET, l,(i+SP)	RET l	INT Type 3	INT (Any)	INTO	IRET
D	ESC 0	ESC 1	ESC 2	ESC 3	ESC 4	ESC 5	ESC 6	ESC 7
E	CALL d	JMP d	JMP l,d	JMP si,d	IN v,b	IN v,w	OUT v,b	OUT v,w
F	CLC	STC	CLI	STI	CLD	STD	Grp 2 b,r/m	Grp 2 w,r/m

b = byte operation
d = direct
f = from CPU reg
i = immediate
ia = immed. to accum.
id = indirect
is = immed. byte, sign ext.
l = long ie. intersegment
m = memory
r/m = EA is second byte
si = short intrasegment
sr = segment register
t = to CPU reg
v = variable
w = word operation
z = zero

where

mod ☐ r/m	000	001	010	011	100	101	110	111
Immed	ADD	OR	ADC	SBB	AND	SUB	XOR	CMP
Shift	ROL	ROR	RCL	RCR	SHL/SAL	SHR	—	SAR
Grp 1	TEST	—	NOT	NEG	MUL	IMUL	DIV	IDIV
Grp 2	INC	DEC	CALL id	CALL l,id	JMP id	JMP l,id	PUSH	—

Mnemonics © Intel, 1978.

APPENDIX F

DATA SHEETS

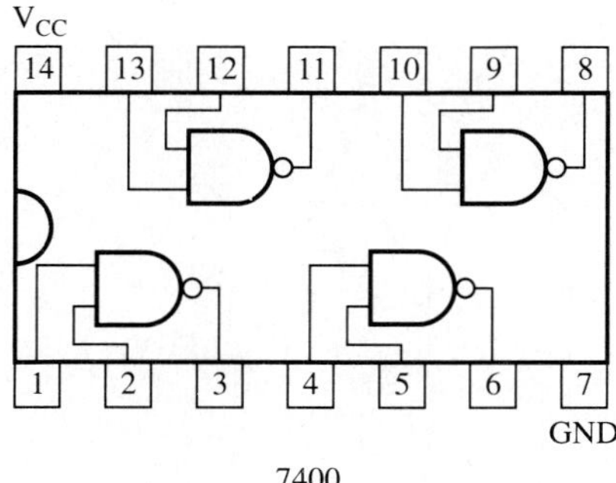

7400

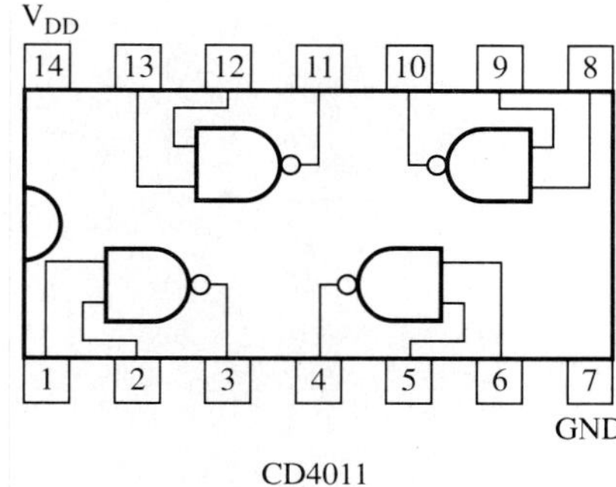

CD4011

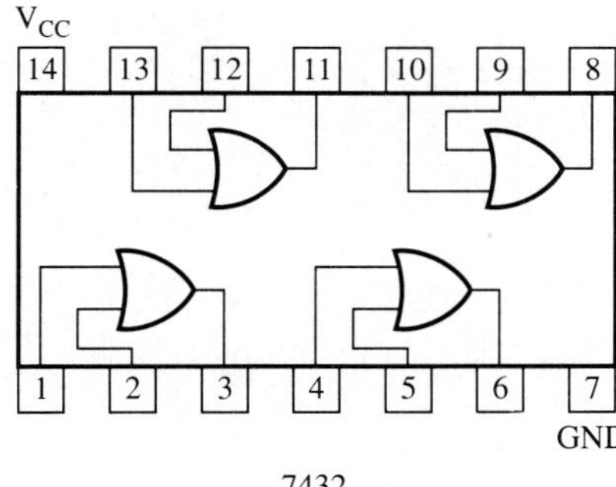

7432

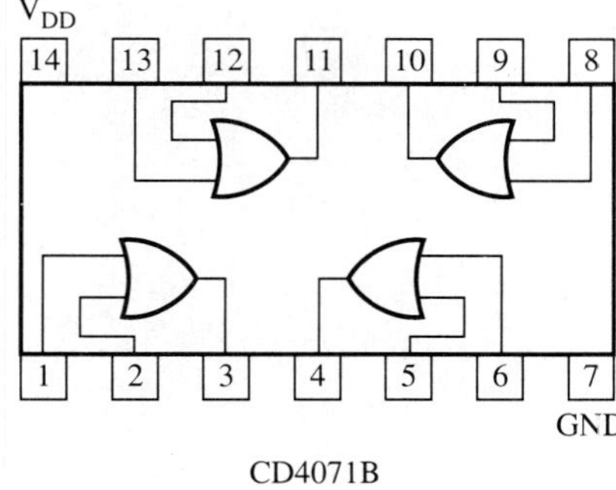

CD4071B

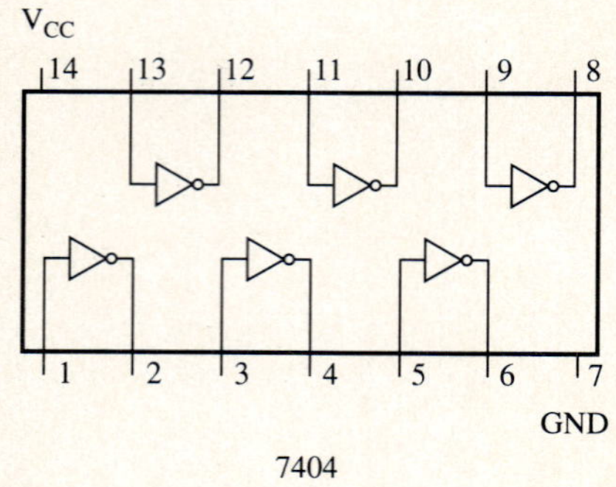

7404

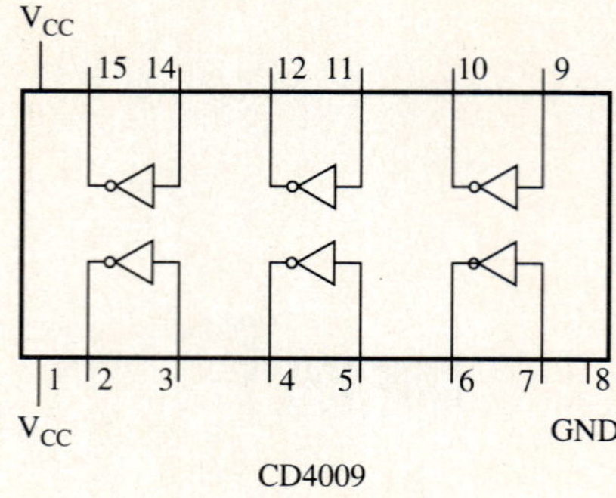

CD4009

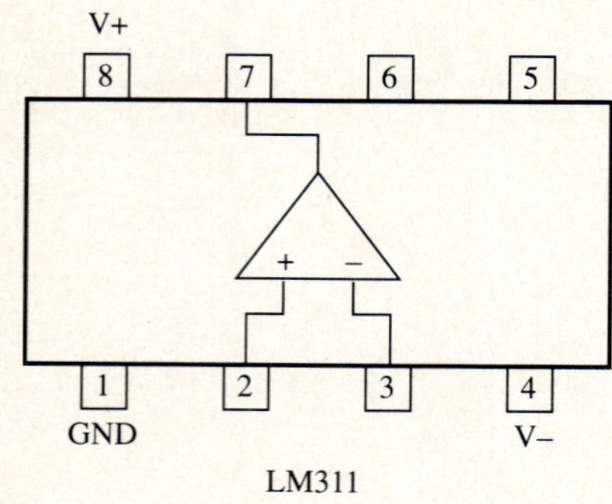

LM311

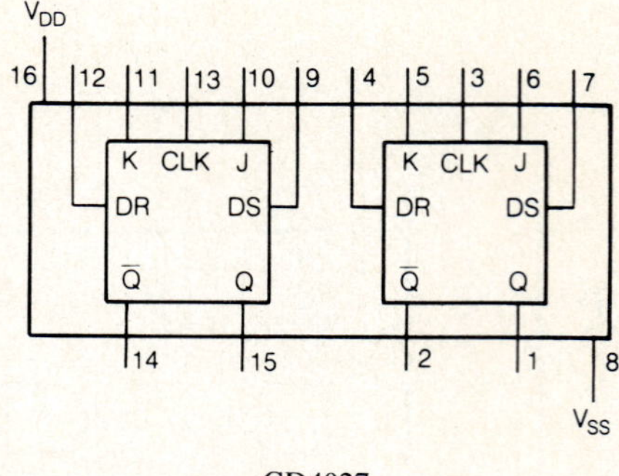

CD4027

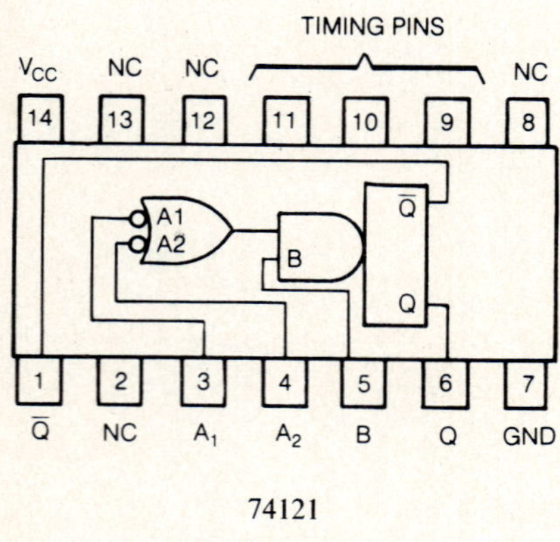

74121

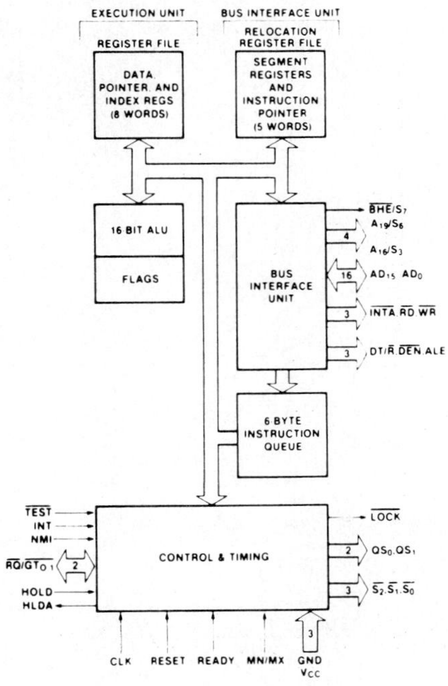

iAPX 86/10 CPU Block Diagram

1	GND	40	Vcc
2	AD14	39	AD15
3	AD13	38	A16/S3
4	AD12	37	A17/S4
5	AD11	36	A18/S5
6	AD10	35	A19/S6
7	AD9	34	BHE/S7
8	AD8	33	MN/MX
9	AD7	32	RD
10	AD6	31	RQ/GT0 (HOLD)
11	AD5	30	RQ/GT1 (HLDA)
12	AD4	29	LOCK (WR)
13	AD3	28	S2 (M/IO)
14	AD2	27	S1 (DT/R)
15	AD1	26	S0 (DEN)
16	AD0	25	QS0 (ALE)
17	NMI	24	QS1 (INTA)
18	INTR	23	TEST
19	CLK	22	READY
20	GND	21	RESET

8086 CPU

40 LEAD

iAPX 86/10 Pin Configuration

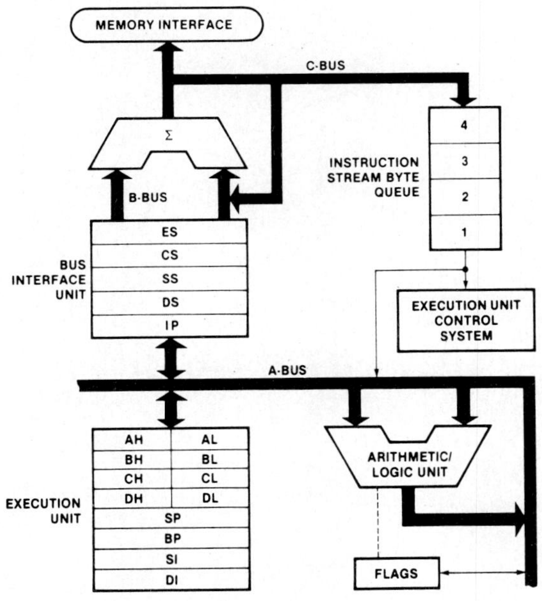

iAPX 88/10 CPU Functional Block Diagram

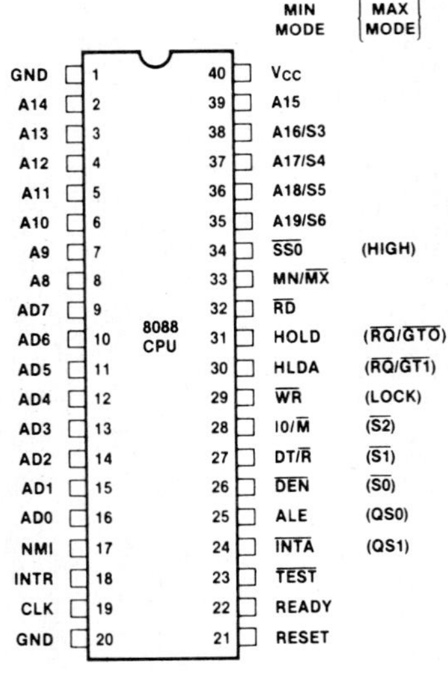

iAPX 88/10 Pin Configuration

(Courtesy Intel Corporation.)

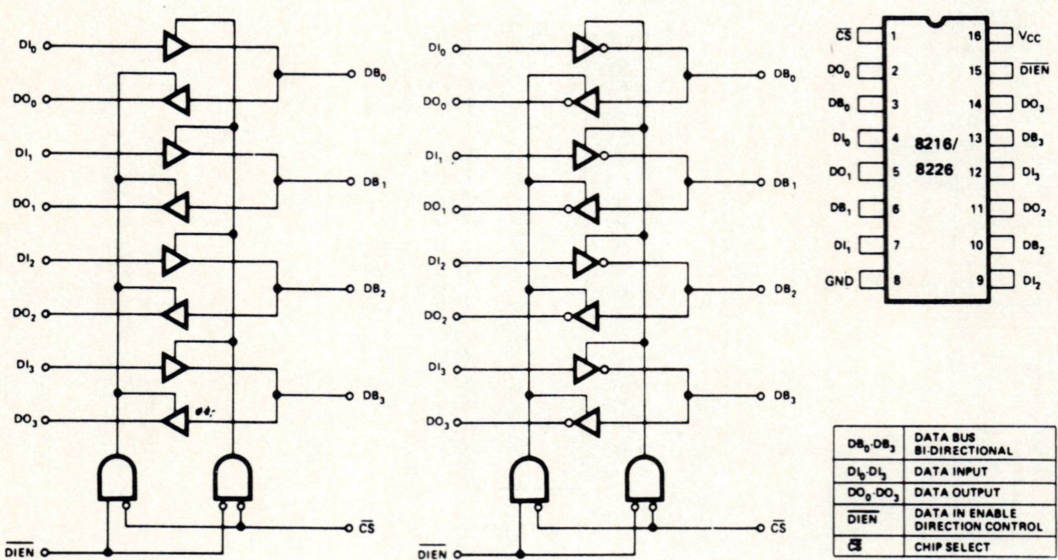

DB_0-DB_3	DATA BUS BI-DIRECTIONAL
DI_0-DI_3	DATA INPUT
DO_0-DO_3	DATA OUTPUT
$\overline{DIEN}$	DATA IN ENABLE DIRECTION CONTROL
$\overline{CS}$	CHIP SELECT

Figure 1. Block Diagrams

Figure 2. Pin Configuration

8216

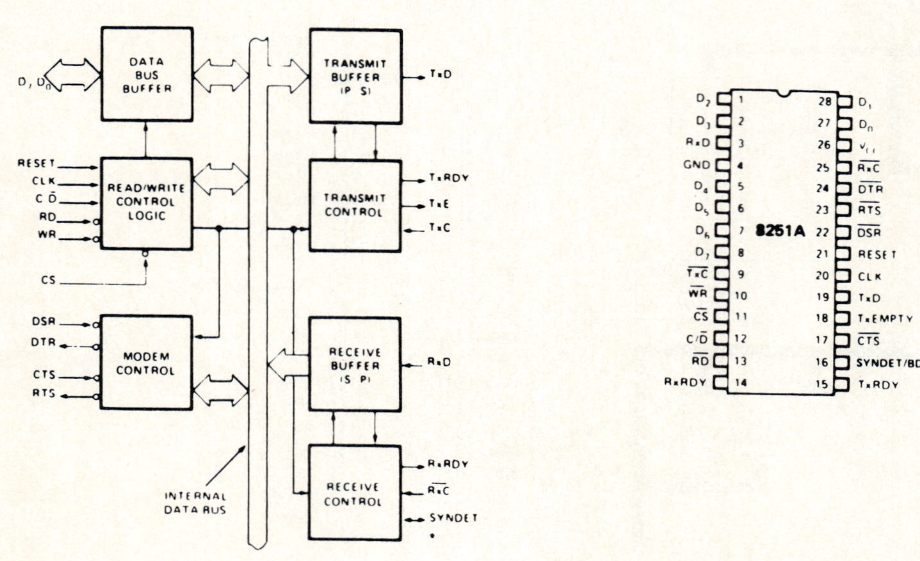

8251A

(Courtesy Intel Corporation.)

PIN CONFIGURATION

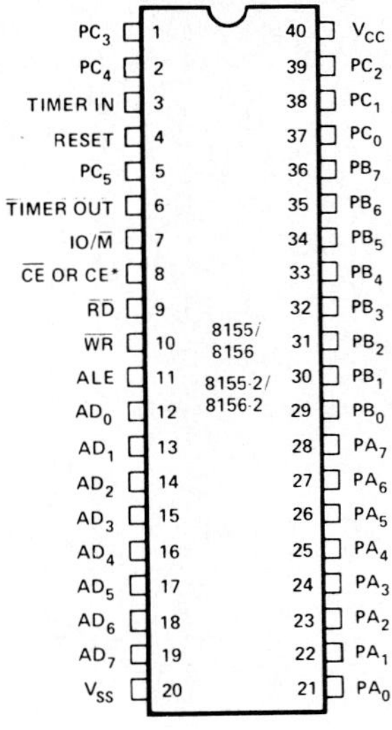

BLOCK DIAGRAM

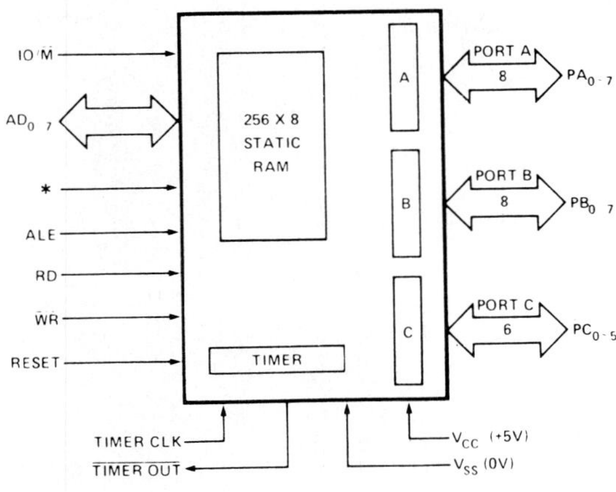

8155/8155-2 = $\overline{CE}$, 8156/8156-2 = CE

8155

PIN CONFIGURATION

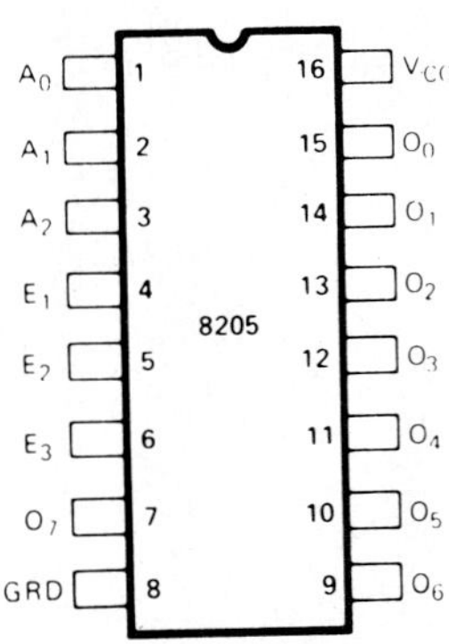

LOGIC SYMBOL

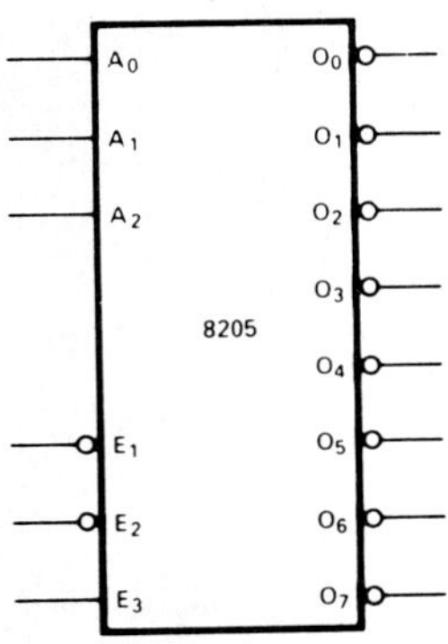

PIN NAMES

A_0-A_2	ADDRESS INPUTS
$\overline{E_1}$-$\overline{E_3}$	ENABLE INPUTS
$\overline{O_0}$-$\overline{O_7}$	DECODED OUTPUTS

ADDRESS			ENABLE			OUTPUTS							
A_0	A_1	A_2	E_1	E_2	E_3	0	1	2	3	4	5	6	7
L	L	L	L	L	H	L	H	H	H	H	H	H	H
H	L	L	L	L	H	H	L	H	H	H	H	H	H
L	H	L	L	L	H	H	H	L	H	H	H	H	H
H	H	L	L	L	H	H	H	H	L	H	H	H	H
L	L	H	L	L	H	H	H	H	H	L	H	H	H
H	L	H	L	L	H	H	H	H	H	H	L	H	H
L	H	H	L	L	H	H	H	H	H	H	H	L	H
H	H	H	L	L	H	H	H	H	H	H	H	H	L
X	X	X	L	L	L	H	H	H	H	H	H	H	H
X	X	X	H	L	L	H	H	H	H	H	H	H	H
X	X	X	L	H	L	H	H	H	H	H	H	H	H
X	X	X	H	H	L	H	H	H	H	H	H	H	H
X	X	X	H	L	H	H	H	H	H	H	H	H	H
X	X	X	L	H	H	H	H	H	H	H	H	H	H
X	X	X	H	H	H	H	H	H	H	H	H	H	H

8205

(Courtesy Intel Corporation.)

8255A BLOCK DIAGRAM

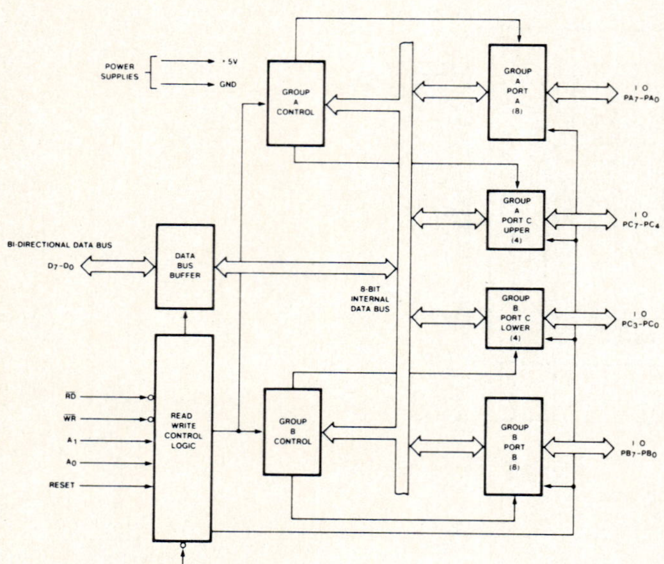

PIN CONFIGURATION

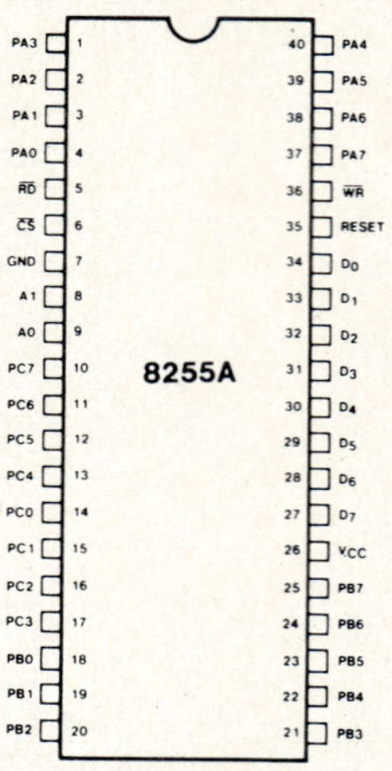

PIN NAMES

D_7-D_0	DATA BUS (BI DIRECTIONAL)
RESET	RESET INPUT
$\overline{CS}$	CHIP SELECT
$\overline{RD}$	READ INPUT
$\overline{WR}$	WRITE INPUT
A0, A1	PORT ADDRESS
PA7-PA0	PORT A (BIT)
PB7-PB0	PORT B (BIT)
PC7-PC0	PORT C (BIT)
V_{CC}	+5 VOLTS
GND	Ø VOLTS

8255A

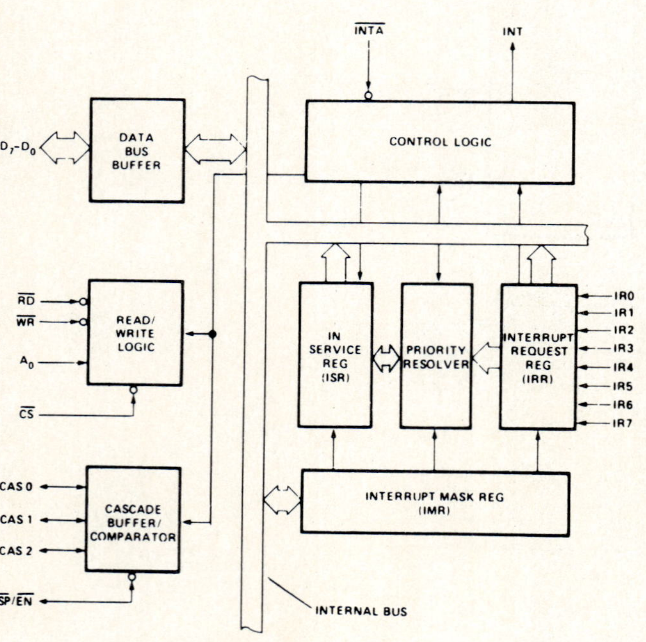

Figure 1. Block Diagram

1	$\overline{CS}$	28	V_{CC}
2	$\overline{WR}$	27	A_0
3	$\overline{RD}$	26	$\overline{INTA}$
4	D_7	25	IR7
5	D_6	24	IR6
6	D_5	23	IR5
7	D_4	22	IR4
8	D_3	21	IR3
9	D_2	20	IR2
10	D_1	19	IR1
11	D_0	18	IR0
12	CAS 0	17	INT
13	CAS 1	16	$\overline{SP}/\overline{EN}$
14	GND	15	CAS 2

8259A

Figure 2. Pin Configuration

8259A

(Courtesy Intel Corporation.)

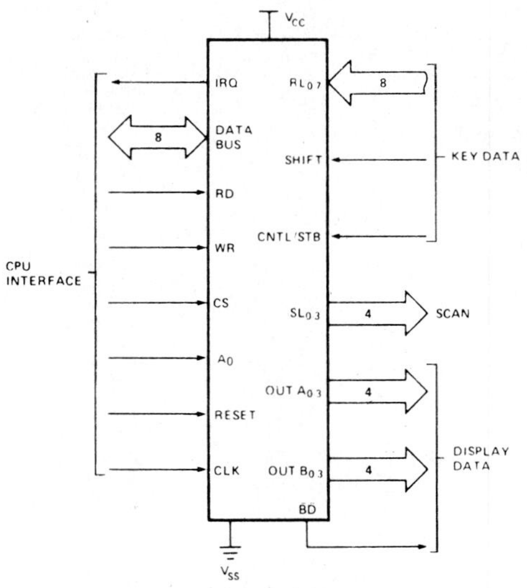

Figure 1. Logic Symbol

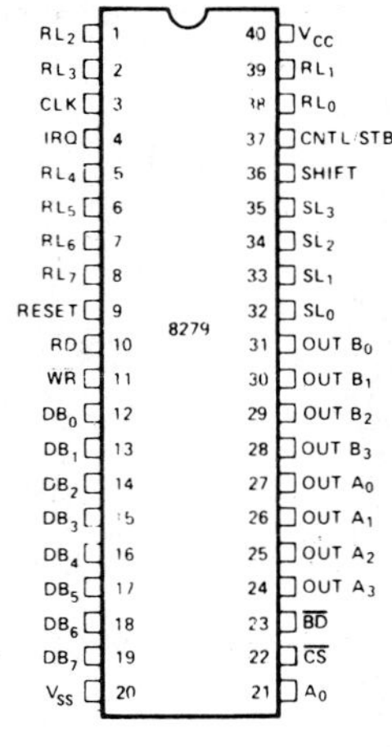

Figure 2. Pin Configuration

8279

PIN CONFIGURATIONS **LOGIC DIAGRAMS**

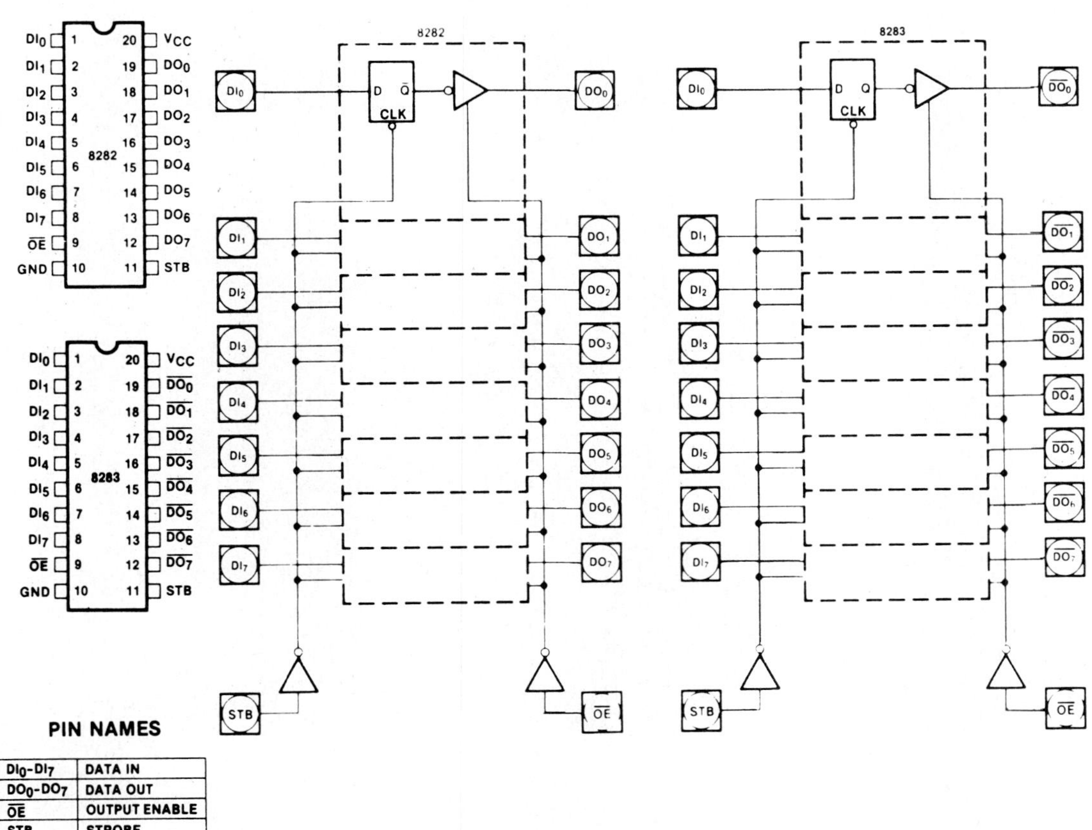

PIN NAMES

DI0-DI7	DATA IN
DO0-DO7	DATA OUT
$\overline{OE}$	OUTPUT ENABLE
STB	STROBE

8282/8283

(Courtesy Intel Corporation.)

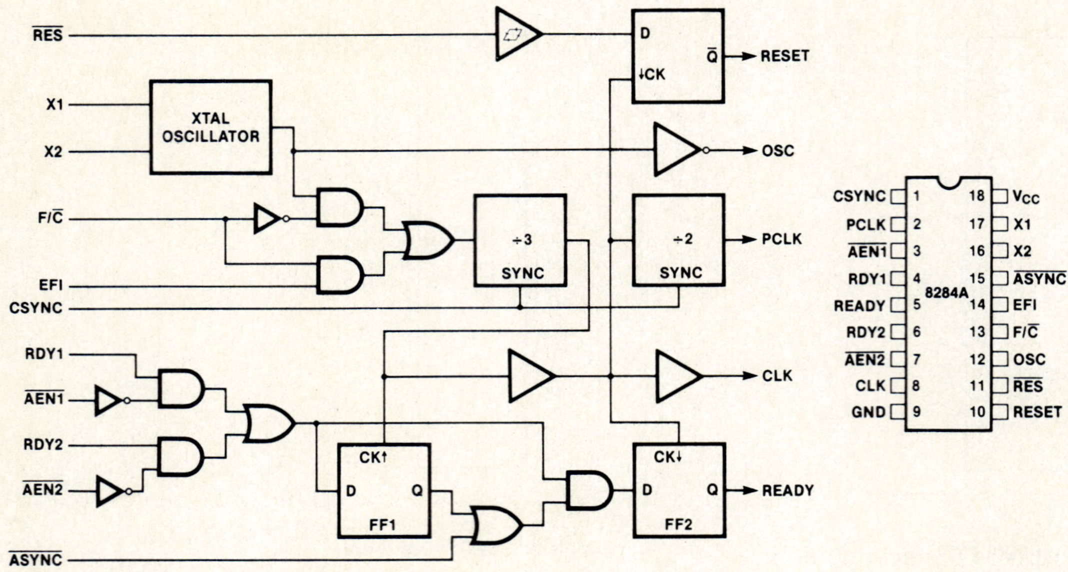

Figure 1. 8284A Block Diagram

Figure 2.
8284A Pin Configuration

(Courtesy Intel Corporation.)

APPENDIX G

CODEVIEW SAMPLE SESSION

This appendix includes a sample troubleshooting session using the major Codeview commands on demonstration program NEXT_WEEK of Figure C2.4(a). It is designed to follow procedure steps 1 through 6 of Chapter 2.

This first section (steps 7 through 26) demonstrates the essential commands and operations and should be learned thoroughly. *In this section we assume that the bus-extender is not present.*

7. Upon entering Codeview, observe that the screen is divided into two major sections: the *window* (top portion) and the *dialog box* (bottom portion). Note program NEXT_WEEK displayed in list file format in the window and the *current location marker* in inverse video over the first executable instruction.
8. There are four ways of giving commands to Codeview: the window menu, the dialog box, the function keys, and the Ctrl (control) key.
   - Note the main menu across the top of the window.
   - Note the prompt (>) in the dialog box at the bottom of the screen.
   - Note the function keys (F1 through F10) on the keyboard.
   - Note the position of the Ctrl key on the keyboard.

   We will use all four of these command-entry methods during this session. Note that Codeview is designed so that many of the commands can be entered in several different ways. Because there is not enough space here to cover all alternatives, we have selected a variety of entry methods that seem in each case to be the easiest to use.
9. Use Ctrl/G and Ctrl/T to set the desired window size.
10. Press F2 to toggle the register/memory box off and on. Leave in the "on" state.
11. Press F3 to switch among source, list, or mixed display. Exit this step with the original *list* format displayed. (Currently, the list and mixed displays are the same.)
12. Press F4 to toggle between the present screen display and the view display. (The "view" display is used for programs that output to the screen.) Return to the screen display.
13. Press F8 to single-step through the program. The inverse video (the current location marker) shows the *next* instruction to be executed. Note the AX and IP register values as you single-step. Also note the DS:0000 memory value of 07 (under the register/flag display) each time you step to the instruction that references variable *seven_days*.
14. To simulate an input port operation (without the use of bus-extender ports), perform the following steps:
    - Step one instruction past the *in al,0* instruction. (The IN instruction was executed and the inverse video is on the ADD instruction.) The value in AL (shown in the register box) is the random value input from the "floating" data bus.
    - To place a desired value (such as 4) into AL, use upper- or lowercase letters to enter the following from the dialog box (bottom of screen):

    ```
    RAX = 4 <E> (Where <E> means "enter")
    ```

    Note the change in the register display.

    We have just simulated the input of byte 04 from an external (embedded) input port to the AL register.
15. To simulate an output port operation, perform the following steps:
    - Step to the *out 1,al* instruction. (The inverse video is over *out 1,al,* the next instruction to be executed.)
    - Note the value to be output in AL and change if desired.
    - Press F8 once to execute the OUT instruction.

We have just simulated the output of AL to an external byte port.

16. To set a *breakpoint,* use F6 to place the cursor in the window (top of screen). (F6 toggles the cursor between the window and the dialog box.) Using the arrow keys, move the cursor to the desired break location—for example, the ADD instruction. Press F7 to execute the program from the current location marker to the breakpoint.
17. We use the "D" (*display*) dialog box command to show memory contents. The D command defaults to the data segment, and the desired offset address can be entered symbolically or numerically. DB (or just D) displays bytes, and DW displays words.

    Move the cursor to the dialog box (F6) and (using upper- or lowercase letters) enter the command shown below to display a block of memory in the data segment beginning with symbolic offset address *seven_days:*

    `DB seven_days` <E>

    Is 7 the first byte displayed? What is the numerical offset address of variable *seven_days*?
18. Enter

    `DB seven_days 3 (or DB 0 3)` <E>

    to display the first 4 bytes of the data segment beginning from offset location *seven_days* (0000). Is the first byte displayed a 7?
19. Enter

    `DW seven_days 2 (or DW 0 2)` <E>

    to display the same information as two words. Note the position of the 7.
20. We use the EB and EW (EXAMINE) commands to change memory contents. Enter the following to place 5 into variable *seven_days:*

    `EB seven_days 5` <E>

    Use DB to verify that variable *seven_days* now holds 5.
21. Enter the following to place 2, 4, 6, 8 into the first 4 locations starting from *seven_days.*

    `EB seven_days 2 4 6 8` <E>

    Use DB to verify the operation. (Note that *seven_days* now holds 2.)
22. Single-step through the program. Does output = input + 2?
23. Press Alt/W to open the "watch window" submenu. With the cursor (inverse video) over "Add watch," press <E>. In the box enter:

    `seven_days` <E>

    Note the top of the screen. What is the displayed value of variable *seven_days*? Note the C notation (0x) for indicating hexadecimal numbers.
24. Using EB, place 7 back into variable *seven_days.* Did the watch value change to 7?
25. Use Alt/R to open the "Run" menu. Press "R" for "reset." Was the present-location-marker reset to the start of the program and all nonsegment registers zeroed out?
26. To exit Codeview and return to DOS (by way of the batch process), type Alt/F (to open the *file* menu) followed by "x" (for exit). (Or enter *quit* from the dialog box.)

This next section (steps 27 through 30) can be done if bus-extender ports are available. (If you are using a bus-extender system different from Figure C2.2, be sure to make any required changes in the initialization data and port addresses.)

27. Batch program NEXT_WEEK of Figure C2.4(b) and enter Codeview.
28. Press F5 to execute program NEXT_WEEK. Change the input DIP switch and note the output on the LEDs. Does output = input + 7? Enter Ctrl/C to stop execution and return to Codeview.
29. To output data byte 55H to bus-extender port 304H, enter the following from the dialog box:

    `O 304 55` <E>

    Is 55H displayed on the LEDs?
30. To input a data byte from bus-extender port 300H, enter the following from the dialog box:

    `I 300` <E>

    Are the proper data displayed on the screen?

This last section (steps 31 through 40) covers more advanced Codeview commands. They offer useful but not essential operations and can be skipped if desired. (Enter Codeview with either version of program NEXT_WEEK.)

31. Make sure the cursor is in the window. Use the arrow keys to move the cursor to the ADD instruction. Press F9 to set a "permanent" breakpoint (one that does not depend on the cursor position). Note the breakpoint indicator to the right of the instruction. (Multiple breakpoints can be set using F9.)
32. Press F5 to execute to the breakpoint.

33. Press F9 to clear the breakpoint.
34. To specify a break-when-TRUE condition ("watchpoint"), press Alt/W, position the cursor over "Watchpoint," and press <E>. To break when register AX equals 0027H, enter:

```
AX == 0x0027
```

(Note the use of C-language syntax.) Observe the "true/false" indicator to the right of the colon in the watchpoint display (top of screen). Is it currently indicating true (1) or false (0)? Comparing the watchpoint value (27H) with the present contents of AX, is the "true/false" indicator displaying the correct value?
35. Using F8, single-step through the loop and note the true/false indicator. Chances are it remained "false" (0). Use the dialog box to change the values of AX. Did the indicator go *true* whenever AX = 0027H and false otherwise?
36. If bus-extender ports are available, press F5 to execute the program. Enter various values into the low-order DIP. Eventually enter 20H or 27H. (Remember, 0020h + 7 = 0027h.) Did the program break when the condition (AX = 27H) turned true, and did the "true/false" indicator go to "true" (1)?
37. Using F8, step to the ADD instruction. From the dialog box, enter the following ASSEMBLE command to change the ADD instruction to SUB:

```
A <E>
    sub al,Byte Ptr[0000] <E>
```

In the window display, was ADD replaced by SUB?
38. Single-step through the program and note the results. Does output = input − 7?
39. Reset the system (ALT/R, R). Was the SUB instruction changed back to ADD?
40. Exit Codeview (ALT/F, x).

For a complete guide to these and other features of Codeview not covered in these sample sessions, enter ALT/H to bring up the help menu—or refer to the appropriate Microsoft literature and software. Appendix C offers a brief summary of the major Codeview commands.

APPENDIX H

ASCII CODE TABLE

DECIMAL VALUE	➡	0	16	32	48	64	80	96	112	128	144	160	176	192	208	224	240
⬇	HEXA-DECIMAL VALUE	0	1	2	3	4	5	6	7	8	9	A	B	D	C	E	F
0	0	BLANK (NULL)	►	BLANK (SPACE)	0	@	P	‘	p	Ç	É	á	1/4 Dots On	└	╨	∝	≡
1	1	☺	◄	!	1	A	Q	a	q	ü	Æ	í	1/2 Dots On	┴	╤	β	±
2	2	☻	↕	"	2	B	R	b	r	é	FE	ó	3/4 Dots On	┬	╥	γ	≥
3	3	♥	‼	#	3	C	S	c	s	â	ô	ú	│	├	╙	π	≤
4	4	♦	¶	$	4	D	T	d	t	ä	ö	ñ	┤	─	╘	Σ	⌠
5	5	♣	§	%	5	E	U	e	u	à	ò	Ñ	╡	┼	╒	σ	⌡
6	6	♠	▬	&	6	F	V	f	v	å	û	ª	╢	╞	╓	μ	÷
7	7	•	↨	’	7	G	W	g	w	ç	ù	º	╖	╟	╫	τ	≈
8	8	◘	↑	(	8	H	X	h	x	ê	ÿ	¿	╕	╚	╪	Φ	°
9	9	○	↓	)	9	I	Y	i	y	ë	Ö	⌐	╣	╔	┘	Θ	•
10	A	◙	→	*	:	J	Z	j	x	è	Ü	¬	║	╩	┌	Ω	·
11	B	♂	←	+	;	K	[	k	{	ï	¢	½	╗	╦	█	δ	√
12	C	♀	∟	,	<	L	\	l	¦	î	£	¼	╝	╠	▄	∞	η
13	D	♪	↔	—	=	M	]	m	}	ì	¥	¡	╜	═	▌	∅	²
14	E	♫	▲	.	>	N	^	n	~	Ä	Pts	«	╛	╬	▐	∈	▮
15	F	☼	▼	/	?	O	_	o	△	Å	ƒ	»	┐	╧	▀	∩	BLANK 'FF'

INDEX